The Special Child

The Special Child

A Source Book for Parents of Children with Developmental Disabilities

SECOND EDITION

by

Siegfried M. Pueschel, M.D., Ph.D., M.P.H.
The Child Development Center
Rhode Island Hospital
Department of Pediatrics
and
Professor of Pediatrics
Brown University School of Medicine
Providence, Rhode Island

Patricia S. Scola, M.D., M.P.H.
The Child Development Center
Rhode Island Hospital
Department of Pediatrics
and
Clinical Assistant Professor
Brown University School of Medicine
Providence, Rhode Island

Leslie E. Weidenman, Ph.D.
Clinical Associate Director
The Groden Center, Inc.
Providence, Rhode Island

and

James C. Bernier, A.C.S.W.
Private Practice in Psychotherapy and Family Therapy
Providence, Rhode Island

with invited contributors

·P A U L·H·
BROOKES
PUBLISHING Cº

Baltimore · London · Toronto · Sydney

Paul H. Brookes Publishing Co.
Post Office Box 10624
Baltimore, Maryland 21285-0624

Typeset by Maple-Vail Composition Services,
Binghamton, New York.
Manufactured in the United States of America by
The Maple Press Company, York, Pennsylvania.

This book is printed on recycled paper.

Library of Congress Cataloging-in-Publication Data

The special child : a source book for parents of children with
  developmental disabilities / by Siegfried M. Pueschel . . . [et al.].
  — 2nd ed.
      p.   cm.
  Includes bibliographical references and index.
  ISBN 1-55766-167-7
  1. Developmentally disabled children.   2. Developmentally disabled
  children—Care.   3. Developmental disabilities.   I. Pueschel,
  Siegfried M.
RJ135.P84   1995
618.92—dc20   ·94-1018
                                                                CIP

British Library Cataloguing-in-Publication data are available from the British
Library.

Contents

About the Authors

Siegfried M. Pueschel, M.D., Ph.D., M.P.H., as Director of The Child Development Center of Rhode Island Hospital since 1975, has worked with thousands of children with special needs. He has published 15 books about various developmental disabilities and has written more than 200 articles relating to many types of disabling conditions. Prior to his appointment at the Rhode Island Hospital, he initiated a lead poisoning program, became director of the first Down Syndrome Program, and provided leadership to the PKU and Inborn Errors of Metabolism Program at The Children's Hospital in Boston.

Certified by the American Board of Pediatrics and a Diplomate of the American Board of Medical Genetics, his academic appointments include Lecturer in Pediatrics, Harvard Medical School; and Professor of Pediatrics, Brown University. During the past 25 years, Dr. Pueschel has been involved in clinical activities, research, and teaching; and continues to pursue his interest in developmental disabilities, biochemical genetics, and chromosome abnormalities, particularly Down syndrome.

Patricia S. Scola, M.D., M.P.H., is a physician at The Child Development Center of Rhode Island Hospital, where she has provided care for children with developmental and physical disabilities for 25 years. She is a Clinical Assistant Professor at Brown University School of Medicine and serves as consultant for several educational programs for children with special needs. Together with her husband and children, she has volunteered in hospitals in developing countries in Africa and South America.

Leslie E. Weidenman, Ph.D., joined the staff of The Child Development Center's Early Intervention Program in 1979, and from 1982 to 1984, directed the Early Intervention Program at The J. Arthur Trudeau Memorial Center in Warwick, Rhode Island. She is currently Clinical Associate Director of The Groden Center, Inc., an agency that provides evaluative, therapeutic, and educational services for children and young adults with behavioral and emotional disorders and autism. She also serves as a consultant to local school systems in Rhode Island, where she is licensed to practice as both a psychologist and school psychologist.

James C. Bernier, A.C.S.W., is a clinical social worker in Providence, Rhode Island. He has been counseling the families of children with physical and emotional disabilities for 21 years and also works with inner-city youth in the Central Falls school system, an ethnically diverse and economically challenged community.

He has authored several articles on subjects related to developmental disabilities and family systems. He has also had his writing published in a professional reference on autism.

From 1979 until 1989 he was the Director of Social Services at The Child Development Center at Rhode Island Hospital. He is a Member of the National Association of Social Workers and the Academy of Certified Social Workers, and holds a Diplomate from the National Association of Social Workers and the American Board of Clinical Examiners in Clinical Social Work. He is a member of several employee assistance programs, where he serves as a specialist in family and marital issues.

Dr. Pueschel, Dr. Scola, Dr. Weidenman, and Mr. Bernier were assisted in their writing by the following colleagues:

Paul W. Austin, M.Ed.
Barbara Bush, R.P.T.
Katherine C. Castree, M.D.
Sarah J. Gossler, M.S.W.
Marita R. Hopmann, Ph.D.
Debra J. Lobato, Ph.D.
Leesa H. Mann, Ph.D.
Daniel T. Marwil, M.D.
James P. McEneaney, M.Ed.
James A. Mulick, Ph.D.

Carol A. Musso, B.S., R.N.
Lucia Paolicelli, Ph.D.
Barbara D. Remor, B.S., R.N.
Ellen I. Rollins, Ed.D.
Edward A. Sassaman, M.D.
Karen E. Senft, M.D.
Peter Stack, M.S.P.T.
Janet L. Tobin, M.S.
Ann S. Zartler, Ph.D.

Preface to the Second Edition

The main purpose for this new edition of *The Special Child* is to convey the enormous progress that has been made in the field of developmental disabilities since publication of the original edition in 1988. The recently accumulated knowledge is the result of outstanding research efforts and clinical investigations in both the medical and behavioral sciences. Moreover, there have been changes in general policy and legislation, as well as in the attitude toward persons with developmental disabilities. We believe that it is extremely important to provide parents with the most up-to-date information about the care and treatment of their children with special needs.

In this second edition, we have incorporated the new definition of mental retardation put forth in 1992 by the American Association on Mental Retardation. We also discuss new tests and procedures available to detect birth defects prenatally; novel thoughts about attention-deficit/hyperactivity disorder, learning disabilities, and autism; and new advances in the study of genetics. This edition also includes an expanded focus on some of the medical and educational issues related to disabilities. Brief sections on facilitated communication, human immunodeficiency virus (HIV) infection, and revisions of psychological tests have also been added. Although there have been numerous other improvements and changes, the main structure and organization of the book has been retained because parents and professionals alike found it to be easy to use.

Thus, this volume provides state-of-the-art, contemporary knowledge in the field of developmental disabilities. It is our sincere hope that this book will be helpful to parents of children with disabilities as well as to other interested people. The more informed and educated parents are about their child's disability, intervention, education, and legal rights, the more effectively they can advocate for their child, and their child will enjoy an enhanced quality of life.

Introduction

The Special Child, in both its editions, is a book for parents. It was written mainly to help parents of children with developmental disabilities.

Children with developmental disabilities, like all children, are unique individuals. No two are exactly alike, even though they may have the same problem or diagnosis. Because of their disabilities, however, they may have many things in common, such as a need for special education, for additional medical care, or for emotional support and counseling. This book focuses on all of these common needs.

The Special Child tells you how to recognize developmental problems and how to obtain an evaluation that may lead to a specific diagnosis. We describe the roles of the various professionals you might meet as your child is evaluated, as well as the types of tests and procedures that can be performed. Other sections of the book focus on families and the adjustments they make when they discover their child has a developmental disability. We also highlight a number of specific disabilities, tests and procedures, medications, treatments, and operations commonly performed. Many other topics of interest, such as going to school, community resources, and legal issues, are discussed as well. We close this book with two resource sections. First is a compilation of resource organizations parents, other family members, or friends may wish to contact. Second, we provide a list of readings; the entries in this list include resources used to write this book and sources readers may wish to consult. Neither of these lists is intended to be comprehensive; rather, we hope readers will use them to get started as they seek new information and become advocates.

Many questions that you will ask about your special child are answered in this book. In fact, this is the reason we decided to write *The Special Child*. Parents so often ask the same questions about various issues concerning developmental disabilities that we realized how valuable a book could be that provided a wide range of information readily.

Obviously, one book will not answer all of your questions. *The Special Child* is not intended to be an encyclopedia. Also, *The Special Child* is not intended to replace the individual counseling, support, and guidance you will receive from the professionals who help you care for your child. Moreover, it is not a "do-it-yourself" book that can be substituted for your personal physician's advice in specific situations. *The Special Child* is a home reference book intended to complement the professional services you and your child receive.

The authors of both editions of *The Special Child* are specialists who work with children with developmental disabilities. These experts, with years of experience, include physicians, psychologists, educators, social workers, therapists, and nurses. All work or have worked at The Child Development Center of Rhode Island Hospital, a University Affiliated Program, which is the major diagnostic and treatment center for children with developmental disabilities in southeastern New England.

Acknowledgments

We are foremost indebted to the many children with special needs we have been privileged to serve in The Child Development Center of Rhode Island Hospital. The lessons they have taught us are invaluable. We also thank their parents, for it was their partnership, devotion, and encouragement that led to the writing of this book.

Moreover, we would like to acknowledge the assistance of our colleagues from The Child Development Center who contributed in numerous ways to this book. We also would like to express our deep gratitude to Esther Brown who singlehandedly prepared the manuscript. Because of her extraordinary efforts throughout the preparation of the manuscript and her outstanding secretarial skills, we were able to complete this work on time.

The Special Child

Children with Special Needs, Their Parents, and the Professionals Who Care for Them

Who Are
the Special Children?

WHAT'S IN A NAME?

When you hear the words *developmentally disabled, handicapped,* or *special needs,* you may think of a specific person or kind of problem. Many people have limited ideas about the effects of disabilities. Some automatically think of children with physical impairments as in wheelchairs; others may picture children with mental retardation. The truth is that there are hundreds of different types of disabilities that can affect many areas of a child's life.

Basically, a developmental disability is any physical or mental condition that can impair or limit a child's skills or that causes a child to develop language, thinking, personal, social, and movement skills more slowly than other children. *Developmental disability* is such a broad term that it is easy to see how two children with very different problems could both be described correctly as having a developmental disability or special needs.

This book uses the terms *developmental disability, disability,* and *special needs* interchangeably. These and other similar terms also have technical definitions. Federal laws and state regulations on special education, for example, include detailed definitions of terms such as *developmental disability, mental retardation,* and other disabling conditions. You will encounter some of these definitions later in this book.

Most people are unfamiliar with the technical definitions of *developmental disability* and *mental retardation* and develop their own ideas of what they mean. Unfortunately, many definitions are inaccurate, based on vague impressions, hearsay, or "horror stories" about individuals with disabling conditions. As a result, the terms and labels used to describe disabilities often have negative connotations that can cause problems for families and children with disabilities. Problems arise in a variety of ways, including fears, prejudices, and discrimination. When specific terms are heard, uninformed people may imagine the worst and then, out of fear, avoid meeting, associating with, and learning about persons with special needs and their families. In *The Special Child*, we hope to dispel many of these misconceptions by sharing what we know about various developmental disabilities. The best way to begin is simply to keep in mind that children with developmental disabilities are children first. They may have disabilities and special needs, but, like all children, they require a great deal of love, care, and affection.

The problems with labels and terminology lead many parents to ask why the use of labels has not been abandoned altogether. After all, children with developmental disabilities are more like children without disabilities than they are different. This problem, however, does not apply only to people with developmental disabilities; racial, ethnic, economic, and religious labels all may bring out prejudices. Mental and physical ability represent two more dimensions by which children and adults can note the array of individual differences present in any group of people, whether a family, classroom, Boy or Girl Scout troop, religious congregation, or neighborhood. Parents also often worry that once a child has been given a diagnosis, the label will remain forever, even if the disability has been "corrected" or if the diagnosis is found to be incorrect.

Despite these problems, there are several good reasons for using specific terms. For example, if a syndrome has been identified and a child has been diagnosed correctly, then parents can be informed about the condition and told what the future might hold for the child. Moreover, parents can be provided with specific genetic counseling, and they can be advised of whether there are risks of having another baby with a similar problem.

Diagnostic labels also provide parents and other family members with a name for the child's condition. Friends, neighbors, and strangers might inquire about the child's disability or ask why the child has not developed like other children. If a diagnosis has been made, the term can help explain the child's problem.

One tangible benefit to being identified as a person with a developmental disability is that as soon as a disability is documented, services often become available. Many government programs base

their eligibility criteria for disability benefits on this kind of information. Moreover, early intervention programs, schools, and community agencies often require a specific diagnosis for enrollment in a special program.

RECENT CHANGES IN ATTITUDES

Fortunately, the care and services available to persons with developmental disabilities has improved greatly in recent years. In the past, children with significant disabilities were hidden in institutions and all but forgotten. Today, attitudes are generally more positive and more realistic. Even the words used to describe disabilities have improved. No longer are expressions such as *imbecile, feeble-minded,* and *moron* used when referring to a child with mental retardation. Instead, more positive expressions have taken their place, including *child with special needs,* or *person with a developmental disability,* or *challenging child.* Condescending and insulting terms are less frequently heard these days and, of course, should not be used at all.

Today, we know that children with many different developmental disorders are able to accomplish much more than was ever anticipated previously. Not only can they participate in family life, but they can go to school, have friends, enjoy recreational activities, live and work in the community, and much more. This knowledge, and the increased focus on the abilities of persons with disabling conditions, not just their disabilities, have resulted in many novel programs and services that are now available from an early age.

Along with the recent changes in attitudes have come insights into how children learn and grow, medical advances, modern technology, and new ideas about the rights of individuals, all of which have revolutionized our thinking and approaches to the care of individuals with developmental disabilities. Many new services, interventions and treatments, and types of adaptive equipment have been devised to help these special children. Even federal laws and state regulations that structure the delivery of services to individuals with disabilities have recognized the importance of equal opportunity for all students, regardless of ability or disability. Special education laws now mandate that children with disabilities be educated alongside their peers without disabilities whenever possible. This concept of inclusion has led to innovative education programs for children. We are fortunate to live in a time of positive thinking, when parents and professionals are striving together to help children with developmental disabilities lead happy, healthy, and productive lives.

ACKNOWLEDGMENTS

Contributions have been made to this chapter by Leslie E. Weidenman, Ph.D., Ellen I. Rollins, Ed.D., and James C. Bernier, M.S.W.

2

Discovering Your
Child Has a Problem

SUSPECTING YOUR CHILD HAS A PROBLEM

Today, because of sophisticated prenatal diagnostic techniques that are available, many birth anomalies, metabolic problems, and chromosome abnormalities can be uncovered during pregnancy. In addition, certain congenital anomalies and developmental disabilities may be identified at birth, shortly thereafter, or during early childhood. In any of these situations, parents usually learn about their child's problem from their obstetrician, pediatrician, family physician, or geneticist.

In other instances, parents are the first to suspect that something is wrong with their child. It may be a vague feeling that something is not quite right or the realization that their baby is not developing at the same rate as the neighbor's child. In particular, parents who are educated in "typical" child development will frequently recognize deviations in their child's motor, language, and/or intellectual progress. At times, questions from close friends or relatives may alert parents that there may be a concern; for example, someone may ask why 10-month-old Kevin isn't sitting up yet, why 1½-year-old Betty isn't walking, or why 2½-year-old Johnny isn't talking yet.

Often the baby's doctor, nurse, or other professionals will notice the child's developmental delay or disability during regular "well-child" visits. There may be other occasions when an older child may tell the parents or a doctor that he or she cannot keep up with other

7

children of the same age; this is sometimes the case in children with muscular dystrophy. Clearly, developmental problems can be discovered in many ways by different people.

Recognizing a developmental disability is sometimes easier if you know something about how children develop "typically." If you have other children or if you have watched someone else's child grow, you may have a general idea of how children develop. Thus, over the years, you may have acquired an understanding of the sequence and ages at which essential skills and abilities generally appear. For instance, you may have noticed that babies usually sit by themselves at approximately 6–8 months and usually start walking some time around their first birthday.

There are numerous indicators or signs of developmental problems in a child. Some may be very subtle and not easily noted; others are more obvious. Careful and repeated observations often are needed before a developmental disability is uncovered. As parents, doctors, and other professionals watch a baby's development, they must keep in mind that the signs of a developmental problem may change as a child matures. A certain behavior that is typical during one stage of a child's development may mean a problem during another. The task of identifying developmental problems is made even more difficult when you consider that every child is unique and no two children will develop in exactly the same way. We must also remember that all children, regardless of whether they have disabilities, are individuals and develop at their own pace, and that there may be considerable variability in developmental progress. The job of parents and professionals is to find out if a particular child's progress and behavior are "typical" or if there are signs of a developmental problem that may need further investigation.

DIFFERENT TYPES OF DEVELOPMENTAL PROBLEMS

To monitor a child's developmental progress, doctors and child care professionals look at how well a baby is doing in a number of areas of development. These areas include basic senses like vision and hearing as well as important developmental areas of language, thinking, social interactions, and movement skills.

Signs of developmental problems also are grouped by area of functioning. Certain signs may suggest a visual problem, whereas others may indicate a hearing impairment. Problems with muscle use are identified in still other ways. There are many signs and symptoms that may indicate problems. Only a few of the common signs are listed here:

If your baby is not startled by loud sounds, does not turn toward your voice when you speak, or at a later age does not respond to his or her name when called or turns the radio or television to "full blast," there may be problems with hearing.

If your baby does not focus on your face, does not follow objects or people as they move, or shows random searching eye movements, there may be a visual impairment.

If your baby is unable to bring his or her hands or certain objects to the mouth, always keeps the hands tightly fisted, is unable to hold the head up by 3 months, is not sitting independently by 10 months, or is not walking by 18 months, there may be a problem with muscles or nerves.

If your baby does not use any words by 15 months or does not speak in short phrases by 24 months, then you probably should be concerned with his or her language development.

If your child does not smile when talked to by family members or friends, stiffens when held, or later avoids making eye contact with you or others and is "in a world of his [or her] own," there may be a social-emotional problem.

If your baby shows one or more of these signs, he or she may have a developmental disability. The best way to be sure is to talk to your child's doctor about your concerns and observations. The doctor then may suggest that you take your child for a thorough developmental evaluation. However, the doctor might reassure you that your child's progress is within the range of typical development and that there is no reason for concern.

WHEN CAN A DEVELOPMENTAL DISABILITY BE DETECTED?

Not all developmental problems are identified during the prenatal period, at birth, or during the baby's first few weeks of life. More often, problems, in particular mild or subtle developmental delays, are not noticed until much later, perhaps during the first few years of life or when the child begins preschool, kindergarten, or elementary school. Part of the difficulty in detecting developmental problems in young children is that many disabilities are not immediately apparent. For example, almost everyone has heard stories of children in excellent health who had no problems during infancy, but later were found to have mental retardation. The opposite situation also occurs, in which children who have had difficult births and a rocky first few days of life bounce back and develop typically.

Detecting Problems During Pregnancy

As mentioned previously, sometimes developmental problems, metabolic disorders, and chromosome abnormalities can be uncovered before a baby is born. A number of screening procedures are now regularly used to detect problems during pregnancy. For example, the amount of a specific protein called alpha-fetoprotein (AFP), which is ordinarily produced by an unborn baby, is often routinely tested in the expectant mother at the end of the fourth month of pregnancy. If too much alpha-fetoprotein is found, the unborn baby may have spina bifida (an opening at the back of the spine) (see Chapter 13) or a related brain or spinal cord defect. If a very small amount of alpha-fetoprotein is uncovered, this may suggest that the mother is carrying a child with Down syndrome, which is the most frequently observed chromosome disorder associated with mental retardation. A recently developed screening test for chromosome anomalies includes not only alpha-fetoprotein but also two hormones—estriol and human chorionic gonadotropin. Although using alpha-fetoprotein screening alone will identify approximately 20% of fetal Down syndrome, the new triple test using alpha-fetoprotein and the two hormones will find about 60% of affected fetuses. A few of the more common tests that are sometimes conducted during pregnancy are described here. A detailed description of these and other procedures is found in Chapter 22.

One procedure used in prenatal diagnosis is called *amniocentesis*. Amniocentesis involves removal of some of the fluid that surrounds the baby in the mother's womb. The cells obtained from the amniotic fluid are grown, or cultured, in a laboratory for 2–3 weeks. Then, the chromosomes, which are tiny, microscopic, rodlike structures containing thousands of genes, are studied or specific biochemical tests are performed. These tests can tell whether or not the unborn baby has any of several disorders known to be caused by chromosome or biochemical problems.

In the 1980s, a new technique for prenatal diagnosis was developed. It is called *chorionic villus sampling* (CVS). During this procedure, a small part of the placenta, which is also called the afterbirth and which nourishes the unborn baby in the womb, is obtained, usually during the third month of pregnancy. The advantage of chorionic villus sampling over amniocentesis is that a chromosome analysis can be performed immediately on a fresh sample of tissue without using lengthy culture procedures. Thus, the time period between obtaining the chorionic villus sample and obtaining the results of chromosome analysis can be shortened significantly. With this procedure, it may only take a few hours to get an answer, whereas cultures after amniocentesis may take 2–3 weeks or sometimes longer. Another advantage of chorionic villus sampling is that it can be performed earlier during pregnancy than amniocentesis. In addition to fast chromosome analysis, the tissue sample can also be used for biochemical studies and DNA analysis. (DNA stands for *deoxyribonucleic acid*, a basic component of living tissue, containing the genetic code.) In addition to the above mentioned advantages, there are also disadvantages involved in using chorionic villus sampling. The risk of a miscarriage after chorionic villus sampling is slightly higher (.5%–1.5%) when compared with amniocentesis. In addition, limb defects and small tongue have been reported in some children who were tested prenatally using chorionic villus sampling.

Ultrasound, or sonography, is another technique frequently used to identify structural problems in the unborn baby. Sonography uses sound waves to form an image of the baby. In particular, spina bifida, major skeletal deformities, enlarged kidneys, and certain congenital heart defects can be detected by ultrasound primarily during the second half of pregnancy.

Fetoscopy is also used in prenatal diagnosis, usually during the second trimester of pregnancy. During this procedure, a tubelike instrument is inserted through the mother's abdominal wall into the womb. With this instrument, the doctor can see body parts of the baby and look for abnormalities. This same instrument also can be used to obtain blood from the developing baby, which then is tested in the laboratory.

Prenatal diagnostic tests are not recommended for everyone, because each test involves some risk to the unborn baby and to the expectant mother. Doctors recommend such prenatal studies only in certain circumstances, if there are valid indications. For example, amniocentesis or chorionic villus sampling is suggested for pregnant women who are 35 years and older, or for those who have already had a child with a genetic problem or chromosome disorder, or if one of the parents has a chromosome abnormality. Fetoscopy is used only in rare situations, such as a suspected blood disorder in the unborn baby.

For the most part, the results of such tests during pregnancy will be normal, which is reassuring to expectant parents. However, if the results are abnormal, meaning that the baby is likely to have a serious problem, you, as parents, are faced with the difficult question of what to do. There is never an easy answer. What is decided will depend on many factors, such as your personal beliefs about complex issues such as termination of pregnancy and right to life of the unborn baby. It will also depend on your understanding of the specific disorder detected, implications for the quality of both the child's and family's lives, the types of services needed, assistance and support available to parents of children with disabilities, and your personal feelings about raising a child with a disability. Your religious convictions and ethical values may also be important factors in your decision-making process. The more informed you are, the better you will be able to make a decision. For this reason, your obstetrician may refer you for genetic counseling. Parents often appreciate the detailed information a genetic counselor can provide in a nonjudgmental manner. Also, talking to other parents who have a child with the identified disorder may give you another perspective. Whatever decision you make then deserves the support of caring professionals.

It should be emphasized that optimal prenatal care, appropriate nutrition, prevention of infections, and avoidance of drugs, alcohol, and smoking will help to preserve the mother's health and aid in the birth of a healthy baby.

Birth and Newborn Difficulties

Doctors usually examine babies as soon as they are born and carefully look for abnormalities during this initial examination. Obvious physical anomalies, such as cleft lip or spina bifida, will be noticed right away. Other congenital anomalies, although present at birth, may not be as visible. They may be uncovered later, perhaps in the newborn period or during the first few years of life.

At times, the process of being born can cause developmental problems. If, during birth, the baby does not get enough oxygen, brain injury can ensue, as too little oxygen (a condition called *anoxia* or *hypoxia*) can harm nerve cells. The extent of brain injury depends on how long the brain was without oxygen. Babies injured at birth or deprived of oxygen sometimes develop cerebral palsy, seizures, or other developmental disorders.

Soon after the baby is born, your doctor or other delivery room personnel will check the infant's heart rate, respiration, skin color, reflexes, and muscle tone. Based on this quick evaluation of your baby at 1 and 5 minutes after delivery, the doctor develops a score (Apgar score) indicating the baby's condition at this particular time. Each of the just-mentioned physical findings are scored from 0 to 2, for a total of 10 points. For example, if the baby's heart rate is more than 100 beats per minute, then the baby will get a score of 2; if the heart rate is below 100 per minute, a score of 1 is given; and if the heart is not beating at all, then a 0 score is obtained.

Premature infants born weeks or even months too early are at a higher risk of developing disabilities than full-term infants. These babies often are very sick and require intensive treatment in a neo-natal intensive care unit (NICU). Most of their problems occur be-cause their vital organs, such as the brain, lungs, liver, kidneys, and intestinal tract, are underdeveloped and are not yet functioning properly. Often, premature infants will need mechanical support systems in order to live. A respirator, for example, may be needed if a baby is born with immature lungs and has difficulties breathing. Other problems common to premature babies are heart defects, feeding difficulties, and metabolic problems. Heart defects may im-pede circulation and delivery of oxygen to the brain and other vital organs. Feeding difficulties may lead to nutritional deficiencies. Met-abolic problems, such as extremely low blood levels of calcium or sugar, may cause seizure disorders. Any of these problems, if severe or prolonged, may potentially lead to developmental disabilities later.

Another source of concern for premature babies is their suscep-tibility to infection. Due to an underdeveloped immune system, in-fections can be very dangerous for a premature infant. If the infec-tion occurs in the brain (termed *meningitis* or *encephalitis*), there may be injury to nerve cells. Some very small, premature infants may sustain brain injury because of bleeding inside the brain called *intra-cerebral* or *intraventricular hemorrhage*. This also may lead to develop-ment of hydrocephalus, which is increased fluid in the brain.

Other concerns in the newborn period require special attention. During the first week of life, all babies are tested for specific meta-bolic problems such as hypothyroidism (a condition in which there is insufficient thyroid hormone) and phenylketonuria (PKU) (a meta-bolic disorder in which a building block or part of a protein called *phenylalanine* cannot be broken down, or metabolized, by the body). In the United States, and many other countries, babies are screened for these and sometimes other metabolic disorders shortly after birth before they leave the hospital. Although these conditions are rare, if detected in the newborn period, appropriate intervention or treat-ment can begin immediately and developmental disabilities can be prevented. Before screening for and treatment of these disorders were available, children with these disorders often developed men-tal retardation.

Uncovering Developmental Problems During Early Childhood

Also during the first few years of life, parents, neighbors, doctors, or a preschool teacher may notice signs of developmental problems in a child. Regular checkups by your child's physician can be helpful in monitoring development and finding possibly existing developmental disabilities early. During these well-child visits, your pediatrician may ask how you think your child is developing and when specific developmental milestones were achieved. Most pediatricians value parents' observations and rely on this information to obtain a true picture of the baby's current level of development.

The pediatrician or family doctor will also examine the baby and obtain his or her weight, height, and head size. (The latter may be an indication of brain development.) Many physicians often conduct developmental screening tests to assess the child's developmental progress more systematically. With this information, then, the pediatrician can compare your child's progress to the average child's development. If any of the results are significantly below the average range, the child may need a more detailed evaluation.

In many communities, public health nurses and/or child development specialists routinely conduct developmental screenings. These professionals give brief screening tests that provide an estimate of the child's level of functioning in several areas of development. The results of such a quick assessment can tell you one of several things: they might show that your child could have a developmental delay and thus might indicate that your child should have a more thorough examination; they may reassure you that everything is fine; or, if the results are unclear, they may suggest that your child's development should be monitored closely and that the screening test should be repeated in a few months. Also, many school districts now offer Child Find services for young children and provide early screening of developmental problems before kindergarten entry.

Infants and toddlers, like newborns, also can be affected seriously by infections of the brain, including meningitis and encephalitis. Other common sources of developmental problems at this age are childhood accidents, lead poisoning, endocrine (glandular) disturbances such as an underfunctioning of the thyroid gland, and specific chronic illnesses. Surely, your pediatrician will discuss these health care issues with you and the ways many of these problems can be prevented.

Finding Problems in School-Age Children

Mild developmental delays and minor disabilities may go unnoticed during early childhood and only become apparent when a child begins school. It may be a child's inability to keep up with others, immature or unusual behaviors, or difficulties making and keeping

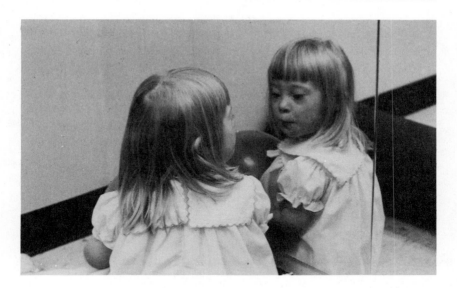

friends. At other times, the teacher may be the one who notices that the child is having difficulties in certain academic areas. Learning disabilities and attention deficit disorders including hyperactivity, poor concentration, distractibility, and similar signs are most often uncovered during the first few years of school.

As you can see, developmental problems can be detected at any time beginning with pregnancy and continuing throughout childhood. Keep in mind, however, that all problems cannot be found at the same time. As a rule, the milder the disability, the later it is uncovered.

COMPREHENSIVE EVALUATIONS FOR CHILDREN WITH DISABILITIES

We have previously mentioned that it might be appropriate to have a child who is suspected of having a disability examined by specialists in a Development Evaluation Center. Such centers, specializing in comprehensive developmental evaluations, are located throughout the United States. Your pediatrician, family physician, state health department, or school can provide you with information about the nearest Development Evaluation Center and can be helpful in obtaining a referral. At these centers, children are evaluated by professionals from a variety of disciplines who work together as a team. Generally, these teams include pediatricians, psychologists, speech-language specialists, social workers, educators, physical and occupational therapists, nurses, nutritionists, and others. At times, additional laboratory procedures and special tests are needed to find the cause of the child's problems. Sometimes the exact cause of the disability remains unknown. When the evaluations have been completed, team members carefully consider all of the information gathered during the various assessments. Then, together they develop recommendations for the child's best care and management.

Many Development Evaluation Centers provide coordinated followup and care through special clinics. Individual therapy, counseling, and support services for parents and family members also are available in a number of places. Continued followup of the child, together with support to the family, appropriate education, and the availability of other needed services, should help the child with a developmental disability to thrive optimally.

ACKNOWLEDGMENTS

Contributions have been made to this chapter by Siegfried M. Pueschel, M.D., Ph.D., M.P.H., Patricia S. Scola, M.D., M.P.H., and Leslie E. Weidenman, Ph.D.

Developmental Disabilities Are a Family Affair

All of us have expectations and dreams of what our children will do when they grow up, who they will look like, and what they will accomplish in life. Such expectations can help us by providing guidelines for planning our children's future. Most of us modify these plans as our children's unique personalities and abilities unfold.

Discovering that a child has a developmental disability is another matter. No one is ever completely prepared to be a parent of a child with a disability.

WHEN YOU ARE TOLD OF YOUR CHILD'S DISABILITY

Being told that your child has a disability always is a shock, even if you suspected that something was wrong. It may seem that your hopes have been shattered and your worst fears realized. At the same time, you may not believe what you have been told and think that this only happens to other people.

Parents of children with developmental disabilities often describe these and other feelings of sadness and desperation upon learning that their child has a developmental disability. We hope that, when you were told of your child's disability, it was done with tact and sensitivity. Unfortunately, this is not everyone's experience. All too often parents are hurt unnecessarily by insensitive but well-meaning individuals or by those who are misinformed.

17

Giving bad news is a difficult task for anyone—professionals included. In your experience, you may have found that certain people are more sympathetic and easier to talk to than others. Some professionals have a special ability to relate to people. For others, developing a rapport does not come easily. Also, some professionals are unaware of the impact their style of communication has on parents. In general, professional training has not included communication skills. Fortunately, this is changing. Increasingly, physicians and other professionals are being taught effective ways of talking to and listening to parents and patients.

Inaccurate information about persons with developmental disabilities is a major source of emotional pain for families. The field of developmental disabilities has advanced rapidly in recent years. What we now know about the potential of children with a variety of disabilities far surpasses our knowledge of only 25 years ago. Unfortunately, not all professionals are aware of these changes, causing them to give parents discouraging information based on outdated views.

Whatever your experience, the initial shock usually is followed by a grieving period during which denial and feelings of guilt and anger often prevail. Subsequently, during the time of adjustment, most parents adapt to the change brought about by the birth of a child with a disability. It is important to remember that everyone adapts in his or her own way. One mother may express her pain and feeling of loss openly, whereas her husband may suppress his grief by immersing himself in work. Another parent may feel numb or waver between periods of acceptance and depression. Other emotions may surface such as anxiety, shame, hatred, self-pity, and loneliness. You may feel a variety of emotions, each with a different intensity, at different times or all at once. Contradictory feelings occasionally may make you feel out of control or cause you to wonder if you are still able to think rationally. Individuals who ordinarily are stable and mature may sometimes feel as if the world is coming to an end. If you are feeling this way, it is likely you are having a normal response to a very stressful situation.

FINDING SOMEONE TO TALK TO

You may find that you are isolating yourself during this difficult time. However, it can be helpful for parents to seek out someone, perhaps a relative or close friend, who will listen. Although you may think that talking only makes things worse, keep in mind that sharing concerns often relieves stress. For example, talking to a parent of a child with a similar problem may convince you that you too can survive this crisis and adjust to the changes in your life. In addition, a parent who has experienced similar disappointment often is more sensitive and can be helpful in ways a professional never can. Fortunately, in recent years, parents have recognized how helpful they can be to each other and numerous support groups have been formed in local areas. Many of these organizations have national and state affiliations.

Beyond the assistance and support of relatives, friends, professionals, and other parents, the most important factor in the adjustment process is time. Initially, you may feel that you will never be able to cope, but with time you will. One mother describing the first 2 years of life after the birth of a child with spina bifida said:

> I can now admit that having Laura is mostly a blessing. . . . Much of the experience has been positive, challenging, and rewarding, and I have grown as a person in ways I may not have without her. . . . In fact, the past 2 years have changed me for the better in just about every way. Nevertheless, I still don't want to be the mother of a handicapped child. But I am Laura's mother, I love her deeply, and that makes all the difference.[1]

Although time generally heals, there are times when parents become significantly depressed. This is particularly true when events surrounding a child's birth have been traumatic. If, for example, a child has a disfigurement or if the professionals attending the family are callous, the results can be deeply distressing. Previous psychological traumas can also make some individuals more vulnerable to stress. In this situation, you may find that you are provided great relief by talking to a professional. For example, psychologists, psychiatrists, and social workers are professionals trained to help people adjust.

HOW DOES THE BIRTH OF A CHILD WITH A DISABILITY AFFECT YOUR MARITAL RELATIONSHIP?

So far this chapter has focused primarily on individual adjustment. Yet, the birth of a child with a disability is bound to affect a husband's and wife's relationship. The birth of any child brings changes in lifestyles and daily schedules. Parents find themselves devoting much of the time and energy once reserved for each other to their baby. And when the baby has special needs, an extra dimension of stress is added to the marriage.

[1]Sutton, B. (1982). A mother's view. Clinical proceedings. Children's Hospital National Medical Center. *The Child with Spina Bifida: II Psychological, Educational, and Family Concerns, 38*(4), 213.

Parents of children with developmental disabilities often experience a range of intense emotions as they adapt to their youngster's disability. Such emotional distress can affect a couple's relationship. Just how the marriage is affected depends, in part, on its strength before the baby's birth. Even healthy marriages may be stressed for a time as husband and wife struggle to cope with, accept, and understand the changes in their lives. As they adjust, they may discover that they have grown closer and that their marriage is stronger than ever. Some marriages, however, have problems unrelated to the child's disability that may become more evident during this period of stress. Old conflicts tend to reappear. In most instances, such problems can be resolved. There are situations, however, where the gap between husband and wife is so great that a resolution is not likely. In addition, during this time of crisis, parents' individual needs often conflict. Each partner looks to the other for support and comfort at a time when it is often difficult to provide.

When a child with a disability is born, parents frequently are faced with many unexpected choices and decisions. Pressures mount and you may feel like everything has to be attended to at once. However, a good rule of thumb is to try to avoid making major life decisions until you have had time to step back and look at your situation objectively. A crisis is not the time to decide your family's future. If possible, take the necessary time to sort out the facts and your feelings. Do not make hasty decisions you may regret later. Your relationship will need some time to adapt to the changes you are experiencing. Some suggestions to help you in this time of transition are provided later in this chapter. However, if serious conflicts or feelings of isolation occur, you may wish to seek assistance from a counselor. Sometimes this can be threatening to persons who take pride in being self-reliant. When one member of a marriage believes there are problems and requests intervention, it is best for a partner to acquiesce because these unresolved questions are likely to become a source of conflict or resentment. Agreeing to seek help is itself a message that you are willing to be supportive and that you are committed to one another.

DIVORCED, SEPARATED, AND SINGLE PARENTS

If maintaining the integrity of an existent marital relationship is complicated by the arrival of a child with disabilities, bringing peace to the strained relationships of separated and divorced parents demands greater care. Although separated couples need not necessarily be in conflict with each other, the probability that misunderstandings will occur are multiplied significantly. Where a child with disabilities is concerned, there is a need for a concerted effort to coordinate parental involvement. Because of this, it is important that parents keep each other informed and that they maintain an interest in their child's care and education.

It can be easy for the noncustodial parent to assume the other will take care of the special needs of their child. This can cause resentment and further alienation. Moreover, the custodial parent can project disinterest onto the absent parent or actively seek to avoid conflict by keeping the other parent uninformed. Because the issues of denial, pessimism, and optimism are weighted differently in each individual, strained communication must be avoided. Children need to love and be loved by each parent, and miscommunication will interfere with fulfilling this need.

To the extent possible, separated parents should share responsibility for caregiving and advocacy, as well as the myriad of other considerations raising a child engenders. Of course, this will not be possible in many cases because of the issues that caused the separation in the first place. All you can do is make your best effort.

It may become necessary to seek the help of qualified professionals when disagreements arise. This may take the form of arranging a simple conference or, in the case of significant conflict, scheduling therapeutic intervention for the family.

Single parents carry the added burden of not having anyone with whom to share the burden of parenthood. There are some who try to do everything themselves. Although this may be necessary in certain situations, try to make use of the agencies, support groups, and, above all, any concerned family members who are available to you.

WHAT TO TELL THE CHILD'S BROTHERS AND SISTERS

While most of your attention is focused on the child with a disability, it is easy to put aside your other children's needs. Remember, people of all ages can feel stress. Even the youngest child can sense when you are sad or something is wrong. Most of us want to know the truth, and children are no exception.

Avoid thinking you must protect your children from emotional pain, and keep in mind that you must remain compassionate. Children, like adults, need accurate, understandable information to help them comprehend what has happened. By discussing the unique needs of the child with developmental disabilities and how they may affect family life, parents will help their children adjust. This is par-

ticularly important if the child has medical or physical problems requiring much of the parents' time and attention. If no explanation is
offered about why so much of your time is spent with the child with
special needs, your other children may draw their own conclusions.
For example, they might think erroneously that you are angry with
them or perhaps that you love the child with a disability more than
them. Without information about the disability, fears may arise
about their sibling's well-being or their parents' sadness. Brothers
and sisters might also fear that they may get sick or develop disabilities. Siblings who are of childbearing age may be concerned about
their own offspring. It is important to acknowledge your children's
fears and concerns and reassure them of your love and their valued
place within the family.

HOW WILL OTHER FAMILY
MEMBERS AND FRIENDS REACT?

In addition to the immediate family, other family members and close
friends are affected by the arrival of the special child. Just as parents'
reactions may differ, so will those of relatives and friends. Relatives,
upset by the news, may insist that the problem will go away or that
the doctors are wrong. Some may argue that "these children" are
better off among themselves and therefore should be institutional-
ized. Other well-meaning friends may point out that Einstein did
not talk until he was 4 years old or that "so and so" took forever to
walk and now is perfectly "normal."

Some family members may look for someone to "blame" for the
child's disability. Comments such as "our side of the family is
healthy, so the bad genes must come from your side" unfortunately
are not uncommon. It is best to avoid such discussions, as they can
be divisive and destructive at a time when the family needs extra
support from everyone.

At times you may find that close friends and family fail to understand or are reluctant to talk to you about your feelings. They
may even avoid you or at the least avoid asking about your child for
fear of hurting you further. Some parents find they are unable to tell
others of their child's problems because it is too painful. Others cannot talk about anything else. If you want to discuss your concerns
and feelings, sometimes it is necessary to let others know that you
would like to talk. Remember, grandparents, aunts, uncles, brothers, sisters, and friends are making their own adjustment to the situation and at the same time may be trying to spare your feelings. The
best solution is to help each other by providing support and assis-

tance when needed. Like it or not, having a child with a disability is a family affair.

SPECIAL PROBLEMS OF ADOPTIVE PARENTS

Adoptive parents can experience special stresses when their children have disabilities, although in some ways they are very similar to those of biological parents. Adoptive parents may have had to come to terms with issues of infertility and the problems associated with the adoption process. If they opted to wait for an infant, rather than an older child, the discovery that their child may have a hidden disability is every bit as devastating as that a biological parent experiences, but with some unique stresses.

Because of policies of confidentiality, which adoption agencies put in place to protect the privacy of the adopted child, adopted parents, and birth parents, adoptive parents may be concerned that something concerning the birth family has been hidden from them, and a new dimension is added to the grief they experience. They may wonder what else has been concealed and how this will affect their attachment to their child. Guilt associated with their natural feelings of ambivalence is a common consequence. If their adaptation to the pain of childlessness has been especially difficult, the added trauma of a disability may make their adjustment especially poignant.

Another set of challenges awaits the couple who adopt a child they know has a disability. In one sense this couple is not presented with the trauma of the unexpected; but, in another sense, the complications that develop due to probable difficulties in the pre-adoption home can be formidable. For example, the child's ability to form an attachment and demonstrate affection and trust may have been affected by abuse or neglect in some cases. In other cases, there are separation problems associated with the loss of a caring foster home. There is some evidence that there are fewer separation problems if the previous placement was an institution or hospital. However, children who have formed a good relationship in the past tend to fare better. In the case of the adoption of an older child, much depends on the expectations of the new parents and the child's previous experiences and temperament.

YOU WILL NEED TO SETTLE IN

After the initial shock has passed and the disappointment, confusion, and grief begin to fade, life will become more normal as you settle into a daily routine. Although it may not be the routine you anticipated, the daily tasks of child care and of maintaining a home and a job do provide a structure that will help stabilize your life.

Every family develops its own system to meet the needs of the individual as well as those of the whole group. This is true whether or not there is a family member with disabilities. For example, some families sit down together for every meal, whereas others see each other only at Sunday dinner.

When a child has a disability, you may find that you must fit many additional activities into your family's schedule. Frequent doctor's visits, appointments with therapists, parent meetings, and so forth, although important, are very time-consuming. In addition, other duties such as giving medicine or doing physical therapy exercises may be daily chores. Adapting to your child's needs can take a lot of energy—intellectual and emotional, as well as physical. Because of such demands, it is important to pace yourself. Having a clear picture of your child's needs will help you settle in and plan for the future.

Have Realistic Expectations for Your Child

Developing a clear understanding of your child's strengths and weaknesses can help prevent unnecessary disappointment and discouragement. Suitable expectations are a protection against the extremes of deep pessimism or overoptimism. Focusing on what your child can do will help you recognize what can be accomplished and how you can help your child progress. Sometimes this is difficult to do. It is not always easy to pinpoint a child's capabilities. At such times, professionals from early intervention programs or Development Evaluation Centers may be of help (see Chapter 4).

Establish Priorities

As you identify the various tasks that need to be performed, including activities suggested by professionals, it is important for you, your child, and the entire family to establish priorities. Therapists, physicians, teachers, or others can unwittingly add to the stress a family feels. In their desire to be thorough and supportive, they may offer ideal intervention or treatment plans that tax you beyond what is necessary. You may need to be assertive in clarifying the extent to which certain exercises or follow-up visits are vital to your child's development. Otherwise, you can find yourself feeling guilty at not having performed tasks that are not essential. No one knows as well as you the demands on your time, as well as your financial and emotional resources. Recognizing the limits of your family's re-

sources is one way to begin. As you plan, consider the time, energy, and cost of each task required and compare this to the benefits. You will want to make sure that the needs of all family members, not just those of your child with special needs, are considered. You also may want to guard against a plan in which one family member makes all of the sacrifices. Some compromises should be expected of everyone. A realistic plan will diminish frustration, resentment, and unnecessary anger.

You may find that your priorities shift as your child grows and your family changes. Therefore, as time passes, routines and schedules should be reassessed and modified to meet changing needs.

There Will Be Ups and Downs

As your child grows and enters new worlds, feelings of disappointment, frustration, and grief may resurface. One day you may be on top of the world, only to find that the next day you are short on patience and angry at everyone. At times, feelings of sadness and sorrow may overwhelm you, often without warning. For example, you may experience both joy and a sense of sadness when your child begins to walk or talk. Although you may be thrilled with your child's accomplishments, you also are reminded painfully of how long it has taken. Major milestones in a child's life, such as the first day of school, the beginning of puberty, or turning 21, often are times when parents are reminded of their child's developmental disability.

These feelings usually are not as intense as those you felt when you first learned about your child's disability. And they typically do not last as long as they did initially. As someone explained, "You never get over having a child with a disability, but you do get used to it." Some professionals use the term *chronic sorrow* to describe the occasional return of painful feelings. Each family member may experience this at different times and in varying ways.

Your Marriage Is Important

Having a child with a disability should not mean that your marriage is disabled as well. As we have mentioned, healthy marriages can become stronger, but they also can be affected by the added stress of having a child with a disability. Just as your child has special needs, so does your marriage. In a way, it is easy to take care of your child's needs and neglect those of your marriage. Many parents feel there just is not enough time to attend to everything. Yet, you will be doing yourself and your family a favor if you take the time and give your relationship some extra attention.

How can this be achieved? First, parents need to spend time together. In a busy family, this can be difficult to arrange. There always seems to be something important that needs attention. When time alone is limited, parents may find that they focus only on significant family matters and never get around to just being with each other. Save some time just for yourselves, even if it means postponing other important matters for a while. Allowing yourselves to enjoy something together, when you do not talk about family routines and problems, can do much to relieve stress and preserve intimacy.

Another way of strengthening marital relationships is preserving communication between you and your partner. Being able to share concerns and feelings and discuss important issues is an important goal, but one that is not always easy to attain.

A good rule of thumb for fostering healthy communication is to avoid making assumptions about your partner's thoughts and feelings. Likewise, you should not take for granted that your mate knows where you stand on various issues. Even if it is "the same old story," listening to what really is meant and not only what is said can improve understanding of each other. After ample discussion, partners often realize that their views are quite similar and that the real obstacle was that they assumed too much and listened too little.

It is also important that you and your partner share responsibilities. There are many tasks to be considered: managing the finances, making decisions about health care, determining the best program for your child, and taking care of household chores. It is not unusual for partnerships to be lopsided. One parent may take on certain jobs and have minimal involvement with others. For example, mothers often take children to the doctor and attend clinics. As a result they may assume the responsibility for managing health care issues. Although it may be necessary for one person to be more familiar with certain problems, this should not mean that the other does not need to show an interest.

Single Parents Need a Break, Too

The burdens of a single parent of a child with disabilities are extensive. Despite budget cutbacks and hard economic times, there are sometimes opportunities for respite provided by state and private agencies. In some cases, this may take the form of an afternoon of recreation for the child; in other cases, weekend respite with approved providers may be available. If you are fortunate a family member or your ex-partner may be of help.

Whatever your circumstances, if there is a chance for you to receive some support or rest, you should avail yourself of the opportunity. Single parents often must do things themselves. However, some, for reasons of guilt or pride, think they owe it to their children to be all things at all times. It is important to realize that you cannot help others if you are exhausted or run down. Take care of yourself so that you will be able to better care for your child.

If a weekend alone, or even just an afternoon off, is not available, find some way to reward yourself.

Brothers and Sisters Also Have Needs

One question parents often ask is: What is the long-term effect on brothers and sisters when a child with a disability is in the family? Studies of brothers and sisters of children with special needs have found that many siblings possess greater tolerance and compassion toward persons with developmental disabilities than their peers. They also are more accepting of individual differences. Moreover, many of the siblings feel good about their role in the progress made by a brother or sister with special needs. Experience with a brother or sister who has a disability has led a number of siblings to careers in the field of human services, including social work, education, medicine, and psychology.

Not long ago, it was assumed that the care of children with developmental disabilities required an inordinate amount of parents' time. Therefore, many professionals concluded that brothers and sisters might feel neglected. Fortunately, most research has not found this to be so. Many parents do make allowances and consider the needs of all of their children. In addition, studies have found that brothers and sisters do not perceive substantial differences in the amount of attention given to them as compared to their sibling with special needs.

How Can You Help Your Other Children? When confronted with novel or unusual situations, children usually model their reactions after those of their parents. Reactions to a sibling with developmental disabilities are no exception. As a parent, how you respond to any situation will set the tone for your children. Because your reactions to the needs of your child with a disability will be numerous and mixed, you can expect that brothers and sisters will have varied reactions as well.

Before you can help your children cope with their emotions, you should be aware of your own feelings. Typically, children experience many of the same emotions as their parents, although the frequency and intensity might differ. Sometimes, children display love as well as resentment toward their sibling with special needs. It is not at all surprising to find occasional frustration, jealousy, and anger directed toward the child with a disability. These emotions commonly are also seen in children adjusting to the birth of a healthy brother or sister. However, when directed toward a child with a disability, these feelings can elicit guilt, fear, or perhaps protectiveness. Everyone needs to know that these feelings are not unusual. Keep in mind that with support from parents, children can learn to manage their emotions as well as resolve problems. As your children grow and mature, their understanding of complex issues will increase. Moreover, their feelings and perceptions will change, and each change may require additional support and guidance.

You may find that explanations must be repeated or expanded upon and that frequent reassurance is necessary. At all times, remember to keep your children well-informed. Without accurate information, fears and misunderstandings can develop, which in turn can affect a child's behavior.

WHEN TO SEEK PROFESSIONAL HELP

There are times when you lose confidence in your abilities as a parent. You may be faced with a difficult problem and find you are unsure of what to do. As we mentioned, talking to a close friend or parent who has had a similar experience may be all that is needed to work out a solution.

Unfortunately, this is not always enough. Concerns can linger or perhaps even worsen. If a problem begins to interfere with your ability to carry out daily activities, getting professional help should be considered. This does not necessarily mean ongoing therapy or counseling. Many issues can be resolved and stress can be reduced in just a few meetings with a professional counselor or therapist. Basically, counseling helps you to look at a problem from another perspective. It also provides an opportunity to talk to a professional who has been trained to help people resolve personal difficulties.

To determine if you need professional help, take a good look at your actions and reactions to daily events. If you discover that one or more of the following describe your behavior or the behavior of anyone in your family, then professional assistance could be beneficial: intense unprovoked anger, prolonged grief, marital problems, difficulty holding a job, loss of interest in typical social activities, and/or abusive behavior toward oneself or others. Chronic depression, excessive drinking, or use of drugs also are signs that help is needed. Sometimes, one family member's emotional problems are a sign that the family as a whole is having difficulties. In such instances, family counseling can be helpful.

It is important to note that not all emotional problems are obvious. Signs of trouble can take various forms. With children and adolescents, the sudden appearance of problem behaviors can be a sign of trouble. Symptoms also can be physical. For example, chronic headaches, loss of appetite, stomachaches, and other ailments may be physical expressions of an emotional problem. If a good student's school performance suddenly fails or a sociable child no longer gets along with peers, help may be needed. Regression (acting in an immature manner) may suggest a problem. For example, a school-age child may revert to thumb sucking, bed wetting, clutching a security blanket, and so forth. It is important to know that children often show their inner concerns through their behavior rather than by talking about them. You can think of these signs as barometers of the family's well-being. When there are significant concerns, help from a professional may be the best remedy. Professional counselors may help you look at problems in new ways and identify resources you may not have considered. However, the actual work involved in making long-term changes will remain the family's responsibility.

LOOKING TOWARD THE FUTURE

Having a child with a developmental disability is not something you expected. Although your child may involve you in many trying experiences, there are also many positive things in your life that happen because of this child. Often you will feel enthusiasm, pride, love, and a great deal of gratification in your role as a parent. You will realize capacities and strength within yourself that you never believed were there, and you will learn to cope in the face of adversity. You may wish things were different, but you may find that you have grown in ways that you never thought possible.

ADJUSTMENT OF THE CHILD WITH A DISABILITY

Until now, this chapter has focused on how you and your family might react and adjust to the special needs of a child with a disability. You also may be concerned about how your child will adjust to his or her own disability. Questions like "Will my daughter with mental retardation recognize that her life is different from other girls her age?" or "Will my son with a physical disability become a loner because he cannot participate in sports with his peers?" or "Will my child with special needs have friends to play with?" are asked frequently by parents (and siblings) of children with developmental disabilities. Such questions reflect a family's concern not just for themselves but for the feelings of their child.

Personal adjustment basically refers to the way individuals respond to the happy, sad, and challenging moments in their lives. In the population with disabilities, individuals considered to be well-adjusted generally are those who have a positive outlook on life, care about others, recognize their strengths, and are proud of their accomplishments. However, poorly adjusted individuals tend to have a negative outlook, often are bitter and unnecessarily dependent on others, and may be overly critical of those around them.

Helping a child develop into a well-adjusted individual is no easy task whether or not the child has a disability. Countless factors influence one's adjustment to personal challenges. For people with disabilities, some of the more obvious influences include the type and extent of the disability, the age of onset of the condition, the stability and support available from family and friends, as well as the child's inherited traits and biological characteristics. The manner in which family members, friends, and strangers react to the child and the disability is particularly significant for the child's attitude. For example, consider the effects on a child with a physical disability of constant attention, pampering, and assistance from others. Before long, this child begins to expect such attention and treatment from others. Such treatment, although meant to be helpful, in the long run may be teaching the child to be dependent. If, however, the child is encouraged from the beginning to do as much as possible for him- or herself, an appreciation of the rewards of self-sufficiency and personal accomplishment are much more likely to develop. Remember, the expectations of others do influence our behavior. Thus, parents' expectations for all of their children will affect their attitudes and outlook on life. In general, to help children with disabilities develop positive attitudes, a good rule of thumb is to try to maintain a balance between encouraging independence and providing enough assistance to prevent frustration.

As children grow and mature, the issues of adjustment change. In infancy and early childhood, for example, important influences on adjustment are the characteristics of the child and the interactions between the infant and family members. During this early stage, it is through interactions with the baby that parents learn about what is comforting, pleasing, distressing, or stimulating to the baby. Not all babies will respond the same way, and all parents learn to tailor their interactions to obtain the best results. Certain babies, however, because of their handicapping conditions, have more difficulty than most others in tolerating stimulation. Premature infants, for example, are much more easily overstimulated than full-term infants. When overstimulated, these infants respond by withdrawing—perhaps by turning their heads, averting their gaze, crying, or stiffening when held. It is important for family members to adjust their styles of interaction to accommodate these sensitive infants. Otherwise, the child will continue to withdraw from human contact, which easily can be misinterpreted by parents as a dislike for them. By adjusting the style of interaction to one the baby can tolerate, parents and the rest of the family adjust to the child's needs.

During the preschool and school years, interactions with people outside the family begin to play an important role in the adjustment of a child with a disability. Teachers, babysitters, neighbors, and peers become part of the child's everyday life and thus help shape attitudes. Many issues of adjustment appear in terms of learning adaptive skills (e.g., getting dressed or eating without help) and self-control (e.g., sharing voluntarily, learning to take turns in a group). Through experience with groups of adults and children, youngsters learn to control their individual desires. The ways in which people respond to the child's natural attempts to control the situation will influence the child's future expectations and approaches. Affection and consistent, fair discipline are as important with a child with a disability as they are with children who do not have disabilities. Feeling sorry for and indulging a child because of the disability is not an uncommon parental reaction. But it is one to avoid if you want your child to be accepted and valued by siblings and peers.

Avoiding discipline or stifling a naturally angry reaction to a misbe-havior because a child has a disability simply emphasizes to the child how different he or she is from other children. Most children with developmental disabilities, however, yearn for the daily re-minders that they are more like other children than unlike them. They want to be recognized as capable people, who deserve and can tolerate the same privileges and treatments received by others. In this regard, the best preparation parents can undertake to ensure that their child is well-adjusted is to acquaint themselves with typi-cal child development. Every child goes through difficult periods during maturation. Most often these phases of emotional turmoil are short-lived. Sometimes they are related to a particular develop-mental stage. A child's emerging need for independence is one ex-ample. Early adolescence, with its emphasis on acceptance by the peer group, entry into sexual maturity, and the desire for adult sex-ual relationships, is another. Any environmental or personal factor adds to the complexities of emotional growth.

By being acquainted with typical psychological stages, parents become better able to differentiate between what are typical cycles and those that represent more serious issues. It is easy for a parent to begin to ascribe deeper significance than is necessary to what could be typical adjustment difficulties to children with disabilities. In other words, with children who have disabilities, we may read more into a situation than is warranted. Conversely, true emotional disturbance can be overlooked because of our own need to reassure ourselves that everything is "normal." Observing other people's children, listening to other parents, and observing your other chil-dren will help you to be attuned to the usual problems your child with disabilities will face as well as those that are more directly re-lated to the areas in which he or she is challenged.

Some disabilities make the tasks of self-control more frustrating for everyone involved. But they are important to master, neverthe-less. If, for example, parents consistently ignore the early, nonverbal requests of a child with a hearing and language impairment but fi-nally respond once that child throws him- or herself on the ground and cries, then the child will learn that the most successful way of gaining attention is by having a tantrum. This same child might never have tantrums in school because the teacher has learned to respond to the earlier nonverbal signals, or when the teacher missed those, he or she never "gave in" as a response to a tantrum. If the child has a learning or memory problem, it is especially important that you be extremely consistent in your reactions to misbehaviors. The child with a learning disability has difficulty applying a lesson learned one day or in one context to another circumstance. This child is likely to make the same mistake over again, requiring repeated consequences. If the consequences are the same each time the behavior occurs, the child will learn the lesson infinitely more rapidly and will be able to turn attention to new learning.

No matter how carefully the parents introduce new challenges so that a child's frustrations are minimized and his or her accomplishments are optimal, once the child enters school, the lessons he or she is expected to learn may not always be so individually planned. In the process of learning the necessary lessons outside of the home, children are likely to encounter failure and perhaps rejection. Much research has demonstrated a strong relationship between personality adjustment and achievement. Encountering insurmountable and regular failure often results in an increase in maladaptive behaviors (e.g., excessive drinking or smoking, yelling, violence). This has been demonstrated repeatedly, even among people without disabilities who beforehand had been considered even-tempered and well-adjusted.[2] Unfortunately, because of the disability, even routine tasks may be difficult for a child. If the child is aware of others' accomplishments, it will be relatively easy for him or her to lose interest and become frustrated when laboring over a task that others do without a second thought. It is, therefore, important that the child be praised regularly for persisting with tasks that are difficult but necessary to master. Furthermore, you and your child's teachers should assist the child to find and pursue activities that accentuate strengths so that his or her feelings of self-worth can survive even outside of the family.

ACKNOWLEDGMENTS

Contributions have been made to this chapter by James C. Bernier, M.S.W., Sarah J. Gossler, M.S.W., and Debra J. Lobato, Ph.D.

---

[2]Szymanski, L.S., & Tanguay, P. (1980). *Emotional disorders of mentally retarded persons: Assessment, treatment, and consultation.* Baltimore: University Park Press.

4

Parents and Professionals
A Working Partnership

There are many reasons your child might need a thorough examination involving a number of professionals and specialists. In the past you may not have needed the services of these specialists, so you may be unfamiliar with what each professional does. If this is the case, you may want to know why particular specialists are seeing your child and how they can contribute to his or her evaluation and care.

WORKING TOGETHER

The idea of parents and professionals sharing information and responsibility for the care of a child with a disability is so important that it merits special attention here. At long last, parents are being recognized as the people who are most important in caring and planning for children with disabilities. In a way, parents are the real experts on their children. They often have the best understanding of the ways their children behave and communicate. They know their children's likes and dislikes as well as their motivations. Many parents have become skilled as teachers and advocates and are quite knowledgeable about their children's special needs and problems. In fact, the expertise of parents has been recognized by the federal government. Recent legislation, such as PL 102-119, the Individuals with Disabilities Education Act (IDEA) Amendments of 1991, mandates parent involvement in planning an appropriate education program for a child with special needs.

Although professionals may be able to suggest many ways to help a child who has a disability, parents know what activities are practical for their particular household. They can take into consideration schedules, finances, and other family needs when planning for the child. This parental perspective is extremely important and should be shared with professionals when intervention and treatment programs are being developed. Recognizing parents' abilities, however, does not mean that their contribution can replace the work of trained professionals. Professionals bring a background of rigorous training, as well as specific knowledge and experience, to evaluation and planning for children with disabilities.

Disabilities often involve complex biological and environmental factors. Advances in the understanding of these factors have come from scientists working in the fields of medicine as well as the social and behavioral sciences. This improved understanding has enabled professionals to develop more effective interventions for the education and treatment of children with developmental disabilities as well as programs to prevent future disabilities. The complexity of some of the disabilities and the diversity of the fields of study contributing to the new knowledge, however, make it necessary for professionals to specialize in order to keep up with even part of the useful information. Thus, numerous professionals from various specialties may be required to work with parents and children with disabilities at different times.

Children with disabilities benefit most when parents and specialists work together. Professionals can provide assistance by working directly with children, consulting with parents and teachers, and participating in the development of plans for care and management. Professionals also help parents solve specific problems and improve their teaching and caregiving skills. In turn, the professionals may rely on parents for specific observations and current information about their children. This give and take, respecting each other as equally important partners in the child's care, will contribute to a trusting relationship between parents and professionals, which is so important for the child's optimal development.

COORDINATING SERVICES

At times, the seemingly endless rounds of appointments and evaluations for your child may leave you feeling confused and exhausted. It may seem like you are running in circles only to get different, and occasionally conflicting, pieces of advice. Coordinating the services for a child with a disability can help reduce some of the stress this confusion can cause. If an evaluation has been done at a major child

Development Evaluation Center, then the chances are that one person from the team of professionals has been assigned the role of coordinator. Or, if your child is receiving early intervention services through a state-funded program, then you probably have a service coordinator. This professional may be a pivotal person you can contact when questions arise about services or upcoming appointments, or perhaps when you want to discuss new problems and concerns. The coordinator may be responsible for making sure that all necessary appointments have been scheduled, recommended tests have been performed, and appropriate follow-up care is being provided. Service coordination is considered so important that it has been included as a mandated service for early intervention programs receiving federal funds through IDEA.

If you have not been to a Development Evaluation Center and do not have a coordinator for your child, there are several options available. One is to assume the responsibility yourself. This would require that you keep accurate, up-to-date records on your child and make sure that all information is shared among the professionals involved in your child's care. This can be time-consuming and, at times, difficult, yet it is an effective way to make sure your child's needs are being met. Another possibility is to contact local associations for individuals with disabilities, such as the Spina Bifida Association, Down Syndrome Congress, or The Arc (formerly called the Association for Retarded Citizens of the United States), for assistance. You also may want to ask your child's pediatrician for help. You can request that all doctors and professionals involved in your child's care be informed of test results, intervention and treatment decisions, and future plans. Moreover, if your child is of school age and receives special education services, someone at the school may be able to assist you in coordinating services.

FINDING AND CHOOSING SPECIALISTS

Referrals to specialists may be made for a number of reasons, such as:

To evaluate specific skills as part of a complete diagnostic workup
To do further testing after a diagnosis has been established
To ensure ongoing intervention and treatment after a problem has been identified
To obtain a second opinion regarding a diagnosis, prognosis, or course of intervention and treatment

Choosing a specialist, like selecting your family doctor, is not always easy. A good place to begin is by asking for recommendations from respected professionals, family members, or trusted friends. If you are new to an area, the public health department, visiting nurse associations, hospitals, the medical bureau, and the directory of medical specialties can provide useful information.

You should feel comfortable with your choice, particularly if you expect a long-term relationship. You should be able to discuss available services, ask questions, and consider the cost of service with the professional without being intimidated or overly embarrassed. Feeling good about the way a professional interacts with your child and the extent of his or her experience in working with children who have special needs are also things to consider. Some professionals might feel uneasy working with a child who has a disability or may not recognize how certain disabilities affect a child's behavior. Remember that your neighbor's favorite doctor may not be the right one for you! If you find that you are uncomfortable or that you do not like the way your child is treated, it is up to you to change doctors, therapists, counselors, and so forth. The better you communicate with the professional, the more likely it is that better services will be obtained for your child.

SOME PROFESSIONALS YOU MAY MEET

The professionals described in this section are people you may meet in Development Evaluation Centers. Also included are specialists your child may be referred to by your family physician or the child's pediatrician. (Note that many of the procedures mentioned here are described in more detail in later chapters.)

Anesthesiologist

An anesthesiologist is a medical doctor who administers anesthesia such as a drug or gas to a patient about to undergo surgery or an obstetrical or other medical procedure, in order to block the feeling of pain. The anesthesiologist examines the patient before an operation; then, in consultation with the other doctors involved, selects the type of anesthesia to be used.

Audiologist

An audiologist is a specialist trained to evaluate a person's hearing. A variety of instruments and/or tests may be used to determine a person's hearing ability. In testing a child's hearing, the audiologist may observe the child's reactions to environmental sounds and to specific sound frequencies presented to each ear. The audiologist also may examine the flexibility of the eardrum using a special instrument in a procedure called *tympanometry* (see Chapter 22). Nerve responses to sounds can be assessed by examining brainwave patterns measured after an eardrum has been exposed to a sound. This is a special procedure called *auditory evoked response* (AER), sometimes called *brain stem evoked response* (BSER) (see Chapter 22). Often, an audiologist will have to test a small child's hearing more than once before an accurate picture of the hearing abilities can be determined. Audiologists frequently work closely with other professionals interested in the child's hearing such as speech-language therapists, otolaryngologists (ear, nose, and throat doctors), pediatricians, psychologists, educators, and so forth. Sometimes, more sophisticated forms of testing may also be used, such as central auditory processing, which assesses a child's listening skills.

If a hearing loss is detected, the audiologist may be the key person involved in planning and coordinating a remediation program. And, if hearing aids are prescribed, the audiologist will teach family members about their proper care, fit, and use.

Cardiologist

A cardiologist is a medical doctor who specializes in the evaluation and treatment of diseases of the heart. The cardiologist examines individuals for symptoms of heart problems, and, in the process, uses various instruments and procedures. Commonly, the doctor listens to the heart sounds using a stethoscope; and, if necessary, conducts special tests such as an electrocardiogram, echocardiogram, or cardiac catheterization. (For descriptions of these procedures, see Chapter 22.) Children with heart problems are treated according to their specific needs. A treatment plan might include one or more of the following: careful monitoring of a child's condition, a change in the child's diet, daily heart medication(s), and surgery to correct a specific defect of the heart. The latter is done by a cardiac surgeon.

Counselor

A counselor is a professional who has been trained to provide individual and/or group counseling services. Counselors may work in a variety of settings such as a clinic, hospital, mental health center, university, or public school, or have their own private practice. In general, counseling aims at helping people improve their feelings about themselves as well as their social relationships with others. A counselor may help an individual pinpoint specific problems and identify potential solutions through personal interviews, individual or group discussions, observation of specific behaviors, or assessment using a variety of tests or inventories. A counselor may work with a parent and a child individually or together, or perhaps with an entire family. It is important to select a counselor based on your needs as well as the counselor's area of expertise. Not all counselors can help solve all problems. (See also **Psychiatrist, Psychologist,** and **Social Worker.**)

Dentist

A dentist is a doctor who has been trained in the care of the mouth as well as prevention, diagnosis, and treatment of diseases of the mouth, particularly of the teeth and gums. Most people have experienced a dental examination and treatment of common dental problems such as cavities. Most will recall that a dental examination involves inspection of the teeth and gums with various instruments and sometimes requires a series of X rays of the teeth. Treatment of cavities or tooth decay usually consists of drilling out the decayed portion of the tooth and filling the hole with a substance to prevent further decay. Other common procedures used in the treatment of dental problems are: cleaning, pulling of teeth, capping or crowning diseased or broken teeth, root canal treatments, and gum care. Professionals in the field of dentistry may specialize and focus their practice on certain types of dental problems. For example, an **orthodontist** corrects irregular tooth alignment through the use of braces or other dental appliances, and a **periodontist** focuses on treating diseases and problems of the gums.

Dietitian (see Nutritionist)

Educator

An educator is a specialist trained to teach others. Educators, or teachers, are professionals who have been trained to instruct students in various fields of study. Teachers must qualify to teach in public schools by successfully completing a course of study that meets the state's requirements. Most states grant teaching certificates for specific areas such as elementary education, secondary education, early childhood or preschool education, and special education. The field of special education is the one with which most parents of children with developmental disabilities will come in contact. Students majoring in special education receive specific training in various disabilities, such as learning disabilities, hearing and visual impairments, and mental retardation. As more children with developmental disabilities are included in education programs with their peers, all educators will have to become familiar with special education practices.

Endocrinologist

An endocrinologist is a medical doctor who specializes in the study and treatment of disorders of the endocrine, or ductless, glands in the body. The endocrine glands include the pituitary, thyroid, parathyroid, adrenal, pancreas, ovaries, and testes. They are called ductless glands because they secrete their hormones directly into the blood stream. Problems with hormone production may result in either too much hormone being released (hypersecretion), too little being released (hyposecretion), or other glandular disorders.

Gastroenterologist

A gastroenterologist is a medical doctor who specializes in the study and treatment of problems of the stomach and intestinal tract. This doctor also might be concerned with other parts of the body related to digestion, including the esophagus, liver, gall bladder, and pancreas. Patients usually are referred to a gastroenterologist for further evaluation, diagnosis, and treatment of stomach and intestinal problems by their regular physician.

General Practitioner or Family Physician

A general practitioner is a medical doctor who attends to and treats a range of medical conditions in a general practice. The general practitioner conducts physical examinations and may order and/or perform specific tests to diagnose a patient's problem. The general practitioner, often referred to as a G.P., provides preventative care by inoculating or vaccinating patients against certain diseases and by advising people about proper diet, exercise, hygiene, and methods of avoiding diseases. A general practitioner also may provide prenatal care to pregnant women and may deliver babies.

Genetic Counselor

A genetic counselor is a specialist trained to advise expectant or potential parents about the risk of their children having hereditary birth defects. People may want to see a genetic counselor for one of the following reasons: they previously may have had a child with either an inherited disorder or a congenital anomaly; someone in the immediate family has a congenital anomaly or genetic disorder; the potential mother is 35 years or older; the mother has had repeated miscarriages or stillbirths; or the couple is worried about exposure to drugs, alcohol, or radiation. The genetic counselor will gather background information about the couple and other family members concerning inherited problems or congenital anomalies. In some situations, chromosome or other genetic studies will need to be done to determine if either parent is a carrier of a chromosome or genetic disorder that could be passed on to the baby. (Chromosomes are structures of the cell nucleus containing DNA, which transmits genetic information.) Usually, results are given in terms of probability, or percent chance, that a baby will or will not have a genetic defect or a congenital anomaly. It must be emphasized that the counselor cannot tell with absolute certainty whether or not a problem will occur. Moreover, the genetic counselor does not tell parents what plan of action should be pursued, but only informs couples about the possible risks.

Geneticist

A neonatal geneticist is a physician who is concerned with the relationship between heredity and certain diseases. The role of the clinical geneticist is often similar to that of the genetic counselor and would include performing a complete examination of the potential parents, discussing all of the information obtained in a genetic counseling session, and describing the chances of having a child with a genetic disorder.

Gynecologist

A gynecologist is a medical doctor who specializes in the diagnosis and treatment of disorders of the female reproductive system. Gynecologists conduct general physical examinations and special examinations of such organs as the vagina, uterus, and ovaries. They prescribe appropriate health care regimens including medications, exercises, and hygiene procedures. A gynecologist may perform surgery as needed to correct a malfunction or remove a diseased organ. A gynecologist also has training as an obstetrician and may provide care for pregnant women.

Intern

An intern is a professional who has just graduated from medical school and is starting to practice medicine under the supervision of licensed doctors in a hospital setting. Internships most often continue for 1 year. The purpose of the internship is to provide young doctors with supervised training and to allow them to gain valuable experience in examining and treating patients.

Internist

An internist is a medical doctor who specializes in the treatment of diseases of internal organ systems. The internist deals with problems and diseases that usually are not treated surgically.

Neurologist

A neurologist is a physician who specializes in the diagnosis and treatment of disorders of the nervous system, including the brain, cranial nerves, spinal cord, and peripheral nerves. The neurologist traditionally deals with problems such as seizures, brain injury, muscular disorders, brain tumors, and so forth. The neurological examination conducted by the neurologist attempts to determine how the nervous system is developing, how it is functioning, and if any problems exist. By observing things such as eye movements, vision, and hearing, neurologists look at, among other things, muscle strength, motor coordination, reflexes, ability to perceive sensations, and the function of the major cranial nerves. A neurologist may use a variety of instruments or laboratory tests to assist in the evaluation of a person's nervous system. The brainwave test (electroencephalogram [EEG]) is used primarily in the evaluation of seizure disorders. The neurologist also may order brain scans (see Chapter 22), spinal taps (see Chapter 12), and other tests to diagnose a patient's condition. Parents seeking neurological evaluations for their children with disabilities should look for a pediatric neurologist who specializes in examining and treating children. A pediatric neurologist is trained to evaluate the developing nervous system and is skilled in assessing problems that may be particular to children.

Neurosurgeon

A neurosurgeon is a medical doctor who has had special training in operative procedures of the brain, spinal cord, and nerves. Neurosurgeons usually perform neurological examinations similar to those done by a neurologist. Neurosurgeons are often asked to treat children with hydrocephalus by inserting a *shunt*, which involves a plastic tube being placed into the middle of the brain (the ventricle), in order to drain the surplus liquid (cerebral spinal fluid) into the abdominal cavity (see Chapter 25). Neurosurgeons are also consulted in cases of head injury, brain tumor, bleeding into the brain, and other brain problems.

Nurse

A nurse is a professional who is trained to care for those who are sick or injured, or who have disabilities, and to provide advice on appropriate health care and prevention of illnesses. Nurses work in many settings including hospitals, clinics, physicians' offices, and the community. The nurse's specific role depends on his or her training, professional background, and job requirements. A nurse's training can lead to several professional degrees. The most common ones are licensed practical nurse (L.P.N.) and registered nurse (R.N.). An L.P.N. is licensed to care for patients under the direction of a physician or registered nurse. An R.N. is a graduate of a nursing training program who has completed all of the requirements for registration and licensure demanded by a state board of nursing. The type of nursing a particular nurse practices often is indicated by the title. For example, the titles district, community, or visiting nurse all refer to registered nurses who work in the community, caring for persons in their homes or in community centers. A school nurse is a registered nurse who provides care to children while they are in school, and a clinic nurse usually works in a hospital setting.

Nurse Practitioner

A nurse practitioner is a registered nurse who has had additional, specialized training enabling him or her to perform physical examinations and to provide general medical care and treatments to patients. Such treatment is usually carried out in a medical facility (e.g., health clinic, health center, hospital, other public health agency) and is provided under the direction of a physician. The expanded role of the nurse practitioner, who sometimes is referred to as the primary care nurse practitioner or nurse clinician, typically includes performing physical examinations; recording physical findings; ordering, interpreting, and evaluating diagnostic tests; and formulating a care plan and expected outcome based on the individual's condition. Nurse practitioners recommend physical therapy or other therapeutic procedures. In developing comprehensive treatment plans for their patients, nurse practitioners collaborate and consult with physicians and other health care professionals. Nurse practitioners are licensed by state licensing authorities, as required of any other health professional. You will recognize a nurse practitioner by the letters R.N.P., which stand for registered nurse practitioner.

Nutritionist

A nutritionist is a specialist in the study of food intake. Nutritionists who work directly with patients most often are found in clinical settings such as hospitals or diagnostic centers. In the field of developmental disabilities, the nutritionist can be an important member of an interdisciplinary team of professionals. The role of the nutritionist generally involves assessing the child's past nutritional history and current status. The assessment might include a study of the child's daily food intake, feeding abilities, food tolerances, and so forth. If a nutritional problem is discovered, the nutritionist, along with the other members of the interdisciplinary team, will develop a treatment plan. Nutritionists are often involved in the care of children with specific metabolic disorders.

Practicing nutritionists usually are registered dietitians, which is indicated by the initials R.D. A registered dietitian has completed a specified course of study in dietetics or nutrition, as well as an internship in a professional setting.

Obstetrician

An obstetrician is a medical doctor who specializes in the care of women during pregnancy, birth, and the period immediately following the birth of a child. The obstetrician typically is the doctor who delivers the baby. Obstetric care usually involves frequent visits to the doctor's office during pregnancy. During the visit, the doctor will monitor the growth of the unborn baby (fetus) and examine the mother's condition. The obstetrician also provides valuable advice about proper nutrition and exercise; and the importance of immunizations, of getting adequate rest, and of avoiding the use of drugs, cigarettes, and alcohol, and the unnecessary use of prescription and nonprescription medications.

Occupational Therapist

An occupational therapist is a professional who specializes in helping individuals with disabilities to improve their skills of daily living in order to function as independently as possible. With children, the focus of occupational therapy (O.T.) concentrates on rehabilitation or the acquisition of new skills. The occupational therapist may work with children in a number of different settings including hospitals, residential facilities, and diagnostic centers, as well as the child's home. The occupational therapist primarily helps the child to improve fine motor skills (i.e., the function of the smaller muscles of the body such as those found in the hands and arms). Examples of such skills include reaching and grasping objects, self-feeding, drinking from a cup, and using crayons. The occupational therapist also devises splints and other adaptive equipment to improve the child's functional abilities. Occupational therapists may work directly with children on a regular basis or consult with family members, teachers, or other professionals who work with the individual child.

Ophthalmologist

An ophthalmologist is a medical doctor who specializes in the diagnosis and treatment of injuries, diseases, and functional problems of the eye. The ophthalmologist examines the eyes and tests visual abilities. The examination may include looking into the eye with a special instrument as well as having the patient look through a variety of lenses. If a vision problem is detected, the doctor may prescribe corrective lenses or glasses.

Optometrist

An optometrist is a professional specifically trained to test vision and prescribe corrective lenses when necessary. The optometrist's professional degree is a doctor of optometry (O.D.). Optometrists are not medical doctors and therefore are not qualified to treat eye diseases or injuries.

Orthopaedist

An orthopaedist is a medical doctor who specializes in the diagnosis, prevention, and treatment of disorders of the bones, joints, and muscles. Of particular interest to the orthopaedist are the body structures involved in various movements such as walking and positions such as sitting or standing. An orthopaedic examination includes an evaluation of muscle strength, range of motion, flexibility, and the presence or absence of any deformities. Often, one or more X rays are needed to determine if an orthopaedic problem exists. Children with certain developmental disabilities, such as cerebral palsy or spina bifida, may need to see an orthopaedist for evaluation and possible treatment at various points during their lives. These disabilities may affect muscle control, which in turn may cause bony deformities. Orthopaedic treatment may consist of a prescription for exercises, physical or occupational therapy, splints, casts, braces, adaptive equipment, or surgery. Orthopaedists often work closely with physical and occupational therapists who are carrying out the treatment plan.

Otolaryngologist

An otolaryngologist is a medical doctor who specializes in the diagnosis and treatment of diseases of the ear, nose, and throat. An otolaryngologist, usually referred to as an E.N.T. specialist, examines the ear, nose, and throat using various tools and instruments such as an audiometer, which measures the acuity of hearing; X rays; an otoscope, which is used to inspect the ear; and so forth. Some physicians may choose to specialize further and focus their attention on only the ear, nose, or throat. Respectively, these doctors are called **otologists, rhinologists,** and **laryngologists.**

Pediatrician

A pediatrician is a medical doctor who specializes in the care of children from the time they are born through adolescence. The pediatrician provides routine health care services such as regular checkups and immunizations. This often is called *well-baby* or *well-child* care. The pediatrician also cares for the child who has become ill or hurt. Parents frequently turn to the pediatrician for advice about many childrearing issues. For example, the pediatrician may be asked questions about behavior management techniques, toilet training, sibling rivalries, discipline strategies, development of independent feeding skills, and so forth. Many pediatricians can offer excellent suggestions about these and other topics.

Physiatrist

A physiatrist is a medical doctor who primarily uses physical agents to treat persons with physical disabilities or neuromuscular disorders. Physical agents may include heat, light, water, electricity, massage, exercise, and radiation. In the field of developmental disabilities, the physiatrist may be involved with those children who have disorders of the nerves and muscles or other physical disabilities requiring intervention or treatment. The physiatrist usually works closely with orthopaedists, and physical and occupational therapists. The physiatrist may be instrumental in prescribing splints, braces, wheelchairs, and other pieces of adaptive equipment for children with physical impairments.

Physical Therapist

A physical therapist is a professional trained to help individuals with disabilities improve and develop skills for balance and movement. The physical therapist (P.T.) is concerned mainly with the function of the larger muscles of the body. These muscles are needed for gross motor activities such as walking, crawling, rolling, and moving from one stationary position to another. Physical therapists can provide therapy to adults and children alike in a variety of settings, such as in hospitals, clinics, rehabilitation centers, schools, and homes. Physical therapists are important members of interdisciplinary teams that provide diagnostic and treatment services to children with developmental disabilities. In this context, the physical therapist's role usually involves conducting an evaluation of the child's current level of motor development and determining if there is a need for therapy. As part of the evaluation, the therapist examines the child's muscle tone, muscle strength, range of motion of the joints, reflexes, posture, movement patterns, and motor skills. The physical therapist also will look for any structural deformities.

Psychiatrist

A psychiatrist is a medical doctor who specializes in the diagnosis and treatment of mental, emotional, and behavior disorders. The psychiatrist obtains information about an individual's condition through observation, physical examination, interviews, and testing. Family members and friends of the patient may be interviewed in order to learn more about the patient's medical and personal history. By carefully evaluating all of the data that have been gathered, the psychiatrist develops a diagnosis of the individual's problem and formulates a plan of intervention or treatment. Psychiatric treatment methods vary considerably, depending on the person's problems, and may include the use of prescribed medications and/or participation in one or more types of individual or group therapy.

Psychologist

A psychologist is a professional who specializes in the study of intellectual functioning and behavior. There are many types of psychologists, including clinical, educational, school, child, and counseling psychologists. Each area has a different focus and prepares the psychologist for a different type of practice. Despite the different emphases in training, all psychologists are concerned with the analysis, interpretation, and application of information that has been obtained about an individual, group, specific problem, or area of investigation.

Parents of children with developmental disabilities are most likely to encounter clinical, school, or child psychologists. Psychologists working with children who have disabilities are skilled in evaluating the child's developmental, social-emotional, and intellectual abilities. As part of the evaluation process they are likely to administer and interpret intelligence tests. Many psychologists also are skilled in other types of evaluation such as behavioral assessment. Upon completion of the psychological evaluation, the psychologist formulates recommendations or develops specific programs for particular problems. The psychologist may work directly with children or consult with parents, teachers, or other professionals involved in the child's overall care.

Respiratory Therapist

A respiratory therapist (R.T.) is a professional trained to help persons who have breathing problems. Assistance can be provided either directly by inhalation and chest physical therapy or indirectly through the use of special equipment designed to make breathing easier. Equipment used in respiratory therapy may include oxygen masks, respirators, mist tents, and intermittent positive pressure breathing (IPPB) machines. The latter technique helps breathing by inflating the lungs with pressurized air. Respiratory therapists most often are employed in medical settings such as hospitals and nursing homes, but also work in agencies providing home care services.

Social Worker

A social worker is a professional whose role, in general terms, involves helping others get along in society. Social workers provide assistance in many different types of human services agencies. For example, they are employed routinely by hospitals, schools, welfare agencies, diagnostic centers, residential facilities, and public health agencies. The specific function of the social worker depends on both the job setting and the individual's professional background and training. Many social workers function as counselors and psychotherapists. In addition, they may help families locate and obtain services from appropriate agencies or other available sources of assistance. In the field of developmental disabilities, social workers often help families to obtain emotional and financial support. For example, they may help families contact other families experiencing similar problems; provide individual, group, or family therapy; introduce a parent to relevant national and/or local organizations; or show parents how to apply for appropriate federal or state aid programs.

Speech-Language Pathologist

A speech-language pathologist is a professional who is trained to evaluate speech and language disorders in children and adults. In addition, speech-language pathologists plan and carry out intervention and treatment plans for these disorders. The speech-language pathologist, who also may be referred to as a speech-language therapist, evaluates speech and language skills primarily by observing the child and conducting specific tests. Speech-language pathologists, like audiologists, also are concerned about hearing problems and the impact they have on the development of language and communication skills. Many children with developmental disabilities are seen by speech-language pathologists because of delayed language development. After the evaluation is completed, the speech-language pathologist will determine the need for direct speech-language therapy. If a child has not developed vocal communication skills, speech-language pathologists will examine the type of communication system the child could use (e.g., a sign language system, modern communication devices).

Surgeon

A surgeon is a medical doctor who specializes in the use of operative or surgical techniques to treat infections, tumors, and injuries; correct deformities; and improve functioning. A surgeon may practice general surgery or specialize further. For example, hand surgeons restrict their practice to problems of the hand; plastic surgeons use surgical procedures to restore or repair parts of the body that have been damaged, lost, or deformed; and cardiovascular surgeons use operative procedures to correct problems of the vascular system, which includes the heart, lungs, and blood vessels. Prior to an operation, the surgeon will examine the patient, select the most appropriate surgical procedure, and evaluate the risks involved. Part of planning for an operation may include consulting with other doctors who have cared for the patient and are familiar with the specific problem necessitating surgery.

Urologist

A urologist is a medical doctor who specializes in the diagnosis and treatment of problems of the urinary tract and kidneys. The urologist also is the doctor who diagnoses and treats diseases and structural problems of the male and female genital tracts. A urological examination might require use of special equipment such as catheters, cystoscopes, X rays, and other instruments. Treatment of urological problems includes prescribing medicine, use of antiseptics to prevent infection, or surgery. In the field of developmental disabilities, children who have spina bifida or a spinal cord injury may need to see a urologist because urological problems are common with these disorders.

ACKNOWLEDGMENTS

Contributions have been made to this chapter by Leslie E. Weidenman, Ph.D., and James A. Mulick, Ph.D.

II

Common Problems
and Disabilities
in Children
with Special Needs

5

Mental Retardation

DESCRIPTION AND INCIDENCE

Although most people have some idea of what *mental retardation* means, not everyone is aware that there are technical definitions of the term. The most commonly used definition was developed by the American Association on Mental Retardation (AAMR), a professional organization that specializes in problems of people with mental retardation and developmental disabilities. This definition, which was revised in 1992, is written in complex language and has several important parts.

According to the American Association on Mental Retardation:

> Mental retardation refers to substantial limitations in present functioning. It is characterized by significantly subaverage intellectual functioning, existing concurrently with related limitations in two or more of the following applicable adaptive skill areas: communication, self-care, home living, social skills, community use, self-direction, health and safety, functional academics, leisure, and work. Mental retardation manifests before age 18.[1]

The phrase "significantly subaverage intellectual functioning" usually means that a child has an IQ score of 70–75 or below on one of the individually administered, standard intelligence tests (see Chapter 27 for a discussion of intelligence tests).

"Adaptive skill areas" refers to the skills needed for personal independence and social responsibility such as dressing, toileting,

---

[1] American Association on Mental Retardation, Ad Hoc Committee on Terminology and Classification (Luckasson, R., Chair). (1992). *Mental retardation: Definition, classification, and systems of supports* (special 9th ed.). Washington, DC: Author.

feeding, behavior control, independence in the community, and interaction with peers. *Adaptive behavior* is a general term that often is used to mean self-care and social skill areas.

Using this definition, a valid diagnosis of mental retardation can be made if the following three criteria are met:

1.   *Intellectual functioning level:* The principal measure of intellectual functioning is the intelligence quotient (IQ). An IQ is obtained from a standardized intelligence test such as the Stanford-Binet Intelligence Scale or Wechsler Intelligence Scales for Children. An individual receiving an IQ score of approximately 70–75 or below would meet the first criterion for the definition of mental retardation, as such a score would fall in the range of subaverage intellectual functioning. Individuals achieving scores above 75 would not be considered to have mental retardation.

2.   *Adaptive skill level:* The second criterion is an individual's adaptive skill level. The generally accepted definition of mental retardation outlines 10 areas of adaptive behavior including communication, self-care, social skills, health and safety, and so forth. If a person with limited intellectual abilities as measured by one or more IQ tests also displays significant limitations in at least two areas of adaptive behavior, then two criteria for a diagnosis of mental retardation have been met.

3.   *Age of onset:* The third criterion that must be met in order to diagnose mental retardation is that the condition was apparent prior to the age of 18 years. This includes the time period from conception to the individual's 18th birthday. If this requirement and the two mentioned above are met, then a diagnosis of mental retardation would be made.

The 1992 AAMR definition of mental retardation takes a more practical approach than previously used definitions and focuses on the intensity and pattern of support an individual with mental retardation needs in order to function in the community. The definition requires that an individual's strengths and weaknesses in each of the 10 adaptive skill areas be considered and that the individual's need for support be described in each area. Four levels of intensity of support have been established. They are intermittent, limited, extensive, and pervasive; they are described briefly in Table 1.

By identifying the strengths and weaknesses of the person with mental retardation and outlining the support the individual needs to live as independently as possible, parents and professionals as well as the individual together can develop a detailed service plan to meet specific needs. The definition also provides a focus on personal growth and development for each individual with mental retarda-

Table 1.   Levels of intensities of needed supports

Level of intensity of support	Description
Intermittent	Uses supports on an "as needed" basis. A person with mental retardation requiring intermittent support might only need assistance during life-span transitions (e.g., loss of a job, change in housing, a medical crisis).
Limited	Requires consistent support over time, but of a time-limited nature (e.g., time-limited job training may be required or support by staff during transitions from school programs to adult services).
Extensive	Requires daily involvement and support in work or home environments. Extensive support is long-term and not time-limited.
Pervasive	Requires high-intensity, constant support across environments. This level of support would involve more staff and is likely to be more intrusive than extensive or time-limited supports.

Source: American Association on Mental Retardation, Ad Hoc Committee on Terminology and Classification (Luckasson, R., Chair). (1992). *Mental retardation: Definition, classification, and systems of supports* (special 9th ed.). Washington, DC: Author.

tion and moves away from out-of-date practices in which maintenance was often the only concern.

The 1992 definition of mental retardation differs from previous versions in several ways. A major change is that it eliminates the levels, or severity, of mental retardation. Formerly, the terms *mild, moderate, severe,* and *profound* were used to describe the degree of mental retardation. The determination of level of mental retardation was based primarily on an individual's score on a standardized IQ test. Although such categorization is no longer part of the 1992 definition, the previous terms are still in use in many professional circles. For example, the American Psychiatric Association includes levels of retardation in its *Diagnostic and Statistical Manual of Mental Disorders* (4th ed.).[2] It is very likely that parents and family members will encounter these terms so they are included here. The four levels of mental retardation, as well as "normal" and "borderline" intelligence, are described here and summarized in Table 2.

Normal Intelligence

According to the 1983 definition, people are considered to be of average intelligence if they score between 84–85 and 115–116 on an intelligence test. This group makes up approximately 68% of the population. People who score above 116 would be considered to be of above-average intelligence or gifted.

---

[2] American Psychiatric Association. (1994). *Diagnostic and statistical manual of mental disorders* (4th ed.). Washington, DC: Author.

Table 2.   Levels of intelligence in relation to IQ score

Level of intelligence	Intelligence test score	% of population in each group[a]
Normal	Between 84–85 and 115–116	68
Borderline	Between 68–70 and 84–85	14
Mild mental retardation	Between 50–55 and 68–70	2
Moderate mental retardation	Between 35–40 and 50–55	< 1/2
Severe mental retardation	Between 20–25 and 35–40	< 1/4
Profound mental retardation	Less than 20–25	< 1/4

Source: Grossman, H.J. (1983). Classification in mental retardation. Washington, DC: American Association on Mental Deficiency.

[a]Approximately 15% of people score above 115–116 IQ.

Borderline Intelligence

An IQ score that falls in the range from 68–70 to 84–85 suggests that an individual is of borderline intelligence. These people are not considered to have mental retardation, as they do not have impairments in their independent living skills. This group represents approximately 14% of the population.

Mild Mental Retardation

Mild mental retardation applies to IQ scores in the range of 50–55 to 68–70, depending on the test used. Many persons with mild mental retardation are indistinguishable from the general population, but they usually will learn more slowly in school and may be limited in their choice of vocation. They are frequently quite independent in the community and most often take responsibility for their own basic daily needs. They are often capable of working and living either independently or with a minimum of assistance and supervision.

Moderate Mental Retardation

Moderate mental retardation includes the IQ score range of 35–40 to 50–55. Children with moderate mental retardation generally will learn the basic arithmetic skills necessary for daily living. As they get older, their school programs often will concentrate on important adaptive, or self-help, skills, community living, and vocational preparation. As adults, they may be employed in supervised work settings.

Severe Mental Retardation

Severe mental retardation refers to IQ scores that fall in the range of 20–25 to 35–40. People with severe mental retardation may have associated disabilities, such as motor problems or significant speech and language deficits. School programs will emphasize basic developmental skills, communication, and adaptive behavior. Many people with severe mental retardation usually will need some supervision in their employment settings.

Profound Mental Retardation

Profound mental retardation refers to IQ scores that fall below the range of 20–25. Again, there may be significant associated disabilities. With proper training, many persons with profound mental retardation can learn basic adaptive skills. If their functioning is very low, if other disabilities such as hearing problems or visual or motor impairments are significant, or if their health status is precarious, special living arrangements may be necessary.

WHAT IT MEANS TO HAVE MENTAL RETARDATION

Mental retardation can be a frightening term. Frequently parents are able to recognize and accept other disabilities in their children, but are devastated by the term *mental retardation*. Many people have strong prejudices or misconceptions about mental retardation. For example, they may think children with mental retardation are very different, that they will not learn or grow or have typical emotions, that their appearance will be unusual, that they always will be children, or that they will be unable to care for themselves.

The various words used to describe a child who receives significantly subaverage scores on psychological tests can be confusing. Parents may have heard terms such as *slow learner, developmental delay,* or *learning disability,* and may not be sure how they differ.

Basically, a child with mental retardation is one who learns slowly. However, the term *slow learner* usually is reserved for children who function slightly below average intellectually, but not so far below that he or she would be considered to have mental retardation. A young child diagnosed with mental retardation will continue to learn, change, and grow intellectually, but the speed with which new skills are acquired will be much slower than that of the average person. Mental retardation is not drastically different from many other kinds of learning problems, but it means that a large number of skill areas are affected, especially those skills that are needed for success in school.

It is important to know that children with mental retardation are not helpless. Unless some other disorder or medical problem is present, or the environment is deprived, children with mental retardation continue to progress.

A child with mental retardation also could be considered to have a learning disability, but only in the broadest sense of the term. Children with mental retardation have disabilities because they have trouble learning or because they learn very slowly, compared to the average child. *Learning disability,* however, is a specific term that refers to a different kind of problem (see Chapter 7). Children with learning disabilities most often have one or more specific deficits in skills necessary for learning, but do not have globally subaverage intelligence. They may receive average or even above-average scores on psychological tests, but fall 2 or more years behind their peer group academically for reasons that cannot always be identified. In these very important ways, learning disabilities and mental retardation are different types of disabilities.

MENTAL RETARDATION VERSUS DEVELOPMENTAL DELAY: MAKING AN ACCURATE DIAGNOSIS

It is very difficult to determine with certainty whether very young children have mental retardation. Infants and preschoolers who are slow in some or all of their developmental skills initially may be said to have *developmental delays* to describe the lag. This term may imply to some parents that the child will catch up at some point and will develop typically afterward. Indeed, some children with developmental delays do "catch up"; however, others do not. Some children who have delays at a young age are found to have mental retardation later. In many children with developmental delays, it is impossible to predict whether or not they will have mental retardation until they are older. *Developmental delay* is often the term used to describe a child's below-average functioning until a more specific determination of the child's cognitive functioning can be established.

It is possible that a developmental delay in a young child is not recognizable because typical development is so variable and unpredictable. Especially if children are typical in appearance, are socially engaging, and are doing well in their muscle development, mental retardation may not be evident until the youngster is 2 or 3 years old or older. For that reason, any suspicion of delays in development, especially in language, deserves a thorough evaluation by a team of professionals.

It is also possible to mistakenly identify a child as having mental retardation. Children who are deprived, uncooperative, withdrawn, ill, tired, frightened, on medication, or very young (birth to 3); who have emotional disturbances or physical disabilities; or who dislike the examiner or the testing environment may perform poorly on certain tests. Also, for reasons that are not well known, a few children can show major variations in test performance over the course of months or years. A child who appears to have mental retardation at one time might seem to be a slow learner at another time when evaluated by another examiner or when given a different test. The opposite can also occur. Usually, these discrepancies are not serious, but they can be upsetting to parents. Therefore, great care must be taken in testing and labeling children. Routine retesting at regular intervals may be important, and a frank discussion with the psychologist whenever a question arises may be of benefit.

Does mental retardation mean that a child has brain injury? In most situations, it is true that something is wrong with how the brain works in children with mental retardation. However, there may not be a specific, identifiable area of injury in the brain to which the retardation can be traced. Not all mental retardation is caused by injury to brain structures. For example, chemical imbalances or "miswiring of nerves" can cause various problems in brain function. Certain neurological tests, such as the brainwave test or electroencephalogram (EEG) and computerized tomography (CT scan) (see Chapter 22), and spinal fluid examination may indicate that there are problems, but usually these tests cannot indicate exactly what is wrong inside a child's brain that may result in mental retardation.

CAUSES OF MENTAL RETARDATION

Medical science has discovered numerous causes of mental retardation. Yet, for many persons with mental retardation, the specific cause remains unknown. Mental retardation frequently is part of a specific developmental disorder or syndrome. As you will see, many of the disabilities discussed in Part III of this book include mental retardation as one of their characteristics.

Mental retardation may be caused before, during, or after birth. Of course, accidents, infections, or injuries to the brain can happen at any time and may result in mental retardation, although according to the definition of mental retardation, onset must occur before 18 years of age. Some of the known causes of mental retardation during early development include the following:

Inherited (genetic) disorders or chromosome abnormalities
Alcohol or certain drugs taken during pregnancy
Specific infections during pregnancy
Malnutrition during important periods of brain development before and after birth

Metabolic problems of the mother, such as diabetes or phenylketo-
    nuria
Complications of prematurity
Severe bleeding at the time of birth
Birth injury or lack of oxygen during delivery
Glandular problems, such as hypothyroidism
Serious brain infections, such as meningitis or encephalitis
Toxic effects on the brain, such as in lead poisoning
Accidents that cause severe head injuries

PARENTAL EXPECTATIONS

To hear that their child has mental retardation can be excruciatingly
painful for some parents. However, the concept continues to be applied because it can be useful. When used appropriately, it conveys
to parents that the disability is real and that it is lifelong. It can help
parents to be realistic about the child's education program and long-
term vocational goals. Yet, it can also be damaging to the extent that
it may cause parents to have low expectations for their child, or it

may create a self-fulfilling prophecy in which the label guarantees that the condition, that of below-average functioning, will remain.

It can be equally damaging, however, to use softer, more vague terms to protect parents from the truth. Avoiding a discussion of the issue of mental retardation can result in years of struggling with inappropriate education programs, poor school curricula, pressure on the child at home, and a long, painful history of failure and frustration on the part of the child. The concept of mental retardation does not need to be discarded. Rather, it must be recognized and defined so that parents as well as the public will come to understand what it means to have mental retardation and how high-quality education programs can help to remediate the condition.

ACKNOWLEDGMENTS

Contributions have been made to this chapter by Leslie E. Weidenman, Ph.D., Leesa H. Mann, Ph.D., and Siegfried M. Pueschel, M.D., Ph.D., M.P.H.

6

Attention-Deficit/ Hyperactivity Disorder

Attention-deficit/hyperactivity disorder (AD/HD) is a syndrome having as its primary features inattention, hyperactivity, and/or impulsivity. Other terms that have been used to describe AD/HD include hyperkinetic child syndrome, minimal brain dysfunction, hyperactivity, and attention deficit disorder. With the publication of the fourth edition of the American Psychiatric Association's *Diagnostic and Statistical Manual of Mental Disorders* (DSM-IV) in 1994, children who exhibit developmentally inappropriate degrees of attention, impulsivity, or overactivity are identified as fitting into one of several subtypes of the disorder.

- Children who display significant signs of inattention, distractibility, and disorganization but not overactivity would be classified as having *attention-deficit/hyperactivity disorder, predominantly inattentive type.*
- Individuals whose primary difficulties are in the areas of overactivity and impulsivity would be categorized as having *attention-deficit/hyperactivity disorder, predominantly hyperactive-impulsive type.*
- The term *attention-deficit/hyperactivity disorder, combined type* is used when an individual presents with features of both inattention and hyperactivity/impulsivity.
- A diagnosis of *attention-deficit/hyperactivity disorder, not otherwise specified* is used when there are clear difficulties in the person's ability to focus and sustain attention, impulsivity, and/or a high activity level but these are not sufficient to meet full criteria for one of the above diagnoses.

Children who exhibit developmentally inappropriate degrees of attention, impulsivity, or overactivity are frequently referred to medical and mental health practitioners. Signs of AD/HD, particularly of the hyperactive-impulsive type, are frequently apparent between the ages of 2 and 5 years, with the average age of onset between 3 and 4 years. Parents are likely to first notice an extremely high activity level and limited attention span. Descriptions such as "he is always on the go," "she never can sit still for a second," "he jumps from toy to toy," and "she never seems to listen" are common. Many of these children are difficult to discipline, have a low frustration tolerance, and have difficulty forming and maintaining relationships with other children. Other common findings are general immaturity, motoric clumsiness, and sleep disturbances.

Although signs and symptoms of AD/HD are usually evident in the preschool years, in some children, particularly those diagnosed with the predominantly inattentive subtype, they may not be obvious until the child enters school. Typically, the increased social and academic demands, as well as stricter requirements for behavioral control in educational settings, make the difficulties of the child with AD/HD especially noticeable. Common observations of parents and teachers at this time are that the child has extreme difficulty working independently, completing seat work, and organizing his or her work. Restlessness and distractibility are also commonly noted. These difficulties are observed much more often during repetitive or taxing tasks, or tasks the child perceives as boring (e.g., completing worksheets or doing homework). They may not be evident when the child is engaged in a pleasurable or novel activity such as playing computer games or watching a fast-paced television show. It is important to remember that even if the AD/HD is not diagnosed until school age or adolescence, a careful study of the child's history will show that signs of the disorder existed before the age of 7.

CAUSES

Definitive causes of AD/HD have not yet been found. No one has found a part of the brain that when damaged results in AD/HD. There are, however, many hypotheses about possible causes of AD/HD. Many studies suggest that a low level of certain neurotransmitters (chemicals that carry messages or nerve impulses throughout the brain) leads to AD/HD. Environmental factors such as toxic substances (e.g., lead) or pre- or perinatal (before or during birth) injuries are thought to be associated with some cases of AD/HD. However, in most cases no specific cause is ever found. He-

redity appears to play a role in many families; up to 30%–50% of children with AD/HD have a sibling or parent who also has the disorder.[1]

The role of diet has been suggested as causative. Particularly in the 1980s, children were placed on highly restrictive diets in an attempt to control their intake of sugar, food additives, and/or artificial colorings. However, carefully controlled research has not supported a link between diet and symptoms of AD/HD except in an extremely small group of children, most of whom were quite young.

INCIDENCE

Approximately 3%–5% of school-age children in the United States are thought to meet the criteria for attention-deficit/hyperactivity disorder. The disorder appears to be much more common in boys than in girls; the male:female ratio ranges between 4:1 and 9:1.[2]

---

[1]Wodrich, D.L. (1994). *Attention deficit hyperactivity disorder: What every parent wants to know.* Baltimore: Paul H. Brookes Publishing Co.

[2]American Psychiatric Association. (1994). *Diagnostic and statistical manual of mental disorders* (4th ed.). Washington, DC: Author.

IDENTIFICATION

Ideally, the process used to identify AD/HD, or any disability, is multidimensional. This means that information about a number of the child's characteristics is gathered from several sources. A comprehensive evaluation includes detailed information about the child's developmental history (medical history, acquisition of milestones such as walking and talking, early behavioral characteristics), and past and current functioning at home and at school. Usually, parents and teachers are interviewed, standardized rating scales are completed, and/or the child is observed in naturalistic settings (home and school) by trained professionals. In addition, psychological and educational testing can provide valuable information about the child's strengths and weaknesses. Certain psychological tests can also help determine the child's ability to maintain attention and organize information.

A diagnosis of AD/HD should only be made after adequate information is gathered from several sources; it should never be based solely on the child's behavior in any one setting (doctor's or psychologist's office, a particular classroom) or with any one person (mother or father). It is also important that alternative explanations for the child's inattention, hyperactivity, and/or impulsivity be explored before a diagnosis of AD/HD is given. Children who are depressed, anxious, or who have learning disabilities may have difficulty paying attention or may appear overactive. The treatments for these difficulties, however, are different from those for AD/HD.

INTERVENTION

Helping children with AD/HD usually involves a combination of treatments such as the use of medications, educational adaptations, counseling, and behavior management techniques.

Medication

Many children diagnosed with AD/HD will respond to treatment with stimulant medications such as Ritalin (methylphenidate hydrochloride), Dexedrine (dextroamphetamine sulfate), and Cylert (pemoline). These medications are thought to work by releasing neurotransmitters. A child should receive a trial of medication only after a complete evaluation that includes a physical examination. Usually, a small dose is administered as a trial to assess for positive effects as well as side effects. If the child appears to be tolerating the medication well, the dosage can be gradually increased until an optimal level is reached. Several dosages a day may be required, except for Cylert, which has a longer course of action than the other stimulants.

Side effects are usually minor and often temporary. They may include headache, stomachache, irritability, difficulty sleeping, and loss of appetite. In many cases, side effects can be easily controlled by altering the dosage or giving the medication at different times of the day (e.g., right before lunch rather than an hour before). There had been concern in the past that stimulants were responsible for growth suppression in children who had taken them for many years. More recent research suggests that such suppression, if it occurs, is very minor ($1/4$–$1/2$ of an inch), and children regain the lost height following a brief medication-free period. In a very small percentage of children, stimulants may precipitate the development of a tic disorder (involuntary motor and/or vocal movements). Frequently, children who develop tics have a family history of a tic disorder or Tourette syndrome, and thus may be predisposed to the development of such a disorder.

Educational Adaptations

Appropriate education for children with AD/HD is essential. Under Part B of the Individuals with Disabilities Education Act (IDEA), children with diagnosed AD/HD may qualify for special education services if it can be shown that their difficulties adversely affect their ability to learn from a standard education program. Many children with AD/HD can participate in a regular classroom setting, but would benefit from accommodations such as shorter work assignments, more frequent breaks, one-to-one assistance, repetition of directions, and behavior management strategies utilized in the classroom. Some children may require more intensive services, as can be found in a self-contained classroom.

Counseling

The development of secondary emotional reactions (e.g., depression, anxiety) and behavioral difficulties are not uncommon in children with AD/HD. Families and children with AD/HD can thus often benefit from counseling. Counseling can assist in educating the child and family members about the behaviors associated with AD/HD and teach them how to compensate for and cope with these difficulties. For the child, counseling affords an opportunity to explore feelings related to weaknesses, and can also engender a sense of positive self-worth by identifying areas in which he or she has demonstrated competencies.

Research has also found that many children with AD/HD have significant problems in peer relationships, as they may tend to be more controlling, impulsive, and aggressive in their interactions with other children. Children with the best outcomes later in life tend to have been able to form positive relationships. Social skills training may thus be a vital component of an overall treatment program.

Behavior Management Techniques

Many of the challenging behaviors of children with AD/HD can be modified by the careful application of behavioral principles. The use of reinforcers to increase positive behaviors may be very helpful. Reinforcers may be an item such as a favorite dessert, or a privilege such as being able to stay up late to watch a television program. Children with AD/HD may need reinforcement more frequently than other children. Over time, they often do not require this continued intensive reinforcement.

Consistent consequences for misbehavior are also important. A child needs to learn what behavior is expected in different situations and what will happen if those expectations are not met. All too often parents or teachers may repeatedly threaten but not follow through with the consequences.

Parents and other caregivers can also prevent problematic situations from arising by anticipating and planning for these situations. For example, if a child typically has difficulties whenever the parent brings him or her into a store, reviewing with the child guidelines for appropriate behavior before entering the store may prevent misbehavior. Finding the strategies that work with a particular child may require some trial and error. Consulting with a specialist trained in the application of behavior management techniques (usually a school or clinical psychologist or a social worker) may assist parents in the development of appropriate strategies.

EXPECTED OUTCOMES

Some children with AD/HD will outgrow many of the core symptoms of the disorder in adolescence or adulthood. The majority, however, will continue to experience difficulties with sustained attention, impulse control, and/or motor restlessness. These difficulties can in some cases lead to lower educational attainment despite adequate intelligence, more frequent job changes, and/or difficulties in personal relationships. With proper psychological support and/or medications (which in some cases continue throughout life), most individuals with AD/HD are able to lead happy, productive lives.

ACKNOWLEDGMENTS

Contributions have been made to this chapter by Lucia Paolicelli, Ph.D., Leslie E. Weidenman, Ph.D., and Daniel T. Marwil, M.D.

7

Learning Disabilities

Children with learning disabilities are a heterogeneous group who are identified as not having such traditional disabilities as mental retardation, a behavior disorder, or a visual or hearing impairment, but who, nevertheless, have disabilities due to their significant learning difficulties.

DEFINITION

Although there is considerable debate and disagreement about the definition of a learning disability, the Individuals with Disabilities Education Act (PL 101-476) has set forth a definition that is mandated for use by all school systems in the United States.

Learning disabilities are defined as deficits in one or more of the basic psychological processes. They may include difficulties in understanding or using language, when it is spoken and/or written. Other learning difficulties occur as an imperfect ability to listen, think, speak, read, write, spell, or do mathematical calculations. The mandated definition includes such conditions as perceptual disabilities, brain injury, minimal brain dysfunction, dyslexia, and developmental aphasia. The definition does not apply to students who have learning problems that are primarily the result of visual or hearing impairments; motor disabilities; mental retardation; behavior disorders; or environmental, cultural, or economic disadvantages.

PREVALENCE

The definition of learning disabilities is not precise in that it can be a discrete disability or a combination of lesser problems with an overall effect. Because of this imprecision, it is essentially impossible to determine the exact prevalence of learning disabilities. However, some estimate that 10%–20% of all school children have learning disabilities.[1]

CAUSES

There are many possible causes of learning disabilities, which are generally presumed to be neurologically based. Interestingly, the same factors are associated with other disabilities, such as mental retardation and behavior disorders. Among these factors are genetic abnormalities, biochemical influences, brain injury, and environmental conditions such as increased amounts of lead in the blood. It is often very difficult to pinpoint a specific cause of a learning disability. In fact, it is more likely that there are multiple interrelated causes than that there is a single cause to explain a child's learning disability.

CHARACTERISTICS OF CHILDREN WITH LEARNING DISABILITIES

According to the federal definition of specific learning disabilities, the characteristics of learning disabilities exist in three areas: 1) reading and writing, 2) mathematics, and 3) receptive and expressive language. Many professionals also identify motor, memory, and perceptual weaknesses as learning disabilities.

Learning problems usually become apparent as children become involved in instructional activities. For example, it may become apparent a child has difficulty in learning to read. There may be a number of indications that this task is presenting a challenge; for example a child may have trouble with decoding or associating letters with sounds. However, this same child may be able to master basic math concepts, just as a child who reads well may have an isolated math disability. Another child might have fine motor planning problems, which affect his or her written output.

If a child has a more fundamental problem, such as a language disorder, a teacher or parent might observe an inability to follow a series of directions or to express him- or herself clearly.

---

[1]Hynd, G., & Cohen, M. (1983). *Dyslexia: Neuropsychological theory, research, and clinical differentiation.* New York: Grune & Stratton.

IDENTIFICATION

Interdisciplinary teams of professionals are best for identifying children with disabilities. This applies to children with other disabilities, too. Individual psychological evaluations (of intelligence) and educational assessments are needed to use as bases for determining if a child has a learning disability. Other evaluations may then be requested as necessary. Depending on individual needs, specialists in the areas of pediatrics, physical therapy, occupational therapy, social work, speech-language therapy, and psychiatry can be consulted.

In preschool children, the team members are frequently helpful in identifying disabilities in gross and fine motor areas and in receptive and expressive language. Input from parents and teachers is considered before arriving at a final diagnosis.

For the school-age child, level of intelligence must be determined as well as the child's present level of educational achievement. After these levels have been established, the diagnostic team must determine whether there is a significant gap or discrepancy between the child's ability (i.e., intelligence) and his or her level of educational achievement. In this manner, the team determines whether the child's performance matches his or her potential.

In addition, tests to assess visual-perceptual motor skills, language, and memory may be used.

EDUCATION AND PROGRAMMING

The most common approach to treatment of learning disabilities is through special services using an individualized education program (IEP) and curriculum that is specific to the child's individual needs (see Chapter 29 for a discussion of IEPs and school programming). Most children with learning disabilities are educated in a regular class. The school's special educator generally consults with the regular class teacher and provides instruction to remediate the learning disability. The instructional plan is based on the child's identified strengths and weaknesses in basic subjects such as reading, mathematics, and writing. Other services, such as the provision of audiotaped books, notetakers, and lesson seat work, may also be provided.

As is suggested by the use of an individualized education program, each child's situation is unique, and a specific methodology for instruction is selected based on the results of testing. Some teaching methods may not be effective for some children. After a

new method has been introduced, the child's progress is monitored carefully. If there is not sufficient academic gain, the method is discontinued and another implemented. Continued research should help teachers to choose appropriate curricula, teaching methods, and materials that will more specifically meet the child's individual educational needs.

Children with learning disabilities may face many problems that affect their academic performance. Because they often have struggled with learning, they sometimes experience emotional difficulties as they attempt school work. Most children come to enjoy reading to some degree, but children with learning disabilities may view reading as a chore. As a result, they tend to avoid it because it is difficult. And, because so much school work is based on understanding written material, children with learning disabilities may become frustrated, which in turn may affect self-esteem. These children tend to equate academics with feeling bad about themselves and practice academic skills less than the average child. This can compound the problem and it becomes difficult to sort out whether the lack of academic progress is due to the disability, reduced practice time, or an aversion to the school task because of its negative emotional impact.

In the latter case, children may exhibit behavior problems as they try to cope with their feelings of failure or inadequacy. This can lead to conflict with teachers, the very individuals who are trying to assist them. At times the children see their teachers or the school as causing the problem when in fact the distress they feel comes from their own struggle with their learning disability. Special education teachers are trained to be sensitive to these problems and try to use techniques that heighten the child's interest and sense of accomplishment. Some children also benefit from counseling to deal with these issues; however, early identification and remediation will help prevent these problems, thus preserving confidence, self-esteem, and emotional well-being.

EXPECTED OUTCOMES

The outlook for children with learning disabilities generally is quite good, although most learning disabilities are lifelong. Most children grow up to lead typical lives and to work productively in the community. Some learn to compensate well and choose careers that demand rigorous academic training. For others, it may be necessary to consider career choices that minimize the impact of the learning disability and capitalize on the child's strengths. Parents can help to ensure success by being supportive and understanding while maintaining appropriate expectations for the child to perform and take pride in his or her ability to work.

ACKNOWLEDGMENTS

Contributions have been made to this chapter by James McEneaney, M.Ed., James C. Bernier, A.S.C.W., and Daniel T. Marwil, M.D.

8

Sensory Disorders

Of the sensory disorders, parents are more likely to detect a severe visual or hearing loss during infancy. A milder degree of visual or hearing impairment may go undetected until screening tests are performed by the pediatrician or during preschool testing. Difficulty with sensation may be noted as toddlers sustain falls or other injuries and fail to react to the pain. Defects in taste or smell are much harder to diagnose in early childhood and may easily go unrecognized.

VISUAL IMPAIRMENT AND BLINDNESS

Description

Visual impairment simply means less than typical vision. More specific information about the type and severity of the problem is needed in order to determine how impaired the vision is. A diagnosis like this is usually provided by an eye doctor or ophthalmologist.

Most people have heard typical vision described as "20/20." This measure of visual acuity, or sharpness, means that an individual can see well at a distance of 20 feet what the typical eye is supposed to see at 20 feet. If a person has a visual acuity of 20/40 this indicates a mild visual impairment. Then the individual can only see at 20 feet what ordinarily can be seen at 40 feet. A significant visual impairment would be 20/200. A person with such poor vision would be considered legally blind.

A restricted visual field is another type of visual impairment. When looking straight ahead, most people also see peripherally in a

180-degree field of vision. If for some reason the visual field is reduced to 20 degrees, a person is designated legally blind. It is thus possible to be legally blind and still have some sight. If an individual has no vision at all, he or she would be considered totally blind.

Causes and Specific Impairments

There are numerous causes of visual impairment. Any defect in the eye itself; in the optic nerve, which carries visual messages to the brain; or in the vision center in the brain may result in a visual impairment. Damage from injuries, accidents, or illnesses to any part of the visual system, and genetic disorders, metabolic diseases, or congenital abnormalities can cause visual impairment. To understand how a visual impairment can develop, it helps to know something about how we usually see.

As seen in Figure 1, light enters the eye through the cornea (1). It passes through the anterior chamber (2), pupil (3), and lens (4). It continues through the vitreous humor (6) until it reaches the retina (7) at the back of the eyeball. The retina contains light receptors that transform the image seen to nerve impulses that are carried by the

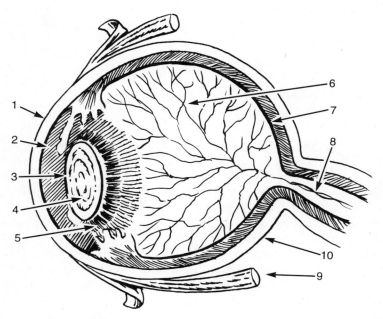

Figure 1.   Cross-sectional view of the eyeball, showing structures of the eye: 1, cornea; 2, anterior chamber; 3, pupil; 4, lens; 5, iris; 6, vitreous humor; 7, retina; 8, optic nerve; 9, eye muscle; 10, sclera.

optic nerve (8) to the vision center at the back of the brain. Only then, when the image reaches the brain and the image is interpreted, do we know what we have seen.

Vision is a complex process. A problem at any step in the sequence can result in a visual impairment. Some common visual problems are described here.

Cataracts affect the lens of the eye by preventing light from passing through in the typical way. Cataracts can enlarge over time, gradually causing the lens to become opaque. Many people associate cataracts with the elderly. However, children also may have cataracts, including infants who may be born with cataracts.

Premature infants who require extensive oxygen after birth may develop a condition called *retrolental fibroplasia* or *retinopathy of prematurity* (ROP) (see Chapter 14). The retina may then become damaged and may not be able to respond appropriately to light.

Other conditions that affect the retina and impair vision are retinitis pigmentosa (i.e., an atypical accumulation of pigment) and retinoblastoma (i.e., a tumor of the eye). Also, a damaged optic nerve may be unable to carry light impulses from the eye to the brain. Moreover, when the eye itself and the optic nerve are intact, it is possible to have visual problems if the parts of the brain that receive and interpret visual images function improperly or are damaged.

An imbalance in the eye muscles can cause a number of visual problems. Coordinated eye movements require that the six eye muscles, which are controlled by three different nerves, work together in perfect harmony. It is easy to understand why this complex process may be a problem in very young infants.

Squint, or strabismus, is a common problem in infants. There are two types of strabismus: esotropia (crossed eyes, or eyes that turn in) and exotropia (wall-eyes, or eyes that turn out). In addition, if a child fails to coordinate eye movements, amblyopia, or "lazy eye," eventually may develop. This occurs when one eye becomes dominant and the brain ignores messages from the other eye in order to avoid double vision.

Nystagmus is another eye condition in which there are atypical eye movements. In this case, a jerky motion of the eyes occurs in a horizontal, vertical, or circular manner. If you suspect that your child has either strabismus or nystagmus, you should discuss your concerns with your physician to determine if the child should be seen by an ophthalmologist.

Near-sightedness (i.e., myopia) and far-sightedness (i.e., hyperopia) are common conditions that usually can be corrected with eyeglasses or contact lenses. These conditions are most often caused by a deviation in the length of the eyeball or changes in the lens so that the light image is projected either a little in front of or a little behind the retina.

Detection and Diagnosis

During infancy and early childhood, parents and pediatricians usually are the first to suspect that a child may have a vision problem. If your child has difficulty coordinating eye movements, appears to hold objects very close to the face, or seems to have poor eye–hand coordination, you probably should have him or her examined by an ophthalmologist.

Visual acuity becomes easier to evaluate after a child develops basic skills such as following directions and naming pictures or letters of the alphabet. Visual acuity testing generally involves reading a chart of letters or pictures using the Snellen Eye Chart for an older child or an E Chart or Picture Chart (Figure 2) for a younger child. For the latter two charts, the child has to respond by pointing to the

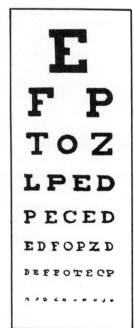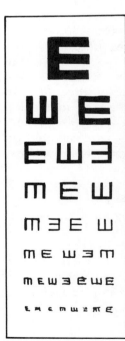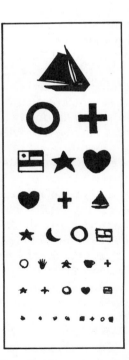

Figure 2.   The Snellen Eye Chart, the E Chart, and the Picture Chart. The latter two are used to assess the ability of young children to see.

direction of the "legs" of the E on the E Chart or identifying the object on the Picture Chart.

Very young children or those with significant developmental delays are frequently difficult to test. If there is a question about whether or not a child can see, one procedure that can be used is a visual evoked potential examination. This involves stimulating the eye and then recording the brain's response in a manner similar to that of a brainwave test or an electroencephalogram. By placing electrodes on specific areas on the back of the head, the electrical activity received in the brain's vision center can be recorded. The pattern of responses is then compared to that of a child with typical vision.

Treatment and Expected Outcomes

Many visual impairments can be corrected easily with eyeglasses or contact lenses. If amblyopia has been diagnosed, patching of one eye is frequently done to strengthen the "lazy eye." At times, eye surgery is performed to correct a muscle imbalance or to remove a cataract. In general, the earlier the problem is detected and treatment is begun, the better the outcome.

Parents and teachers frequently suspect that school-age children who have difficulty learning to read have eye problems. Visual screening by a pediatrician or at school can determine which children should be seen by an eye doctor. Special eye exercises and training programs have been suggested by some optometrists for children with learning disabilities. However, there is no proof that these exercises provide any long-term gains in reading skills. Parents need to consider carefully whether they want to spend time and money on a program of questionable value.

For children who are blind, the onset of blindness is an important factor. A child who is blind from birth will have more difficulties in certain developmental areas than a child who becomes blind after having had a few years of vision. For instance, a child who is blind from birth usually will have difficulty with spatial concepts such as large and small or how much liquid a container will hold. Motor skills also tend to develop more slowly in a child who cannot see the movements of others and thus does not learn by imitating. Because children who are blind cannot explore with their eyes, they have to rely on their other senses. The tactile (touching) sense becomes highly developed in many children who are blind. Caregivers should be aware of how important it is for the child with visual impairments to touch objects. Fortunately, language development generally is not affected by a visual deficit.

HEARING IMPAIRMENT AND DEAFNESS

Description

Hearing is a complex process involving the three major parts of the ear—the outer, middle, and inner ear—as shown in Figure 3. Each part contains several components such as the tympanic membrane or eardrum (3), the ossicles (4) or small bones that conduct the sound in the middle ear, and the auditory, or hearing, nerve (7), which carries sound messages to the brain.

Each component of the ear must work properly if a child is to have adequate hearing. Hearing impairments may result from problems in any part of the ear or in the hearing center of the brain. There are three major types of hearing problems: conductive, sensorineural, and mixed. A conductive hearing loss indicates a problem in the outer or middle ear. A sensorineural hearing loss refers to problems of the inner ear, such as the auditory nerve. When both conductive and sensorineural hearing problems are present, the impairment is referred to as a mixed type of hearing loss.

Many children have hearing problems in only one ear, which is called a *unilateral hearing loss*. If both ears are affected, it is a *bilateral hearing loss*.

The intensity of a hearing loss is determined by how loud a sound must be before it can be heard. Sound intensity is measured in decibels, abbreviated dB. People with typical hearing can detect a variety of sounds at 20 decibels or less.

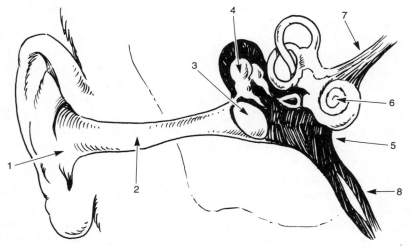

Figure 3.   Structures of the ear: 1, outer ear; 2, ear canal; 3, tympanic membrane (eardrum); 4, ossicles; 5, middle ear; 6, inner ear; 7, auditory, or hearing, nerve; 8, eustachian tube.

There are generally four levels of hearing impairment. A mild hearing loss means that sounds must be between 20 and 40 decibels and above before they can be heard. An individual with a mild hearing loss can hear and participate in conversations but may have difficulty hearing sounds and noises from a distance or whispered sounds. Although children with mild hearing problems may be delayed in language development, speech and articulation generally are unimpaired.

A moderate hearing impairment means that sounds cannot be heard until they reach 41–70 decibels and above. Conversation at a usual level of loudness is difficult to hear, and articulation often is impaired. Language development in these children is usually delayed.

A severe hearing impairment means a hearing loss in the 71–85 decibels range. At this level, an individual generally cannot participate in typical conversations. Most of what is said will not be heard. Hearing aids can be very helpful to persons with both moderate and severe hearing impairments. School children may require FM (i.e., frequency modulation) amplification systems for classroom use.

A profound hearing loss means that sounds must be 85 decibels or louder in order to be heard. These individuals usually do not have speech that sounds typical, and hearing aids are only partially beneficial. Individuals with profound deafness generally learn an alternative system of communication such as sign language, a communication board, voice synthesizers, and so forth.

Causes

Infections and head injuries are some of the most common causes of hearing problems in children. During the preschool years, many children are prone to frequent throat and middle ear infections (the latter is also called *otitis media*). Chronic middle ear infections may result in a mild to moderate conductive hearing loss. This type of hearing problem may be temporary, but may affect academic performance.

Another common problem in children that can cause a temporary hearing loss is the buildup of wax, or cerumen, in the ear canal. When the ear canal is totally blocked, sounds cannot reach the eardrum, and hearing is impaired.

Sensorineural hearing impairment can be caused in numerous ways. It may be inherited, in which case these children are often born deaf. A viral infection or the use of certain drugs during the early stages of pregnancy may cause injury to the unborn baby's hearing mechanism. A difficult birth causing a lack of oxygen to the baby's brain also may result in a sensorineural hearing impairment. In infancy and childhood, a number of antibiotics (e.g., streptomycin) and certain serious illnesses (e.g., bacterial meningitis) may be associated with later sensorineural hearing loss.

Excessive noise in the environment sometimes causes mild to moderate sensorineural hearing impairment. These problems may be temporary. If the exposure to excessive noise continues, it can become permanent. For adolescents, a common source of excessive noise is listening to loud music or attending rock concerts. Some reports indicate that noise levels at rock concerts have reached 120 decibels, similar to the noise of a jet engine. Although numerous causes of hearing impairment have been discovered, children may also develop a hearing loss for unexplained reasons.

Incidence

Approximately 1 in every 1,000 children has a profound hearing loss and is considered deaf. Of these, it is estimated that 65% were deaf from birth. When mild, moderate, and severe degrees of hearing impairment are added to this statistic, estimates of children with hearing impairments increase to 15–30 in 1,000. Hearing problems frequently occur along with other disabilities. A survey of children in schools for individuals with hearing impairment found that 40% had an additional disability.[1]

Detection and Diagnosis

During infancy and early childhood profound hearing losses usually are detected by parents and family members. They may notice that the baby does not react to loud sounds and voices and does not seem to know his or her name. Milder or fluctuating hearing problems are more difficult to detect. However, if a child has frequent ear infections, responds inconsistently when spoken to, or is slow to acquire language skills, a thorough hearing evaluation should be obtained.

Audiologists, or hearing specialists, have ways of testing the hearing of children of all ages. Some of these methods are outlined in Chapter 22. Most audiometric tests involve presenting a variety of sounds of different intensities and frequencies to each ear and having the child indicate when the sound is heard. Depending on the age and ability of the child, the audiologist may use headphones

[1]Batshaw, M.L., & Perret, Y.M. (1992). *Children with disabilities: A medical primer* (3rd ed.). Baltimore: Paul H. Brookes Publishing Co.

to present sounds or may observe the child's reactions to sounds in a testing room via speakers.

Audiologists also may test the flexibility and mobility of the eardrum using a procedure called *impedance audiometry*. For very young children and children who are difficult to test, auditory evoked response (AER) (sometimes called *brain stem evoked response* [BSER]) testing often is recommended. Further descriptions of these tests are provided in Chapter 22.

Treatment and Expected Outcomes

Conductive hearing problems resulting from frequent ear infections, or fluid in the middle ear, generally improve with medical treatment. Many children respond well to antibiotics, whereas others may require minor surgery in order to drain the fluid buildup. A common surgical procedure involves a myringotomy with tube insertion. In this procedure, under general anesthesia, a tiny cut is made in the eardrum, and a small tube is placed in the middle ear to drain the fluid from this space.

Sensorineural hearing loss generally cannot be cured. In some persons with profound hearing loss, special implants have been attempted with moderate success. Hearing aids can be very useful for certain children with sensorineural impairments. Although they may not restore perfect hearing, they do make many sounds loud enough for the child to hear. The most common type of hearing aid is the behind-the-ear type, as illustrated in Figure 4.

Children with hearing impairments often are delayed in learning language. The more severe the hearing loss, the harder it is to

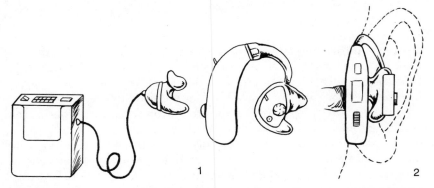

Figure 4. The body-style hearing aid at left is usually attached to straps or clothing. A behind-the-ear hearing aid is depicted on the right. A frontal view (1) and a side view (2) are shown.

acquire typical language. Some children never learn to speak, but they do develop other ways to communicate such as through sign language or use of a communication board or voice synthesizer. Children with significant hearing impairments who speak often have articulation problems. The improper pronunciation reflects the child's inability to hear sounds accurately.

Special education services usually are required for children who have a permanent hearing loss. Extra help from early intervention programs designed for these children is particularly important during the preschool years. Some type of special help may be required throughout the school years for children with serious hearing impairment. Some children may also require the use of a wireless FM auditory training system.

LACK OF SENSATION

Description

Difficulty in feeling various sensations is common in disabilities associated with paralysis or nerve injury such as spina bifida. Sensations include touch, as well as the ability to feel pain, temperature changes, vibration, and a sense of position in space. A loss or impairment of sensation may be partial or total as well as temporary or permanent.

Causes and Incidence

Any disease, injury, or disability that affects the nerves and sensory receptors may affect the ability to feel sensation. Conditions such as cerebral palsy, which involve the motor system, may affect the ability to interpret sensations. There also is a rare condition known as *congenital insensitivity to pain*, in which children cannot feel pain. Exact data on the number of children or adults with impaired sensation or a lack of sensation are not available.

Diagnosis and Detection

By observing a child's reactions to various sensations, you generally can tell if there is a specific concern. A pediatrician or neurologist can evaluate your child's sensory abilities more systematically to determine if there is a problem with sensation.

Treatment and Expected Outcomes

The cause of the sensory problem will determine the type of treatment the child will receive. Temporary impairments caused by illnesses, for example, generally disappear with the treatment of the illness. Children with permanent disabilities may not be cured, but their ability to feel or interpret sensation can be improved with therapy.

In cases where the loss of sensation is total and no improvement is expected, children and parents are taught how to avoid injury to insensitive body parts. For example, children with paralysis who spend hours at a time seated in wheelchairs learn to shift their positions to avoid skin sores.

ACKNOWLEDGMENTS

Contributions have been made to this chapter by Patricia S. Scola, M.D., M.P.H., Janet L. Tobin, M.S., and Paul W. Austin, M.Ed.

9

Communication Disorders

Communication can be defined as a process of exchanging information, thoughts, and ideas. It encompasses the ability to interpret, transmit, and express messages. Communication not only involves the vowel and consonant sounds we use and the sentences we create but also tone of voice, rate of delivery, eye contact, facial expression, and body movement. Some of these communication skills are present at birth. As infants develop, their ability to communicate expands to using and understanding spoken and written language.

DESCRIPTION

Communication disorder is a general term comprising any number of concerns affecting the development of language and the ability to exchange information both verbally and nonverbally. Communication disorders can be categorized into problems of articulation, voice disorders, stuttering, and language disorders. These disorders affect a child's ability to understand and/or formulate a message and then to transmit that message to another individual. Difficulties in communication can result from both organic or nonorganic factors. The development of communication skills encompasses such factors as biological readiness and cognitive, social, and environmental factors.

ARTICULATION

Articulation refers to the ability to pronounce vowel and consonant sounds correctly. Appropriate coordination of movements of the lips, tongue, palate, and jaw are necessary for proper articulation.

Development of this coordination begins in infancy with the process of sucking, chewing, and swallowing. As the child grows, drinking from a cup refines coordination of the muscles of the mouth and prepares the child for production of vowel and consonant sounds. Early speech usually is a poor approximation of actual words. However, as children learn to speak and practice pronunciation, articulation gradually improves. By the age of 6–7 years, most children have learned to produce all of the sounds of their language correctly.

Articulation problems are likely to be present in children who have physical problems causing interference with coordinated movements of the lips, tongue, and other anatomical structures that take part in speech production. Children who have language delays (i.e., who are late in acquiring their first words) or youngsters with structural defects such as cleft palate may have problems with articulation. Infants with swallowing or chewing difficulties or excessive drooling may also develop articulation problems. In some children, articulation difficulties are caused by difficulties learning the rules for sequencing vowel and consonant sounds and the rules for the position of these sounds in actual words.

VOICE DISORDERS

Voice disorders are less common in children than in adults; however, they do occur. Voice disorders also are referred to as *abnormal phonation*.

Judgment about whether a child's voice sounds "normal" can be very subjective. However, conditions of excessive or prolonged hoarseness or a nasal or denasal voice (i.e., a voice that has a head cold quality) usually are identified readily by parents. If this unusual quality persists, parents may adapt to it so that it no longer sounds strange to them. Therefore, it is important to monitor closely any voice changes in the developing child. If changes persist for more than 2–4 weeks, an evaluation is indicated.

Hoarseness can be caused by chronic irritation of the throat, infection, allergy, and vocal abuse such as yelling or screaming. Hoarseness must be evaluated medically to determine the cause and to initiate care if indicated. Hypernasality exists when too much sound is passing through the nose; its opposite, hyponasality, refers to too little sound passing through the nose. Both conditions require medical evaluation. Blockage of the nasal passages, allergies, and chronic colds can cause hyponasality and may contribute to a speech pattern that is difficult to understand. Hypernasality occurs when the soft palate fails to close the nasal passages, thus allowing air to pass through the nose. Children with cleft palate often have this type of voice pattern due to insufficient palatal tissue.

STUTTERING

As the child progresses toward sentence production, occasional repetitions, hesitations, or long pauses can be heard in the child's speech. Often this is labeled *stuttering* or *stammering*. This type of nonfluency is a common part of the typical language development process, although if this pattern of communication is causing concern it is important to have it evaluated early by a speech-language pathologist as this pattern can become habituated and can result in the development of anxiety and reluctance on the part of the child to communicate.

Nonfluency is a part of typical conversation for both children and adults and is not necessarily a problem; therefore, calling little attention to these differences will make it easier for the individual to produce a more fluent pattern. It is, however, important for parents who are concerned about the disruptions in the rhythm of their child's conversational speech to consult a professional for evaluation to determine the most appropriate method of intervention.

LANGUAGE DISORDERS

Language disorders are generally categorized either by cause or in descriptive terms. Due to the variety of difficulties children can experience during the process of development of communication, a concise definition or description is difficult to formulate. The American Speech-Language-Hearing Association provides the following definition:

> A language disorder is the abnormal acquisition, comprehension or expression of spoken or written language. The disorder may involve all, one or some of the phonologic, morphologic, semantic, syntactic, or pragmatic components of the linguistic system. Individuals with language disorders frequently have problems in sentence processing or in abstracting information meaningfully for storage and retrieval from short and long term memory.[1]

In essence, a language problem can refer to difficulties with sounds (phonological), grammatical structure and use (morphological and syntactical), word meanings (semantic), and the social skills involved in adjusting language to varied situations (pragmatic).

Language Disorders Caused by Central Nervous System Defects

In the development of speech and language, the central nervous system and the nerves that control our senses and muscles play a vital role. In order to absorb information from the environment, children must see, hear, and feel what is happening around them.

If damage has occurred to any of these sensory systems, delays or disruption of the typical process of speech and language development can occur. It is important to recognize these problems early in order to aid the child in developing strategies to compensate for these deficiencies.

Two communication disorders caused by problems in the brain itself are *expressive aphasia* and *apraxia*. These terms refer to the inability to produce language due to problems in processing information and producing responses. These difficulties often are described as a short-circuit in the system of receiving and sending messages. Often inconsistencies in language abilities are seen in children with aphasia and apraxia. This suggests that the brain's system is working at times and failing at others. These children often have echolalic speech (i.e., they repeat or echo what is said to them). They also tend to be distractible, nonverbal, and easily frustrated by conversations they do not understand. On occasion, they can use words meaningfully. But if asked to repeat what they said, children with

---

[1]American Speech-Language-Hearing Association, Committee on Language, Speech and Hearing Services in the Schools. (1980). Definitions for communicative disorders. *Asha, 22,* 317–318.

aphasia and apraxia often are unable to respond correctly. Both of these disorders require the assistance of professionals and a rehabilitation program.

Language Processing Disorders and Language-Based Learning Disabilities

The school-age child who begins to have difficulty learning academic subjects may have problems in one or more of the following areas: understanding spoken or written language; expressing ideas either orally or in writing; finding the appropriate words; and processing or discriminating information through the senses of hearing, seeing, touching, or movement. The prevalence of this type of disorder is believed to be between 40% and 60% of the population with learning disabilities.[2]

Because language-based learning disabilities are subtle and not easily recognized, they often are not detected in the preschool years. However, there are early signs that may indicate a language-based learning disability. For example, the family may observe the child having difficulty focusing on tasks, becoming confused easily by lengthy directions or conversations, having difficulty attending to and following stories read aloud, being unable to express ideas in an orderly fashion, and verbally rambling without actually communicating an idea. As these language problems usually affect a specific area of the total language process, they can be overlooked easily, unlike the child who fails to talk at an appropriate age or has difficulty pronouncing words.

Language-based learning disabilities include specific deficits such as difficulty using the correct words in a given situation; substituting an explanation for a specific object label; using nonspecific words (e.g., *that thing, this stuff*); inability to understand and express the how and why of a situation; or difficulty making appropriate judgments in social situations. In the comprehension area, children sometimes misinterpret words that represent time or space concepts (e.g., *yesterday* or *tomorrow, near* or *far*); have difficulty understanding multiple meanings of words (e.g., *trunk*—a suitcase or part of an elephant); or interpret figurative language literally (e.g., *she is a backseat driver, he is falling apart*).

These language disorders affect how the child reasons, reacts to family members and peers, and performs in the classroom. Without

[2]Shames, G., & Wiig, E. (1985). *Human communication disorders* (2nd ed.). Columbus, OH: Charles E. Merrill.

the abilities to understand and use language, many children fail to progress beyond routine repetitious learning. For example, they may be able to count, recite the alphabet in order, and memorize mathematic facts without understanding the concepts involved.

Evaluation of a child's language abilities and disabilities, together with an assessment of educational, cognitive, and social development, are necessary to identify the area(s) of difficulty. Once identified, appropriate intervention programs can be developed. It is the team process—professionals working together with family members—that is most important in determining the problems and piecing together all of the components of an educational intervention program to help the child progress through the elementary and secondary school years.

Specific language impairment (SLI) is sometimes observed in children who have average cognitive function. This may be due to specific involvement of areas of the brain that concern language processing.

CAUSES

The causes of communication disorders in children are as varied as the problems themselves. In many instances, the exact reason cannot always be determined. In the case of stuttering, a cause for the disorder has never been documented, although many theories have been proposed. Some researchers believe it is caused by emotional or psychological factors in the family environment or in the children themselves. Others attribute the problem to a malfunction of the central nervous system. Voice disorders in children frequently are caused by physical anomalies or misuse of the voice mechanism. A physical examination by a physician, most often an ear, nose, and throat specialist (i.e., otolaryngologist), X-ray studies of the voice box (i.e., larynx), and assessment of the oral mechanism often are needed to determine the presence of a structural defect that may be contributing to the child's unusual sounding voice. Articulation disorders may be due to a delay in maturation; imitation of another child with pronunciation problems; physical or structural abnormalities of the mouth, lips, tongue, jaw, or throat; or a neurological impairment. Language disorders are often caused by specific brain injury, which may occur pre-, peri-, or postnatally. There are three factors that are most frequently cited as possible causes of language difficulties: perceptual abilities, cognitive development, and brain injury.

INCIDENCE

The incidence of communication disorders is variable, depending upon the age of the population discussed and what disorders are included in the total number. It has been reported that approximately 6% of children ages 6–18 years have problems in the area of voice, articulation, and stuttering.[3] The study did not include those children with specific language impairments or language-based learning difficulties.

ASSESSMENT

The evaluation of communication disorders generally consists of four parts. When a parent or physician suspects a child to have a speech or language problem, the child may be sent to a speech-language pathologist for an evaluation. This professional examines the physical mechanisms for speech production, hearing ability, speech quality, voice and rhythm patterns, and comprehension and expression of verbal language. The speech-language pathologist first evaluates the oral mechanism, usually by looking at the structure of the mouth and observing the movements of the tongue, lips, and jaw during the production of speech. In addition, the examiner usually will ask the child to imitate various mouth movement patterns, sounds, and words. A referral to a physician may be necessary for a more complete assessment of the vocal mechanism if a physical problem is suspected.

Second, articulation or pronunciation usually is tested by asking the child to name a specific series of pictures or to tell a story. It is important for the speech-language pathologist to hear how a child pronounces each consonant and vowel sound in isolation, in single words, and in conversational speech. Pronunciation often seems better in one-word responses than in conversation. This is directly related to the amount of fine motor coordination that is involved in producing a long sentence as opposed to producing a single word. When sounds are mispronounced, the evaluator may ask the child to try to imitate the appropriate pronunciation to help determine if therapy is needed and the type of program that may be indicated.

The third aspect of assessment, that of the language process, probably is the most time-consuming part of the evaluation. The

[3]Lahey, M. (1988). *Language disorders and language development*. New York: Macmillan.

speech-language pathologist usually administers a series of standardized tests to determine a child's ability to understand and use spoken language. The type of tests used varies, depending on the child's age, ability, and attention span. Most tests involve the use of pictures or toy objects. Comprehension, the ability to understand spoken language, is usually evaluated by asking a child to point to the one picture in a group that has been named by the examiner or to follow a series of directions. The tests typically measure comprehension of nouns; action words; adjectives; concepts such as size, quality, and quantity; and grammar. Some of the more frequently used tests are the Test of Auditory Comprehension of Language, Zimmerman Pre-School Language Scale, Sequenced Inventory of Communication Development, Tina Bangs Vocabulary Comprehension Scale, Bracken Basic Concept Scale, Test of Language Development, Clinical Evaluation of Language Function, the Peabody Picture Vocabulary Test, MacArthur Communicative Inventory, and the Communication and Symbolic Behavior Scales.

The evaluation of expressive language includes a child's use of vocabulary; sentence structure; thought sequence; ideas; and responses to simple what, when, how, where, and why questions. The evaluation of language usage also involves the use of common pictures or toys. The child may be asked to imitate sentences produced by the evaluator. Specific questions are asked in order to assess how children formulate their thoughts and how well they can communicate these ideas to the listener. The examiner observes the body movements, gestures, and facial expressions that the child uses in addition to, or in place of, words. This becomes especially important when evaluating children who have difficulty expressing themselves verbally. Instruments used to evaluate all of these functions include the just-mentioned tests and the Word Test, Test of Problem Solving, Expressive One Word Picture Vocabulary Test, and Test of Language Competence.

Audiological evaluation makes up the fourth area of assessment. It is discussed in Chapter 8.

After testing, the scores and observations are compiled by the evaluator, and a judgment is made as to whether the child is functioning on par with other children of similar age. Further evaluation, which may include medical, educational, or psychological testing, may be recommended at that time to determine the cause of the child's language problem. In the school-age population, language assessment is completed using a battery of standardized tests as well as varied published checklists. These checklists are often completed while observing the child's verbal interaction with peers and/or teachers during class discussions; they help to assess the pragmatic language areas. Tape recordings of actual discourse are also sometimes made and later scored according to specific scoring standards to assess structure and form of language, as well as the appropriateness of the child's responses or conversational content.

Following completion of the language evaluation, a team of professional school personnel compare all of the test results and discuss appropriate remediation, intervention or treatment, curricula, and accommodations that might be made. The classroom teacher often is available and the parent will have the opportunity to discuss all recommendations and plans and to participate in the process of designing a specific education program, called an *individualized education program* (IEP), if the child qualifies under state and federal guidelines for services.

THERAPY AND PROGRAMS

The type and severity of the communication disorder, as well as the child's age, will determine if specific language or speech-language therapy is needed. Very young children often require ongoing language stimulation activities to foster the development of communication skills. Such activities may be recommended by a speech-language therapist or a professional in early child development to be carried out by parents and family members. The activities are designed to aid the child in acquiring skills or in some cases to teach the child to compensate for a physical problem.

For school-age children, speech-language therapists may provide individualized therapy or design programs to be carried out in the classroom. Again, the individual needs of the child determine the type of services to be provided.

COMMUNICATION AIDS

For many reasons, oral communication, or speech, is so difficult for some children with developmental disabilities that it is virtually impossible for them to make their needs known verbally. For these children, one of the numerous forms of alternative and augmentative communication (AAC) aids available may enable them to express their needs to others.

Every day we use alternatives to speech to communicate. Facial expressions, gestures, and writing are common examples of nonverbal communication. Many people with deafness or hearing impairment use sign language as the primary mode of communication. For children with disabilities who are unable to speak, these and other alternatives are used if possible. Often simple picture, word, or object systems are devised specifically for the individual child. In other situations, technologically sophisticated electronic aids with voice synthesizers or printers are used. The type of communication aid to be selected for the individual depends on the child's age, physical ability to use various body parts to operate such a device, intellectual functioning, sensory adequacy (hearing and vision), and other economic and environmental factors.

Communication Boards

The simplest type of communication aid is the communication board or book. Depending on the child's abilities, the board or book presents a display of pictures, drawings, words, or symbols. To communicate, the child simply points to or touches the items shown. A child who wants a snack may make the request by pointing to the words, "I want a cookie." A younger child might simply point to a picture of a cookie to make the same request. Children with severe cognitive deficits may communicate with object boards, on which replicas or miniature objects are displayed. Because communication boards can be cumbersome to carry around, many children use communication books instead. The books, like the boards, display pictures, words, or symbols on the pages. Children are required to flip

to the necessary page and then to point to the pictures or words that communicate their ideas.

Mechanical Aids

Mechanical aids refer to those that have moving parts but are not electronically operated. An old-fashioned nonelectric typewriter is an example of a mechanical communication aid. Many children with poor fine motor control are unable to write legibly but are able to press keys on a typewriter and thus to express their thoughts.

Electronic Aids

The effectiveness and the variety of available electronic communication aids have increased dramatically in recent years. The advantages of electronic aids are that they can provide a much larger vocabulary, can be connected to a digital display, monitor, or printer, and can be programmed or updated relatively easily. Some electronic aids have voice synthesizers that "speak" for the child. Many voice synthesizers have a monotone voice quality and resemble "robot" speech. However, the quality of speech of recently developed voice synthesizers is much improved. Some electronic communication aids are no bigger than a desktop calculator, whereas others look like a small communication board mounted on a briefcase. Other more sophisticated devices resemble small computers.

The variety of communication aids now available has opened up a world of social interactions and communication for many individuals with developmental disabilities who otherwise would be passive participants in social activities.

FACILITATED COMMUNICATION

Facilitated communication is the term used for a communication technique in which a person with a language impairment is assisted by another individual to use an alternative communication device, such as a typewriter; computer; picture, letter, word, or symbol board; or other augmentative system. It is the participation of a facilitator that makes facilitated communication different from other communication systems. The facilitator assists the individual with a language impairment by physically supporting the hand, wrist, or forearm, as he or she points to the letters or types a message. The main action required by the person communicating is to lower his or her hand toward a desired picture, letter, word, or symbol. The facilitator's support reduces the motor control needed to make the selection. After the selection is made, the facilitator assists by pulling the person's arm back to a ready position so he or she is prepared to make another choice. The role of the facilitator is to give just enough support to enable the person to point to chosen words or letters. With practice, many individuals have increased their degree of independence and facilitators have been able to reduce the amount of support provided. What has been so exciting about facilitated communication is that many individuals who did not have the motor control to operate an alternative communication device on their own are now able to communicate.

According to some reports, facilitated communication has dramatically changed some children's lives. Children who had been labeled as having mental retardation and even being "unteachable" are now reported as only unable to talk. Other professionals argue that these personal accounts are merely anecdotal. They cite testing done under more controlled conditions as revealing a consistent pattern with the content of the message coming from the facilitator, not the person with a disability.

Facilitated communication should be examined and evaluated using the same set of questions used for all interventions. The effectiveness, consequences, and alternatives must all be considered.

When the effectiveness of facilitated communication is assessed by anecdotal reports, families and others sometimes describe enormous joy at the sense of being able to communicate with a son or daughter whose contributions to conversations had previously been minimal or nonexistent. An awesome barrier of silence, they report, is broken, if not lifted. Relationships with peers and adults may suddenly shift as others now regard the individual who does not speak as possessing thoughts and feelings. In addition, unexpected literacy skills have been reported, sometimes demonstrated by individuals who had received no formal reading instruction.

When the testing circumstances have been monitored carefully in research studies, however, no evidence has been found to support the view that facilitated communication provides a "miracle intervention" for individuals with communication impairments. It was found that facilitators, contrary to their intentions, in fact have a substantial impact on the content of the typed messages. An unanticipated consequence of facilitated communication concerns the content of some of the messages produced. Typed messages describe inspiring thoughts and feelings, but also have revealed dissatisfaction on the part of the individuals with disabilities with important aspects of their environments, including people, activities, living arrangements, and even sexual abuse.

Although more research concerning facilitated communication should be forthcoming, children with communication impairments cannot wait until definite research results on this subject have been produced, nor do they need to. Any individualized communication program should incorporate basic components to provide the best possible intervention. Such a program should assume that the child wants to communicate, use the assistance of others in teaching how to compose meaningful messages, encourage multiple ways of communicating, and involve appropriate interests and skills. In working with an individual, it should be noted that communication skills can vary from one environment to another. Frequent reassessment by a qualified professional is necessary. The ultimate goal is to enable the child to communicate with the people who are important to him or her.

ACKNOWLEDGMENTS

Contributions have been made to this chapter by Janet L. Tobin, M.S., Marita R. Hopmann, Ph.D., Leslie E. Weidenman, Ph.D., and Paul W. Austin, M.Ed.

10

Autism
A Pervasive
Developmental Disorder

INTRODUCTION

During the toddler years, many children go through a stage commonly described by parents as the "terrible 2s." This time period is not actually terrible, but is a typical developmental phase when many children begin to assert themselves—often through extreme behavior, such as yelling, hitting, crying, and throwing tantrums. Behavioral outbursts may be quite common, but when they are the *predominant* means of expression, they may indicate a significant developmental problem. In this chapter, pervasive developmental disorders (PDD), which are rare lifelong conditions that affect a child's social, behavioral, and interpersonal abilities, are described. Autism, the most common of the pervasive developmental disorders, is the primary focus of the chapter.

DESCRIPTION OF PERVASIVE
DEVELOPMENTAL DISORDERS

Pervasive developmental disorders is a category of disorders of infancy, childhood, and adolescence as outlined in the medical classification system developed by the American Psychiatric Association.[1]

---

[1] American Psychiatric Association. (1994). *Diagnostic and statistical manual of mental disorders* (4th ed.). Washington, DC: Author.

Autism is the most widely recognized of the disorders included under the heading of PDD. The other disorders are Rett syndrome, childhood disintegrative disorder, and Asperger syndrome. A final subgroup is pervasive developmental disorder—not otherwise specified (PDD-NOS), a diagnosis for those individuals who have a pervasive developmental disorder that does not fit into any of the established disorders mentioned above. Most people are more familiar with autism than PDD, but in recent years the use of PDD as a diagnosis has become more common.

Pervasive developmental disorders are complex developmental disabilities in which there are severe impairments involving language and communication skills and social interactions. Most of the pervasive developmental disorders become apparent during the first 3 years of life. Some conditions, such as Rett syndrome, involve motor problems. Children may stop using their hands purposefully and have difficulty walking. Individuals with childhood disintegrative disorder often have restricted or repetitive patterns of behavior. Asperger syndrome is characterized primarily by difficulties in social interactions without the delays in language development and cognitive abilities that are seen in other pervasive developmental disorders. Because autism is the most common of the disorders, it is discussed in more detail below.

ASPERGER SYNDROME

Because of the similarities in individuals diagnosed with Asperger syndrome or disorder, and those with autism, a brief description of Asperger syndrome is included here. The rest of this chapter focuses on autism.

In 1944, the Austrian psychiatrist Hans Asperger first described the syndrome that today bears his name. Characteristics of Asperger syndrome include abnormal content of speech, unusual verbal and nonverbal communication, impaired social interaction, presence of repetitive activities, resistance to change, poor motor coordination, and intense interest in one or two subjects. Upon meeting an individual with Asperger syndrome, one of the most obvious characteristics is impaired social interaction. Unlike individuals with autism, people with Asperger syndrome do not withdraw from social contact, although they have difficulty participating in two-way interactions. They do not seem to recognize and understand the basic rules of social behavior. They tend to dominate conversations, typically talking about one or two topics to the exclusion of everything else. Often the areas of interest are specific and narrow, such as bus timetables, prehistoric monsters, or the characters in a television series. Often, the discussion is a one-way, lengthy discourse on the topic of interest. Grammar is generally acquired but often there is some difficulty in using pronouns correctly. Persons with Asperger syndrome seem to have limited facial expression and unusual vocal intonation. In addition, gestures are limited or exaggerated and inappropriate for the conversation. Children with Asperger syndrome tend to be clumsy and have difficulty playing games that require good motor coordination. Because of their peculiar social interactions, children with Asperger syndrome have difficulty developing and maintaining friendships.

People diagnosed with Asperger syndrome usually have average or above-average intelligence; their verbal IQs are often higher than their performance IQs. In recent years, it has been reported that some children with Asperger syndrome have mental retardation. School-age children with Asperger syndrome may experience problems with writing, reading, and mathematics. As adults, they usually are capable of living independently and supporting themselves through work, but they are often loners. Psychiatric problems such as depression, antisocial behavior, and suicide attempts have been reported.

Although the exact cause of Asperger syndrome is not known, evidence suggests that there may be a genetic component involved. One study of six generations of a family with several individuals with Asperger syndrome found an X-linked inherited pattern; that is, with sons being affected more often than daughters. Other medical and laboratory tests reveal that some individuals with Asperger syndrome have brainwave abnormalities. So, like autism, there is evidence that this disorder is biological in origin. The incidence of Asperger syndrome is not known as there have not been any large-scale studies to determine its prevalence.

AUTISM

Individuals with autism exhibit impairments involving the senses, thinking abilities, language and communication, and social interactions. They often display ritualistic and self-stimulatory behaviors, such as rocking, spinning, and finger flicking. Unusual responses to the environment are common for individuals with autism. The word *autism* refers to the tendency to withdraw into oneself, ignoring much of what goes on in the environment.

Autism is now believed to be the result of neurological differences or problems in the brain. As a result, children and adults with autism may experience distortions in any one or more of their sensory capacities. Thus, sights, sounds, tastes, and feelings may be experienced very differently. Some adults with autism have been able to describe their unusual sensory experiences. For example, one woman reported that to her rain on a window sounded like a thundering locomotive and the sound hurt her ears. Another person reported a visual preference for certain colors and orientation of letters. Many individuals seem to have different reactions to pain and touch. Some are overly sensitive to light touch, whereas others seem to crave deep pressure. No two people with autism are likely to have identical responses to sensory stimulation. It is likely, though, that an individual with this disorder may have unusual reactions to certain sensations.

Because of their impairment in managing sensory information, children with autism may react to sensory stimulation in different ways. Severe overreactions, such as screaming, throwing tantrums, head banging, tensing, or self-biting, occur with varied frequency. Some children may overreact like this many times a day and others may do so only once a week. A careful behavioral analysis (an examination of the conditions that lead to outbursts and their consequences) of these outbursts may indicate that the child is reacting to a specific type of sensory stimulation. Other, less dramatic reactions might include social withdrawal in which the child seems to be in his or her own world. Children with autism often show a lack of responsiveness or indifference to people, including family members. Repetitive motor movements, such as rhythmic rocking or spinning, are common in children with autism. This type of response might reflect the person's attempt to shut out sensory stimulation.

Infants with autism commonly are fussy and resist comforting. Parents describe their children with autism as difficult to hold or resistant to cuddling. When held, these infants may seem stiff or rigid and fail to mold to their parents' bodies. Difficulty with feeding is frequently a problem. Many children have very limited diets, refusing to add or try new foods. Mood abnormalities are another characteristic of children with autism. Very often these children display rapid mood changes, show unusual fear or other reactions to harmless objects, exhibit bodily tension, show lack of fear to real dangers, and display an apparent absence of emotional reactions in social situations. At times, they avoid eye contact with others. Unusual motor movements also are commonly seen. For example, repetitive motions, such as waving the arms and flapping the fingers, may be observed in response to excitement or certain stimulation.

Odd hand and body posturing and walking on tiptoes are also noted in many individuals.

Also, the children's thinking skills, or cognitive abilities, show definite abnormalities. Although mental retardation is present in the majority of children with autism, there are some individuals who have average or above-average intelligence. However, these people still may have some distortions of thinking. Difficulty in interpreting facial expressions and gestures is a common problem. A lack of imaginative or pretend play is also reported in young children with this disorder. Children will repeat the same actions with toys, such as lining up blocks, or doing the same puzzle over and over again. Older children may be very insistent on following the same routine each day, and they may become distressed if the routine changes even slightly.

Communication problems are one of the essential features of autism. Speech and language may be absent or delayed. For children who develop speech, problems with intonation, voice quality, rate of speech, and ability to express themselves may be present. Very often, the speech consists of repetitive phrases, which is referred to as *echolalia*. The ability to comprehend what is said by others is often affected. People with autism often are unable to understand sarcasm, jokes, puns, and idiomatic expressions commonly used in everyday language.

CAUSES OF AUTISM

Medical research has demonstrated that biological differences are observed in the brains of persons with autism, and therefore, it is said to be a neurological disorder. There can be a number of causes of the neurological problems that result in autism as well as the other disorders in the category of PDD. Some documented causes include viral and/or chemical exposure during pregnancy and certain diseases, such as celiac disease, rubella, and untreated phenylketonuria. Genetic factors also may play a role, but specific genes involved in autism have not yet been identified. It is very possible that autism may result from a combination of several of these causes.

Years ago, it was a popular but erroneous belief that unresponsive parents and psychological stress somehow caused children to develop autism. It should be emphasized that there never has been any evidence that autism is caused by unresponsive parents or any other aspect of the child's psychological environment. Current research clearly supports the notion that autism is a neurological disorder; however, the definitive cause is often unknown.

INCIDENCE OF AUTISM

The incidence of autism is rare. Estimates range from 2–4 cases in every 10,000 live births to a high of 15 in every 10,000 live births. Autism occurs approximately four times more often in males than in females.

DIAGNOSIS OF AUTISM

A diagnosis of autism is made after careful observation and evaluation of the individual. Although autism is considered a neurological disorder, there is no specific medical test or procedure that can confirm a diagnosis of autism. Instead, professionals look at all of an individual's symptoms and compare them to the established criteria for diagnosing the disorder. If the individual has a majority of the symptoms listed in the criteria, the diagnosis will be made. If the diagnosis is questionable, the physician, psychologist, or another professional may want to observe the child over a period of time before labeling him or her with the diagnosis of autism.

Criteria for a Diagnosis of Autism

The American Psychiatric Association describes specific diagnostic criteria for autism and other disorders in its *Diagnostic and Statistical Manual of Mental Disorders*. In the most recent edition of this manual (4th ed.) (1994) autism is one subgroup of pervasive developmental disorders. The diagnosis of autism is made if a child demonstrates at least six characteristics of the 12 that are organized under the following three main headings:

1. *Qualitative impairments in social interactions,* which refers to difficulties in developing friendships, making eye contact, recognizing emotions, and using facial expressions
2. *Qualitative impairments in communication,* which refers to the delay in development or total lack of speech, unusual or repetitive speech, and an inability to carry on a conversation
3. *Restricted repetitive and stereotyped patterns of behavior, interests, and activities,* which refers to preoccupations with particular objects and unusual repetitive mannerisms such as spinning, finger flicking, and a tendency to complete routines in the same way

Despite the specific criteria detailed by the American Psychiatric Association, making a diagnosis of autism often is not easy or straightforward. In numerous cases, children display some, but not all, of the characteristics listed. Whether the label should be applied becomes a difficult issue for parents and professionals alike. If an individual does not meet the specific criteria for a diagnosis of autism, but shows significant impairments in the areas of social interactions and communication and displays a limited repertoire of activities and interests as described above, other diagnoses in the PDD category may be considered; these include Rett syndrome, childhood disintegrative disorder, Asperger syndrome or disorder, and pervasive developmental disorder—not otherwise specified. Although many of the criteria for the different disorders overlap, it is believed that each disorder is distinct.

Many parents report that their children with severe behavior and communication problems have been diagnosed simply as having PDD. The use of PDD as a diagnostic label is not universally accepted by professionals who specialize in the care and treatment of these children. Some feel that a more useful label would be "autistic spectrum disorder" to reflect the range of severity and diversity that is seen in the population of individuals with autism. As of 1994, the category of "autistic spectrum disorder" has not been adopted by the psychiatric community. PDD is likely to continue to be used as a diagnosis for children who do not meet the specific criteria for autism or related developmental disabilities.

TREATMENT OF AUTISM

Because autism is a brain-based developmental disability, there is no cure for it. However, comprehensive treatment and intervention can make a difference in the ability of the person with autism to function independently and lead a productive life. There are many approaches to treatment including educational, behavioral, and vocational programming, and sensory approaches designed to reduce the impact of overly sensitive tactile, visual, or auditory senses. The use of a variety of prescription medications, dietary changes, and food supplements to alleviate symptoms of autism has been tried with varying degrees of success. Use of food supplements and restricted diets is considered controversial by many professionals as these treatments have not been proven to be effective through controlled research.

Because no two persons with autism or other pervasive developmental disorder are alike, an individualized treatment plan must be developed to meet the individual's special needs. A team approach in which professionals from a variety of disciplines and family members work together to devise treatment strategies is one of the best ways to create an individualized plan. Together, parents and professionals can set priorities for the particular stage of the child's life. Goals are likely to change as the child develops, matures, and acquires skills. For the majority of individuals with autism and other forms of PDD, language and communication skills, social interaction abilities, and behavioral goals (both to reduce undesirable and disruptive behaviors and to increase appropriate alternative behaviors) will be a focus of a treatment plan.

Beginning treatment early in life is now possible through early intervention programs and preschool special education programs available throughout the United States. The earlier intervention begins, the better the chances of the child making a good adjustment. Studies of the effects of early intervention on children with autism have demonstrated positive results, including improved behavior and the ability to attend public school classes. Early intervention seems most effective when it is intensive and involves active participation of the parents and other family members.

Many children with autism or other pervasive developmental disorders receive education services in specialized classrooms or centers designed to provide a high degree of structure with opportunities for individualized teaching or small-group instruction. Depending on the extent of the disability, some children may spend all of their school years in specialized programs whereas others may require only a few years before being included in public school settings. In addition to well-structured classrooms, highly skilled teachers who are proficient in designing and implementing programs to foster appropriate behavior are essential. Special methods such as behavioral procedures have been effective in helping children with autism learn to communicate and develop social interaction skills. Behavior modification relies on rewarding or reinforcing the child when appropriate behaviors are displayed and ignoring or withdrawing reinforcement when inappropriate behaviors occur. In rare, severe cases, disruptive or self-injurious behavior is so serious that family members and professionals may determine that more intrusive punishment procedures are necessary. Whatever the treatment plan, active parent participation in its development is critical.

EXPECTED OUTCOMES FOR CHILDREN WITH AUTISM

Although autism is a lifelong disability, the impact it has on an individual's life can be lessened through continuous efforts of parents and professionals. Although there is no cure, individuals with autism do learn to compensate and cope with their disabilities. The degree of adjustment depends on the severity of the disorder and

whether there are associated problems such as a seizure disorder, hearing or vision problems, or other health conditions. Approximately one sixth of children diagnosed as having autism eventually make a reasonable social adjustment, which may include the ability to work independently in the community. Another one sixth are reported to have a fair outcome; the remaining two thirds are significantly affected throughout life. With specialized intervention and services, however, more and more people with autism are making use of their abilities through supported employment programs and supported living arrangements.

ACKNOWLEDGMENTS

Contributions have been made to this chapter by Leslie E. Weidenman, Ph.D., and Ann S. Zartler, Ph.D.

Inherited and Acquired Developmental Disabilities

In a book of this nature, it is impossible to include all of the disabilities that have been identified in the past. Instead, we have chosen to give an overview of the most common developmental disabilities as well as a few of the less frequently occurring disorders, including those that have been described more recently.

Specific disabilities may refer to problems in a single area of functioning or might represent a cluster of problems. When problems or symptoms occur in groups, they generally are referred to as a *syndrome*. A number of syndromes are discussed in this section.

For each topic, we define and describe the disability and provide information about the incidence; cause, if known; expected outcomes; and intervention or treatment. In addition, methods used to diagnose the disorder are mentioned.

A number of medical terms and some examples of professional jargon that you are likely to hear are included and explained. Familiarity with such terms will help you to improve your ability to communicate with the professionals you meet.

Chromosome and Genetic Disorders

DESCRIPTION

Certain developmental disabilities may be the result of too much or too little chromosome material or of atypical genes. Chromosomes are microscopic, rodlike structures that contain thousands of genes, and genes are the hereditary material that determine how we grow, how tall we are, what color hair we have, and how our bodies and brains work.

CHROMOSOME PROBLEMS

Our bodies are made up of millions of cells. The cells typically contain 46 chromosomes each, except for sperm and egg cells, which have 23 chromosomes each. At conception, when the sperm and the egg unite, the newly formed cell again has 46 chromosomes, as shown in Figure 1. Because a human being receives a set of 23 chromosomes from the father and another set of 23 chromosomes from the mother, there is a total of 23 pairs of chromosomes. Twenty-two pairs are called *autosomes*. The remaining 23rd pair contains the sex chromosomes, known as X and Y *chromosomes*. A person with two X chromosomes is a female. In contrast, a male has one X and one Y chromosome, as noted in Figure 2.

Occasionally, during the formation of the egg or sperm, an accident occurs with the chromosomes, causing an imbalance in the amount of chromosome material in the egg or sperm. If there is too

117

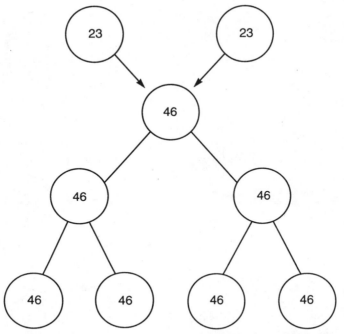

Figure 1.　Twenty-three chromosomes derive from each sperm and egg cell. At the time of fertilization, the first cell has 46 chromosomes. Under "normal" circumstances, this cell contin- ues to divide, and in subsequent generations, each cell will have 46 chromosomes.

much or too little chromosome material in either the egg or the sperm that come together at conception, abnormalities in the devel- oping individual may be observed. Most embryos with chromosome problems are miscarried. It has been estimated that between 8% and 10% of all embryos are miscarried.

There are three major types of chromosome disorders:

1.　If there is an extra chromosome, the disorder is referred to as *trisomy*. One less chromosome is called *monosomy*. If a piece of chromosome is missing, it is a *deletion;* if a small piece within a chromosome is upside down, it is called an *inversion*.
2.　Some parents have two chromosomes that are attached to each other, a condition known as *translocation*. If this translocation is passed on to a child, and the other parent contributes the typical number of chromosomes, then the offspring may have too much chromosome material and may develop physical and mental ab- normalities. Translocations are also observed in some children whose parents have normal chromosomes.

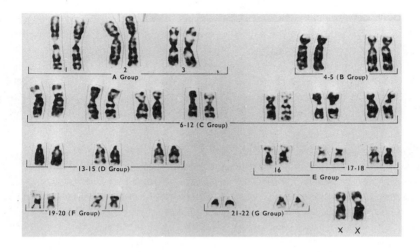

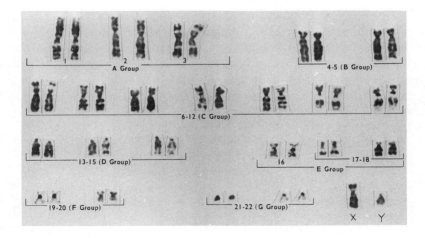

Figure 2. A karyotype (chromosome pattern) of a typical female is shown on the top; a karyotype of a typical male is depicted on the bottom.

3. Not all chromosome problems occur before conception. Some may occur after conception and thus do not affect all of the cells in the developing embryo. This condition, in which some cells have the normal number of chromosomes and the other cells have too much or too little chromosome material, is called *mosaicism*. When mosaicism occurs, the child may show typical features of the syndrome, although sometimes to a lesser degree. The extent of the problem depends on the percentage of cells with abnormal chromosomes present in the child's body.

Through analysis of chromosomes, the specific pair of chromosomes affected is identified by a number. For example, trisomy 21, observed in children with Down syndrome (see discussion later in this chapter), is caused by an extra chromosome added to the 21st pair, as seen in Figure 3. Similarly, trisomy 13 refers to an extra #13 chromosome, and in trisomy 18, three #18 chromosomes are noted.

GENETIC PROBLEMS

Abnormalities in a parent's genes may cause health problems or a disorder in a child. Whether a child is adversely affected by a genetic

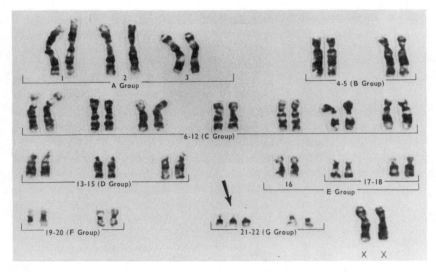

Figure 3.   A karyotype of a girl with Down syndrome. Note the extra #21 chromosome as shown by the arrow.

condition depends in part on the pattern of inheritance of the disorder. Genetic disorders are classified according to the method of inheritance. The four basic categories are autosomal dominant, autosomal recessive, X-linked recessive, and multifactorial inheritance. In addition, there are a few recently described disorders that are inherited in a different (nonmendelian) way. Some of the more common genetic disorders are described later in this chapter.

Autosomal Dominant Inheritance

Children of an adult with an autosomal dominant disorder have a 50% chance of inheriting the disease, as shown in Figure 4. Occasionally, a child is born with an autosomal dominant disorder that was not present in the parents. This is called a *spontaneous mutation* and means that the disorder developed as a result of an accidental change in the child's genetic material. This child then has a 50% risk of passing the disease on to his or her children. Examples of autosomal dominant disorders include achondroplasia (a form of dwarfism) and Huntington disease (a disorder affecting the brain).

Autosomal Recessive Inheritance

An individual with an autosomal recessive disorder inherits two abnormal genes, one from each parent. If a child inherits only one abnormal gene, the disease will not become evident. A person carrying only one abnormal gene is known as a *carrier* or *heterozygote*. Carriers do not get the disease, but can pass the abnormal gene on to their children.

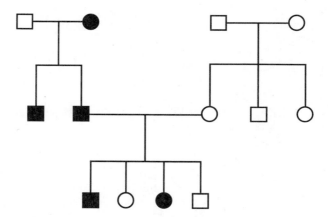

Figure 4.   In autosomal dominant inherited patterns, individuals with the disorder are often observed in each generation, as noted in this pedigree (square = male; circle = female; solid shading = individual with disorder).

When parents who are carriers of the same disease have children, each child born to that couple will have a 25% chance of being affected, a 50% chance of being a carrier, and a 25% chance that the gene pair will be normal. Autosomal recessive disorders are more likely to occur when an individual marries a close family member because of the shared genetic background, as seen in Figure 5. For example, phenylketonuria (PKU), a disorder caused by a deficiency of the enzyme phenylalanine hydroxylase that usually results in mental retardation if not treated appropriately, is an autosomal recessive disorder (see also Chapter 19 for a discussion of metabolic disorders).

X-Linked Recessive Inheritance

X-linked recessive disorders are transmitted by abnormal genes on the X chromosome. They also are called *sex-linked disorders*. Common X-linked disorders are muscular dystrophy, hemophilia, and color blindness. The abnormal gene is carried by the mother on one of her two X chromosomes. The mother usually is not affected by the disorder but she can pass the gene on to her children, as noted in Figure 6. There is a 50% chance that a son will have the disorder.

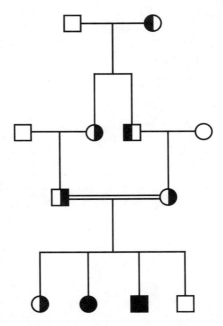

Figure 5. Examples of autosomal recessive inheritance. The parents who are first-degree cousins are heterozygotes; they have two children with the disorder they carry (half-shading = carrier individuals).

Daughters usually do not have the disorder, but they have a 50% chance of inheriting the abnormal gene and becoming carriers (see generation 2 in Figure 6). In rare instances in which a man with an X-linked disorder mates with a woman who is a carrier for the same disorder, there is a 50% chance that a daughter will be affected by the disorder.

Multifactorial Inheritance

Multifactorial disorders are those in which several genes and environmental factors together seem to cause a disease. Simply having the affected genes or just being exposed to an adverse environment will not cause the disorder; there must be some interaction between these two components. Examples of conditions that are inherited in a multifactorial manner include cleft lip and cleft palate, clubfoot, spina bifida (opening at the spine), hip dislocation, and congenital heart disease. In a family with one child who has such a disorder, the risk of another child in the family having the same defect is generally 2%–5%. If there are two children with the same disorder, then the recurrence risk increases to 5%–10%.

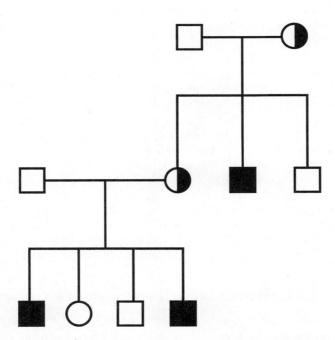

Figure 6.   Example of X-linked recessive inheritance in which the mutant gene is carried by the female, but only males have the disorder (half-shading = carrier individuals; full-shading = affected individual).

Nonmendelian Inheritance

Enormous progress has been made in the past few decades in the field of genetics. It has been found that in addition to disorders caused by autosomal dominant, autosomal recessive, X-linked, and multifactorial disorders, there are other diseases that do not fit into these modes of inheritance. As of 1994, three other forms of inheritance have been observed; they are briefly described here:

- Mitochondrial inheritance is caused by a mutation of mitochondrial DNA (mitochondria are located in the cell plasma and produce energy; DNA is the molecular basis of heredity). Mitochondrial disorders are inherited from the mother because mitochondria are found in the egg, not in the sperm. If the mitochondrial DNA is defective, the child may have severe brain and muscle disorders.
- Genomic imprinting is the influence of either paternal or maternal abnormal genes on the expression of a genetic disorder. For example, in a child with Prader-Willi syndrome (which is characterized by obesity, small hands and feet, short stature, small genitalia, and mental retardation), a part of chromosome #15 inherited from the child's father is deleted. However, if the same deletion of chromosome #15 is inherited from the mother, the child will have Angelman syndrome (small head, characteristic facies, atypical walk, paroxysms of laughter, and mental retardation).
- Uniparental disomy occurs when two chromosomes of a pair are derived from one parent, instead of having one chromosome of the pair come from the mother and the other from the father. This is thought to be due to an abnormal cell division. For example, it has been reported that in a child with cystic fibrosis, two copies of chromosome #7 both came from the mother. (Usually cystic fibrosis is inherited in an autosomal recessive mode where one abnormal gene comes from the father and the other abnormal gene from the mother.)

These inheritance patterns do not fit the usual mendelian mode of inheritance. They were discovered because of recent technical advances. As newer genetic methods become available, it is possible that new forms of inheritance will be identified.

CAUSES OF CHROMOSOME AND GENETIC DISORDERS

No one knows what causes most chromosome abnormalities. Some scientists believe that viral infections, abnormal hormone levels, X rays, potent drugs, or a genetic predisposition may lead to chromosome problems. However, there is no definite proof that any of these conditions causes chromosome problems in particular children.

Some chromosome disorders seem to occur more frequently in mothers who are 35 years or older; for example, this is true of Down syndrome. The older the mother, the greater the chance that she may have a child with Down syndrome. There also is a slightly increased risk of having a child with Down syndrome if the father is older than 50. We do not know what is responsible for changes in genes that may result in genetic disorders.

INCIDENCE

The incidence, or the frequency of, specific chromosome and genetic disorders varies with each disability. In the chapters that follow, the incidence of individual disorders is listed, if known.

After parents have had a child with a chromosome disorder, they usually wonder about the likelihood of having another child with the same problem. If neither parent has an abnormality in their chromosomes, their risk of having a second child with a chromosome disorder is considered small—approximately 1%. However, even this risk is somewhat higher than that for the general population.

One way parents can learn more about their particular risk of having children with genetic or chromosome disorders is through genetic counseling (see Chapter 4 for a discussion of the role of a genetic counselor).

DETECTION AND DIAGNOSIS

If a chromosome disorder is suspected, a physician may order a special blood test to analyze the chromosomes. When the chromosomes are lined up according to size, a karyotype is constructed (as shown in Figure 2). The karyotype shows the 23 pairs of chromosomes. The chromosomes are then examined for any abnormalities. If there are problems, such as an extra chromosome (i.e., trisomy), deletion, translocation, or other structural chromosome abnormalities, it will become apparent in the karyotype.

A chromosome analysis usually is done to confirm a doctor's clinical impression of a specific disorder or syndrome. Many chromosome and genetic disorders are associated with specific physical features. Recognizing the presence of these features is the first step in making a diagnosis. For example, when a physician sees a newborn with the facial features associated with Down syndrome, he or she may order a chromosome analysis to confirm the clinical impression.

EXPECTED OUTCOMES

The impact of a chromosome or genetic disorder on a child's life depends entirely on the specific disorder. Whereas some disorders are associated with mental retardation, health problems, and specific physical characteristics, others may affect the individual's reproductive ability only. At this time, there is no effective medical treatment to correct chromosome disorders. However, many of the management aspects of developmental disabilities that are discussed later in this book (e.g., early intervention) help children to reach their fullest potential.

COMMON CHROMOSOME DISORDERS

Some of the more common chromosome disorders, including Down syndrome, cri du chat syndrome, trisomies 18 and 13, Turner syndrome, Noonan syndrome, fragile X syndrome, and Rett syndrome, are described in the sections that follow.

Down Syndrome

Perhaps the most familiar chromosome abnormality is Down syndrome. As stated previously, individuals with Down syndrome, or trisomy 21, have an extra 21st chromosome, giving them a total of three #21 chromosomes (see Figure 3). This means there are a total of 47 chromosomes in each cell instead of the usual 46. Down syndrome occurs in approximately 1 in every 800–1,000 births. There is quite a range of intellectual functioning in children with Down syndrome. The majority of children with Down syndrome have mental retardation. However, there are some children with Down syndrome who do not have mental retardation.

Children with Down syndrome have a number of similar physical characteristics that make them easily recognizable. The back of the head is often flattened, the eyes may be slightly slanted, skin folds at the inner corners of the eyes—called *epicanthal folds*—may be present, the bridge of the nose often is depressed, and the nose and ears are usually smaller than in typical children. A newborn baby with Down syndrome frequently has excess skin at the back of the neck. Typically, the hands and feet are small. Children with Down syndrome also have loose or lax ligaments, and during infancy their

muscle strength and muscle tone are usually diminished. About 40%–50% of children with Down syndrome have congenital heart disease. Other problems may be present at birth, such as block-e of the bowel or cataracts. There is a wide variation in physical features, mental ability, behavior, and developmental progress in children with Down syndrome. In spite of their limited intellectual abilities, their various physical concerns, and health problems, children with Down syndrome can participate in education programs, often are vocationally productive and are contributing members of society. Many individuals with Down syndrome live well into their 50s and 60s.

Cri Du Chat Syndrome

Cri du chat (a French term meaning "cry of the cat") syndrome is a rare condition resulting from a loss of some genetic material from chromosome #5. Cri du chat syndrome occurs in approximately 1 in every 20,000 births. Children who have cri du chat syndrome may be recognized at birth. They tend to be small and grow slowly. They typically have a distinct cry that may sound like a meowing cat. Children with cri du chat syndrome have mental retardation. Most learn to walk, but their language and their mental development are significantly affected. The physical appearance of a child with cri du chat syndrome includes a small head with a round face, widely set eyes, and small folds of skin over the inner corners of the eyes. These children often have strabismus (crossed eyes). The face may lack symmetry and the ears may be shaped atypically. In addition to these features, congenital heart disease and other abnormalities may be present. Children with cri du chat syndrome usually survive into adulthood.

Trisomy 18

Trisomy 18 is a disorder arising from the presence of an extra #18 chromosome. It occurs in approximately 2–3 babies in every 10,000 births. In general, infants with trisomy 18 are small and have a weak cry at birth. Children with trisomy 18 have an unusually shaped long head, atypical ears, narrow eyelids, and a small mouth and chin. The hands are characteristically clenched, with overlapping fingers. The fingernails may be very small. Many additional anomalies may be seen in these children. Children with trisomy 18 are usually weak. They often have episodes in which they fail to breathe, a condition called *apnea*. They may have limited sucking capability and may require feeding by tube. Only 10% of these children survive the first year of life, and those who do have significant mental retardation.

Trisomy 13

Trisomy 13 is another serious chromosome disorder. It occurs on the average of 1 in every 10,000 births. As the name implies, there is an extra #13 chromosome present causing the brain to be malformed with incomplete nerves for sight and smell. Children with this syndrome have mental impairments and may develop seizures. In addition, many have cleft lip and cleft palate, congenital heart disease, and other abnormalities. Less than 10% of these infants survive the first year of life. The survivors have seizures, fail to grow typically, and often have mental retardation.

Turner Syndrome

Children with Turner syndrome are girls who most often have only one X chromosome instead of the normal two. Their appearance is characterized by frequent swelling of the back of the hands and feet at birth, a low hairline at the back of the neck giving the appearance of a short neck, and a broad chest with widely spaced nipples. They also may have heart disease, most commonly a narrowing of the aorta, which is the major vessel coming from the heart. As these children develop, the swelling of hands and feet diminishes. Their growth is slow and their stature is usually short, often less than 5 feet. Their ovaries are underdeveloped; to mature sexually, these individuals require female hormone therapy starting in adolescence.

Growth hormone treatment has also been suggested. The majority of these women are infertile. Individuals with Turner syndrome usually have average or low to average intelligence. The incidence of this rare syndrome is estimated to be 1 in every 10,000 births.

Noonan Syndrome

Noonan syndrome may affect males or females. Individuals with Noonan syndrome are similar in appearance to those with Turner syndrome. Noonan syndrome most often is inherited as an autosomal dominant disorder. Unlike Turner syndrome, no chromosome abnormality has been identified in these children. Noonan syndrome is said to be more common than Turner syndrome. These children often have congenital heart disease that is more severe than that found in Turner syndrome. In addition, children with Noonan syndrome may have mental retardation or learning disabilities.

Fragile X Syndrome

Fragile X syndrome is a disorder that runs in families. It is X-linked inherited and is marked by the presence of unusually structured lower parts of some X chromosomes. This is seen only when a special method is used in the chromosome analysis. Males who have fragile X syndrome have mental retardation. Atypical facial features and large testes also have been described. Some females with fragile X syndrome have mental retardation; others have average intellectual functioning.

Rett Syndrome

Rett syndrome occurs only in females. During the first year of life most children with Rett syndrome develop typically. However, in the beginning of the second year of life, most girls with Rett syndrome regress in their development and lose some of their previously acquired skills. They often exhibit autistic-like features, have significant mental retardation, develop no or very little language, and display poor social interaction. Irritability, poor sleep habits, and inconsolable crying episodes are also often observed. In addition, many of the girls have difficulties with equilibrium and may walk with a broad-based gait. The head is usually small, and most children with Rett syndrome are underweight. Many girls with Rett syndrome have seizures and a curvature of the spine (i.e., scoliosis). They may hyperventilate and have breath-holding spells. Most characteristic is the stereotypic use of the hands, which has been described as "wringing of hands" or "hand-washing movements." Although it is thought that Rett syndrome is an X-linked genetic disorder, the cause of Rett syndrome is not known. There is currently no effective medical treatment.

ACKNOWLEDGMENTS

Contributions have been made to this chapter by Siegfried M. Pueschel, M.D., Patricia S. Scola, M.D., M.P.H., and Karen E. Senft, M.D., Ph.D., M.P.H.

Environmental Events

INFECTIONS

During the past several decades, much has been learned about the causes, treatment, and prevention of infections. Numerous childhood deaths and ill effects from infections such as whooping cough (i.e., pertussis), diphtheria, lockjaw (i.e., tetanus), poliomyelitis, and measles have been prevented by immunizations. Naturally, the serious physical and intellectual damage that sometimes accompanied these infections does not occur in children who are properly immunized. Unfortunately, there are other infections for which immunizations are not available, and infections that can affect babies before they are born.

Description

Serious developmental problems can be caused by certain infections that affect children in the prenatal (before birth), perinatal (shortly before, at, and immediately after birth), or postnatal (after birth) periods. Prenatal infections are transmitted to an unborn baby through the infected mother. Any serious bacterial, viral, or parasitic infection in a pregnant woman may harm her unborn baby. The effect of prenatal infections on the fetus varies, depending on the type of infection and the time during pregnancy in which it occurred. Perinatal infections occur around the time of delivery, and postnatal infections can be contacted any time after birth.

Toxoplasmosis, rubella (German measles), cytomegalic inclusion disease, and human immunodeficiency virus (HIV) are some of the infections that can infect an unborn baby prenatally. Herpes simplex

131

and HIV can infect the baby perinatally during the birth process. In the postnatal period, meningitis and encephalitis pose the most serious risks to children. These infections, their incidence, and possible effects on the child are described in the following sections.

Toxoplasmosis *Toxoplasmosis gondii* is a parasite found throughout the world. Cats serve as the major host for the parasite. The transmission of the parasite is caused primarily by contact with infected cat feces or with contaminated, improperly cooked meat. A toxoplasmosis infection transmitted to the fetus in the womb can result in premature birth or an infant who is small for gestational age (length of pregnancy). In addition, early infant death, mental retardation, and visual problems including blindness may occur in infected children. The child's head may be unusually large or very small. Approximately 0.5–1.0 per 1,000 live-born infants are infected with toxoplasmosis, 25% of whom will have symptoms.

Rubella Rubella, or German measles, usually is acquired from other infected humans through their cough or moist expired air. An infant, infected prenatally, may be smaller than expected at birth. The baby also may be deaf, have congenital heart disease, and have visual problems due to cataracts and inflammation of the retina. The baby may have a small head and mental retardation. Because almost all females in the reproductive age have been immunized against German measles, congenital rubella syndrome is now rarely seen. Many states require that a woman have a blood test to determine her immunity to rubella at premarital screening. If her immunity is not adequate, then she is advised to be immunized before starting a family.

Cytomegalic Inclusion Disease Cytomegalovirus (CMV) is a common virus found throughout the world. Most infants infected in the womb do not have signs and symptoms at birth, but they may be at risk for hearing loss detected at a later age. The infants who have symptoms at birth may be smaller than expected, have blood spots on the skin (i.e., petechiae), a yellow cast to the skin (i.e., jaundice), a small head (i.e., microcephaly), delayed development, and mental retardation. It has been estimated that approximately 0.2%–2% of newborns are infected with CMV, and only a few of these children display the symptoms described here.

Herpes Simplex Herpes simplex virus infections are caused by one of two types: type 1 is known as oral herpes; type 2 is genital herpes, which is spread by sexual contact. A newborn infant, however, may contract type 2 herpes simplex by passage through an infected birth canal. Pregnant women known to have genital herpes are watched very carefully throughout pregnancy and if there are signs of infection, delivery is by Cesarean section to prevent infection of the baby. A baby with herpes simplex usually shows signs of the infection during the first month of life. The symptoms range from skin problems to the involvement of many organs, including the brain. Mental retardation or even death may occur. Approximately 0.1–0.5 of 1,000 live-born infants are infected with herpes simplex virus, more than 95% of whom develop symptoms.

Human Immunodeficiency Virus (HIV) Human immunodeficiency virus (HIV) is the virus that causes acquired immunodeficiency syndrome (AIDS). Common causes of HIV infection include intimate sexual contact with an infected partner, intravenous drug use with contaminated needles, and transfusion with blood or blood products prior to screening tests. Pregnant women known to be infected with HIV have a 30%–50% risk of having a baby who is also infected with the virus. In addition, breast milk may contain HIV, and mothers who are HIV positive should not breast feed.

Women and infants who have been infected by HIV are at risk of developing AIDS. The virus attacks cells that are important in fighting infection. Blood tests confirming evidence of HIV infection and low levels of immunity, in association with recurrent and severe infections, are the basis for the diagnosis of AIDS. Children with AIDS may have pneumonias such as lymphoid interstitial pneumonia and *Pneumocystis carinii* pneumonia.

It is not always easy to determine the HIV status of an infant on the basis of the usual HIV antibody test, and further diagnostic tests may be required. Many infants infected with HIV will develop symptoms by 2 years of age. An infected infant may have developmental problems because of progressive neurological disease, but also as a result of multiple serious illnesses and hospitalizations.

Because children with HIV or AIDS may reside in a home with a parent who has AIDS or may have lost a parent to the disease, there may be additional serious strains within the family.

Meningitis Meningitis is an infection of the membranes covering the brain and spinal cord and the adjacent neural tissue. Many kinds of bacteria can cause meningitis, and specific names are applied to the diagnosis depending on the type of bacteria—for example, *pneumococcal meningitis* or *hemophilus influenzae meningitis*. The age of the child, the type of bacteria causing the infection, the severity of the infection, and the effectiveness of the specific treatment determine the outcome. Some children recover completely after an episode of meningitis, whereas others may survive with blindness, deafness, paralysis, seizures, or mental retardation.

Encephalitis Encephalitis usually is caused by a virus. Encephalitis refers to an inflammation of brain tissue, whereas *encephalomyelitis* indicates involvement of both brain and spinal cord, and *meningoencephalitis* is an infection of both the brain and its covering membranes. When a prolonged coma is a symptom associated with such an infection, the term *sleeping sickness* has been used. The type of virus, the age of the child, and the severity of the infection determine the individual outcome and whether or not a disability develops. Certain childhood illnesses, including rubella and mumps, may lead to encephalitis. Also, the herpes simplex virus and many others can cause encephalitis. The subsequent brain injury may lead to mental retardation and behavior disorders.

The immunizations used to prevent childhood illnesses may themselves cause encephalitis, although this is extremely rare. The risk of such a postimmunization encephalitis is far less than the risk of complications from the childhood diseases.

Causes

Certain bacteria and viruses, as well as drugs, alcohol, and other harmful substances that cause an unborn baby to develop atypically are called *teratogens* (see the section about Drugs, Alcohol, and Smoking later in this chapter). Why certain infectious agents act as teratogens when contracted prenatally is not completely understood. What is known is that at critical stages of embryonic and fetal development, infections can have serious, long-lasting effects.

During the first trimester of pregnancy, when the basic structures of the body, including the brain, are formed, the embryo or fetus is particularly vulnerable to infections. Also, during birth and during the postnatal period, certain infections, especially those that attack the brain and nervous system, can cause brain injury and developmental disabilities.

Diagnosis

When a newborn baby is suspected to have been infected prenatally, various tests can be done in an attempt to determine whether or not an infection occurred and, if so, what kind of infection. Some physicians then ask that a TORCH titer be done to determine whether there has been exposure to certain infectious agents. This test requires blood samples from both mother and baby, which are then examined for antibodies against TORCH organisms, whereby T stands for toxoplasmosis, O for other germs, R for rubella or German measles, C for cytomegalic inclusion disease, and H for herpes simplex. If a very high antibody titer for one of the organisms is found, then there is a possibility that a prenatal infection has taken place.

If meningitis or encephalitis is suspected in a child, the doctor most often will do a lumbar puncture or a spinal tap. These tests involve placing a needle between the spinal cord and its membranes and withdrawing some spinal fluid. The spinal fluid is then examined for bacteria and viruses. Also, blood cell counts and certain chemical tests can be done on spinal fluid, which will help to make the diagnosis.

Expected Outcomes

The type of treatment a child receives and the effects of the illness depend on the particular infection and the severity of the disease. Antibiotics are given immediately if meningitis has been diagnosed. The type of antibiotic used will depend on the specific bacteria found and their sensitivity to various antibiotics. However, a baby who has been infected prenatally by the rubella virus or cytomegalovirus will not receive medical therapy because most of the damage has already been done. If a child contracts encephalitis after birth, new antiviral drugs are now available for treatment.

DRUGS, ALCOHOL, AND SMOKING

There may be times when a pregnant woman needs to take prescription drugs or over-the-counter medicines. Unfortunately, medicines that help the expectant mother sometimes harm the unborn baby. A number of medicines, illicit drugs, and other substances have caused abnormalities in fetal development. One of the most publicized catastrophes in medicine occurred in the 1950s and early 1960s in Europe and some other countries and involved the use of the drug thalidomide during pregnancy. Women who took this drug as a mild sedative during the first few months of pregnancy gave birth to children with shortened or absent limbs. This cluster of abnormalities led to studies indicating that thalidomide caused the birth defects.

Description and Incidence

Serious medical conditions such as seizure disorders, cancer, infections, and blood diseases may necessitate a mother's use of medicine during pregnancy. Drugs commonly used to treat such conditions, but that may also damage the baby, are described here.

Seizure Medications Seizure medications, or anticonvulsant drugs, must be given with utmost care during pregnancy, because they are potentially dangerous to the unborn baby. These medications should be administered by a physician aware of the potential effects on the fetus.

Dilantin   Dilantin (or the generic drug phenytoin) causes congenital anomalies in approximately 43% of infants exposed to it prenatally. Of these infants, 33% are mildly affected, and the remaining 10% have the so-called fetal hydantoin syndrome. These children have unusual facial features with wide-set eyes, a short nose, and small fingernails and toenails. Occasionally, these youngsters have mental retardation.

Tridione   Tridione (or the generic name trimethadione) is an anticonvulsant medication known to cause abnormalities in more than two thirds of the children exposed to it in the womb. These children generally have characteristic facial features such as a short, upturned nose, a broad and low nasal bridge, a prominent forehead, atypical genitalia, congenital heart disease, and mental impairment.

Depakene   Recent studies have indicated that spina bifida, or meningomyelocele, occurs in approximately 1% of children exposed in the womb to Depakene (or the generic drug valproic acid).

Anticlotting Medications   Anticlotting, or anticoagulant, medications are occasionally necessary for the pregnant mother. When Coumadin, a common brand of anticoagulant medication, is taken during pregnancy, affected children may have numerous congenital anomalies including short fingers, low birth weight, a small nose, and unusual facial features. Five of 16 reported children have shown significant mental retardation. Approximately two thirds of exposed infants will be unaffected, and one third will show bodily effects and brain anomalies or will be miscarried.

Anticancer Drugs   Women who develop cancer during pregnancy and who are in need of life-saving but toxic medications will require careful medical management by both their obstetrician and their oncologist (physician who treats cancer). In order to save her life, the expectant mother may need to take many drugs that may be harmful to the unborn baby.

Other Medications   Many drugs are marketed each year, and careful surveillance is necessary to identify those that may be harmful to the fetus if taken during pregnancy. One of the more recent drugs found to be harmful if taken during pregnancy is an acne medication Acutane (or the generic drug cis-retinoic acid). Women who have taken the drug during pregnancy have had children with brain malformations.

The list of drugs known to be hazardous to the unborn child undoubtedly will expand as more studies are done and more drugs are released on the market. During pregnancy it is wise to use only those drugs that are absolutely essential. Even drugs that can be purchased without a prescription may be potentially dangerous and should not be taken without the obstetrician's knowledge.

Illicit Drugs As many as 10% of pregnant women may use illicit drugs such as marijuana, cocaine, heroin, amphetamines, and LSD. In addition, many of these women also use alcohol and cigarettes, making it difficult to determine the effects of each substance on the developing baby. Cocaine, for example, is known to alter the circulation in the womb and thus can cause birth defects. Prenatal substance exposure has also been reported to be associated with premature birth, delayed growth in the womb, and the birth of infants who have symptoms of addiction at birth. Furthermore, children raised by parents with continued substance abuse may not be provided with an appropriately stimulating environment so important for typical development.

Alcohol In addition to avoiding medications, pregnant women have a responsibility to their unborn children to avoid consuming products known to injure fetuses. The best known of these substances is alcohol. Women who consume two or more drinks per day throughout pregnancy may have children with lower than expected birth weights. Those ingesting four to six drinks per day may have children with subtle findings of fetal alcohol effect (FAE), and 8–10 drinks or more per day may result in children with the full-blown fetal alcohol syndrome (FAS). Children with FAS have low birth weights, may have mental retardation, often are irritable during infancy, and frequently are hyperactive later in childhood. They usually have characteristic facial features including narrow eyelids. Congenital heart disease also may be present. A child of a woman who is an alcoholic has the greatest risk of showing FAS symptoms. To date, the question of whether binge drinking in pregnancy is harmful has not been answered. Studies are ongoing, but until this question is answered, it would be wise for pregnant women to avoid alcohol totally.

Smoking Many women who smoke continue to do so during pregnancy. Some of the many studies on the effects of smoking on the fetus have shown an increased rate of spontaneous abortion and death in the newborn period. Most studies show that children born to mothers who smoke during pregnancy tend to have lower birth weights than those born to nonsmoking mothers.

Causes

Like other teratogens, when drugs, alcohol, and tobacco are taken by a pregnant woman, they can cross the placenta and affect the baby. These substances are particularly dangerous during the early stages of development. Yet, the manner in which these substances interfere with embryonic fetal development is not fully understood.

Diagnosis

Diagnosis of a developmental disability caused by substance abuse is made primarily by a detailed medical history and a thorough physical examination of the baby. Reports of a mother's use of drugs, alcohol, and/or tobacco during pregnancy, considered with unusual physical features in the baby, and the infant's slow growth and development, suggest that such substances may have had harmful effects.

Expected Outcomes

As with other causes of developmental disabilities, the severity of a child's problems will determine the amount and type of services needed. The long-term effects on the baby of teratogenic substances consumed by the mother during pregnancy depend to a large extent on the substance, the amount taken, and the time during pregnancy when it was consumed. As mentioned in the descriptions of specific substances, the effects range from mild anomalies to severe deformities and mental retardation.

LEAD POISONING

Description

Lead poisoning occurs primarily in children who have ingested chips of lead-containing paint peeling from walls and woodwork in old houses. It has been known for many years that high levels of lead in the blood are associated with serious neurological disorders such as seizures, swelling of the brain, and mental retardation. During recent years there has been increasing concern about low levels of lead in the blood causing subtle developmental problems and learning disabilities.

Causes

When children eat paint chips containing lead or plaster crumbs soaked with lead paint, they often will develop lead poisoning. Also, when renovating old houses to eliminate old lead paint, lead may be distributed in the air and the soil outside of the houses. Children who breathe this air or play in the dirt may absorb lead into their systems. Previously, leaded gasoline and water from lead pipes or lead-soldered pipes contributed to lead poisoning in child-

hood. Lead pencils, toys painted with lead paint, and the burning of battery cases were other sources of lead poisoning. Children who have a history of pica (eating or chewing nonfood-containing materials) are at a higher risk for lead poisoning.

Diagnosis

It is recommended that physicians who care for children conduct routine annual screenings for lead in the blood between the ages of 6 months and 6 years. A small amount of blood is sent to the laboratory to obtain a blood lead level. Sometimes an X-ray examination of the abdomen will reveal paint chips throughout the intestinal tract. It is also important that the environment be inspected and samples of paint from walls and from other suspected sources be examined for lead content.

Expected Outcomes

After a diagnosis of lead poisoning is made, children should be followed carefully. Medications such as penicillamine, calcium disodium edetate, or succimer may need to be administered. It is of utmost importance that children are removed from environments where there will be continued exposure to lead-containing materials. If paint removal is carried out, it should be done in a safe manner. The best approach is prevention.

ACCIDENTS

Description

Prevention of accidents is of major concern to parents. The developmental stages at which specific types of accidents occur are reviewed by pediatricians during well-child visits. Public health programs emphasize measures such as seat belt use and safety in the home. Even under the best circumstances, children are involved in a variety of accidents in the process of growing up. Most accidents are relatively minor and result in only scrapes and bruises. Injury to the brain or spinal cord are most likely to contribute to significant developmental delays, although serious injury to any part of the body may cause permanent disability.

Causes

Young children are more apt to sustain injuries from falls. As children grow older, motor vehicle, bicycle, and pedestrian accidents are more frequent causes of trauma. Sporting and recreational activities are important childhood experiences, but may also result in injury. There is mounting concern about the increased risk to children of all ages from physical assault that occurs at home as a result of domestic violence or in unsafe neighborhoods where they may be innocent bystanders.

Numerous factors influence the incidence and type of accident. For instance, motor vehicle accidents may occur at a higher rate in a congested metropolitan area while children in a rural area are at risk from complex farming equipment. Injuries are more common in good weather and during those times when school is not in session. Boys are almost twice as likely to experience a head injury as are girls.

Diagnosis

At the time of an accident it is helpful if witnesses can provide information to determine the site of possible injury. The potential for head injury must always be considered even when the child is conscious. Diagnostic studies are conducted at the facility where the injury is treated, and may range from a simple X ray to more sophisticated imaging studies. After very severe injuries, the diagnostic process may continue throughout an extended hospitalization. Parents and professionals should remain aware of subtle long-term effects upon school performance and behavior after a head injury.

Expected Outcomes

The outcome of a severe accident can be influenced by the rapid availability of skilled care. Individuals trained in cardiopulmonary resuscitation (CPR) can initiate measures to maintain oxygen flow to the brain while awaiting emergency support and transportation by emergency medical technicians. Increasingly, geographic areas have designated trauma centers that specialize in the care of major injuries. If necessary, a child may be evaluated at such a center until he or she is stable enough to be transferred to an even more specialized center that treats only children. Hospitalization in pediatric intensive care units provides supervision by intensivists who monitor the needs of critically ill children. Once a child becomes well enough, intensive rehabilitation may be initiated in a rehabilitation program that can offer appropriate speech-language, physical, and occupational therapy.

ACKNOWLEDGMENTS

Contributions have been made to this chapter by Patricia S. Scola, M.D., M.P.H., Karen E. Senft, M.D., and Siegfried M. Pueschel, M.D., Ph.D., M.P.H.

13

Birth Defects

TYPICAL FORMATION AND FUNCTION OF THE CENTRAL NERVOUS SYSTEM

The formation and development of a human being is a complex process. What begins at conception as a single cell starts dividing, differentiating, developing, and maturing finally forms a complete human being. Within 2 weeks after conception, the primitive central nervous system, called the *neural plate,* already is present. By approximately 3 weeks, after further differentiation, the neural plate develops into what is called the *neural tube* and the *primitive brain.* During the next several weeks and months, the complete formation of the nervous system occurs.

At birth, the central nervous system, which is composed of the brain and spinal cord, is nearly fully developed. The brain is a complex organ that has a number of areas with specialized functions. Some of these functions direct movements of the body and limbs, whereas others are responsible for vision, language, memory, thinking, hearing, feeling, and many other important functions. Deep inside the brain are small hollow spaces, called *ventricles,* that contain fluid. This fluid also cushions and bathes the brain's outer layer. In the lower part of the brain are the midbrain and brain stem, which direct basic functions such as sucking, swallowing, and breathing. Another part, called the *cerebellum,* which controls refinement of movements and equilibrium, is located at the back of the brain. Finally, there is the spinal cord, which runs down through the bones of the spine (i.e., spinal canal) and contains nerves that carry impulses to the muscles.

In order for a child to function adequately, a well-formed central nervous system is needed. If there are disruptions in brain development that may lead to permanent malformations, serious developmental disabilities may become apparent.

ATYPICAL DEVELOPMENT OF THE CENTRAL NERVOUS SYSTEM

Common birth defects involving malformations of the brain or spinal cord are described in this section. Two conditions, hydrocephalus and spina bifida, are discussed in greater detail because of their more frequent occurrence.

Anencephaly

If during early development the neural tube does not close at the section that ordinarily forms the brain, the child may be born with major parts of the brain missing. This condition is known as *anencephaly*. Children with anencephaly may have enough brain stem function at birth to breathe and suck initially. However, most of these infants do not show any appreciable developmental progress, and they almost invariably die of infection or respiratory complications in the newborn period. Anencephaly is estimated to occur in 0.1–6.7 per 1,000 live births.

For a mother who has had a child with anencephaly, there is a 2%–4% chance of recurrence of a neural tube defect in a future pregnancy. However, prenatal tests are available to detect anencephaly and related disorders during pregnancy (see Chapter 22 for a discussion of prenatal diagnosis).

Hydranencephaly

In hydranencephaly, the skull is intact and usually of average size or somewhat larger than usual. However, the space inside the skull, which should contain brain tissue, mainly is filled with fluid. The brain stem may be functioning, allowing the child to suck and breathe for some time. However, most children born with hydranencephaly do not have the potential for intellectual growth, and most of them die during the first few months of life.

Holoprosencephaly

Holoprosencephaly is another problem of early brain development. During the third week of pregnancy, when the basic structures of the central nervous system are being formed, the cells that are destined to become the person's face and the front of the brain fail to develop correctly. As a result, the brain forms abnormally and cannot function properly. In addition, the face shows abnormalities in that the eyes are very close together and the nose is very small or almost nonexistent. A large cleft palate is often present. Children with very severe holoprosencephaly usually die in the newborn period. Other children may live beyond infancy, but their capacity for intellectual achievement is poor. Some youngsters have uncontrollable seizures originating in the malformed brain. Holoprosencephaly is seen in some children with trisomy 13 and occasionally in other chromosome anomalies, but often no specific cause can be found.

Hydrocephalus

Hydrocephalus (also called "water in the brain") refers to increased fluid in the hollow spaces, or ventricles, of the brain. As the ventricles fill and enlarge, two effects will be observed: the head will expand and the brain tissue will be compressed, which, if not treated promptly, eventually may result in brain injury.

Causes and Incidence Hydrocephalus may be caused by overproduction of fluid in the brain, a blockage in one of the passages that ordinarily drains fluid from the ventricles, or severe bleeding into the ventricles in the newborn period. Hydrocephalus occurs in approximately 0.8–1.6 of 1,000 live births.

Expected Outcomes The expected outcome for children with hydrocephalus depends on many things including the cause, the severity of the condition, and how quickly treatment is provided. Children who have hydrocephalus because the brain is severely deformed are less likely to do as well as youngsters in whom hydrocephalus results from blockage of the drainage system. Children with long-standing hydrocephalus more often have brain injury than those who are treated early in the development of the hydrocephalus.

In some families, hydrocephalus is inherited as an X-linked recessive trait (for a description of the recessive inheritance pattern, see Chapter 11). In another very small group of families, hydrocephalus recurs in subsequent offspring, but in most instances, hydrocephalus is not hereditary and the risk to future children is small.

An effective treatment of hydrocephalus is the placement of a plastic tube or shunt into the fluid spaces of the brain, which then drains the excessive fluid into the abdomen (for a description of the procedure, see Chapter 25). Sometimes special medicines that reduce fluid production can be used.

Ultrasound techniques are available that permit physicians to visualize the baby in the womb. This technique, which is described in more detail in Chapter 22, can show the size of the head as well as the brain's fluid spaces. If repeated ultrasound images indicate that the ventricles are getting larger and if hydrocephalus is diagnosed, the obstetrician may elect to deliver the baby early so that shunt placement can be done before too much of the brain is injured. When hydrocephalus is detected and it is too early for the child to survive outside of the womb, an operation can be performed while the baby is still in the womb to drain the excess fluid from the baby's ventricles into the surrounding amniotic fluid. Although this type of surgery remains risky and experimental, it offers a great deal of hope for the future.

Spina Bifida

Spina bifida, or meningomyelocele, is a defect of the spinal cord and the bones of the spine that ordinarily surround the spinal cord (Figure 1). Spina bifida develops when the spinal canal does not close completely (i.e., neural tube defect), and the spinal cord, the surrounding tissue, and the membranes covering the spinal cord bulge out through the back of the spine as shown in Figure 1. The delicate nerves in the spinal cord that protrude through the back are injured, leaving the child paralyzed in the lower part of the body. The severity of paralysis depends on where the nerves protrude through the

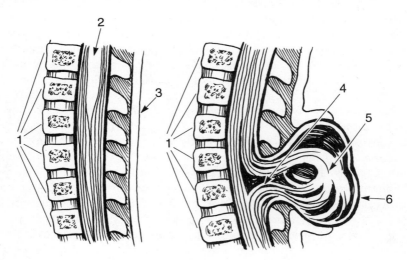

Figure 1.   Cross-sectional views of a normal spine on the left and spine of a person with spina bifida on the right. In the drawing of spina bifida, note the opening at the spine and the protrusion of the spinal cord and its nerves through the back. Shown are: 1, bones of the spine; 2, normal spinal cord; 3, normal skin covering; 4, opening of the spine; 5, damaged spinal nerves; and 6, sack with spinal fluid and nerve tissue.

spine. When the opening is high on the back, paralysis is the greatest, and these children usually will have to use a wheelchair later. Children with spinal cord lesions at the midback also may have to use a wheelchair, although they may be able to stand, and some may walk short distances with appropriate bracing. Lower-back spinal cord lesions generally permit walking some distance with braces and crutches. Children with even lower lesions near the end of the spine may walk with light-weight ankle braces or without any bracing at all.

Because the nerves have been injured, many children with spina bifida will have numbness of the feet, legs, and buttocks. The extent of the numbness depends on the level of the spinal cord lesion. The injury to the nerves also affects the child's bowel and bladder control. Children often cannot feel the urge to pass urine or stool, and they lack the muscle control to do so voluntarily. In addition, urinary tract infections are common. Many of these children develop reflux, a backing up of urine from the bladder into the kidneys. Of children with spina bifida or meningomyelocele, 70%–90% also have hydrocephalus.[1]

Cause and Incidence   The exact cause of spina bifida is unknown; however, both genetic and environmental factors are thought to play a role. An estimate of the incidence of spina bifida, one of the most common birth defects, is 1 affected child in every 1,000 live births. Once a woman has a child with spina bifida, the chances of having another child with the condition are approximately 2%–4%. Today prenatal tests are available to detect meningomyelocele in the unborn baby (see Chapter 22 for a description of the alpha-fetoprotein blood test for spina bifida).

Expected Outcomes   Because meningomyelocele involves so many areas of functioning, a team approach to intervention is especially important. With such an approach, parents can receive appropriate counseling, and children will be provided with optimal medical care and educational services. Medical, and often neurosurgical, treatment are necessary immediately after birth. Infants usually are transferred to a special care nursery. The opening in the back is then closed surgically, and a shunt operation is performed if development of hydrocephalus is noted. If these operations are carried out promptly, and if there are no complications such as infections or shunt malfunctioning, then the outlook for the child's cognitive development usually is good. In fact, the greatest danger to the

[1]Thompson, M.W., McInnes, R.R., & Willard, H.F. (1991). *Genetics in medicine* (5th ed.). Philadelphia: W.B. Saunders.

newborn with spina bifida is an infection of the fluid spaces in the brain, called *ventriculitis*. If this can be prevented, it is likely that the child will have average or near-average intellectual abilities later.

Urinary problems caused by nerve damage may be dealt with in many ways. If a child has a very large bladder that does not empty on its own, it can be emptied manually by applying manual pressure over the bladder. This procedure is called *Credé method*. Previously, many children with meningomyelocele underwent surgery for an ileal loop, whereby the ureters (tubes coming from the kidneys) were brought to the surface of the abdomen (see Chapter 25). The child then wore a bag attached to the stoma (opening in the abdominal wall) to collect urine coming from the ureters. Today, a nonsurgical approach, called *intermittent catheterization*, is used most often. This involves placing a small plastic tube into the bladder for urine drainage several times a day. Bowel continence can be encouraged with regularity of timing of bowel movements, diet, and laxatives or suppositories as needed. Most children find the best program for themselves through experimentation.

As mentioned before, damage to the nerves causes numbness of certain parts of the skin. Skin that is numb may break down, and sores may develop easily. Therefore, meticulous skin care is very important.

Adaptive equipment and physical therapy are essential for children with spina bifida. Professionals can help these children achieve as much independence as possible with proper equipment and practice. The type of equipment needed will depend on the level of the lesion and the degree of paralysis (see Chapter 23).

With appropriate prenatal care, skillful neurosurgical approach in the newborn period, and optimal follow-up care by a team including a neurosurgeon, urologist, orthopaedist, physical therapist, developmental pediatrician, and others, children with spina bifida have a much brighter future today than ever before. In addition, early intervention and adapted education services will foster the child's developmental and academic progress.

Prevention   There is ample evidence that prenatal vitamin supplementation containing folic acid, which is taken from the time of conception, can decrease the incidence of neural tube defects.

CLEFT PALATE AND CLEFT LIP

Cleft palate is a birth defect in which the two halves of the palate (roof of the mouth) fail to join properly. This usually leaves an opening (i.e., a cleft) at both the hard (bony part) and soft (fleshy part) palates and sometimes the lip. When the development is interrupted during the early stages, the result may be a cleft in the lip only. The cause of the interruption in development is not always known. Certain environmental events such as use of specific drugs, German measles, and vitamin deficiencies have been associated with clefts. Cleft lip and cleft palate are also often observed in specific syndromes such as trisomy 13. In other instances, there seems to be a genetic predisposition for the development of a cleft. Cleft lip and cleft palate are multifactorially inherited disorders (see Chapter 11), with a recurrence risk of approximately 2%–4%.[2]

Clefts are known to occur at different rates in various racial groups. Reports list the incidence of clefts in Caucasians as 1 in every 550 live births. The incidence among African Americans is much lower, approximately 1 in every 2,500 live births.

A child with a cleft lip and cleft palate often will have feeding problems, as normal sucking will not be possible. Specialized feeders and specific nipples are utilized, and instructions for home feeding are given to the parents before the baby is discharged from the nursery. To correct the palate and/or the lip defect, a series of surgical procedures are performed, usually within the first year and a half of life. A child with a cleft palate may have speech problems, depending on the size of the cleft and the success of surgical repair. In addition to oral surgery, the child's dental development often requires monitoring by both a dentist and an orthodontist (dentist who specializes in correcting irregularities of the teeth and jaw), as missing, malformed, or malpositioned teeth occasionally are observed, in particular, if the cleft extends into the front area of the palate.

Ear infections and conductive hearing loss are common in this group of children. Therefore, careful followup of the youngsters' hearing is needed. Special attention should be paid to these conditions so that they do not interfere with language, speech, and cognitive development.

CONGENITAL HEART DISEASE

To understand birth defects of the cardiovascular system, it helps to know how the heart and blood vessels are structured and how they function. The following is a brief description of the various parts of

---

[2]Thompson, M.W., McInnes, R.R., & Willard, H.F. (1991). *Genetics in medicine* (5th ed.). Philadelphia: W.B. Saunders.

the heart and how they work together to pump blood throughout the body. The various types of heart defects are then explained.

The Heart

The heart is a muscular organ that acts as a pump and circulates blood to the body and all of its organs. The heart has four chambers—right and left upper chambers known as *atria,* and right and left lower chambers called *ventricles.* The right and left atria and right and left ventricles are separated from each other by a wall of mainly muscle tissue called the *septum.* Blood from the right atrium flows into the right ventricle through a valve known as the *tricuspid valve.* The left atrium connects to the left ventricle by the mitral valve, as shown in Figure 2.

Under normal circumstances, blood is pumped from the left ventricle through arteries to all parts of the body. After flowing through the vessels and capillaries, where the cells receive oxygen and nutrients from the blood, the blood returns to the heart through the veins. The blood then enters the right atrium and subsequently flows to the right ventricle. From there it is pumped to the lungs through the pulmonary arteries, where the blood is enriched with oxygen. The oxygen-rich blood returns to the left atrium of the heart, flows to the left ventricle, and then again is pumped to all parts of the body.

In the unborn baby, the blood follows a slightly different path. Some of the blood that arrives at the right atrium is directed through a hole, called the *foramen ovale,* to the left atrium. In addition, most of the blood that is pumped from the right ventricle through the pulmonary artery is shunted to the aorta which is the main artery coming from the heart through a special vessel called *ductus arteriosus.*

Defects of the Heart

In most infants the ductus arteriosus closes within hours after birth. In a condition known as *patent ductus arteriosus* (PDA), the ductus arteriosus remains open and part of the blood going to the aorta is pushed into the pulmonary artery. This increase in blood flow to the lungs may cause heart and lung problems. Like the ductus arteriosus, the hole between the upper chambers, the foramen ovale, usually closes shortly after birth as the pressure in the left atrium increases. There are occasions when it does not close spontaneously.

Congenital heart defects can be differentiated into those that cause cyanosis (blue discoloration of the skin, lips, and tongue), indicating a low concentration of oxygen in the blood, and those that

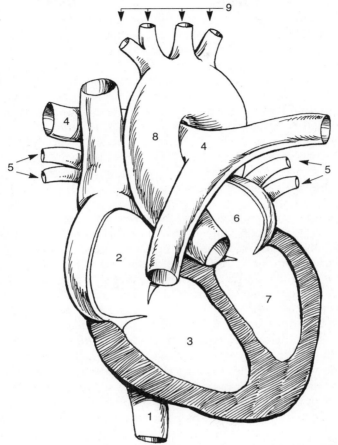

Figure 2. The human heart. The blood enters through the veins (1) into the right atrium (2). From there it flows into the right ventricle (3) and then enters the lungs through the pulmonary arteries (4). The blood returns from the lungs through the pulmonary veins (5) into the left atrium (6), and then continues into the left ventricle (7). From there, blood is pumped into the body through the aorta (8) and the entire arterial system (9).

are not cyanotic. Cyanotic heart disease usually is detected in the first few days of life. Any structural abnormality of the heart that inhibits blood flow to the lungs, where blood is oxygenated, or that causes a mixing of oxygenated and unoxygenated blood will produce cyanosis. Another way of looking at congenital heart disease is to consider the ways that structural defects obstruct or create abnormal blood flow through the heart and lungs.

In *transposition of the great vessels*, the arteries that leave the heart—the aorta and the pulmonary artery—are reversed; this means the right ventricle is connected to the aorta instead of to the pulmonary artery, and the left ventricle is attached to the pulmonary artery instead of to the aorta. In this situation, oxygen-poor blood is not returned to the lungs to get oxygen. Rather, it is pumped directly into the body's circulation, causing cyanosis.

Tetralogy of Fallot is a cyanosis-producing, congenital heart defect in which both obstruction of blood flow to the lungs and mixing of oxygenated and unoxygenated blood occurs. In tetralogy of Fallot, there are four defects: a narrowed passage between the right ventricle and the pulmonary artery; a thickening of the walls of the right ventricle because of obstruction to blood flow; a defect of the wall between the two lower chambers; and a misplacement of the root of the aorta.

Endocardial cushion defect, or *atrioventricular canal*, occurs frequently in children with Down syndrome. This type of heart defect usually involves holes between the right and left atria and right and left ventricles. Often a defect of the mitral valve is present as well. In addition, there may be other heart lesions. Endocardial cushion defect can range in degree from mild to severe.

A *ventricular septal defect* (VSD) is an opening in the wall that separates the right and left ventricles. As a solitary defect (not grouped with others), ventricular septal defects rarely produce cyanosis. Ordinarily, the pressure in the left ventricle is greater than that in the right ventricle. When a ventricular septal defect is present, the unequal pressure in the chambers causes blood to be shunted from the left ventricle into the right ventricle. This increases the blood flow to the lungs, which ultimately increases the volume of blood delivered from the lungs to the left ventricle. Because of the increased blood volume, the left ventricle has to work harder to pump blood throughout the body. Small ventricular septal defects often close spontaneously. Complications of large ventricular septal defects may include recurrent pneumonia, poor growth, and congestive heart failure.

Atrial septal defects (ASDs) are of two types. When the hole in the wall separating the right and left atria is high near the foramen ovale, it is called an *ostium secundum defect*. When the hole in the septum is low, it is called an *ostium primum defect*. Again, because of pressure differences in the two upper chambers, blood tends to flow across the atrial septal defect from the left atrium into the right atrium. In turn, an increased volume of blood is delivered to the right ventricle, which may lead to thickening of the walls of the right ventricle, called *right ventricular hypertrophy*. In an ostium primum atrial septal defect, frequently one of the valves between the upper and lower chambers, usually the mitral valve, also is defective. This may lead to mitral insufficiency, a condition in which some blood from the left ventricle flows back into the left atrium when the left ventricle pumps blood through the aorta into the body. This condition may lead to congestive heart failure.

Partial obstruction of blood flow through the heart and lungs can occur at any of the valves in the heart. *Pulmonic stenosis* refers to a narrowing of the valve between the right ventricle and the pulmonary artery. *Aortic stenosis* is a narrowing of the valve between the left ventricle and the aorta. The greater the obstruction, the harder the ventricles must work. Over time, the ventricles adjust to the obstruction by developing thickened muscular walls. But there is a limit to the effectiveness of this thickening. Heart failure may develop when the heart becomes overtaxed.

Another form of circulatory obstruction is *coarctation of the aorta.* This is a defect in which part of the aorta is narrowed or absent, and blood flow must be diverted through small branches, or collateral vessels, of the aorta.

A discussion of the assessment of congenital heart defects is provided in Chapter 22. Operations to correct these defects are described in Chapter 25.

ACKNOWLEDGMENTS

Contributions have been made to this chapter by Karen E. Senft, M.D., Katherine C. Castree, M.D., and Siegfried M. Pueschel, M.D., Ph.D., M.P.H.

Problems
in the Newborn Period

Expectant parents may experience various emotions during pregnancy. There is usually excitement, joy, and anticipation as the date
of the birth comes closer. However, pregnancy also may cause anxiety as the delivery approaches and the reality that the baby will be
arriving soon settles in. In addition, many parents worry about the
possibility that their child might have a disability.

In today's modern health system, prenatal care is available to
nearly everyone to ensure optimal health of both expectant mothers
and their future children. During prenatal checkups, the baby's
growth is followed closely and the mother's medical condition is
monitored carefully for any potential problems. During labor, fetal
monitoring may be used to check the baby's heartbeat. If significant
changes in the heartbeat are detected, in particular if it slows down
markedly signaling fetal distress, prompt delivery by Cesarean section (incision through the walls of the abdomen and uterus, also
called a *C-section*) may be life-saving for the baby.

Immediately after birth, a newborn's condition is evaluated and
given a numerical rating from 0 to 10, called the *Apgar score* (see
Chapter 2). Apgar scores are assigned by delivery room personnel
at 1 and 5 minutes after the baby's birth. Five characteristics—
the baby's color, respiratory effort, muscle tone, reflex activity,
and heart rate—are evaluated, and each one is given a 0, 1, or 2
rating. The Apgar score thus reflects the condition of the baby
within the first few minutes of birth. A score of 7–10 indicates that
the baby is in good shape, whereas a score of 0–4 may mean

that the baby has serious difficulties and requires immediate attention.

Despite today's sophisticated health care, complications can develop during pregnancy, labor, and delivery that may affect the baby's future well-being. In this chapter, some of the more common problems observed in the newborn period that may lead to developmental disabilities are discussed. For example, problems noted in some premature infants such as respiratory distress syndrome, bronchopulmonary dysplasia, retinopathy of prematurity, necrotizing enterocolitis, and intraventricular hemorrhage are highlighted, as are other problems that also may occur in full-term infants following a difficult birth.

PROBLEMS OF PREMATURE INFANTS

Typically there are approximately 280 days from the time of conception to the birth of the child. This period is referred to as *gestation*. During this time period, children are growing and developing so that at birth they will be ready for life outside the womb. If a child is born prematurely and thus is underdeveloped, he or she may have difficulties surviving. *Prematurity* is defined as delivery before the 36th week of gestation.

Causes of Prematurity

There are many reasons why a baby may be born prematurely. For example, the membranes, or bag of water (i.e., amniotic sac), may break early, in which case labor pains often begin. An infection, especially of the mother's kidney or bladder, may also irritate the womb and cause contractions leading to early labor and delivery. Premature birth is also more likely to occur in adolescent mothers, in women who have had many babies, and in twin pregnancies. Smoking and illicit drug use have also been associated with prematurity. Some women have a weakness of the cervix (the narrow, lower end of the uterus), called *incompetent cervix*, which may lead to early labor. In addition, when there are serious complications in pregnancy, labor sometimes is induced early by the obstetrician to avoid endangering the life of the baby and/or the mother. Toxemia of pregnancy (a combination of high blood pressure, fluid retention, and protein in the urine) is a condition that can be life-threatening if the pregnancy is allowed to continue. Another serious condition is placenta previa whereby the placenta is implanted over the inner part of the cervix instead of in the wall of the uterus. In this condition, onset of labor may lead to serious bleeding often necessitating premature delivery. Abruptio placenta, or the premature separation of the placenta from the wall of the uterus, may be life-threatening for the baby because the blood supply from the mother is interrupted. This may require immediate delivery to save the baby's life.

Incidence

Estimates of the number of pregnancies ending prematurely are between 8% and 10%.

Expected Outcomes

In general, the earlier a baby is born and the smaller and less developed he or she is, the greater the chances that there may be a serious problem. With recent medical advances, some babies with a birth weight of 1–2 pounds who are born as early as the 26th week of gestation now are surviving. Approximately 10 years ago these infants would have had little chance of living.

Mothers who are at risk for complications of pregnancy or who experience premature labor are increasingly sent to perinatal centers for delivery. These centers provide specialized obstetrical and perinatal care for the mother. Once the infant is born, neonatal intensive care units (NICUs), staffed by specialized pediatricians known as *neonatologists,* are available to care for premature infants and full-term infants who develop serious illnesses. When necessary, the neonatologist begins helping a premature infant to breathe immediately after delivery and continues to follow the infant until discharge from the NICU is possible.

The expertise of neonatologists and intensive care nurses allows for anticipation and early treatment of problems that may arise from prematurity, and has contributed to increasingly favorable outcomes for premature infants. Neurological, metabolic, and respiratory difficulties combined with very low birth weight are important determining factors in predicting the eventual course for infants born prematurely. Unfortunately, despite the medical advances and special care provided in an intensive care nursery, some premature infants who now survive have problems in the newborn period that may result in long-term developmental disabilities.

SPECIFIC COMPLICATIONS OF PREMATURITY

Respiratory Distress Syndrome

A severe breathing problem that affects many premature infants is respiratory distress syndrome (RDS), which is also referred to as *hyaline membrane disease.* Respiratory distress syndrome may develop within a few hours or days of birth and is characterized by grunting and rapid respirations. Babies with respiratory distress syndrome have to expend a great deal of effort to breathe. Approximately 20% of premature infants develop respiratory distress syndrome.

Respiratory distress syndrome is caused by an inability to produce surfactant, a chemical substance, in the premature baby's lungs. Normally, after the first few breaths, the air sacs in the lungs are kept open by surfactant. Babies begin to produce surfactant between the 32nd and 36th week of gestation. Thus, a baby born prior to 32–36 weeks may be at risk for developing respiratory distress syndrome because of lack of surfactant.

The severity of respiratory distress syndrome will determine the type of treatment a premature infant receives. Children with a mild condition may need oxygen by mask. If the disease is more severe, an endotracheal tube may have to be placed in the windpipe or trachea, to help the baby breathe. This tube is connected to a respirator, which assists the baby with breathing or actually takes over breathing by pumping air and oxygen into the lungs. Children with mild respiratory distress syndrome usually recover rapidly as their lungs mature. In recent years it has become possible to instill surfactant into the trachea and bronchial tree, making breathing easier for the infant.

Bronchopulmonary Dysplasia

A few babies, usually those who are very premature, may develop damage to the lungs leading to a condition known as *bronchopulmonary dysplasia* (BPD). Bronchopulmonary dysplasia is a serious complication of prematurity. Children with this disease may require oxygen for months to years. They also may have heart problems and may be more susceptible to colds and pneumonia than other children. Fortunately, bronchopulmonary dysplasia improves with age and with the growth of new lung tissue. Most children eventually will overcome their breathing problems.

Retinopathy of Prematurity

Retinopathy of prematurity (ROP), formerly known as retrolental fibroplasia, a serious eye problem, is another complication of prematurity. It is due to the overgrowth of blood vessels in the retina (the tissue of the back of the eye). It occurs primarily in very premature infants who have required a great deal of oxygen in early life. ROP may cause near-sightedness. In some instances, it may lead to blindness. Modern neonatal care with careful monitoring of blood gases to determine the amount of oxygen in the blood decreases the frequency of retinopathy of prematurity, but is unable to eliminate it completely.

Necrotizing Enterocolitis

Necrotizing enterocolitis is a serious bowel disorder that occurs often in very small premature infants. In this condition, part of the bowel does not function properly and may become diseased. The causes of necrotizing enterocolitis are not completely understood, but are currently under investigation. Children with mild necrotizing enterocolitis may recover when regular feedings are withheld and when nutrients are given directly into a blood vessel (i.e., hyperalimentation). Babies with severe necrotizing enterocolitis are at risk for developing a hole in the bowel, called a *perforation*, and may require surgery.

Intraventricular Hemorrhage

Intraventricular hemorrhage (IVH) refers to bleeding into brain tissue and the fluid spaces within the brain (i.e., ventricles). This is another major problem in very premature infants. In this condition, blood leaks from the vessels around the edges of the ventricles. Intraventricular hemorrhage is graded by severity, from Grade I, which is a slight leaking of blood, to Grade IV, indicating severe bleeding into the ventricles and seepage into the surrounding brain tissue. Children with Grade IV hemorrhage sometimes develop a blockage in the brain's fluid drainage system that may lead to marked enlargement of the fluid spaces (i.e., hydrocephalus). Hydrocephalus (also known as water on the brain) may require surgical intervention in which a tube is placed in the ventricles of the brain to drain the extra fluid into the abdomen. This *ventricular-peritoneal shunt*, as it is called, is described in more detail in Chapter 25, and hydrocephalus is discussed in Chapter 13.

PROBLEMS OF FULL-TERM INFANTS

Description

When a child is born at full term, as most children are, chances are very good that everything will go well and that the baby will be healthy. However, even with excellent prenatal care and appropriate monitoring at birth, things occasionally may go wrong and the baby may be born with or develop a disability.

Full-term infants, like premature babies, may develop brain damage from injuries, diseases, or events that prevent enough oxygen from reaching the brain. These children may show signs of cerebral palsy during the first few years of life (see Chapter 15). Problems of the mother during pregnancy, such as diabetes or malnourishment, can affect the baby. The use of drugs and alcohol during pregnancy, or infections, also may put the unborn baby at greater risk (see Chapter 12). Because all of these problems can cause developmental disabilities, each is discussed in greater detail below and in other chapters of this book.

Causes

Events that cause lack of oxygen during birth in full-term infants are similar to those for premature infants and include early separation of the placenta, fetal distress, a difficult delivery in which the baby's head becomes lodged in the birth canal for a time, and the umbilical cord becoming tightly wrapped around the baby's neck.

Other less common problems may occur during pregnancy. For example, mothers with diabetes are at risk for delivering large infants. These infants—known as large for gestational age (LGA) babies—have difficulty maintaining their blood sugar levels in the newborn period. If not closely monitored, low blood sugar (i.e., hypoglycemia) may develop, which can result in brain injury. In addition, if the mother's diabetes has not been well controlled during pregnancy, the baby may be born with congenital anomalies.

If a mother has been ill or poorly nourished, if she has a metabolic condition called *phenylketonuria,* or if her placenta does not deliver sufficient nutrients to the fetus, a small and underweight infant may be born. These children are known as small for gestational age (SGA) infants. This means that the child is small, although born after a full-term gestation. Once born, small for gestational age children may have trouble adapting to life outside of the womb. Often, however, the mother of a small for gestational age infant had an uneventful pregnancy, and the reason for the poor fetal growth is not known.

Children of mothers who use unnecessary medications or drugs during pregnancy may be at risk for developmental disabilities. Tranquilizers, narcotics, barbiturates, and illicit drugs, such as cocaine and heroin, can cause addiction in the fetus before birth. After birth, the child is abruptly deprived of the drug and experiences withdrawal. The baby may become very irritable, have tremors, and may even develop seizures. In addition, it has been found that infants of mothers who use strong narcotics, such as heroin, during pregnancy have a much greater risk of dying from sudden infant death syndrome (SIDS) during the early months of life.

Children are also susceptible to many different kinds of infections before, during, and immediately after birth. When the infection occurs in the brain, it may lead to brain injury. This was discussed in detail in Chapter 12.

Incidence

The number of full-term infants who develop disabilities following complicated pregnancies, difficult deliveries, infections, or exposure to drugs or alcohol during fetal development is estimated to be 0.5%–1.5%. In addition to these known risk factors in the newborn period, a certain percentage of apparently healthy full-term infants develop problems or disabilities during childhood.

Expected Outcomes

The treatment needed for full-term infants experiencing problems after birth depends on the type and severity of the disorder. Infants who experience brain injury from lack of oxygen during or after birth may require treatment in the hospital's neonatal intensive care nursery. The extent of the brain injury will determine the extent to which the baby has been affected. As mentioned previously, babies of mothers with diabetes may have difficulty regulating their blood sugar levels. Brain injury may be prevented with careful monitoring of the baby's blood sugar. Provision of intravenous glucose may be necessary for a period of time to control the baby's blood sugar level. Babies born with drug addiction may be treated with gradually decreasing doses of medications such as sedatives or methadone.

Meticulous prenatal care, careful monitoring during labor and delivery with appropriate intervention if problems occur, and the development of special care nurseries staffed by experts in the care of sick newborns have decreased infant deaths in the prenatal period as well as the rate of serious disease.

ACKNOWLEDGMENT

Contributions have been made to this chapter by Karen E. Senft, M.D.

15

Cerebral Palsy

DESCRIPTION

Cerebral palsy (CP) is a general term used to describe disorders of movement that result from injury to the brain. Basically, cerebral palsy is a problem of muscle coordination. The muscles themselves are not affected, but the brain is unable to send the appropriate signals necessary to instruct the muscles when to contract and when to relax.

There are three major types of cerebral palsy. Within each category, there are many degrees of severity. The type of cerebral palsy is determined by the location of the brain injury, and the severity is based on the amount of injury that has occurred.

1. *Spastic cerebral palsy* is found in more than half of all children with cerebral palsy. *Spasticity* means increased muscle tone. Spasticity results from injury to the area of the brain that initiates muscle movement, particularly the bundles of nerves known as the *pyramidal tract*. Thus, another way to describe spastic cerebral palsy is as *pyramidal tract cerebral palsy*. Children with spasticity will have tight, or sometimes rigid, muscles and are unable to move the involved limbs well. The limbs may be drawn into atypical positions by some muscle groups pulling against weak muscles. This imbalance and the increased muscle tone may be slight and appear as clumsiness. However, this imbalance may be severe, so that the child is unable to move voluntarily with good control. If one limb is involved, the term used is *monoplegia*; if two limbs are affected with either both arms or both legs involved it is called *diplegia*; if one side of the

163

body is compromised, the child has *hemiplegia;* and if all four limbs are affected, the child has *quadriplegia.* The term *paraplegia* also is used to describe an involvement of the legs only.

2. *Choreoathetoid cerebral palsy* is a term used when children have abrupt involuntary movements of the arms and legs. The area of the brain that regulates muscle movement and posture is outside of the pyramidal tract. Therefore, choreoathetoid cerebral palsy is also referred to as *extrapyramidal tract cerebral palsy.* For individuals with this type of cerebral palsy, controlling the extremities to carry out activities is extremely difficult. At one time, choreoathetoid cerebral palsy was common, as it was the result of brain injury caused by complications from Rh incompatibility between the mother's and baby's blood. Now that RhoGAM, a type of vaccine, is available to Rh-negative mothers who deliver Rh-positive children, choreoathetoid cerebral palsy is decreasing in frequency.

3. *Mixed-type cerebral palsy* describes the condition of persons with a mixture of spasticity and choreoathetoid movement and reflects a combination of pyramidal and extrapyramidal involvement.

The types of cerebral palsy and the corresponding brain injury are shown in Figure 1.

Many children with cerebral palsy also are affected by other developmental disabilities. Approximately 60% of children with cerebral palsy have mental retardation, 40% are affected with visual problems, 35% may develop seizures, and 20% have language and hearing difficulties. Many children with cerebral palsy, particularly those with mild conditions, are of typical intelligence and do not have any other disabilities.

CAUSES

Cerebral palsy can be caused by numerous problems occurring in the prenatal period, prematurity, labor and delivery complications in the newborn period, and problems during early childhood. During the prenatal period due to genetic or chromosomal abnormality, the brain may not develop in the typical way. Certain environmental factors such as drugs, metabolic problems, intrauterine infections, and placental dysfunctions may also lead to cerebral palsy. In addition, prematurity and associated complications have been recognized as a cause of cerebral palsy. Whereas previously it was thought that most of the infants with cerebral palsy had brain injury because of difficulties during labor and delivery, today only a minority of

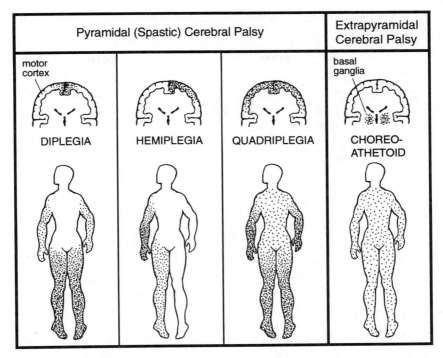

Figure 1. Types of cerebral palsy: The areas of affected brain and the affected body parts are outlined by dots.

children who are later diagnosed to have cerebral palsy had birth injuries or oxygen deprivation during the time of delivery. In the newborn period, severe intraventricular hemorrhage (bleeding into the fluid-filled spaces inside the brain) may result in cerebral palsy (see Chapter 14). During childhood, brain infections (e.g., meningitis, encephalitis), injury to the brain due to accidents, and certain toxins such as lead may cause brain damage leading to cerebral palsy (see Chapter 12). There are also numerous children with cerebral palsy (about 30%) with causes that cannot be identified.

INCIDENCE

Estimates of the number of persons with cerebral palsy vary considerably. A frequently cited figure is 1.5–2 per 1,000 live births. Of these, approximately 60% have spastic cerebral palsy, 20% choreoathetoid, and the remaining 20% mixed-type cerebral palsy. Seizures commonly occur in conjunction with cerebral palsy (see Chapter 16).

Motor difficulties may also affect muscles necessary to coordinate other functions of the body, such as swallowing and vision.

DIAGNOSIS

There is no specific test for cerebral palsy. Rather, it is diagnosed after the doctor has obtained a detailed medical history, examined the child, and observed the child's movements. Signs of cerebral palsy can include delayed development of motor skills, unusual patterns of movement, atypical reflexes, and increased muscle tone. Cerebral palsy usually is not diagnosed until the baby begins to move and atypical patterns of movement are noted. Most children with cerebral palsy are detected between 12 and 18 months of age. Some of the milder forms of cerebral palsy may be identified later. Often, a physician will examine the child several times before making a definite diagnosis. It may take time to determine if the problems in motor skills are the result of cerebral palsy or simply due to late-developing motor skills.

INTERVENTION

Although there is no cure for cerebral palsy, there are many ways to help persons with cerebral palsy improve their abilities and independence. Because of the complexities of the problems associated with cerebral palsy, a transdisciplinary treatment approach often is needed. This treatment approach emphasizes teamwork by a group of professionals from a variety of disciplines. Physical therapy programs provide exercises to keep muscles stretched and supple and to improve the functioning of imbalanced muscles. An occupational therapist can teach the child independence and self-sufficiency in skills such as dressing and feeding. Orthopaedic care can prevent contractures, permanent deformities, and limitations of joints due to very tight muscles through a prescription of exercises, braces and other adaptive equipment (see Chapter 23), and occasionally surgery. Provision of braces and other needed special equipment can make the child more independent and able to participate in a wide variety of activities (see also Chapter 23). Speech-language therapists can monitor language development, provide therapy, or devise alternative communication systems should they be needed.

In addition to these therapies, other members of the team make important contributions to the child's care. Assessment by a clinical psychologist can provide important information about cognitive functioning for planning of educational needs. Special education programs include the recommendations of numerous specialists to carry out an individualized plan for each student. As the result of the concept of inclusive education, more students with cerebral palsy are attending traditional classrooms in their neighborhood schools. If there are emotional concerns, financial issues, or questions about community programs, social workers can be helpful. Developmental pediatricians and nurses are often called upon to integrate the range of services that a child with cerebral palsy requires. Usually they are responsible for coordinating the medical needs, as determined by various medical specialists and therapists, with school and community activities.

Spasticity is often a significant factor in cerebral palsy. Medications such as Valium, Dantrium, and Lioresal are among the more commonly prescribed drugs to help relieve spasticity (see also Chapter 24). There are also numerous orthopaedic surgical procedures to release spastic muscles or improve muscle functioning and thus correct or prevent deformity. Physical therapy and bracing are frequently used to maintain the benefits gained by surgery.

A relatively new neurosurgical procedure called *rhizotomy* has been found to decrease muscle spasticity. During rhizotomy, certain fibers in nerves coming from the spinal cord that contribute to muscle spasticity are identified and cut. The best time for such surgery is thought to be between 3 and 5 years of age when patterns of muscle movement are obvious, but fixed deformities have not yet occurred. Rhizotomy is not generally recommended for ataxic (involving problems with motor control) or choreoathetoid cerebral palsy and is used mostly in spastic diplegia and quadriplegia. After surgery, continued care by other specialists such as orthopaedic doctors or physical therapists is still necessary.

EXPECTED OUTCOMES

Cerebral palsy is the result of brain injury, and its outcomes are determined by the location and severity of injury. Significant involvement may prevent ambulation and require assistance in daily living skills throughout an individual's life span. The mildest injury may result in a child who appears clumsier or less coordinated than other children his or her age. Early intervention programs and innovative school plans provide an increasing array of services that should improve outcomes. The larger community has a new awareness of the importance of accessibility since passage of PL 101-336, the Americans with Disabilities Act of 1990. With changes in the U.S. and world economy, there is hope that technology will play an increasingly important role in enabling individuals with the most severe motor involvement to improve their functional mobility and communication skills.

ACKNOWLEDGMENTS

Contributions have been made to this chapter by Karen E. Senft, M.D., and Patricia S. Scola, M.D., M.P.H.

16

Seizure Disorders

DESCRIPTION

Seizures may occur in children with developmental disorders. A child with a seizure disorder, however, may not have a developmental delay and, in fact, often will be typical in all other aspects. The terms *seizures* and *convulsions* are used interchangeably here. *Epilepsy* refers to recurrent seizures due to a central nervous system disorder.

Nerves and nerve cells and their interactions cause electrical activity in the brain. This activity can be recorded by means of a brain-wave test, also called an *electroencephalogram* (EEG). A seizure is the result of atypical electrical discharges within the brain that often, but not always, can be detected by a brainwave test. In many instances, different types of seizures show specific patterns of the brainwaves.

Seizures are described as *generalized* when both sides of the brain are involved with seizure activity. *Partial* seizures are those in which specific localized areas of the brain are usually affected. Some common terms used to characterize seizures are *tonic, clonic,* and *atonic.* Tonic means that during the seizure the muscles are in a rigid state. Clonic refers to fast, jerky movements of the muscles. A combination of tonic-clonic seizures is characterized by tense, rapid muscular movements; these seizures were previously termed *grand mal convulsions.* An atonic, or drop, seizure describes a loss of typical muscle tone that causes the person to fall. The duration of the atypical movements and the loss of consciousness that often accompanies a seizure are important in differentiating the types of seizures. Although watching someone have a seizure can be frightening, it is

169

helpful to the doctor if parents or others note the various characteristics and the duration of the seizure.

A child with a seizure disorder may experience a warning sign (i.e., aura) just prior to the seizure such as an unusual odor, a strange feeling, or a brief motor movement. The seizure itself is called the *ictal stage* and is followed by a *postictal* period, during which the person may be drowsy or may sleep. There are numerous types of seizures; some of the more common ones are described below.

Generalized Tonic-Clonic Seizures

Of those seizures that are grouped together under the term *epilepsy*, the type most often observed is the generalized tonic-clonic seizure. This type of seizure disorder may develop at any time from infancy to adulthood. Associated with the tonic-clonic seizures are loss of consciousness and often the temporary loss of bladder control.

Absence Seizures

Absence seizures were previously referred to as *petit mal* seizures and are brief in duration, often less than 30 seconds. They may happen anywhere from a few to 100 times a day. Frequently, they consist only of brief staring spells, but motor signs such as twitching of the eyelids also may be seen. A specific brainwave pattern (slow spike and wave) is characteristic of such seizures.

Myoclonic Seizures

Myoclonic seizures include several forms, such as minor motor seizures, infantile spasms, and massive myoclonic jerks. Myoclonic seizures are characterized by sudden flexion or bending of the body and neck while the arms are outstretched. Children who develop myoclonic seizures before 2 years of age usually have developmental delays and continue to have a poorer outlook than children whose seizures develop later in childhood.

A special form of myoclonic seizure is the infantile spasm. During such a seizure, brief tonic contractions of the muscles are observed involving both sides of the body equally and in clusters. As a result the infant may exhibit rapid stiffening of the body or a bowing forward movement. A disorganized electrical pattern of the brainwaves known as *hypsarrhythmia,* is characteristically seen in young infants with this seizure disorder. The association of infantile spasms, developmental delay, and hypsarrhymthia is called *West syndrome.*

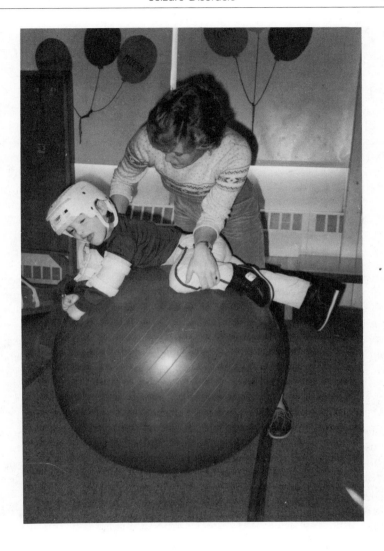

Partial Lobe Seizures

Temporal lobe, or psychomotor, epilepsy is an example of a partial seizure and usually occurs in later childhood and in early adult life. Signs of simple partial seizures include inappropriate movements and behavioral patterns previously called *psychomotor* seizures. Although some features such as staring spells or repetitious movements may be common to both simple and complex seizures, the duration of the seizure is longer in complex seizures, which usually originate in the temporal lobe of the brain. Facial grimacing, lip smacking, chewing movements, and eye blinking are often observed and can last from 30 seconds to 5 minutes.

Simple Febrile Convulsions

One common type of seizure that is not considered epilepsy is a simple febrile convulsion. A simple febrile convulsion usually occurs for the first time between the ages of 6 months and 6 years. The seizure is associated with a sudden rise in temperature and usually is brief and generalized. A child who has had a simple febrile convulsion is not at great risk of developing epilepsy, although he or she may have a repeat febrile convulsion if a high fever recurs.

CAUSES AND INCIDENCE

Many causes of seizure disorders have been discovered, although in most instances the reason the seizure disorder develops remains unknown. Known causes of seizures include genetic factors, brain injuries, infections, lack of oxygen, and brain hemorrhage. It is estimated that seizure disorders affect approximately 1%–3% of the general population. The number of children with developmental disabilities who have seizures is reported to be between 5% and 10%.

DIAGNOSIS

Medical and physical examinations determine how your doctor will begin to investigate your child's seizures. An electroencephalogram, or brainwave test, is usually carried out to determine what type of seizure is occurring. New electroencephalographic telemonitoring is available to assess unusual presentations of seizures. Imaging techniques such as a computed tomography (CT) scan or magnetic resonance imaging (MRI) may also provide useful information (see Chapter 22).

EXPECTED OUTCOMES

Children with seizures usually are treated with one or more anticonvulsant medications. These medications are used to prevent or reduce atypical electrical activity of the brain that characterizes seizures. Monitoring of medication blood levels has been of great assistance in controlling seizures while decreasing undesirable side effects. For a detailed description, see Chapter 24 about medications.

Many children's seizures are well controlled with proper medication. For some, however, the severity of the disorder makes control of seizures difficult. In instances of very severe seizures that do not respond to medication, some children may benefit from neurosurgery. Some individuals with seizure disorders have fewer or no seizures as they grow older. Often, these individuals can stop taking medication and remain seizure free. Others may need to take medication throughout their lives. The use of specific seizure medications and monitoring of drug dosage by means of blood levels have been of great assistance in controlling seizures. Continued public education and elimination of misinformation about seizure disorders are equally important to allow the child with seizures to participate in all life experiences.

ACKNOWLEDGMENTS

Contributions have been made to this chapter by Karen E. Senft, M.D., and Patricia S. Scola, M.D., M.P.H.

17

Neurological Disorders with Associated Skin Findings

There is a group of serious diseases of the brain and nervous system in general that can be diagnosed because of their associated skin abnormalities. As a class, these are known as *neurocutaneous syndromes* or *phakomatoses*. This chapter describes the common neurocutaneous disorders.

TUBEROUS SCLEROSIS

Tuberous sclerosis is a neurological disorder that affects primarily the brain and the skin. Children with this disorder often have seizures, mental retardation, and an overgrowth of certain brain cells, causing small tumors to develop. Calcium deposits in certain parts of the brain also are common. Specific skin lesions of tuberous sclerosis include: adenoma sebaceum, an acne-like skin condition on the cheeks, nose, and chin; shagreen patches, which are thickened areas of skin with an orange peel texture; and ash-leaf marks, which are pale areas of the skin that are seen more easily when ultraviolet light is held close to the skin. Other manifestations of this disease include tumorous growths in many parts of the body. In the back of the eye a tumor known as a *mulberry lesion* may develop. Tumors also may be found in the kidneys, bones, lungs, and on the skin. Problems with endocrine glands also are associated with tuberous sclerosis.

Cause and Incidence

Tuberous sclerosis is a genetic disorder with an autosomal dominant inheritance pattern. However, approximately 80% of all people with this disorder have new mutations. The incidence of tuberous sclerosis is reported to be 1 in every 20,000 live births. If a parent has tuberous sclerosis, there is a 50% chance with each pregnancy that the child will have the disease.

Expected Outcomes

Specific therapy to treat tuberous sclerosis is not available at this time. However, children with this disorder who have seizures should be treated for the seizure disorder. Occasionally surgical intervention is necessary to remove tumors. The course of tuberous sclerosis is variable. In many cases, the neurological progression of the disease shortens the life span of affected individuals.

Depending on the extent of the neurological involvement and the degree of mental retardation, the person with tuberous sclerosis will participate in educational programs and will become involved in vocational endeavors.

NEUROFIBROMATOSIS

Neurofibromatosis may affect the brain, nerves, bones, muscles, skin, and glands. The two common skin findings are café-au-lait spots (light brownish marks) and tumors along the nerve fibers, which are called *neurofibromata*. Café-au-lait spots generally resemble very large freckles. Neurofibromatosis may range from a mild problem to a very serious and debilitating disorder.

Years after café-au-lait spots are noted, neurofibromata of various sizes may appear beneath the skin. Symptoms depend on where these tumors appear. Tumors of the nerves of the ears and eyes may affect hearing and sight, respectively. There may be multiple tumors appearing beneath the skin, resulting in deformity. Tumors of the bone may lead to fractures and skeletal changes such as scoliosis (curvature of the spine). Most individuals with this disorder are of average intelligence. Of those affected with neurofibromatosis, 10%–25% have mental retardation. Seizures and hypertension (high blood pressure) also are common.

Cause and Incidence

Neurofibromatosis is an autosomal dominant inherited disorder (see Chapter 11 for a discussion of inheritance patterns). The incidence rate of type I neurofibromatosis, which includes most of the signs and symptoms described above, is approximately 1 in 4,000 live births. The incidence of type II neurofibromatosis, which includes tumor development along the nerves of the ears (i.e., acoustic neuroma), is about 1 in 50,000 live births.

Expected Outcomes

There is no definitive treatment available for neurofibromatosis. At times, surgical removal of tumors may be indicated. Seizures should be treated with anticonvulsant medications in the same manner as any other seizure disorder. Regular monitoring is recommended for scoliosis and hypertension, and when these conditions become apparent, appropriate treatment should be initiated. The severity of this disease varies widely. The bodily difficulties experienced by individuals with neurofibromatosis may range from minimal to severe. Most individuals with this disorder function well with optimal medical treatment and psychological support. Generally, these youngsters will be able to learn as other children do, will be able to hold a job, and will participate successfully in society.

STURGE-WEBER SYNDROME

Sturge-Weber syndrome is characterized by a large, dark, red birthmark, called a *port-wine stain*, most often seen on the forehead and cheek on one side of the face. The lip, nose, and eyelid also may be involved and may appear swollen. Sturge-Weber syndrome is a neurological disorder in which the brain may have a blood vessel abnormality similar to that seen on the skin. The resulting brain involvement causes seizures in 90% of persons with the disorder. Mental retardation occurs in 30% of individuals with Sturge-Weber syndrome and may be accompanied by psychological problems. About half of the children with this syndrome will have hemiplegia (one-sided paralysis). This disease is not genetic, and therefore, familial recurrence is unlikely.

ATAXIA-TELANGIECTASIA

Ataxia-telangiectasia is an autosomal recessive disorder, and is characterized by progressive ataxia (uncoordinated movements) and choreoathetosis (involuntary movements). A child with this disorder may start to walk normally, but later develop increasing unsteadiness. The involuntary jerky movements also may start earlier. As the muscles around the mouth are involved, the child's speech may become progressively more difficult to understand. As children become older, they may lose the ability to sense where their bodies are in space. At approximately 5–6 years of age, spidery dilated blood vessels, known as *telangiectasia*, become apparent in the whites of the eyes and later on the face and neck. The children's mental functioning decreases gradually. Many people with ataxia-telangiectasia also have defective immune systems and, therefore, have difficulty fighting infections. There may be multiple bouts of pneumonia and sinusitis, which can lead to progressive permanent lung damage or bronchiectasis and eventual respiratory failure. There is no specific treatment available for ataxia-telangiectasia at this time. Antibiotics are used vigorously to control infections.

SUMMARY

The neurocutaneous disorders discussed in this chapter can be devastating when the brain is severely involved and when deformities affecting the skin become apparent. However, many people with any of these disorders frequently live fulfilling lives. Whatever their intellectual abilities, these children will benefit from educational experiences and later become contributing members of society.

ACKNOWLEDGMENT

Contributions have been made to this chapter by Karen E. Senft, M.D.

18

Diseases of
Muscles and Bones

Well-coordinated body movements are the result of nerve impulses that travel from the brain and through the spinal cord, to connect with nerves that carry messages to the muscles. These nerve impulses tell the muscles when to relax, when to tighten, and how to move the limbs. For smooth, coordinated movements, bone joint structures must be in good working order, and the muscles must be attached to the bones properly by ligaments. If one of these parts is not working well or is defective, normal muscle function and well-coordinated movement will not be possible. This chapter describes a number of developmental disabilities in which the primary areas affected are the muscles and bones. In each case, problems with movement and coordination are the primary disabilities.

FRIEDREICH ATAXIA

Friedreich ataxia, or spinal cerebellar degeneration, is a progressive disorder involving degeneration of nerves in the spinal cord. Individuals who develop this disease show unsteadiness and loss of coordinated movement because their muscles are no longer receiving appropriate signals from the spinal cord. They may lose the ability to know where their arms and legs are in space. The muscles of the heart also may be involved, and sometimes intellectual limitations are noted. This disease usually has its onset in the first 20 years of life.

SPINAL MUSCULAR ATROPHY

Spinal muscular atrophy, or anterior horn cell disease, is an inherited disorder that involves severe wasting of muscle. The actual problem is in the nerve cells of the spinal cord that ordinarily convey messages from the spinal cord to the muscles. Because of this defect, the impulses cannot travel down the nerve, and the muscles cannot work properly and gradually will waste away.

There are three subgroups of this disease, each of which has a different level of severity. The most severe form, known as *Werdnig-Hoffmann disease*, is recognized at or shortly after birth. These children have very weak muscles; they will later experience difficulty swallowing and have frequent respiratory infections. Most children with the severe form of Werdnig-Hoffmann disease usually do not survive the first year of life. Children affected by the intermediate form of spinal muscular atrophy have a somewhat better survival rate. Intensive physical therapy, appropriate orthopaedic intervention, and bracing may allow some of these youngsters to walk.

Kugelberg-Welander disease is the mildest form of spinal muscular atrophy. Again, physical therapy and orthopaedic care can help these children retain some motor skills.

The spinal muscular atrophies are autosomal recessive disorders, meaning that both parents must be carriers of the gene for the disease in order to have an affected child (see Chapter 11 for a discussion of inheritance patterns). Recent reports indicate that the gene for spinal muscular atrophy is located on chromosome #5. A finding such as this is important for potential gene therapy.

CHARCOT-MARIE-TOOTH DISEASE

Charcot-Marie-Tooth disease also is known as *peroneal muscular atrophy*. Children with this disease lose function of the peripheral nerves leading to certain muscle groups. The earliest symptoms usually occur by 10 years of age, and include foot deformities such as a high arch and curled toes, as well as gait abnormalities. The disease progresses slowly; as it develops, weakness and wasting of foot muscles occurs. Later, the hand muscles may be involved. This disease is inherited in an autosomal dominant fashion (see Chapter 11 for a discussion of inheritance patterns).

ROUSSY-LÉVY SYNDROME

Roussy-Lévy syndrome is similar to Charcot-Marie-Tooth disease, but affected individuals may have more disabilities. In addition, they usually have tremors. These individuals also may develop diabetes mellitus, a metabolic disorder in which blood sugar levels are usually significantly elevated because of lack of insulin.

MYOTONIC DYSTROPHY

Myotonic dystrophy is a disease of the muscles. The basic problem is an inability to relax muscles. For example, after shaking hands, the person with myotonic dystrophy will have difficulty letting go. This disorder is most often passed on in an autosomal dominant manner.

MUSCULAR DYSTROPHIES

The muscular dystrophies are a group of inherited disorders characterized by progressive degeneration of muscle tissue. There are several forms of muscular dystrophy.

Duchenne Muscular Dystrophy

Duchenne muscular dystrophy is the most common of the muscular dystrophies. It is an X-linked recessive disease and therefore affects boys almost exclusively. The onset is usually in the first few years of life. An atypical gait usually is the first symptom noticed. Parents also report that the child falls frequently, has difficulty climbing stairs, and cannot keep up with his or her friends. The gait often is described as waddling and wide-based, which is a result of weakness in the pelvic and hip muscles. There is a steady deterioration in muscular dystrophy, with most children becoming wheelchair users early in their second decade of life. Weakness is most noticeable in the muscles closest to the body's center, such as the trunk, shoulders, and hip muscles. The calf sometimes appears larger, a condition called *pseudohypertrophy*. However, larger in this case does not mean stronger. The heart muscles also may be affected. Once an individual loses the ability to walk, scoliosis (curvature of the spine) may develop. As the disease progresses, other muscles, including those used for breathing, become weaker, which may lead to frequent colds and pneumonia.

In recent years, much progress has been made in molecular genetics. The gene that causes Duchenne muscular dystrophy and the gene product (i.e., dystrophin) have been identified. Current research activities attempt to introduce the normal genes into the diseased muscles of people with Duchenne muscular dystrophy. It is hoped that the normal gene will be incorporated into the affected muscle cells and will lead to production of dystrophin, which ultimately should result in average muscle strength.

Becker Muscular Dystrophy

Becker muscular dystrophy is similar to Duchenne muscular dystrophy, although it is a milder form. People with Becker muscular dystrophy generally are able to walk and maintain this ability into adolescence and sometimes into early adulthood. Becker muscular dystrophy is also an X-linked recessive genetic disorder.

Limb Girdle Muscular Dystrophy

In limb girdle muscular dystrophy, there is a predominant weakness in the musculature of the pelvic region. The prognosis varies greatly and must be assessed individually. Inheritance of this form of muscular dystrophy is autosomal recessive.

Facioscapulohumeral Muscular Dystrophy

Facioscapulohumeral muscular dystrophy affects mainly the muscles of the shoulders and face. This disease usually is relatively mild with slow progression, but more severe forms do occur. The inheritance is autosomal dominant.

OSTEOGENESIS IMPERFECTA

Osteogenesis imperfecta, or brittle bone disease, is a disorder in which the bones break easily. In the most severe form, many bone fractures are already present at birth and the infants might not survive the newborn period. In milder forms, fractures are frequent and may cause some degree of dwarfism in some children. The effects of osteogenesis imperfecta on individuals vary greatly. In some children, fractures rarely occur, whereas in others even normal movements can cause fractures. Individuals also may have deficiencies of tooth enamel, as well as a hearing impairment. The whites of the eyes, or sclera, may appear blue. The basic abnormality in osteogenesis imperfecta is a defect in formation of connective tissues. This disease is inherited in an autosomal dominant manner. It also may occur as a new mutation. There is no specific treatment available, but meticulous orthopaedic management and preventative care will minimize deformity.

ACHONDROPLASIA

Achondroplasia is a term that describes the failure of bones to grow normally. It causes extreme shortness of arms and legs. As a result, affected individuals are of short stature. The head of an individual with achondroplasia often is enlarged. Youngsters with achondroplasia usually are of average intelligence. Achondroplasia is an autosomal dominant inherited disorder, which means the risk of recurrence is 50% in each pregnancy. This disorder occurs in approximately 1 in 10,000 births.

CAUSES AND INTERVENTION

The diseases discussed in this chapter are genetic in origin. A definitive cure is not available for any of these disorders at this writing, but supportive treatment can help. The principles of treatment include physical therapy and appropriate orthopaedic management to prevent deformity and to increase and maintain function for as long as possible. In addition, appropriate genetic counseling of families with these disorders should be provided. Parents should also be informed of the availability of prenatal diagnosis for some of these diseases.

EXPECTED OUTCOMES

Although many individuals' life expectancies are reduced and their nerve, muscle, and/or bone involvement may often be severe, many of these individuals can live productive lives. Depending on the type and the severity of the neuromuscular disorder, many children develop fairly well during early childhood. All children will have educational opportunities available to them that are similar to those provided for children who do not have disabilities. Vocational training and higher education are recommended for those who are able to pursue these goals. In addition, there are numerous modern treatment modalities available that will improve quality of life. Most importantly, as mentioned previously, exciting research pursuits in molecular genetics point to novel and more effective therapies for some disorders that will constitute major breakthroughs.

ACKNOWLEDGMENT

Contributions have been made to this chapter by Karen E. Senft, M.D.

19

Metabolic Disorders

The biochemical processes of the human body are extremely complex. Often many steps are needed to break down or build up bodily materials. Specific proteins called *enzymes* regulate many of the metabolic processes in the human body. Defective or absent enzymes can lead to dangerous excesses of some biochemical products and deficiencies of others that the body needs to function properly. The excesses and deficiencies of certain chemical products can cause serious disabilities. The degree of disability varies with the specific chemical process that is disturbed, the type of chemicals that are deficient or produced in excess, and the availability and efficacy of treatment.

Metabolic disorders usually are categorized by the chemical product that is affected, such as parts of protein or amino acids, fats or lipids, and sugars or carbohydrates. If the metabolic product associated with the disease is detected in the blood, a term ending in *emia* is used. When the product is detected in the urine, the descriptive term ends in *uria*. Thus, hyperphenylalaninemia indicates that there is too much of a specific part of the protein or amino acid called *phenylalanine* in the blood, whereas phenylketonuria refers to the presence of certain chemicals called *phenylketones* in the urine.

DESCRIPTION

This chapter describes three major types of metabolic disorders; these include disorders of amino acid metabolism, lipid metabolism, and carbohydrate metabolism. Each section includes information about the cause, incidence, and treatment of the disorder. The

chapter concludes with a brief discussion of lysosomal storage diseases.

DISORDERS OF AMINO ACID METABOLISM

Amino acids are chemicals that when linked together form proteins. Amino acids frequently are called the building blocks of protein. The most common amino acid disorder is *phenylketonuria* (PKU). This disorder is caused by the lack of a specific enzyme known as *phenylalanine hydroxylase*. This enzyme is needed to change the amino acid phenylalanine into another amino acid, namely tyrosine. If phenylalanine is not broken down and an excess of it is building up in the body, mental retardation may be the result. Because most protein foods contain phenylalanine, it is important to detect and treat children with phenylketonuria as early as possible. Otherwise, phenylalanine will begin to accumulate in infants with phenylketonuria, causing serious disabilities. Untreated infants with phenylketonuria may become irritable, vomit, develop a skin rash, have a distinctive odor described as musty, and have developmental delays andmental retardation. Fortunately, phenylketonuria can be detected in the newborn period, and all babies born in the United States and many other countries are screened for phenylketonuria. This test, which requires only a few drops of blood, is usually done before a baby is discharged from the hospital. Infants found to have phenylketonuria can be treated with a special diet that has limited amounts of phenylalanine. Early treatment can prevent mental retardation. Most children with phenylketonuria who are treated in infancy and throughout childhood are of average intelligence.

Phenylketonuria, like most metabolic disorders, is inherited as an autosomal recessive trait. Therefore, parents who have a child with phenylketonuria have a 25% chance of having another affected child in each future pregnancy. Phenylketonuria, the most common of the amino acid disorders, is actually quite rare and occurs in approximately 1 in 10,000–14,000 live births.

Another example of an amino acid disorder is *maple syrup urine disease*, so called because the urine of children with this disorder smells like maple syrup. The defect involves a group of amino acids termed *branched chain amino acids*. Maple syrup urine disease is much rarer than phenylketonuria, occurring in 1 in every 120,000–200,000 live births. This disorder also can be detected in the newborn period, and if a child is found to have maple syrup urine disease, he or she can be treated with a special diet. When undetected and thus untreated, many infants die within the first few weeks of life. Dietary treatment has saved the lives of many infants with this disease.

Numerous amino acid disorders have been discovered in the past decades, but not all of them are amenable to treatment. Many of the amino acid disorders cause irritability, feeding problems, seizures, and other neurological problems in the newborn period. If left untreated or if no treatment is available, mental retardation and growth failure may be observed in the survivors of many of these disorders.

DISORDERS OF LIPID METABOLISM

In disorders of lipid metabolism, large amounts of certain fats are stored in body tissues. This group of metabolic diseases is called *sphingolipidoses*. There are subgroups of this disease entity that are classified by the particular fat, or sphingolipid, involved and the respective enzyme defect.

Tay Sachs disease is perhaps the most widely known example of this group of disorders. Tay Sachs disease is a degenerative disorder resulting from a deficiency of the enzyme hexosaminidase A, which causes an accumulation of a sphingolipid called *ganglioside GM_2*. Infants with Tay Sachs disease appear to be healthy at birth, but as the sphingolipid accumulates in the nervous system, muscle weakness, failure to thrive, blindness, and developmental regression leading to mental retardation are observed. Most children with this disease die between 3 and 5 years of age.

Tay Sachs disease is an autosomal recessively inherited disorder (see Chapter 11 for a discussion of inheritance patterns). It occurs in approximately 1 in every 3,000 live births in people of Jewish background. There is a 25% chance in each future pregnancy that a family with an affected child will have another child with this disease. Carrier detection and prenatal diagnosis now are available for this disorder.

Other sphingolipidoses include *metachromatic leukodystrophy, Gaucher disease,* and *Niemann-Pick disease.* Because the onset of symptoms and the eventual outcome of the different sphingolipidoses and their subtypes vary with the specific biochemical defect, it is important to establish the diagnosis by means of specific laboratory studies and to provide appropriate counseling to the family. Although for most of the sphingolipidoses no specific therapy is available at this point in time, in recent years people with Gaucher disease have been treated effectively with enzyme replacement.

DISORDERS OF CARBOHYDRATE METABOLISM

A group of metabolic diseases in which complex sugars or carbohydrates accumulate in the urine is called *mucopolysaccharidoses.* Their classification has been complicated by the fact that they were recognized as diseases long before biochemical tests were available to differentiate them. Thus, they were initially labeled *Hurler, Hunter, Sanfilippo, Maroteaux-Lamy,* and *Scheie* syndromes, to name a few.

Hunter syndrome is a sex-linked disorder, whereas the other mucopolysaccharidoses are autosomal recessively inherited (see Chapter 11 for a discussion of inheritance patterns). Hurler syndrome is the most severe of these disorders. It is caused by an accumulation of chemical products in the bones and other organs of the body, including the brain. As a result, children with Hurler and Hunter syndromes deteriorate physically and mentally. In these syndromes, marked changes are observed in the shape of the face, hands, joints, and spines of these children. Enlargement of liver and spleen are often present. Mental retardation, as well as visual and hearing impairments, accompany the disorders. At present, no effective treatment is available. It affects approximately 1 in 100,000 children, and most die in early childhood.

Galactosemia is another disorder of carbohydrate metabolism in which a specific sugar called *galactose* cannot be metabolized, or broken down, because the body lacks an essential enzyme called *galactose-1-phosphate uridyl transferase*. If a baby with galactosemia is given a milk-based formula, symptoms, such as vomiting and other gastrointestinal disturbances, listlessness, and poor muscle tone, occur. Jaundice and liver problems also may be present. If untreated infants survive, they often develop cataracts and mental retardation. Galactosemia occurs in approximately 1 in 40,000 newborns. Dietary treatment, in which galactose is eliminated from the diet, should be started as early as possible to prevent both physical and mental retardation or early death.

LYSOSOMAL STORAGE DISEASES

In addition to classifying diseases by their biochemical and enzymatic defects, it is now possible to determine where in the cell the biochemical problem is situated. For example, there are certain small structures within a cell called *lysosomes*. These are enzyme-containing particles that ordinarily break down certain chemicals. If a lysosomal enzyme is defective, then the material to be metabolized may be stored within the lysosomes, instead of being broken down. The diseases that result are called *lysosomal storage diseases*. This category includes some of the sphingolipidoses, mucopolysaccharidoses, mucolipidoses, and other similar disorders. A great deal of research now is being carried out in the area of metabolic diseases, since abnormalities of metabolism can result in severe disabilities.

ACKNOWLEDGMENTS

Contributions have been made to this chapter by Siegfried M. Pueschel, M.D., Ph.D., M.P.H., and Patricia S. Scola, M.D., M.P.H.

Endocrine Disorders

Endocrine glands produce hormones that regulate many functions of the body. For example, hormones control water balance, blood sugar level, growth, sexual maturation, and many other bodily functions. Although the lack of these hormones may cause significant effects, most are not directly related to developmental disabilities. There is one notable exception, however, in which a deficiency of thyroid hormone leads to hypothyroidism, which was previously known as *cretinism*.

HYPOTHYROIDISM

Description
At birth, children with hypothyroidism ordinarily appear to be healthy. In the newborn period, constipation, lethargy, prolonged jaundice, poor feeding, and low body temperature may be present. If hypothyroidism is not treated with thyroid hormone, the child eventually will develop a puffy face, a dull appearance, a protruding tongue, a prominent abdomen with an umbilical hernia, and mental retardation.

Cause and Incidence
Congenital hypothyroidism results from a lack of thyroid hormone or is caused by an absent thyroid gland. Approximately 1 in 4,000 infants is born with this disorder.

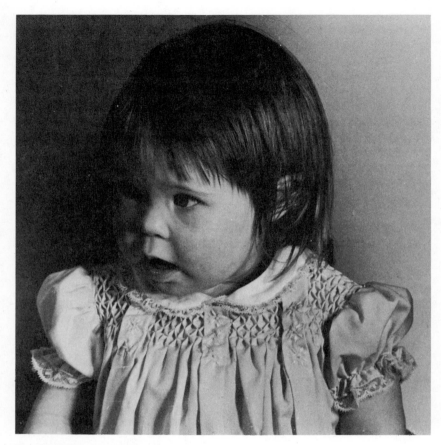

Detection and Treatment

Today, most infants born in the United States and other countries are screened for hypothyroidism before they are discharged from the hospital nursery. If the screening test is positive, the child's physician is notified, and treatment with thyroid hormone is begun immediately after the diagnosis of hypothyroidism is confirmed.

Expected Outcomes

With early treatment, the expected outcome for a child with hypothyroidism is good. If a child with hypothyroidism is not identified and treatment is delayed, then the child may develop mental retardation. Thus, the time at which treatment is started plays an important role in the outcome.

ACKNOWLEDGMENT

Contributions have been made to this chapter by Karen E. Senft, M.D.

Special Care for Your Child

Procedures, Assistive Devices, and Medical and Surgical Treatments

21

Strategies for Helping Your Child

When a child is found to have a developmental delay or another disability, most parents and families are anxious to begin helping their child in any way possible. Depending on the child's particular problem, a number of strategies may be useful. This chapter briefly outlines the various types of strategies and interventions that generally have proven helpful for children with developmental disabilities. As you read the description of each intervention, keep in mind that not all children require all types of services. Your child's individual needs, which have been identified during the evaluation process, will determine the specific kinds of interventions that are necessary. Also, remember that the various treatments, therapies, and interventions described here do not necessarily cure children of their disabilities. In many cases, the interventions help the children to become more active participants in everyday activities. In other instances, the assistance or therapy may enable children to learn or improve basic skills such as feeding and dressing.

Some strategies are primarily educational in nature and may be provided in a public school or special center. The program may focus on developing the child's thinking and language skills through special instruction with carefully designed materials and specially trained teachers. Whatever the intervention, the aim is to help the child and family in those areas in which assistance is needed.

The process of selecting the appropriate intervention begins with developmental and diagnostic evaluations (see also Chapters 22 and 27 about Tests and Procedures and Assessing Developmental

Disabilities, respectively). During an in-depth assessment, professionals will determine a child's strengths and weaknesses and find out whether a developmental disability exists. This is the first step in planning an appropriate intervention. Obviously, a therapeutic program cannot be developed until the child's needs have been identified. The more thorough the assessment, the more specific and comprehensive the recommendations for services can be.

After an initial evaluation, children with developmental disabilities may need to return for repeated evaluations each year or every few years. Reassessment may be necessary because the child has matured physically and developmentally. The child's growth may make it possible for certain tests to be performed that were difficult to carry out previously. Moreover, the child's specific needs change as he or she grows and develops. For example, an adolescent will have different concerns from a preteenager. In addition, recently acquired knowledge about a particular disorder might suggest new directions for care and management. Thus, assessment must be considered an ongoing process. The results of each reevaluation or new test may affect the type of treatment or services given. Therefore, it is important that the appropriateness of current interventions be monitored carefully and that changes be made whenever new information indicates that they are necessary.

It is also essential that the effectiveness of the intervention program be studied. If the planned program is not meeting the child's needs, or if new knowledge is obtained, additional assessment may be necessary to determine how the program can be improved.

Various kinds of intervention strategies are summarized in the following sections. They are grouped in categories for ease of discussion.

MEDICAL AND SURGICAL INTERVENTIONS

Many children with developmental disabilities have health problems resulting from a birth defect, an injury, or other causes that require medical or surgical intervention. The term *medical intervention* simply means that the child's health problems must be taken care of by a physician. This could be the family doctor, the child's pediatrician, or a specialist such as a neurologist, orthopaedist, or cardiologist. At times, a child with a specific disorder such as spina bifida will need to be followed in a clinic where children with such problems are treated by a number of specialists. The specific treatment or intervention provided to a child may consist of frequent visits to the doctor or other health care provider, such as a physical or occupational therapist; careful monitoring; or taking medications regularly (see Chapter 24). It also could include using special equipment at home (see Chapter 23) or a stay in the hospital (see Chapter 26). A child with multiple problems might need a variety of treatments or interventions combined into a special regimen to be followed daily. For example, a child with a seizure disorder and cerebral palsy might have to take medications as well as participate in a regular physical therapy program.

Surgical interventions may require an operation to correct or alleviate certain problems. Although many minor operative procedures, such as hernia operations or tonsillectomies, are now often performed on an outpatient basis, major operations usually require a stay in the hospital. Decisions to operate are made carefully. A number of factors, such as the severity of the child's problem, and the child's size, weight, and general health, will need to be taken into consideration by the doctor and family, before electing to perform an operation. Surgeons want their patients to be in the best physical condition possible prior to an operation to reduce the chance of complications and to improve the likelihood of a speedy recovery. However, there are situations in which surgery must be performed on an emergency basis to save the child's life.

For children who are facing hospitalization, further information about preparation and aftercare is found in Chapter 26. Operations that are frequently performed on children with various kinds of developmental disabilities are described in more detail in Chapter 25.

NUTRITIONAL INTERVENTIONS

Many parents of children with developmental disabilities may require the assistance of a nutritionist, dietitian, nurse, physician, or other professional to ensure that their child receives the proper kind and the right amount of food. Proper nutrition involves getting adequate amounts of proteins, carbohydrates, fats, minerals, and vitamins that the body needs to grow and develop typically. For children with feeding problems, food allergies, or food intolerances, a nutritional evaluation may be necessary in order for them to eat and develop properly. Nutritional strategies may focus on what, how much, or how often a child eats. Parents might have to increase or decrease the total number of calories fed to a child in a day, change the number of meals provided, or give the child a special food supplement. A nutritional evaluation may be concerned with how or in what position a child is fed. For example, a child who has trouble swallowing may need to be fed with a tube, or a child who is unable to chew may eat strained or puréed foods while efforts are made to develop necessary feeding skills such as proper swallowing or chewing.

Nutritional intervention may be part of an overall treatment plan. Whenever a treatment is prescribed, it is very important that the instructions be followed carefully. In this way the doctor, nutritionist, or other professional involved can evaluate whether or not the intervention is working. This is particularly important because, if the expected improvements do not occur, the plan may have to be adjusted or changed. Therefore, before a change is made, you and the professionals will want to be sure that it was the treatment that was ineffective rather than a failure to implement a good plan correctly.

Special dietary treatment plans or nutritional interventions are essential for children who have certain metabolic disorders. The words *metabolic* and *metabolism* refer to the way the body digests, processes, and breaks down the foods we eat. Some metabolic disorders are caused when a child is born without a certain essential body chemical (i.e., enzyme) needed to break down food. A widely known example of a metabolic disorder requiring nutritional intervention is phenylketonuria (PKU). Children with phenylketonuria are born without a specific enzyme needed to metabolize a building block of protein called *phenylalanine,* which is necessary for growth. When children with phenylketonuria eat foods containing phenylalanine, most of the phenylalanine remains unused and builds up in the body and the brain. This buildup can be harmful and can cause brain injury and mental retardation. Fortunately, children with phenylketonuria can be treated by providing them with a special diet. The diet restricts foods containing large amounts of phenylalanine and includes a special formula that has just enough phenylalanine to ensure proper growth and development. The earlier the treatment for phenylketonuria begins, the greater the chance that the child will grow and develop well. Because early treatment is so important in preventing brain injury and mental retardation, all children born in the United States are screened routinely for phenylketonuria before they leave the newborn nursery (see also the discussion of PKU in Chapter 19).

Babies who are having difficulty gaining weight and growing are likely to need a nutritional intervention. This condition is often referred to as *failure-to-thrive* or *failure-to-gain-weight.* Depending on the cause of the child's problem, part of the plan may involve giving the baby a special fortified formula that will add extra calories and nutrients to the diet. Parents may have to increase the number of feedings offered to the baby each day and carefully monitor how much is actually consumed.

Increased weight gain and obesity can also necessitate nutritional intervention. In American culture, many children are overfed and become overweight from an early age. It is important that parents be provided with information about feeding their children a balanced diet containing an appropriate number of calories. It is easier to prevent increased weight gain than to treat obesity.

EDUCATIONAL INTERVENTIONS

Throughout the United States, special education services are available to help children with developmental disabilities. A major purpose of special education is to ensure appropriate educational programming for children who need special assistance in order to be able to learn. Depending on the particular child, the help required may be a small part of the overall education program, or it may involve all aspects of the program. For example, the only assistance a child of average intelligence and a mild form of cerebral palsy may need is regular physical therapy to improve walking skills. Such assistance easily could be provided in a regular education program. Children with multiple disabilities who demonstrate significant delays in all areas of development will need special assistance in all facets of their education program. Where such services can be best delivered is something that will be determined by the parents and professionals who know the child and the available program options.

When identifying an education program for a specific child, parents and professionals look for the least restrictive environment (LRE) in which services can be delivered. The goal of the LRE is to have children with and without disabilities educated together in their local schools while providing the degree and intensity of services that each student needs. The concept of the LRE is part of the federal law governing special education (PL 94-142, the Education for All Handicapped Children Act of 1975, which is now included in the Individuals with Disabilities Education Act [IDEA]). The law requires that, whenever possible, children with special education needs be included with their peers in regular education settings. More information about special education services can be found in Chapter 29.

The educational options for children with developmental disabilities are numerous. Creative, individualized planning can result in unique programs that offer the needed services in community and school settings. PL 94-142 requires the development of individualized education programs (IEPs) for children with disabilities. Some common arrangements outlined in IEPs include having the child in the regular educational classroom for part of the day and providing individualized services in a resource room for the rest of the school day. For other children with more significant needs, the best program might be a special education classroom where services are available in both the quality and quantity needed. And for others, spending part of the day in school, at a special center, or in the community at a vocational site may be the best way to ensure that the child's educational needs are being met. At times, a child's needs may be so great that the child will require a prolonged school program (about 230 days a year) instead of the usual 180-day program.

PL 94-142 also mandated that special education services begin by age 5. Since 1975 when PL 94-142 was passed, two other federal laws, PL 99-457, the Education of the Handicapped Act Amendments of 1986, and PL 102-119, the Individuals with Disabilities Education Act Amendments of 1991, have gone into effect requiring that services for children with disabling conditions and developmental disabilities begin at age 3. The legislation also provides financial incentives for states to develop and implement early intervention programs for children under the age of 3. As of 1994, all states are providing early intervention programs for this group of children; however, the extensiveness of their programs varies considerably. For information about what is offered in your state, contact the special education office in your community or the state board of special education. These offices can direct you to the agencies in your area that provide early intervention services.

Early intervention is a form of educational programming for infants, toddlers, and preschoolers. In addition, it offers families of children with disabling conditions a means of coordinating a range of services designed to help meet the needs of the child and family. Services to be provided for a particular family are determined jointly by the family and professionals. Together, the priorities for service and intervention are outlined in a document called the individualized family service plan (IFSP). The IFSP indicates what services will be provided, how often they will occur, who will provide them, and where they will occur. This flexibility in service provision enables families to participate in their child's program. It is not unusual for early intervention services to be provided in the home, a child care center, or another agency specializing in the care of children. For more information about early intervention, see Chapter 28.

THERAPEUTIC INTERVENTIONS

Many children with developmental disabilities require at least one form of special therapy at some point during their lives. The most common forms of treatment are physical therapy, occupational therapy, speech-language therapy, respiratory therapy, specific psychological services, and social service interventions. Each type has a unique purpose.

Physical Therapy

Physical therapy (PT) attempts to help children develop their gross motor abilities, those that involve the large muscles of the body. Examples of gross motor skills include walking, running, crawling, and jumping. Physical therapists may work with infants, toddlers, and young children, as well as teenagers and adults. A baby may receive therapy to develop basic skills that will be needed before complex skills like walking can be learned. For example, one baby might need assistance in improving head control or rolling from front to back, whereas another child might need help learning how to get into the sitting position and maintaining balance. An older child's therapy program might concentrate on improving walking skills or helping the child learn to use special equipment such as a wheelchair or walker.

Many physical therapists are trained specifically to work with children. These pediatric physical therapists have learned special ways to provide therapy for children. Techniques used with babies and small children include proper positioning and motivating the child to move by using toys. Other activities performed by the therapist include stretching tight muscles or increasing the range of motion of limbs. Such passive activities may be an important part of a therapy program but generally should not constitute the entire treatment plan. Many therapists today strive to have children actively participate in the therapy program. Active participation is the best way for children to learn what they must do in order to move in a desired way.

Individual physical therapy sessions may last from 15 or 20 minutes to an hour. The duration of the session depends on the individual's needs and tolerance. Some children require therapy several times a week, whereas other youngsters need only to be seen once every month or so.

Usually, physical therapists work closely with the child's parents or other family members. In the case of a school-based physical therapy program, the therapist would also consult with a child's classroom teacher. By keeping in close contact with parents and teachers, the therapist can demonstrate and review methods used to encourage development of the child's gross motor skills. Families are expected to continue working with the child on some of the exercises and activities at home as well. This is essential if improvements are to be made. Without carryover of the program to home and school, where children spend most of their time, the effects of weekly or even monthly therapy sessions would be lost quickly. By working with a therapist, many parents have become excellent co-therapists for their children.

The physical therapist also can be instrumental in helping parents learn to use assistive technology and devices that have been prescribed for their children. (For details on this subject, see Chapter 23 about Adaptive Equipment.)

Occupational Therapy

Many people are confused by the idea of occupational therapy, particularly when it is recommended for young children. The term *occupational therapy* (OT) originally was referred to as a form of treatment for adults with disabilities, who, because of injury or deformity, were unable to participate in activities of daily living. These people, who had difficulty using their hands to complete everyday tasks, were helped by therapists to improve their occupational skills.

Occupational therapy for young children refers to a form of treatment that will enhance their fine motor skills and control of the smaller muscles of the body. This includes muscles of the arms and hands needed for reaching, grasping, and holding objects. It also involves muscles of the face and mouth that are important for chewing, swallowing, and maintaining lip closure. In addition to improving control of particular muscles, an occupational therapist is concerned with improving the way different muscles work together, such as in eye–hand coordination. Some types of occupational therapy can be useful to children who are overly sensitive to touch or whose touch perceptions appear distorted. These children often experience difficulty interpreting information received through their senses, and benefit from a form of occupational therapy called *sensory integration*.

Like the physical therapist, the occupational therapist will want to work closely with parents, teaching them how to incorporate exercises into daily routines. The occupational therapist also can advise parents on the use of special equipment, the application and use of hand splints, and other types of bracing devices. Many occupational therapists have been trained to construct hand and arm splints. For a detailed description of the various kinds of adaptive equipment, see Chapter 23.

Speech-Language Therapy

Professionals who specialize in the treatment of language problems and speech disorders are called *speech-language pathologists* or *speech-language therapists*. Children who show a significant language delay or hearing loss, or who are having difficulty producing speech sounds, may benefit from speech-language therapy. Depending on the individual's problems, speech-language therapy may be provided in a small-group setting or on an individual basis. For very young children, who have not yet begun to talk, therapy may consist of language stimulation activities, sound imitation training, and activities to encourage babbling and to make other sounds. Older children may need articulation training or speech-language therapy to help them produce clearer sounds. For a child with a hearing impairment, speech-language therapy may consist of hearing training and development of a communication system using sounds, gestures, and hand signals. Speech-language therapy, like other therapies already discussed, is more successful when parents and other family members continue with the recommended exercises and activities at home.

Children with severe language or communication problems may require ongoing language and communication training activities. This may be accomplished in the classroom by trained teaching staff who work closely with a speech-language pathologist. In many cases, such ongoing training in the classroom environment is more effective than individual therapy provided in a different setting. In such situations, the speech-language pathologist would play a critical role in planning therapy goals and monitoring the child's progress.

Speech-language therapists share a concern with occupational therapists about the function of the muscles of the face, mouth, and throat because these muscles are primarily responsible for speech production. If a child has a severe speech-language impairment due to marked problems with muscles around the mouth, the therapist and the child's family may decide to develop an alternate means of communication. Alternative forms of communication range from sign language and communication boards (with pictures and/or words) to sophisticated computerized speech synthesizers. The type of alternative communication device depends on the child's age and cognitive abilities. In order to use a communication board with pictures or words, the child has to recognize names of objects, understand that pictures are representations of objects, and comprehend that written words refer to specific things. Implementing an alternative system of communication generally takes considerable time for both planning and training. However, the efforts can be very rewarding, as the system enables a child to communicate with others.

Respiratory Therapy

Children with medical or physical conditions that impair their breathing may require respiratory therapy to prevent lung infections and to improve breathing efficiency. Chest percussion is a form of treatment for respiratory problems that consists of pounding the child's chest in order to loosen the secretions of the bronchial tubes so that the mucus can be coughed up. This type of therapy may be needed several times a day in order to keep the lungs clear. Other forms of respiratory therapy involve the use of mechanical devices that aid breathing, such as a respirator, a mist tent, or an oxygen mask or tent. Children with certain conditions, such as cystic fibrosis, who have problems with chronic lung infection and congestion may also need regular chest therapy at home. For these children, teaching the parents or caregivers the treatment procedures is essential to the child's well-being.

Psychological Services

A psychologist can help children with developmental disabilities and their families in a number of different ways. Often, the initial contact with the psychologist occurs during the evaluation process. The psychologist may have tested the child to determine if developmental delays or behavior problems are present. Beyond evaluation, the range of psychological services also includes individual therapy for the child; counseling or therapy for the parents; family therapy where all members including sisters and brothers are seen together; and consultations on specific problems such as discipline, behavior problems, learning disabilities, and emotional disorders. Many parents seek help because they are having difficulty coping with the stresses of everyday life. These problems may have originated long before their child was born. It is not unusual for the birth of a child with disabilities to reactivate previously existing problems.

For many individuals, a psychologist can be of most assistance by helping parents and family members learn more about their child's problems and understand the impact on their own and their

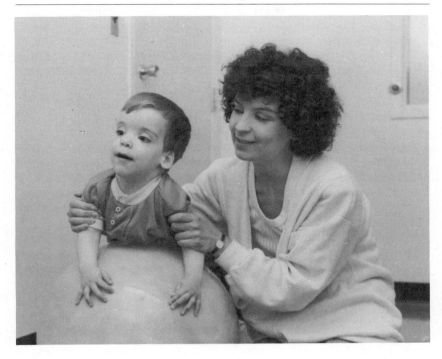

child's lives. Talking to a psychologist or a trained counselor frequently helps people sort out their feelings and come to terms with problems that may have seemed insurmountable. Psychologists may also be consulted by teachers, therapists, and/or other professionals working with children who have disabilities about behavior problems, unusual social interactions, learning difficulties, and discipline strategies. Psychological assistance may consist of suggesting ways to manage behavior problems by working directly with the child and family on behavior management programs. In the case of an emotional problem or unusual social behavior, a psychologist may decide to see the child on a regular basis for individual therapy. The type of therapy provided depends on the child's specific problem. Techniques that are commonly used for treatment include play therapy, behavior management techniques, group therapy, and family therapy.

Social Service Intervention

It is not unusual for families of children with disabilities to feel overwhelmed at times because of the numerous demands and problems presented by caring for their child. All parents face crises with their children at one time or another, but parents of children with disabilities tend to face a never-ending succession of both major and minor crises as their child grows. Whether or not each crisis is handled successfully or results in enormous stress on the family depends on many factors such as the severity of the problem; the parents' coping ability; and resources available to the family including financial, professional, and emotional support from others. Issues that frequently are the focus of family crisis can range from acute health or medical problems of the child, decisions about therapeutic or surgical interventions that have been recommended, concerns about financial resources needed to obtain optimum care, unusual time demands required of the parents, and worries about their child's future. Parents may also be bewildered by the number of agencies and professionals involved in their child's care and confused about the types of services each offers. Other potential sources of stress are the parents' own feelings and emotional responses to their child and to the disability and their experience with friends, neighbors, other family members, and strangers. To help solve some of these problems and relieve the feelings of stress, people often turn to a social worker for assistance. Many social workers are trained in psychotherapy and counseling skills and are knowledgeable regarding community agencies available to families. They can be extremely helpful in directing parents to the appropriate agency for assistance.

The amount and types of assistance a social worker provides vary from family to family. The assistance also may vary from clinic to clinic, as the social worker's role may be different in various settings. Many parents simply need to be pointed in the right direction and then are able to obtain help on their own. Often, these are the families who have an extended support network already available to them and who are coping fairly well with their child's disability. Other families, who have more extensive problems, may benefit from regular counseling.

Various social service interventions available to aid people with disabilities differ from state to state. To learn more about what is available in your area, you will need to contact your state social service or welfare agency, the nearest branch of The Arc (formerly the Association for Retarded Citizens of the United States), local chapters of various associations for different disabilities (e.g., Muscular Dystrophy Association, United Cerebral Palsy Associations, Spina Bifida Association, National Down Syndrome Congress, National Down Syndrome Society), or diagnostic centers offering services to children with mental retardation and disabilities. Most areas have agencies that can assist parents in their efforts to care for their children with disabilities. Sometimes, helping families means finding a way to give parents a break from the demanding responsibilities their child presents. These breaks, or respites, can be for an occasional afternoon or for 1- or 2-week vacations through temporary foster care or placement in a group home if necessary.

As parents find they are having trouble managing the care of the child alone, they may begin to think about alternative arrangements. In these situations, talking to a social worker can be extremely helpful. Social workers may help families to find appropriate programs that are geared primarily to enriching the individual's life. Many localities in the United States offer extensive recreational and vocational programs for their citizens with mental retardation. The Special Olympics program, for example, which has grown considerably since the mid 1970s, has probably done more nationwide for the self-image of the persons who participate in it than any other individual program. In addition to helping its participants, Special Olympics has brought national attention to the needs and rights of persons with mental retardation and other disabilities in the United States.

Thus, the social worker is often a resource broker—that is, a person who may help you to discover what services are available to you and your child with a disability.

ACKNOWLEDGMENT

Contributions have been made to this chapter by Leslie Weidenman, Ph.D.

22

Tests and Procedures

During the past several decades, some of the most dramatic advances in medicine have been made possible because of the development of numerous medical tests and special procedures. Today, the human body can be studied in many ways, not even envisioned as recently as the 1960s or 1970s. More and more physicians are relying on technologically sophisticated tools such as ultrasound, computed tomography, and magnetic resonance imaging to diagnose and treat difficult medical conditions. This chapter describes these techniques and other commonly used tests and procedures, and shows how they may be applied to various medical disorders and developmental disabilities. Several of these procedures have been described briefly in previous chapters of this book. Cross-references are included to guide your reading.

PRENATAL DIAGNOSIS

As genetic counseling has become more effective, greater emphasis has been placed on diagnosing certain disabilities before birth. Through the use of various prenatal studies and tests, many chromosome disorders and genetic diseases can be diagnosed during pregnancy (see also Chapter 11).

Ultrasonography

Ultrasound, or ultrasonography, is a noninvasive procedure during which sound waves are sent into the womb. These sound waves bounce off the fetus and provide a picture-like image of the various structures of the unborn baby. This procedure is most often used to obtain an objective assessment of the baby's size and development, which in turn allows the physician to estimate the approximate due date. In addition, certain structural abnormalities, such as spina bifida, hydrocephalus, certain skeletal disorders, congenital heart disease, and bowel obstruction, can be diagnosed with level II ultrasonography, which provides more details about specific defects than regular sonography.

Amniocentesis

The most widely used test for prenatal diagnosis is amniocentesis. Amniocentesis usually is performed between the 15th and 16th week of pregnancy. More recently some centers have used amniocentesis as early as the 12th or 13th week of gestation. This procedure ordinarily is done on an outpatient basis. It involves introducing a needle through the abdomen into the womb and withdrawing some of the liquid, called *amniotic fluid*, that surrounds the unborn baby. This amniotic fluid then can be studied for various metabolic problems, chromosome disorders, and alpha-fetoprotein. For chromosome analysis, certain cells—called *fibroblasts*—obtained from the amniotic fluid must be grown in a laboratory. After being cultured for approximately 2–3 weeks, these cells can be examined for chromosome problems and for certain biochemical disorders.

The risks associated with amniocentesis are very small, especially when the procedure is carried out by an experienced obstetrician guided by ultrasonography. However, like any invasive procedure, amniocentesis carries a slight risk of infection, and there is a slight increase of spontaneous abortion. These risks must be weighed against the benefits of the procedure. There also may be some discomfort for the mother when the needle is pushed through the skin into the womb.

Amniocentesis is usually recommended for women who are 35 years and older, for families who already have a child with a chromosome or genetic disorder, if one of the parents is a translocation carrier, or if a metabolic problem in the fetus is suspected.

Chorionic Villus Sampling

In the 1980s, a new technique for prenatal diagnosis during the first trimester of pregnancy was developed. It is called *chorionic villus biopsy* or *chorionic villus sampling (CVS)*. The *chorion* refers to the part of the placenta that is near the unborn baby. In this procedure, a plastic tube is passed through the vagina into the uterus and a small sample of the chorion is obtained for diagnostic studies.

This technique is primarily performed at certain university centers. Chorionic villus sampling requires a trained professional in ultrasonography and a skilled obstetrician. Ultrasound is needed to localize the placenta from which the obstetrician can obtain a tissue sample.

There are certain advantages of chorionic villus sampling over amniocentesis. First, a chromosome analysis can be performed immediately, with results made available in a few hours; and second, chorionic villus biopsy can be performed at an earlier time in pregnancy, usually during the third month of gestation. In addition to chromosome analysis, the tissue sample can be used for biochemical studies and DNA analysis.

As with any procedure, there are also disadvantages as well as technical difficulties. There are some reports in the literature indicating rare limb defects as a result of chorionic villus sampling.[1] Future investigations will determine whether chorionic villus biopsy is a safe procedure yielding accurate results.

Fetoscopy

A more invasive diagnostic test used in the prenatal period is fetoscopy, which uses fiber optic techniques. During this procedure, a tube is placed into the womb, through which the fetus can be visualized. Fetoscopy also is being used to obtain blood from the unborn baby. This procedure is performed only if the baby is suspected to have a specific blood disorder that cannot be diagnosed through amniocentesis. Because fetoscopy poses a risk to mother and baby and the rate of complications is somewhat higher than for other procedures, it is used only on a very limited basis. Fetoscopy is being replaced by sophisticated level II ultrasonography.

DNA Analysis

A new diagnostic method involves the use of deoxyribonucleic acid (DNA) analysis. This test can provide information about the actual genetic makeup of the fetus. It is used to detect a variety of blood disorders in the fetus such as thalassemia and sickle cell disease, as well as other genetic disorders.

To do the test, a small blood sample is needed from each parent and their child with the disorder. A fetal sample can be obtained by amniocentesis, chorionic villus sampling, or fetoscopy. The samples are then sent to a special laboratory that is equipped to carry out the DNA analysis. The results are usually available in 1–3 weeks.

---

[1]Goldberg, J.D., Porter, A.E., & Golbus, M.S. (1990). Current assessment of fetal losses as a direct consequence of chorionic villus sampling. *American Journal of Medical Genetics, 35,* 174–177.

In addition, blood or tissue samples may be used for enzyme analysis to confirm or rule out the presence of a suspected metabolic disease.

Alpha-fetoprotein Analysis

To determine if an unborn baby has spina bifida, a birth defect in which the spine fails to form properly, maternal blood can be analyzed for alpha-fetoprotein. Alpha-fetoprotein is a substance produced by the unborn baby. From there it enters the amniotic fluid and then passes into the mother's blood. If the alpha-fetoprotein level obtained from maternal blood samples between the 16th and 18th week of the pregnancy is atypically high, ultrasonography is done to rule out other conditions that could result in high alpha-fetoprotein levels. For example, a twin pregnancy or intrauterine death may bring about high levels of alpha-fetoprotein. Also, if the date of the expected birth has been miscalculated, the alpha-fetoprotein level could be elevated. If such conditions have been ruled out, an atypically high alpha-fetoprotein level could mean that the baby has spina bifida. In such instances, amniocentesis and/or ultrasonography are recommended to enable a more definite diagnosis.

During the 1980s, it had been observed that many women who gave birth to children with Down syndrome had very low alpha-fetoprotein levels. Therefore, an increasing number of alpha-fetoprotein screening programs recommend amniocentesis and subsequent chromosome analysis if the alpha-fetoprotein level is significantly decreased and if there is a high risk that the mother may carry a fetus with Down syndrome or any other chromosome problem. During recent years other tests have been added to alpha-fetoprotein screening such as estriol and human chorionic gonadotropin determinations. If in addition to a very low alpha-fetoprotein level, the mother's blood has a decreased estriol content and an increased level of human chorionic gonadotropin, there is an even higher risk that the mother may be carrying a fetus with Down syndrome. In such a situation, amniocentesis is usually recommended.

NEWBORN SCREENING

Metabolic disorders refer to problems of the body's chemicals. For many years, tests for a variety of metabolic disorders have been performed using samples of blood, urine, amniotic fluid, and other tissues. Since the 1960s, nearly all newborn babies in the United States and other countries have had blood tests for certain metabolic conditions such as phenylketonuria (see Chapters 19 and 20, about metabolic and endocrine disorders). Other screening tests have been added since the 1970s so that most states also screen for hypothyroidism and other rare metabolic diseases such as maple syrup urine disease, homocystinuria, and galactosemia (see Chapter 19). Throughout the United States, different states test for different metabolic disorders. For example, in Massachusetts the Newborn Screening Program also includes toxoplasmosis, sickle cell disease, congenital adrenal hyperplasia, and biotinidase deficiency.

During screening, a few drops of the baby's blood are collected on a filter paper within the first few days of life and are sent to a laboratory for testing. In some states, a sample of the baby's urine also is obtained later to test for specific metabolic disorders. If a child is identified as having a metabolic disorder, appropriate treatment can be started immediately. Treatment for metabolic disorders may mean giving the baby a special diet or administering medications. With early detection and treatment of certain metabolic disorders, mental retardation and physical problems can be prevented in many children who otherwise would have had serious disabilities.

Various biochemical tests also are carried out in older children who are suspected to have a metabolic problem. For example, a urine specimen can be examined for the presence of increased amounts of amino acids or organic acids that, if found, may suggest a specific metabolic disorder. Cells obtained from blood and skin can be checked for certain enzyme deficiencies, as in Tay Sachs disease, Hurler syndrome, and others (see Chapter 19 about Metabolic Disorders).

Many maternity hospitals have started to screen newborns for hearing disorders. This procedure, called *evoked otoacoustic emissions test*, is a simple, inexpensive hearing test whereby inner ear (i.e., cochlear) problems are identified. In Rhode Island, legislation mandates that this hearing screening test be available for all newborns.

SWEAT TEST

A sweat test, or iontopheresis, is used to diagnose cystic fibrosis, a relatively common inherited disease affecting the intestinal and respiratory systems. A sweat test measures the concentration of sodium and chloride in the child's perspiration. In most cases, an excess of sodium and chloride in the perspiration is an indicator of cystic fibrosis. It is important to identify children with cystic fibrosis as early as possible because supportive care, administration of intestinal enzymes, and antibiotic therapy for respiratory infections will improve the expected outcomes of these children. The recent discovery of the gene that is defective in cystic fibrosis brings molecular genetic therapy within reach for this disorder.

CHROMOSOME ANALYSIS

Chromosome analysis is used to diagnose a number of chromosome disorders such as Down syndrome, Turner syndrome, and Klinefelter syndrome. This procedure usually involves taking a blood sample from the child. Also, cells from skin, amniotic fluid, and various other tissues can be used for chromosome analysis. The cells are incubated in a laboratory for approximately 3 days. Then the cells are placed on a glass slide, stained, and specially prepared so that the chromosomes can be examined under a microscope. The number and the structure of the chromosomes are then analyzed.

Various chromosome abnormalities can be detected, such as the presence of an extra chromosome in one of the pairs (called *trisomy*), the attachment of one chromosome to another (called a *translocation*), a missing part of a chromosome (called a *deletion*), or a portion within a chromosome that is upside down (called an *inversion*) (see Chapter 11 about Chromosome and Genetic Disorders).

It is important for a physician to know if a child has a chromosome abnormality. Once detected, appropriate genetic counseling can be provided to the parents.

TESTS FOR NEUROLOGICAL DISORDERS

Electroencephalogram

For many years neurological disorders, or problems with the body's nervous system, have been studied using various tests and procedures. One of the most frequently used tests is the electroencephalogram (EEG), which is commonly known as a *brainwave test*. During an electroencephalogram, a child usually will have 16 small electrodes placed on specific locations of the scalp. These electrodes are connected to the electroencephalogram machine, which then records the electrical activity generated by the child's brain cells on a paper strip. The recording shows the individual pattern of the brain's electrical activity, which is interpreted by a neurologist.

Electroencephalograms of children with tonic-clonic, absence, or other seizure disorders often show characteristic patterns of electrical activity (see also discussion of seizure disorders in Chapter 16). Information obtained from the electroencephalogram, together with the child's medical history, helps the physician to diagnose and treat various seizure disorders. In addition to seizure disorders, abnormal

electroencephalograms may indicate space-occupying lesions such as tumors, abscesses, and other anomalies of the brain. Other tests will be needed, however, to make an accurate diagnosis of such conditions.

Computed Tomography and Magnetic Resonance Imaging

Since the early 1980s, the diagnosis of neurological problems has been revolutionized by the development of two new procedures: 1) computed tomography, also known as CAT scan or CT scan; and 2) magnetic resonance imaging, commonly referred to as MRI. A CT scan is a sophisticated three-dimensional X ray printed out by a computer in two dimensions. Magnetic resonance imaging involves the magnetic sensing of the atoms of the brain to create an image of brain structures. The pictures obtained from the CT scan and MRI allow the physician to see the detailed structures of the brain and other body parts. In addition, in the early 1990s, recearchers described a technique called functional MRI, which refers to the detection of functionally induced changes in blood oxygenation by magnetic resonance imaging. Previously, only invasive procedures were available, such as the injection of dye into an artery or air into the ventricular system. These procedures often were painful and riskier, and provided less information about brain structures than the new imaging techniques. Both CT scans and MRI are extremely helpful in diagnosing tumors, hydrocephalus, atypical blood vessels, bleeding (i.e., hemorrhage) in the brain, and other structural problems of the brain and the rest of the body.

Positron Emission Tomography

During the late 1970s and early 1980s, a new technique, called *positron emission tomography* (PET), was developed to study actual brain function. The PET scan allows measurement of various central nervous system activities, such as blood flow, oxygen consumption, and sugar (i.e., glucose) metabolism. A distinct strategy for the functional mapping of neuronal activity has emerged more recently as a result of PET scan capabilities. Although PET scanning has been used primarily as a research tool in the past, it is now being introduced into clinical medicine.

Anticonvulsant Blood Levels

Children with seizures who are treated with anticonvulsant medications will have a small amount of blood drawn at regular intervals to measure the concentration of the seizure medication in the blood. These measurements, or blood levels, tell the physician whether the child is getting enough medication to control seizures. Medications must be in sufficient quantity in the child's body to be beneficial. The blood levels also will reveal if a child has too much or not enough of a specific medicine in the body. Medication levels that are too high may cause side effects or toxic symptoms (see also Chapter 24 about medications).

PROCEDURES TO DIAGNOSE
NEUROMUSCULAR DISORDERS

Neuromuscular disorders, including Duchenne muscular dystrophy and spinal muscular atrophy, can be assessed in various ways, including blood tests for muscle enzymes, studies of muscle contractions (i.e., electromyography) and nerve conduction, muscle biopsies, and molecular genetic studies.

Muscle Enzyme Test

The presence of high levels of certain muscle enzymes in the blood may mean that the muscles are abnormal or diseased. For example, testing for the enzyme creatine kinase (CK or CPK) will help a physician to diagnose specific muscle diseases, such as Duchenne muscular dystrophy. The procedure for muscle enzyme testing involves obtaining a blood sample and sending it to a laboratory for examination. CK levels are also sometimes used to identify carriers of neuromuscular diseases.

Electromyography

The electrical conductivity of nerves going to the muscles and muscle contractions can be studied by a procedure called *electromyography (EMG)*. During this procedure, a very small needle is inserted directly into the muscle, and the electrical activity during a muscle contraction is recorded. Muscles typically have a specific pattern, whereas diseased muscles show unusual recordings.

Nerve Conduction Studies

Nerve conduction studies involve placing electrodes at two sites on the same nerve, several inches apart. A small electrical charge is sent through the nerve at one end and recorded at the other end. Normal nerves conduct electrical charges at a specific speed, and the readings show distinct patterns. Diseased nerves, however, show unusual patterns of electrical conductivity.

Both electromyography and nerve conduction studies can assist in determining whether a child has a primary muscle disease or whether the nerve tissue in cells or nerve fibers are damaged.

Muscle Biopsy

Muscle biopsy involves surgically removing a small portion of muscle tissue and examining it under both a light microscope and an electron microscope. Before the tissue is examined, it is prepared with special stains and chemicals. These procedures are most helpful in diagnosing several forms of muscular dystrophy and other neuromuscular disorders. In addition, muscle tissue can be examined for dystrophin and DNA analysis (see Chapter 18 for details about muscle diseases).

PROCEDURES TO DIAGNOSE SENSORY DISORDERS

Audiogram

An audiogram, or hearing test, can indicate whether or not a child has a hearing impairment. A child who has delayed language development or who fails to respond typically to sounds should have a hearing assessment (a detailed discussion about hearing impairment is provided in Chapter 8). The techniques used during the hearing examination may vary according to the child's age, cooperation, and cognitive abilities. If the child is younger than 6 months of age, the audiologist will observe the child's responses to sounds of controlled intensities and frequencies. The child may respond to sounds by turning the head, blinking, startling, widening the eyes, or cessation of sucking. In a somewhat older child, visual reinforcement audiometry often is used, which means an animated toy or a flashing light reinforces a localization response to sounds. For children from 2 to 6 years old, a procedure called *conditioned play audiometry* frequently is employed, whereby children engage in play activities, such as putting a toy into a box, each time a sound is heard. In older children, pure tone audiometry may be used, during which a tone is presented at different intensities and frequencies. If a hearing loss is present, the audiogram can tell the degree of the hearing impairment and whether the ability to hear high- or low-pitched sounds is affected.

Tympanometry

Tympanometry involves placing a seal over the front of the ear canal and gently injecting small amounts of air through the seal into the ear canal. The eardrum, also called the *tympanic membrane*, typically will move back and forth slightly against the tiny jet of air. This movement can be measured and compared to established norms. If this movement is markedly reduced, the middle ear may be filled with fluid or pus or the eardrum itself may be diseased. The lack of flexibility of the eardrum observed in various conditions often will compromise the child's hearing significantly.

Brain Stem Evoked Response

Direct measurements of electrical conductivity along the nerves that carry sound impulses into the brain can be made using a procedure called *brain stem evoked response (BSER)* or *auditory evoked potential.* This procedure is quite similar to an electroencephalogram, which was described previously. The child is placed in a quiet environment and measured sounds are presented to each ear. Electrodes placed over certain portions of the scalp measure the rate of sound conduction through the auditory nerve to the brain. A slower than expected rate of conduction or lack of response may indicate a serious hearing problem. Small children often need to be sedated for this test.

Visual Evoked Potential

A process similar to the brain stem evoked response, called *visual evoked potential*, is available for studying visual abilities. In this test, visual stimuli are given instead of auditory stimuli, and recordings of the nerve conduction of the visual information are made from different portions of the brain.

EVALUATION OF RESPIRATORY DISORDERS

Chest X Ray

Respiratory disorders such as pneumonia, asthma, and lung problems in cystic fibrosis are best diagnosed with the help of a chest X ray. The chest X ray is one of the most reliable tools available to the physician because it allows the physician to locate and identify the respiratory problem.

Taking X rays is like taking a photograph. The X-ray pictures are obtained in a special room with lead walls so that no radiation can leave the room. The child's chest is placed against a photographic plate, the child is asked to take a deep breath, and then the picture is taken with special rays that can "see through" the body. Usually the amount of radiation is quite small and will not harm the child. After the X ray has been taken, it will need to be developed like any other photograph. Following this, a radiologist will interpret the X-ray picture. For example, the doctor, usually a radiologist, can determine whether the child has pneumonia, bronchitis, an overinflated lung, a collapsed lung, a tumor, or a collection of fluid in the chest cavity. The X ray also reveals which part of the lungs is diseased.

Pulmonary Function Tests

During pulmonary function tests, a child breathes into a machine that measures the amount of air that moves in and out of the child's lungs. In certain lung diseases, the volume of air moving in and out of the lungs may be reduced significantly. In addition, pulmonary function tests can measure the concentration of specific gases in the expired air. These tests usually are given to children who have cystic fibrosis, muscular dystrophy, or other disorders that affect the lungs. Through pulmonary function studies, a physician can determine the extent of lung disease and if there has been improvement with treatment or if the disease is getting progressively worse.

ASSESSMENT OF HEART (CARDIAC) DISEASES

Cardiac diseases can be studied through the use of chest X ray, electrocardiogram, echocardiogram, and cardiac catheterization.

Chest X Ray

The chest X ray allows the radiologist to find out whether the entire heart or particular heart chambers are enlarged. It also provides information on the configuration of the heart—whether it is round-shaped (i.e., globular), boot-shaped, and so forth. Moreover, if, for example, there is too much blood flow from the heart to the lungs, the vessels (i.e., vascular structures) can be identified.

Electrocardiogram

The electrocardiogram (EKG) provides a direct measurement of electrical activity produced by the nerves in the heart. This procedure is much like the brainwave test described previously, but for the EKG the electrodes are placed on the limbs and across the chest. By analyzing the patterns of the electrical activity shown on the electrocardiogram, the physician can determine many things including whether the heart rhythm is normal, whether the heart chambers are enlarged or the muscles are thickened, whether the heart muscle is stressed or pumping too hard, whether the heart muscle is injured, and whether the heart's nerve conduction system is working appropriately.

Echocardiogram

The echocardiogram is a noninvasive procedure in which sound waves are sent into the chest and the waves then "echo," or bounce off, the structures of the heart to a recording membrane. From the pattern of the echoed sound waves, information can be obtained about the structures of the heart chambers, heart muscles, blood vessels leading to and leaving the heart, and heart valves that regulate the blood flow. The echocardiogram is an excellent tool for looking at certain congenital heart defects, such as holes between the heart chambers (i.e., septal defects) and abnormal structures of the large blood vessels. The echocardiogram also provides information about blood flow.

Cardiac Catheterization

During cardiac catheterization, a dye is injected through plastic tubing that has been threaded through either veins or arteries leading to the heart. After the dye is in the heart, a series of X-ray pictures is obtained in rapid succession. This allows the cardiologist to visualize the inside of the heart as it pumps. In addition, the oxygen content and the pressure in the heart chambers and adjacent vessels can be measured accurately using this procedure. Cardiac catheterization involves certain risks, which the cardiologist should discuss with the child's parents in detail. The risk of catheterization often is outweighed by the information gained about the functioning of the heart. Because the child is slightly anesthetized, no significant discomfort is felt during this procedure.

DIAGNOSTIC PROCEDURES USED IN INTESTINAL DISEASES

Intestinal disorders such as colitis and ileitis (inflammation of the bowels) as well as ulcers can be studied using direct visualization through fluoroscopy, endoscopy, rectoscopy, sigmoidoscopy, and colonoscopy, and with X-ray procedures such as barium swallow, barium enema, CT scan, and MRI.

Fluoroscopy

Similar to echocardiography, sound waves are used during fluoroscopy of the abdomen. The reflections of the sound waves are recorded on a screen. Various structural defects, such as tumors, enlargement of organs in the abdomen, gallstones, hernias, and certain bowel and stomach problems, can be detected using this noninvasive procedure.

Endoscopy, Rectoscopy, Sigmoidoscopy, and Colonoscopy

During endoscopy, a long, narrow, flexible tube is inserted through the mouth and the esophagus into the stomach. The procedure allows the inside wall of the stomach to be examined. Ulcers, tumors, and bleeding are among the most commonly diagnosed problems using endoscopy.

Rectoscopy, sigmoidoscopy, and colonoscopy use a similar, but sometimes longer, tube to study diseases of the rectum and large bowel, which is referred to as the *colon.* Inflammatory bowel disease, such as ileitis or colitis, polyps, diverticulosis, or cancer can be diagnosed this way, because the physician can visualize any changes or abnormalities on the inside of the bowel. At the same time, a specimen of suspicious bowel tissue can be obtained (i.e., a biopsy) during colonoscopy, sigmoidoscopy, or rectoscopy for microscopic studies. These procedures can be done either on an inpatient or an outpatient basis. Although these procedures usually are not painful, there may be some discomfort when the instrument is inserted into the rectum.

Barium Swallow

X-ray studies, including a barium swallow and an upper gastrointestinal (GI) series, can give a picture of the lining of the esophagus, stomach, and the intestinal tract. These procedures involve swallowing a small amount of barium, a whitish chalky material that can be seen on an X-ray film. The barium is followed through the esophagus into the stomach and then through the upper portion of the small bowel. X rays are taken at specific time intervals during this process. Usually no pain or discomfort is associated with these procedures.

Barium Enema

A barium enema is similar to the barium swallow. In this case, the barium is introduced into the rectum and sigmoid, which is the lower part of the large bowel. Again, the radiologist can examine the progression of the barium through the colon and take X-ray pictures of various parts of the large bowel containing barium.

DIAGNOSTIC PROCEDURES
USED IN UROLOGICAL DISORDERS

Urological disorders are studied by using a combination of direct inspection with the cystoscope (a tube-like instrument that is inserted into the bladder) and indirect visualization with X-ray techniques, and fluoroscopy. The most common X-ray studies of the kidneys and bladder are the intravenous pyelogram and the voiding cystourethrogram.

Intravenous Pyelogram

The intravenous pyelogram (IVP) involves injecting dye, most often into one of the veins in the forearm. The dye is carried through the blood stream and then passes through the kidneys, ureters, and into the bladder. X rays are taken of these structures at various times after the injection of dye. By looking at the flow of the dye through the kidneys and ureters into the bladder, the radiologist can determine whether there are any problems such as kidney stones, tumors, kidney injury, areas of narrowing or widening of the tube system (i.e., ureters), or bladder problems.

Voiding Cystourethrogram

A voiding cystourethrogram (VCUG) involves the injection of dye into the bladder. A tube is inserted through the urethra, which is the passageway from the bladder to the outside, into the bladder. The dye then is passed through the tube into the bladder. Subsequently, X-ray pictures are taken, which may show abnormal structures inside the bladder, and which also reveal whether there is a problem with reflux. Reflux occurs when urine from the bladder is backing up into the ureters and kidneys. Typically, a one-way valve in the bladder prevents reflux, but in certain conditions, such as repeated urinary tract infections or abnormal ureters, reflux may occur. Placement of the tube through the urethra into the bladder may be associated with some discomfort, particularly in boys.

Cystoscopy

Direct visualization of the bladder can be accomplished by cystoscopy. During this procedure, a tube is passed through the urethra into the bladder. With the cystoscope, the urologist can see whether inflammation, tumors, bleeding, stones, abscesses, or other structural anomalies are present. During cystoscopy, the urologist also can measure the pressure in the bladder.

Fluoroscopy

Fluoroscopy, as mentioned previously, is a noninvasive procedure that uses sound waves to evaluate certain structures in the body. Often fluoroscopy is used to identify the presence, size, and shape of the kidneys, the size of the ureters, the bladder configuration, and other structural aspects. Pathological concerns can be easily noted using fluoroscopy.

PHYSICIAN'S RESPONSIBILITY

There are, of course, numerous other tests and procedures applicable to children with developmental disabilities. However, they cannot all be detailed in this book.

It is the responsibility of the physician ordering the tests and procedures to explain to the child and the child's family the nature of the test procedures he or she has selected, why the tests and procedures are necessary, what the benefits of the procedures are, the degree of risk and discomfort involved, and the possible course to be followed after the test results are obtained.

ACKNOWLEDGMENTS

Contributions have been made to this chapter by Siegfried M. Pueschel, M.D., Ph.D., M.P.H., and Edward A. Sassaman, M.D.

23

Adaptive Equipment

EQUIPMENT FOR CHILDREN
WITH DEVELOPMENTAL DELAYS

Why Is Adaptive Equipment Needed?

Participation in daily routines of family and community activities may be difficult or nearly impossible for children with significant physical disabilities. However, although a child with a disability may have differing abilities from those of his or her playmates or siblings, the child's curiosity and desire to participate may be quite similar. All children can benefit from a variety of experiences, and all children should have opportunities to be involved in enjoyable events.

Children with physical disabilities can delight in their achievements and independence, but achieving success often takes considerably more effort and persistence than most people without a disability realize. Adaptive equipment can help children with disabilities to improve control of body movements, increase self-reliance, and make daily routines easier. It also can improve the quality of the child's life by expanding opportunities for growth, satisfaction, and learning.

What Is Adaptive Equipment?

The term *adaptive equipment* refers to devices that help people to overcome in some way the limitations caused by their disabilities. Another term, which appears in legislation, is *assistive technology and devices.* Here we refer to "adaptive equipment" such as walkers and wheelchairs that support or hold an individual, and to "assistive technology" such as electronics, programs, and computers used to perform tasks (e.g., environmental control, communication). Assistive technology is discussed in other chapters in this book; for example, hearing and vision aids are detailed in Chapter 8, and communication devices in Chapter 9.

Adaptive equipment may be used for a variety of activities, or for just one specific task. Use of adaptive equipment always should be coordinated with other goals for a child's development. This is important because equipment used to improve skills in one area may disrupt the development of other essential skills. For example, if a headrest needed for head control at mealtimes is used throughout the day, it actually could prevent the child from developing good head control.

There are a number of types of adaptive equipment, including the following:

- *Positioning devices* such as bolsters, wedges, and modified types of furniture
- *Mobility aids* such as scooter boards, walkers, and wheelchairs
- *Transportation aids* such as car seats and travel chairs
- *Items to facilitate daily care* such as bath seats, lifts, and adaptive clothing
- *Communication devices* such as scanners, pointers, nonoral communication systems, and artificial voices
- *Individualized seating systems*
- *Modified tools, utensils, and work surfaces*

In addition, many excellent adaptive devices have been made by modifying standard infant accessories (e.g., walkers, high chairs, swings, jumpers, infant seats) with ordinary household materials.

This chapter describes the problems of children who require adaptive equipment and the benefits they derive from using it. Various kinds of devices are discussed, including how, when, and why to use specific types. Guidelines are provided to help you select, measure, fit, and assess the effectiveness of the equipment. Important information about how to use various items properly also is provided.

ADAPTIVE EQUIPMENT FOR BODY CONTROL: POSTURE, MOVEMENT, AND BALANCE

Children with problems that involve the central nervous system (brain and spinal cord) and the musculoskeletal system (bones, muscles, and joints) often need special appliances to improve posture, stability, balance, and movement for many daily activities. Such devices help a child to be more independent. The following sections describe the various problems of children with developmental disabilities and how equipment can be used to compensate for them.

Problems Involving the Nervous System

The central nervous system controls all of our body's movement and posture by sending messages via the nerves to specific parts of the body. Specific areas of the brain are responsible for control of particular body parts. Certain areas of the brain also determine *muscle tone*, which refers to the degree of tension or slack in the muscles, or to the way muscles feel (e.g., hard, stiff, and firm; or soft and floppy). Muscle tone also refers to how muscles react to the brain's signal to work. Muscles that react well move freely in coordination with one another and adjust readily to changes in movement or posture. Brain injury as well as abnormalities in brain structures can produce atypical muscle tone and control, resulting in problems with coordination, posture, and balance. Children with cerebral palsy (motor disease due to injury to the brain), hydrocephalus (increased fluid in the brain), spinal muscular atrophy, brain malformations or masses, or degenerative neurological conditions often have these problems. Sometimes the spinal cord or the nerves themselves are damaged, preventing the brain's messages from reaching the muscles. This is the case in children with spina bifida, those who have had a traumatic injury to the spinal cord, and those who have defects of specific cells of the spinal cord (i.e., anterior horn cell disease), such as polio or spinal muscular atrophy. These children generally have profound weakness or some degree of paralysis.

Problems Involving the Muscles

Muscles contract and relax in various combinations and degrees, enabling us to maintain stability or move individual body parts. Certain diseases attack the muscle cells themselves, causing degeneration, which leads to muscle wasting and weakness. This is what happens in muscular dystrophy, an inherited muscle disease. Another cause of muscle weakness and wasting is atypical formation or composition of the muscle fibers. Muscular problems contribute to poor posture, balance, and coordination, and can lead to atypical or restricted patterns of movement.

Problems Involving Bones and Joints

Atypical bone and joint formations can cause limitations in movements of the joints. Muscles attached to the deformed bones may be held in atypical alignment, which then limits the ability to produce typical joint motion, maintain body symmetry, and balance. This is the case in children with clubfoot, congenital scoliosis, congenital hip dislocation, arthrogryposis (persistent flexure or contracture of a joint), and many other conditions.

Temporary Muscle Problems

Injuries to bone and muscles often result in temporary limitations of movement. For example, casts or traction following a fracture or surgical procedure may be essential for healing, but at the same time will prevent exercise of the muscles or joints. The lack of activity can cause temporary stiffness in joints and a loss of some flexibility and strength in the muscles.

WHEN TO CONSIDER
ADAPTIVE EQUIPMENT FOR YOUR CHILD

If your child has a disability that causes problems in body control and effective, independent movement, you may find that many daily activities are too difficult for him or her to master alone. However, with your support and assistance, you will notice that your child is able to perform more capably. In this situation, you may be able to substitute adaptive equipment for your physical assistance, which allows the child to be more independent. Although you will need a professional's help in selecting, prescribing, and fitting the proper equipment, some general guidelines for determining when your child is ready for adaptive equipment are outlined here.

First, consider your child's age. An appliance should not be used to position children before they have reached the age when most children gain independence in that particular position. This is the time when children are ready to use the new position to explore their environment and develop skills in other areas of functioning. For example, most children begin to prop themselves up and sit alone by 6–8 months of age. Thus, adaptive equipment to help a baby sit alone and play should not be considered before this age. If a child is unable to sit at the appropriate age, a special sitting device can be designed to help him or her develop fine motor skills and achieve more independence in social activities and other daily living skills.

Second, consider the sequence in which a child gains motor control. Infants first develop motor control lying on their backs (i.e., supine), then lying on their stomachs (i.e., prone). From there they progress to rolling, belly-crawling, sitting, propping up on the hands and knees, creeping, standing, and eventually walking. Motor control generally develops gradually from head to toe and from large muscle groups of the trunk, shoulders, and hips to the smaller muscle groups of the hands and feet. Gaining control in basic areas enables a child to begin to practice more advanced skills. For example, children must be able to prop on their forearms before they can start to belly-crawl. Propping up on the forearms allows the baby to practice shifting weight from arm to arm, an essential component of belly crawling. If adaptive devices are needed, make sure the ones chosen encourage development of skills in a typical sequence. Each new skill becomes a building block for the next, and skipping over intermediate skills only makes it more difficult for a child to use the equipment designed for a more complex skill to his or her best advantage.

By providing appropriate equipment as soon as your child seems ready, you may help to prevent bad posture and movement habits. If, for instance, your child has difficulty sitting up properly during daily activities like meals or play, an appropriate chair can be devised to provide the necessary supports. By using the special chair, slumping over or slouching, which can lead to spinal deformity, can be prevented.

ADAPTIVE EQUIPMENT CAN IMPROVE YOUR CHILD'S ATTITUDE AND INTEREST

A child's ability to enjoy activities and succeed at new tasks is also an important consideration in the use of adaptive equipment. Many parents find that the new independence fostered by adaptive equipment helps their children to develop positive attitudes toward themselves. Building a positive attitude can have far-reaching effects on your child's enthusiasm and willingness to persist in challenging situations.

Think about adaptive equipment when your child's development seems to be at a standstill. This may be a clue that the next developmental step is too difficult to attain without additional assistance. Help in the form of a piece of special equipment or an appliance may be all your child needs to continue progressing in the typical sequence of development. Also, think about adaptive equipment when your child shows a strong interest in a particular skill, but is unable to master it, despite repeated tries over an extended period of time. In such situations, you may want to discuss your concerns with the professionals involved in your child's care. They can guide you toward appropriate devices to foster goals within your child's reach.

WHAT KIND OF EQUIPMENT DO YOU NEED?

As mentioned, before selecting equipment it is important to define the goal for which it is to be used. Deciding on a goal is often a natural extension of identifying a particular problem that disrupts performance and new skill acquisition.

As parents of a child with special needs, you are intimately aware of your child's strengths and weaknesses, as well as his or her successes and failures. You probably cannot help but compare your child's development to that of other children such as cousins, nieces, and playmates. By carefully noting what seems to be different about the way your child tries to sit, reach, creep, or accomplish other motor tasks, you may identify areas in which help is needed. For instance, if your child seems to fall over backward in sitting, a firm, high-back chair may be necessary, or if he or she tends to fall forward, a tray or harness may prove more useful.

Not all adaptive equipment must be specially ordered from an appliance shop. Many useful devices can be created with household materials such as rolled towels, cardboard boxes, stuffed animals, and belts or straps temporarily added to the furniture and equipment you already use. Together, you and your child's therapist can fashion equipment with the features best suited for your child's needs.

If equipment must be ordered, it is wise to see whether you can rent or borrow the item. Appliance shops often rent or loan equipment for you to try prior to purchase. In addition, some organizations (e.g., Muscular Dystrophy Association, National Easter Seal Society, United Cerebral Palsy Associations, Spina Bifida Association of America) often have equipment that can be borrowed. If your child receives regular physical therapy, ask the therapist about borrowing a piece of equipment to try at home.

Additional Considerations Before Purchasing Equipment

Before you decide to buy a piece of equipment, you should consider several other factors. First, think about how the piece of equipment will fit into your family's lifestyle. If, for example, you are an active family, you will want to know if the equipment is portable, how much it weighs, how big it is, and how often it should be used. Often, several manufacturers make similar products with slightly different features. You might find one item designed to fold for convenience, while a comparable model is more rigid and requires more space. Or one device may be heavier than others. An on-the-go family will appreciate a light-weight model. Living conditions also can affect your choice of equipment. If you have to contend with stairs, small living space, and narrow doorways, or if you rely on public transportation, you will want to select a device that can be used easily and conveniently.

The length of time your child needs to use the equipment should also be considered. If you anticipate that an item will be necessary for only a brief period, you will not need to worry about making adjustments as your child grows. However, if long-term use is anticipated, the adaptability or availability of accessories to modify the equipment becomes much more important. A short period of use is also more reason to endeavor to rent or borrow the equipment, rather than spending extra money to purchase it.

What is required to keep the equipment clean and in proper working condition also should be investigated. If you are considering an upholstered piece, find out if it is designed to resist staining, odor, and deterioration from exposure to urine or saliva. It also pays to check on the warranty. Ask the salesperson about repairs or a service contract. Find out if replacement parts are readily available.

Consider your child's comfort and safety. Is the upholstery designed to "breathe" on hot days? Is the padding adequate on the back, seat, and armrest? Are cushions needed at bony prominences such as the spine and hip bone, to prevent skin breakdown? Comfort factors become more critical if the equipment is to be used for long periods of time. Check to see if harnesses and seat belts are secure and comfortably placed. Be sure the brakes of a wheelchair are easy to operate. Examine the equipment for any sharp edges, loose pieces, or other safety hazards.

Do not forget to consider how the equipment looks. Your child is likely to experience more acceptance from peers if the equipment looks like ordinary furniture and is attractively painted and nicely finished. Be sure to ask your child if he or she feels comfortable in the equipment and if he or she likes it. Remember, too, your child may want to specify a favorite color.

Lastly, keep in mind that other parents can be an excellent source of information about adaptive equipment. From their experience, they can advise you about what equipment lasts the longest and which devices are easiest to use, to keep clean, and to repair.

Being Realistic—What Else to Expect from Adaptive Equipment

It is important to be realistic about the effect that any piece of adaptive equipment can have on your child and family. Try to understand that expecting too much from adaptive equipment can lead to frustration. Realistic expectations will make the experience more positive for all involved and will increase your chances for success.

A piece of equipment is not likely to be the perfect solution to all of your needs. If the equipment brings some improvement, but does not do everything you expected, consider it a good start. Even with the best possible equipment, adjustments and new accessories often are needed. Do not give up because you do not see immediate improvement. Be sure to allow enough time to give the device a fair trial. Successful use of adaptive equipment generally is the result of small improvements made specifically for individual owners. With modifications, many devices are "custom-fit" to the child. If you find the equipment simply does not meet your needs, try switching to a new device or consider a different approach to using the device.

When problems arise as your child grows and changes, it is important to make necessary modifications one at a time. If you make several adjustments at once, you will not be able to tell which one made the difference. Many ingenious solutions have been discovered by parents approaching problems in an orderly way.

Periodically, as your child grows and gains skills, expect to reassess the need for equipment. Every so often you may want to check how well your child performs a particular skill when the amount of help provided by the equipment is reduced. If performance is unchanged with less support, your child may have outgrown the need for the amount of support given. You then can modify your child's equipment accordingly. If more help than needed is given when the equipment is used, it becomes less effective. That is, it actually will hinder the development of skills. However, your child could need more assistance and accessories as time goes by, as is the case with certain progressive and degenerative diseases.

HOW TO OBTAIN AND FINANCE ADAPTIVE EQUIPMENT

Before reading this section, be aware that procedures for obtaining and financing adaptive equipment differ from state to state. What is funded in one region may not be in another. Because of the complexities of funding, many of the people who prescribe or sell equipment can help to complete, or actually do, much of the necessary paperwork for you. Your child's service coordinator, if available, may be of assistance in this regard. This can be extremely helpful to parents whose children need equipment, but who do not require ongoing medical treatment or physical therapy and, thus, do not have easy access to professionals who can assist them in obtaining equipment.

First, find out whether a doctor's prescription is necessary to obtain the equipment and whether it is covered by your medical insurance. Most orthopaedic appliances (e.g., splints, braces) require a special prescription, as do many large pieces of adaptive equipment or special accessories. Also, sometimes a prescription is needed only if you want an insurance policy or government-subsidized program to cover the cost. Many items are available without this.

If your child's needs are short-term, consider the advantages of making the equipment yourself, borrowing it from a friend, or renting it from an appliance store. Books are available with simple plans for homemade equipment. Your child's therapist may be able to provide you with plans or books, or put you in touch with parents willing to loan equipment. To find out which alternative is best, compare the cost of each with the expected period of use. If you decide to purchase an appliance, ask your child's therapist and physician for advice and assistance. The physical therapist is usually the most knowledgeable about where to obtain equipment in your area. In some instances, therapists may be willing to do the ordering for you, as they are familiar with the process and the paperwork involved. If you do not have regular contact with a therapist, try consulting one at your child's school or clinic.

Equipment always can be obtained through local surgical supply companies, but the brands and models they carry may vary markedly. To know what is available, it is best to check ahead of time. Some of these companies will send a representative to your home, if you wish, to discuss the product and ordering as well as to take care of any necessary details such as measuring or fitting. These companies usually deliver the equipment you purchase and make any adjustments your child needs. The representative also can teach you about proper use and maintenance of the equipment.

Some items can be ordered directly from the manufacturer. Although you may pay some additional shipping and handling charges when ordering directly, the initial cost of the equipment may be a bit lower. Vendors or retailers may need to charge somewhat higher prices to cover their costs in shipping, as well as the cost of the extra services they provide. It may be worthwhile to compare prices from the manufacturer with those of several vendors, just as you would comparison shop for any major purchase. Remember that when you order directly from a manufacturer, you must know the size, model, and accessories you need. You also will have to make any adjustments on your own, or make arrangements for a therapist to see your child for a fitting.

When the equipment is ordered, ask how long it will take to be delivered. Many vendors keep popular items in stock and can deliver them promptly. Frequently, it is necessary to wait for individualized items, as they are purchased by special order only. Vendors often require prior consent from your insurance carrier or other payment source before they will process your order, and this can cause more delay in delivery.

Ordering accessories that you anticipate your child will need later sometimes can lower the cost, and will ensure that you have everything you need to provide the proper help. Companies may offer options packages at a discount, similar to those for new cars. Also, insurance companies often cover the cost of accessories at the time of the original purchase, if detailed on the prescription, but may refuse to pay for items ordered separately. Call your insurance representative if you have any questions. The same procedures also are used for government assistance programs such as Supplemental Security Income (SSI), Title XIX Waiver, the Medicaid program, and others. If you are unsure about the necessity or worth of some equipment options, it probably is better to order only what you need. That way, you will not be burdened with unnecessary trappings.

Whenever possible, use your medical insurance to cover the costs of your child's appliances. Insurance policies vary considerably. If your policy has Major Medical coverage (or comparable provisions), it may cover as much as 80% of the cost of equipment. You will be responsible for the standard deductible and the balance that is not covered by your policy. To avoid any unpleasant surprises, check with your insurance carrier for details. You may find that your insurance company stipulates a limit on the dollar amount of purchases for what they refer to as "durable medical equipment" in a given period of time.

Governmental assistance programs are another source of help for obtaining equipment. The federal Supplemental Security Income (SSI) program sponsors a program for children with disabilities, which may cover the costs of such items. There are also special waivers, and the federal Medicaid program, in which states may choose to participate, makes certain children eligible for many services. Some states have their own programs for persons with developmental disabilities as well. All of these programs have their own eligibility requirements and limitations. Sometimes there is a limit to the amount of assistance you can receive during a specified time. Ask the social worker at your child's clinic or school, or staff at the local Medicaid office, for specific details about eligibility and the application process.

Support groups, such as the Spina Bifida Association of America, The Arc (formerly the Association for Retarded Citizens of the United States), Muscular Dystrophy Association, United Cerebral Palsy Associations, or National Easter Seal Society, are other sources to investigate. Although many do not fund individual equipment requests, they may provide equipment on loan, as mentioned previously.

Insurance companies sometimes cover the cost of equipment ordinarily not covered by the policy if it is purchased and provided as part of a hospitalization. If your doctors suggest equipment while your child is in the hospital, try to have it delivered, fitted, and checked during the hospital stay. In this type of arrangement, the hospital purchases the equipment and then bills you for it as part of the total cost of the hospitalization.

METHODS TO HELP
COMPENSATE FOR VARIOUS DISABILITIES

You probably can think of many daily activities that are easier to do in one position than in another. For example, lifting a heavy object is easier if your feet are spread apart than if they are close together. Writing is easier when your arm is supported on a table rather than held in the air. The relationship of body parts to one another and their position in space clearly affects our skill and success at a specific task.

When we start to perform a familiar task, most of us assume a comfortable position without much thought or effort. However, as new skills are learned, many positions may be tried before the ones that make the jobs easier are found. Once effective positions are established, we use them quite naturally. Unlike a person without a disability, a child with a disability may not be able to control his or her body well enough to get into a good position for many activities. As a result, the child's ability to perform many tasks may be diminished. Placing a child with a disability in a proper position and providing appropriate equipment may improve his or her ability to succeed at specific tasks. If, for example, your child cannot hold his or her head and body in balance, equipment can provide the support and proper body alignment to allow the child to do things that would otherwise be impossible. Equipment also can be used to reposition a child in such a way that weak muscles are assisted or stronger ones are allowed to do more of the work.

Some children develop deformities because they cannot change positions easily. Special appliances can help children vary their position periodically and prevent or delay such problems. Use of these devices also may diminish the need for additional procedures such as splinting, casting, traction, or even surgery.

There are other benefits as well. Positioning equipment can allow children with a disability to bear weight on their limbs at appropriate ages. Weight bearing is important for bone structure and formation. As children grow, bones change shape and strengthen in response to the weight they support and the pull of the muscles attached to them.

The best positioning devices provide just enough assistance for a child to improve performance, while also encouraging practice in a problem area. For example, a head support should maintain head control loosely, allowing the child to move and adjust his or her head position within a narrow range. The loose fit gives a child the opportunity to improve head control while providing assistance at the same time. A tight-fitting head control device would not allow a child to strengthen the muscles supporting the head. All types of adaptive equipment for positioning and support should be used as directed by your child's pediatrician, orthopaedist, therapist, or other specialist.

GOOD POSITIONING DOES NOT ALWAYS
REQUIRE COMMERCIALLY MADE ADAPTIVE EQUIPMENT

Although the main focus of this chapter is on adaptive equipment, you should be aware that some of the benefits of positioning discussed here do not require specialized devices. There are numerous ways parents and family members can promote proper alignment and positioning when carrying a child, placing him or her in a chair or on the floor to play, or helping him or her to stand and take steps. Your child's therapist can show you the best ways to work with your child. If your child does not need adaptive equipment but does need ongoing help in achieving proper positions, then you might want to establish a working relationship or partnership with the therapist. That way, you can review your child's positioning needs and keep informed about the best ways to provide assistance.

Some relatively simple positional aids have a range of practical applications. Sandbags can be used to support any body part in a correct position. Wedges can help to elevate the head and shoulders. When the child lies on his or her stomach, a wedge or bolster can be used to prop the child on forearms for play. Rolled towels, fuzzy paint rollers, or plastic soda bottles rolled in a towel can be easily transformed into bolsters. An inflatable swim ring can be placed around a child's chest for the same purpose. Therapy rolls of varying sizes also can be purchased commercially.

An adjustable prone board on which a child lies can be used in place of a wedge for propping on the hands or forearms, as shown in Figure 1. Prone boards can be purchased or improvised from cardboard boxes or boards. Commercially available ones have wings at armpit height to prevent the arms from retracting or drawing back out of a good weight-bearing position.

A side-lyer can provide symmetrical support. The side-lying position promotes the child's use of two hands together in front of his or her body. Side-lyers are available commercially, but a sturdy box with a belt for safety also can be used. A small pillow should be placed under the head and between the legs to ensure symmetry. Be sure to alternate sides, unless your child has a persistent right or left asymmetry.

A hammock can help a child who usually keeps his or her body stiff and extended to get into a curled, relaxed position while lying on the back. A hammock can be made easily from a crib blanket gathered and tied at the ends and hung low across a crib or playpen.

Sitting

For sitting, an infant seat can be padded to provide appropriate support for a small child. Sandbags, towel rolls, or paint rollers placed at the sides can be used to make a snug fit. Placed under the knees, they prevent the child from sliding forward and out of the seat.

Bean-bag chairs are sometimes helpful if your child does not require a lot of extra support. For sitting on the floor, swim rings or rubber tubes can be inflated and placed around the child's trunk for

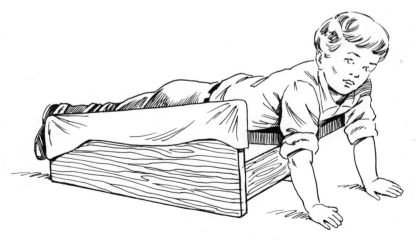

Figure 1. An adjustable prone board allows the child to be positioned on his or her abdomen.

support. You can use one or several of these devices, depending on how much trunk support is needed.

Corner seats are commercially available, or can be made from a sturdy cardboard box. A corner seat may have high sides to support your child's head and trunk, or low sides to control just the lower trunk. The sides of a corner seat should be kept at shoulder height if the child has difficulty keeping the arms forward to reach and manipulate toys. Corner seats may be placed on the floor or elevated. Elevated corner seats will allow the child to sit with feet positioned flat on the floor in order to provide balance. Additional supports may be needed to help keep the legs and feet in proper alignment. A harness or belt will prevent your child from falling forward, and a padded dowel between the thighs will prevent him or her from sliding forward.

For children who have some head and trunk control, booster seats can be used as children begin to use their legs more actively in support. Initially, a booster seat should be used with a small table, or it can be placed in a cardboard box to keep the child's feet from sliding forward. If the sides of the box are high enough, the child can hold on with his or her hands at a comfortable level.

A wide variety of toddler chairs can be adapted to the needs of your child. Many commercially available seats with a variety of attachments can improve a child's ability to sit. These chairs generally offer adjustable backs, side support for the body, adjustable and removable headrests, and other attachments that can properly position both the hips and legs. Firm footrests, which can be adjusted for height and angle, as well as straps for keeping the feet in the proper position, are standard accessories. Trays are usually available for most models.

With the advice and guidance of your child's therapist, you also can adapt a sturdy wooden chair to fit your child's needs. A chair with armrests is best. For extra support, a board can be added in the back, extending the chair's height. Placing the entire chair inside a three-sided cardboard box can help keep a child's arms forward. Improvise a harness or seat belt if you need it, and use a tray or table for support in front. Bathtub appliqués, used to prevent slipping in the bathtub, also can be applied to a chair to prevent sliding forward in the seat. Be sure to provide a firm footrest attached to the chair; or a box of appropriate height can be used for the same purpose. Makeshift straps will help steady the feet in good position.

Stools and bed trays can be used as play trays for corner seats. Although commercial models are often available, you can easily make a tray from a sturdy cardboard box by cutting the sides to the child's chest height and carving a semicircular notch in the top to fit the child's chest. If your child has little trunk control, such a tray should be at chest height. If your child has partial control, you can place the tray at waist height. Foam pipe insulation (tubes) can provide padding along the edge.

Crawling and Standing

Some equipment is also available to help children bear weight on all four limbs when they are unable to balance on their hands and knees alone. Such devices look like small hammocks. They have a sling for the child's trunk, which is attached to a frame by straps or strings. This helps the child to prop on both arms and legs without fear of falling. Some frames are mounted on casters, so that children can experiment with creeping on their hands and knees.

Standers are used for children who are unable to bear weight on their legs unless fully supported. Some are designed to permit standing at an angle, not in a fully upright position. By standing the child at an angle, the body weight is distributed throughout lower limbs, trunk, and arms, instead of resting only on the feet. Such controlled weight bearing in supine standers can help promote bone growth and typical development of the hip sockets in young children. Standers come with a variety of accessories and adaptations, which allow them to be used in many different ways. Some are designed to lean forward at a table, counter, or other surface and are called *prone standers*. Others are freestanding or fixed to a stable base and may support the child vertically. There are many varieties of prone standers and a number of accessories. You may want to shop around to find the one that best meets your child's needs.

Standing tables and standing boxes are used for children who can bear their total body weight on their feet but are unable to stand independently. The child is supported loosely by a box with a tray attached as a play surface. The entire unit is attached to a stable base to prevent tipping. Standing tables provide an opportunity for the child to practice standing balance without fear of falling.

MEASURING YOUR CHILD FOR ADAPTIVE EQUIPMENT

Most large pieces of equipment are available in a variety of sizes and models and are designed to fit your child's size and specific needs. If you plan to use the equipment for a long time, you should consider your child's height, weight, and rate of growth. In addition, you should measure your living space, including doorways, halls, and counter heights, to determine the best size and model for your child. You may want to obtain assistance from a local adaptive equipment clinic so your child's therapist can have the additional resources of other knowledgeable clinicians.

Accurate measurements and careful planning also are essential when you make equipment at home. In addition, your child's therapist may be able to provide plans and helpful hints for construction.

ORTHOPAEDIC APPLIANCES

Orthopaedic appliances make up a special category of adaptive equipment, including prescription items such as traction, casts, splints, braces, shoe corrections, and specialized seating and standing devices. Such appliances are used to improve body position, posture, and symmetry. They also can help to maintain good range of motion in the joints as well as reduce, halt, or reverse various deformities. In addition, orthopaedic appliances can help to correct and maintain joint mobility, with the ultimate goal of avoiding more invasive surgical procedures.

Orthopaedic appliances frequently are used in conjunction with regular home exercises or direct physical therapy. Children who wear orthopaedic devices for prolonged periods need ample time out of the appliances to experience other positions and experiment with independent movements. No one position is appropriate or beneficial all of the time. Tightness can develop if muscles are maintained in the same position for too long, which in turn can lead to other limitations of movement. However, in some cases the benefits of care involving extended use of appliances are considered greater than the risk of new limitations. This is generally true in severe or rapidly progressing problems. In such cases, a therapist or orthopaedic surgeon is faced with a difficult decision of choosing the lesser of the two evils.

Types of Orthopaedic Equipment and Appliances

Traction   Traction is one method used to correct atypical positioning of the joints. Joints are molded by two separate forces: 1) the position of the bones, and 2) the appropriate tension or muscle pull around the joint. Atypical positioning or muscle function can have a lasting effect with respect to how a joint is shaped and how it moves. Traction also is used after an injury or surgery to maintain correct positioning of bone segments for healing.

Traction usually is introduced in the hospital, where it can be monitored closely. If long-term treatment is necessary, traction easily can be transferred to the home. Equipment can be rented from a medical supply company and monitored by a local public health nurse. Traction equipment generally will include a bed frame, pulleys, and weights, as well as cuffs or belts to attach weights at specific angles.

Casts Casts are used to position and stabilize joints or bones after an injury or operation. Usually, they are made of plaster strips that are soaked and wrapped around a body part. Casts most often are applied for 4–6 weeks following muscle surgery and for 6–8 weeks following bone surgery or fracture. Fiberglass casts may be applied over plaster for strength. In addition, there are color and theme casts available for young children.

Splints Splints generally are used for a limited period of time to maintain a stable or functional position of the joints. Typically, they are molded to fit snugly. Some splints are available in standard sizes. However, to ensure a proper fit and to maximize functioning, splints should be fabricated by a trained therapist following a thorough evaluation of your child's needs and abilities. Many different types of materials are available.

Night splints are used primarily for preventing contractures (limited joint movements), maintaining a good range of motion, and stretching of tight muscles. For example, children with very tight inner thigh muscles might be treated with a splint that stretches the muscles and maintains a desirable range of hip mobility. Without treatment, such children would have difficulty separating their legs adequately for typical posture, movements, and hygiene. Such treatment may have the added benefit of preventing hip dislocations.

Some splints improve the function of specific body parts by providing stability and a good position or by counteracting increased muscle tone. A child with spastic cerebral palsy, for example, may use what is called a hip abduction splint in a sitting position to improve independent balance and control. Because the splint keeps the legs separated, it gives the child a broadened base of support for balance and simultaneous control of increased muscle tone.

Splints usually are prescribed by an orthopaedist or physiatrist and are fitted and fashioned by an occupational therapist, physical therapist, or orthotist. If your child needs a splint, you will be given instructions regarding its use and the indicators of possible problems.

Braces Braces and splints perform similar functions. Like splints, braces help to maintain passive range of motion and provide proper joint alignment. However, braces also are used to increase control of body parts while making specific movements easier. In other words, braces align and support particular joints, so other joints can be used in a more appropriate way. For example, a body jacket is a brace that provides the trunk with support, and it can be used to counteract an atypical spinal curvature. When in use, it gives a child enough additional control in sitting to permit more success in daily routines and play. Also head control can be improved dramatically through the use of a body jacket. Similarly, ankle braces provide enough stability for a child to stand and walk in a more typical fashion.

Static splints and braces maintain one position in a part of the body without stopping or actively helping movement in another. *Dynamic* splints and braces position certain joints in the best possible way and also actively assist other body parts in performing useful movements. Dynamic devices usually consist of a stable portion, similar to static splints, with attachments to free-moving body parts that produce or make a specific motion easier. These attachments usually incorporate string or elastic bands, which act as substitute muscles. For example, a dynamic splint to improve voluntary grasp release might consist of a static portion to hold the wrist in one position, plus finger slings attached to elastic bands.

Semidynamic splints are made without moving parts but they position the hand and wrist to allow the extremity to optimize its own movement. An example of this type of splint is a thumb loop. This is designed specifically to decrease tone and put the hand in a more functional position.

Braces, or *orthoses* as they are sometimes called, usually are named for the joints they align and support. An *a*nkle-*f*oot *o*rthosis, referred to as an *AFO*, controls the position of the ankle. A *KAFO* is a *k*nee-*a*nkle-*f*oot *o*rthosis, and controls both the knee and ankle position relative to one another. A *TLSO*, or body jacket, is a *t*horaco-*l*umbo-sacral *o*rthosis, which provides control of the entire spine from chest to pelvis, and an *LSO*, or *l*umbo-sacral *o*rthosis, controls the lower spine. Small, in-the-shoe braces that support the ankle and foot bones during weight-bearing are called *UCBs*. UCB does not stand for particular body parts, but for the university where the braces were first developed, the University of California at Berkeley. An *RGO*, or *r*eciprocal *g*ait *o*rthosis, allows a child with paraplegia (paralysis of the legs) to move his or her legs one at a time, providing that certain muscles are working.

Ankle-Foot Orthoses (AFO)   Ankle-foot orthoses commonly are used to control conditions such as flat arches, tight heelcords, and atypical rolling and turning of the ankle and heel in a standing position. The position of the ankle is controlled by the shell of the brace. Ankle-foot orthoses also can control the amount of knee extension by holding the ankle and foot in an approximate 90-degree angle (Figure 2).

Knee-Ankle-Foot Orthoses (KAFO)   A knee-ankle-foot orthosis controls the alignment of the knee and ankle for proper weight-bearing. It also can prevent the knee from going back too far. In addition, knee-ankle-foot orthoses prevent or limit lateral deformities of the knee, such as knock knees (i.e., genu valgum) and bowlegs (i.e., genu varum). Some knee braces are molded plastic shells, whereas other types are structured from plastic or leather cuffs attached to rigid uprights, which are metal struts that provide a structural frame for the brace components. Metal braces are somewhat heavier than plastic ones, but they provide more stability. When metal uprights are used, they frequently include a locking mechanism at the knee, which allows a locked fully extended knee position for standing and an unlocked bent position for sitting, as noted in Figure 3.

Hips-Knee-Ankle-Foot Orthoses (HKAFO) and Pelvic Bands   Some children will require bracing from their hips to their ankles. These braces are usually constructed with cuffs and uprights. They also provide locks that allow full extension or flexing at the hip and knee to accommodate standing and sitting. Waist or

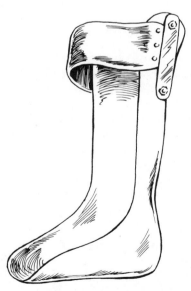

Figure 2.   A commonly used ankle-foot orthosis (AFO) controls the position of the ankle. It is made out of plastic material that should fit well in an everyday shoe.

Figure 3. A knee-ankle-foot orthosis (KAFO) with a locking device at the knee controls alignment of the knee and ankle for proper weight bearing.

pelvic bands are commonly used with bilateral long-legged braces, for both symmetry and control.

Cables Some braces have cables that control the amount of inward or outward rotation of the leg or foot. Most often, they are used to counteract intoeing, which is inward positioning of the feet that may cause a child to trip while walking. Cables usually are attached to ankle-foot orthoses and to a waist belt. Twisting the cables in the direction opposite to the way the child's foot turns will help to bring the foot into a more neutral alignment.

Standing Frames and Parapodiums Children who require full support of the lower trunk and the legs may use standing frames or parapodiums. Standing frames are long-legged braces attached in a rigid position to a broad and stable base. This eliminates the need to balance independently while standing and, therefore, frees the child's hands for all types of activities. Parapodiums are similar to long-legged braces attached to a stable base, but parapodiums have adjustable hip and knee joints for standing and sitting. A parapodium can be worn for longer periods of time, because the child's position can be varied without removing the equipment.

Special Shoes   Children with very mild deformities of the foot and ankle often can be treated with simple shoe corrections or with sturdy, specially fashioned footwear. Some children with flat arches or a tendency to walk on the inside of the feet need arch supports or scaphoid pads, commonly called *cookies*. They are placed inside the shoes and lift the arches, thereby improving the position of the ankles. Other shoe corrections include both inner and outer heel and sole wedges. Outer wedges tip the foot and ankle inward. Inner wedges tip the foot and ankle outward.

If a child has one leg that is longer than the other, a lift usually is placed under the shorter leg to even the leg lengths. By using a lift, a symmetric position of the hips, trunk, and shoulders can be maintained and the development of major deformities, such as scoliosis or sideward curvature of the spine, can be prevented.

Thoraco-Lumbo-Sacral Orthoses (TLSO) and Lumbo-Sacral Orthoses (LSO)   Thoraco-*l*umbo-sacral *o*rthoses (TLSO) and *l*umbo-sacral *o*rthoses (LSO) counteract spinal deformities, such as scoliosis, excessive kyphosis (a rounded back), and increased lordosis (called *swayback*). These braces usually are made from a molded plastic shell, which supports the child's spine in a straightened position, as seen in Figure 4. Milwaukee-style braces, which also are used to treat scoliosis, actually are thoraco-lumbo-sacral orthoses with rigid metal struts that support a neck ring and chin pad to apply slight distraction to the spine. A physician also may prescribe a fabric corset to control and support the trunk. In addition, collars may be used to enhance head control, visual monitoring, and eye–hand skills through increased support of the neck.

Total Support Systems   Children with virtually no muscle control may require specialized total support systems or full body orthoses. These braces enable a child without muscle control to sit and participate in certain daily routines or educational activities. Total support systems must be molded carefully in a precise position and lined with foam to ensure a comfortable fit and to minimize the risk of pressure sores. They are most commonly fitted into wheelchairs.

Proper Fitting and Prescription of Braces

Although braces are individualized for a proper fit, with frequent use the equipment may loosen or stretch and require adjustments.

Figure 4. A molded plastic shell-type body jacket, which supports the child's spine in a straightened position.

Revision also will be needed as your child grows. A brace must fit in order to work properly. Braces usually are measured, fitted, and fashioned by a professional orthotist who works from a prescription written by an orthopaedist or physiatrist. Occasionally, several fittings may be necessary before the final product is ready for use.

When your child needs a brace, make sure you are taught how to apply it correctly, when and how to use it, and how to check for comfort.

Braces are designed to stabilize and align joints. Although this is essential for treatment, it also limits the natural movement of the joint, which is necessary for the development and use of typical balance reactions. Limiting the functional ranges of some joints may cause a child to compensate by developing an atypical posture or movement pattern in other joints. The likelihood of such secondary problems developing can be lessened by careful fitting, frequent observation, and readjustment if needed. You may expect some problems, yet they should not outweigh the gains achieved by the bracing. Review the advantages and disadvantages as you see them with your child's orthopaedist, therapist, and orthotist when deciding whether to change the treatment.

PROSTHESES OR ARTIFICIAL BODY PARTS

Children born with certain defects of the body or limbs may need prosthetic devices, or artificial body parts. Malformations of the limbs can include missing parts, shortened segments, or atypically aligned and formed segments. Some children require a prosthesis because of a trauma or tumor necessitating amputation.

Prostheses for the lower limbs are designed to allow the child with disabilities to stand and walk. They may replace a portion of the foot, the whole foot, foot and ankle, lower leg or entire leg, and thigh or hip. Prostheses for the upper limbs are designed to allow the child to perform routine functional activities such as feeding, dressing, writing, playing, reaching, grasping, and manipulating objects. An entire arm or any part of the arm can be fitted with a prosthesis.

All prostheses are helpful in restoring an even distribution of body weight, which improves symmetry in function and helps with balance. They also can improve appearance, which in turn may help a child develop a positive self-image and promote acceptance by peers in social situations. The cosmetic value of a prosthesis should not be underestimated.

Prostheses are highly individualized and are specially made and fitted by a trained prosthetist, according to a doctor's prescription. Artificial limbs usually are constructed to resemble the body parts they replace and to match the corresponding limbs (Figure 5). They may have movable parts and joints, which can be operated by gravitational pull, pulleys and cables, hydraulic systems, or electrical stimulation in which batteries stimulate the child's nerves. The working ends of an upper limb prosthesis may look like a real hand or may be more like a simple tool such as a claw or clamp.

Prostheses are held in place by the fit of the socket or by a special harness or both. Total contact sockets fit the child's stumps snugly. Some have a suction type of fit, which further increases stability. The prosthesis must be stable if it is to be reliable for daily use.

When a good fit is achieved and the child has learned to use the prosthesis, more complex devices can be added. Simple tools that have a single motion, such as open and close, may give way to

Figure 5.   An example of a simple lower limb prosthesis.

more complex devices offering a wider range of motion and positions that will improve control and function.

MOBILITY AIDS

Children who cannot pivot, crawl, creep, or walk often benefit from equipment that helps them to move about independently and explore their environment. Most frequently, children who need mobility aids have disabilities that affect their central nervous system and musculoskeletal system. A child with poor muscle tone will have difficulties maintaining a stable position, an essential ingredient in achieving purposeful movement. However, increased muscle tone often restricts joint motion and prevents a child from moving about freely. A child with flaccid or weak muscles may not be able to overcome gravity to move about. Other children may have bony deformities that prevent the usual movement patterns. Children with unsteadiness or poor balance, also called *ataxia*, may need the help of appropriate devices in order to move about. Another group of children will require mobility aids on a temporary basis—for example, when wearing casts following an injury or surgery.

In general, mobility aids offer support to improve posture as they make moving around easier. Movement can be made easier when support is increased by allowing children to move their extremities with more freedom. Many mobility aids also improve balance and stability by providing a wider base of support for movement, thus enabling the child to overcome gravity more efficiently.

Types of Mobility Aids

Mobility aids include hammock swings, ramps, wedges, lazy Susans, scooter boards, crawlers, creepers, handcarts, wheelchairs, adapted ride-on toys, and other ambulation aids. Most mobility aids are prescription items that are recommended by your child's physician or therapist. They often need to be adjusted to the child's size and disability.

Hammock swings (Figure 6) and rocker seats can be used to treat children who have difficulty tolerating movement in space. They are designed to provide slow, controlled motion. Through experience, the child begins to predict the changes in position and learns to tolerate movement in space. These devices can be activated by an adult or can be brought into motion by movements children make on their own.

Ramps and wedges can be used to encourage rolling or belly-crawling. Placing a child on the elevated side of the ramp or wedge will permit gravity to assist him or her to slide downward.

A *lazy Susan* allows the child to pivot on his or her stomach with ease. The child is placed on the lazy Susan so the body is supported fully and the hands are free to push against the floor. With the lazy Susan, the effects of friction are minimized. Thus, even slight pushes by the child will cause it to turn in a circle.

Scooter boards (Figure 7) can help a child learn to belly-crawl or creep on all fours. These devices eliminate the need for very coordinated movement of the legs because the body is fully supported by the board.

Crawlers and *creepers*, like scooter boards, provide support for the child in prone by slight lift off the floor enabling the arms and legs to propel the child in a prone position most closely resembling hands-and-knees crawling or creeping.

Figure 6.   This variation of a hammock swing allows controlled movements in space.

Handcarts provide the opportunity to experience propulsion in a seated position by grasping the wheels on either side and moving them as one would move a wheelchair. A handcart is frequently a child's first wheelchair-like experience.

Wheelchairs often are introduced at an early age for children who most likely will not become community ambulators (able to walk

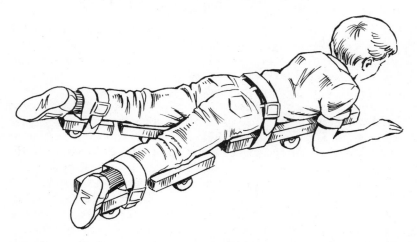

Figure 7.   A scooter board can help a child who is unable to crawl or to creep explore the environment.

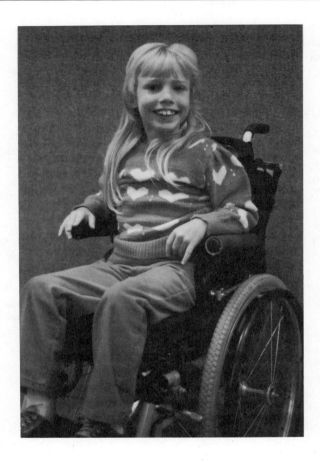

most of the time in most places). Some children will use wheelchairs exclusively, whereas others may need them only in specific locations or when long distances must be covered.

Wheelchairs are prescribed by a physician, often with a therapist's assistance. They vary considerably in size, strength, durability, and weight. Some are more adaptable than others and have more accessories. Some permit a greater number of modifications or are easier to fold. Your child's size, strength, and other musculoskeletal factors will need to be taken into consideration when a wheelchair is selected.

Electric wheelchairs are powered by batteries and can be outfitted with a variety of control systems. For example, wheelchairs have been designed to be operated by hand, foot, mouth, chin, or breath control. They may be adapted to any movement a child can control consistently.

Ride-on toys also can be used to help a child move about in a seated position. Most ride-on toys will need to be adapted to provide more support for the trunk, with a firm, flat seat or high backrest.

AMBULATION AIDS

Ambulation aids are used to help children walk, and include parallel bars, walkers, crutches, canes, and other movable supports. Each device provides a different amount of support. As with other types of equipment, a child should use the aid that provides just the right amount of support. Too much support may interfere with his or her progress.

Parallel bars are used by children who need stable support for their arms in order to move their legs forward. Parallel bars provide a great deal of support. Frequently, they are used as a child begins to learn to walk. As the child gains control of his or her movements, the use of parallel bars is phased out and other aids are introduced.

Walkers are used when a child can balance independently in a standing position for brief periods of time. When using a walker, a child stands alone momentarily as he or she moves the walker forward, either by pushing or lifting and placing it. Walkers come with or without wheels. Walkers with wheels may be more difficult to control, as the child has to prevent them from rolling too fast or too far in front of him or her.

Crutches can be used by children who have good control of their trunk and upper extremities and some independent standing for balance. Using crutches, a child can achieve a more typical and efficient walking pattern than with either a walker or parallel bars. This is because the child moves each limb independently in an alternating, reciprocal pattern. Different types of crutches are available to suit individual needs. Some provide axillary support as well as handgrips. This type of crutch must be well padded at the top to prevent pressure on the nerves that run through the armpit to the muscles of the arm. Other types of crutches provide forearm support and are used by children who have good balance and shoulder control (Figure 8). Platform crutches are used by children who can bear weight on their forearms but not on their hands (Figure 9).

Canes are primarily for balance rather than support. They are available with a single tip or four prongs at the end (the latter called a *quad cane*) to increase stability. Some children use two canes instead of crutches.

Figure 8.   A crutch with forearm support.

Most children who require continued use of ambulation aids wear some type of brace or corrective footwear. Also, following orthopaedic surgery, or while a fracture heals, a child temporarily may need to use crutches, canes, or a walker.

Ambulation aids must be adjusted carefully to the child's height and body position to ensure correct posture and optimal support. Any skeletal problems must be taken into consideration when fitting the equipment. Length should be checked regularly, particularly during periods of rapid growth.

ADAPTIVE EQUIPMENT FOR FINE MOTOR CONTROL

Children who need adaptive equipment for general posture control usually benefit from fine motor adaptations. Fine motor adaptive equipment generally is designed to improve a child's independence

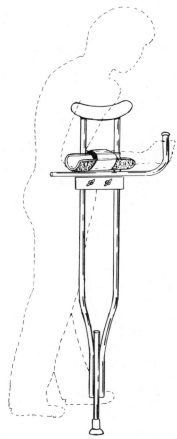

Figure 9.   A platform crutch for children who cannot bear weight on their hands.

in performing specific tasks (e.g., feeding, dressing, other activities of daily living). Typically, fine motor equipment provides stability and positioning for the head, upper trunk, or upper extremities. Usually the arms are supported with the hands in front of the body, so the child can see his or her hands as they are being used. This is important for the development of eye–hand coordination and in all activities involving reaching, grasping, and releasing objects, as well as in motor planning.

Most fine motor appliances aid in learning and enjoyment by increasing opportunities to improve skills using toys, books, tools, and household items. Such equipment also may enable children to become more responsible for their own daily care and grooming.

Equipment to Position Arms and Head

Accessories are available for many seats and standers that can position the head and arms effectively for improved fine motor control. Chair accessories such as head supports, harnesses, lateral trunk supports, and trays help to keep your child's head, upper body, and arms well supported in a symmetrical posture. Trays keep the arms steady so attention can be focused on using the hands. Elbow blocks can be mounted on armrests or trays to keep the arms forward to bear weight in a proper position and to keep the hands together near midline. Dowels can be mounted on trays to enhance and control the arms and shoulders. When the child grasps a stable object such as a dowel with one hand, the child's shoulders are steadied, and as a result the opposite arm can perform with greater control. Dowels and elbow blocks keep the elbow positioned in front of the shoulder for proper weight bearing, and dowels keep the forearm in a midposition, which is essential for many manipulative tasks.

Splints and braces are sometimes worn on the arms and hands to improve their position for a variety of activities. They are used to position and stabilize the shoulders, elbows, or forearms in such a way that wrists, hands, fingers, and thumbs can be used with greater control. Some splints and braces keep the elbows straight to facilitate weight bearing on the hands. Other splints and braces attempt to align the forearm and wrist in a neutral position, which enables the hand to hold a pencil or other utensil. This type of equipment must be small and comfortable to allow some movement of the arm.

Straps can be used to hold the forearms steady against a surface for children who cannot control movements and keep their hands on desired objects. With random motions reduced or eliminated, a child is more apt to be successful in reaching, holding, and manipulating items that are placed nearby. Straps can be used by themselves or in conjunction with other positioning devices.

Because all of these devices restrict motion in some areas by fixing the extremity in a particular position, they should be used sparingly—only when needed for a specific activity. Prolonged use of any positioning device may be uncomfortable, cause frustration, and limit the development of other equally important skills.

Modifying Objects for Grasping

At times, you can improve your child's ability to hold and manipulate toys, utensils, tools, clothing, and other things by altering the objects. Simple modifications often can make a big difference. For example, adding handles to toys and household items such as pull toys, toothbrushes, combs, and books can enable a child with poor grasp to hold and use the items more efficiently. Another way to adapt materials is to increase the length or width of an object. This makes it easier to hold on to it. Thickening the handle of a spoon or toothbrush by wrapping it with tape or adding rubber can make it large enough to be grasped easily. Gluing a clothespin to a light switch can help a child to operate the switch on his or her own. Large tabs can be attached to pages in a book to make it easier to turn pages.

Adding texture to an object or surface can make grasping easier and improve the stability of objects during manipulation. Try putting tub appliqués on smooth surfaces for stability. Sandpaper or double-backed tape can be added to blocks, utensils, and other objects for texture. Use your imagination to create ways to make objects safer and easier to handle. For writing, select implements that need minimal pressure and accuracy in orienting the tip, such as Magic Markers and jumbo crayons. Even removing the paper from crayons can make writing easier, as less precision will be needed in orienting the crayons to the paper.

ADAPTING SWITCHES FOR PEOPLE WITH SEVERE DISABILITIES

Electrical and battery-operated household items and toys such as lights and radios can be adapted for people with severe physical disabilities by wiring a simple switch into the electrical circuit. Some switches are sensitive to the slightest pressure on a large surface. Others are sensitive to either the light or shadow cast upon a surface. Still others such as mercury switches are sensitive to the slightest movement of almost any body part. Certain switches can be operated by sucking or blowing and need very little control of the muscles of the head, neck, and the four extremities. Some children with adequate head control, but poor control of their body and extremities, can be fitted with head sticks and pointers to turn pages, operate simple controls, or point to symbols on a communication board.

EQUIPMENT TO IMPROVE THE LINE OF SIGHT

Many children have difficulty positioning their head and eyes in such a way that they can see their hands as they manipulate objects. Methods to help a child visually attend to a fine motor activity can be devised easily. Strategically placed mirrors, for example, will enable children who have difficulty positioning their head to see their hands at work. Children who have limited range of motion of the arms and head benefit the most from mirrors.

Easels, lap boards, and felt boards can be adjusted to the proper height and angle for easy viewing or manipulation of materials. Book rests also can be adjusted to position pictures and books at the correct level for the child. Some materials can be suspended to achieve a good position, using household items like dowels, hooks, coat hangers, and strings.

The height of chairs and tables or other work surfaces can be adjusted to keep hands and objects in the line of sight. Extenders for table legs often are available, as are adjustable seats and trays for many seating systems.

CLOTHING MODIFICATIONS

Clothing fasteners can be modified for ease of operation by making simple changes such as adding loops or large handles to zippers or replacing zippers and buttons with Velcro closures. Using large buttons and snaps in place of the small ones usually found on children's clothing is also helpful. Selecting clothing with large or loosely elasticized openings, rather than snaps or buttons, can make dressing easier. For older children, the tips of laces on shoes or clothing can be enlarged to facilitate handling, and, if possible, large eyelets can be substituted for small ones. Many companies now offer stylish clothing specially adapted for persons with disabilities.

MEALTIMES

Specialized seats to support a child's head and body in the right position are useful at mealtimes. These items usually are covered with a stain-resistant, water-repellent material for easy cleaning. Feeding seats are designed to keep the child's head in midline with the chin, tucked slightly to encourage proper movements of lips, tongue, and jaw. Most standard high chairs provide inadequate support for the child with poor postural control.

Changing the angle and orientation of the utensils can improve efficiency. Spoons and forks are available with bent handles for children who have trouble turning and rotating their wrist to put them into their mouth. Utensils with swivel handles are available for children who have difficulty keeping them level while bringing food to the mouth (Figure 10). Many different types of bottles and nipples

Figure 10.   An example of an adapted spoon. The bent, easy-to-grasp handle makes self-feeding easier for children with fine motor problems.

are available to make bottle feeding easier for babies who have a weak suck or grasp. When purchasing your mealtime equipment, keep in mind that the weight of the utensil can facilitate or inhibit its use.

BATHING

Bath seats secure a child safely while in the tub and free your hands for bathing. They are particularly helpful if your child requires total body support due to weakness or low muscle tone, or because the child moves about too much or too forcefully. Bath seats generally resemble chaise lounges and often are made from light-weight plastic piping. The seats themselves are of a washable mesh or similar material for easy drainage and drying. The legs usually are equipped with suction cups to secure the seat in the tub. Foam cushions are also available for bathing young infants in a sink. After the bath, the seats can be squeezed out to dry. In addition, the cushions can be used for support on the changing table.

TRANSFER AND TRANSPORTATION DEVICES

Lifts are mechanical devices that can transfer a child with a physical disability from one spot to another—for example, from a bed to a wheelchair or from a wheelchair to a tub. Platform lifts are used to transfer a child while in a wheelchair to and from specially equipped vans. Some public transportation vehicles also are equipped with platform lifts. Simple board-like devices also can be used to provide a surface on which the child can slide.

Children who require total support in almost all situations will need adapted strollers or wheelchairs, safe and supportive car seats, and proper seating in the home. Travel chairs can serve all three purposes. They adjust to several different heights and angles of recline and have multiposition rear wheels that fully retract under the seat, permitting use as a car seat. In the car, a travel chair can be secured with a standard seat belt. Travel chairs can be equipped with trays for home uses, such as meals or play, and can be pushed outdoors like any stroller. These chairs are relatively easy to adjust and maneuver. They have a full range of accessories and usually can be adjusted to fit as the child grows.

With minor adaptations, standard car seats can be used for many children with disabilities. Some are available with hard shells to fully enclose and protect the child from a jolting forward motion. A therapist may be able to help you select the best and safest model for your child and adapt it as necessary. Remember that children and infants never should be transported in an adult's lap or unrestrained in any seat. Many states have laws prohibiting traveling with unrestrained children in the car.

TOILET-TRAINING AIDS

A regular potty seat can be used with many children with disabilities when they are ready to be toilet trained. A few manufacturers offer adaptive potty seats with high backs, side supports, and desk-like front supports. For some children, a standard potty seat positioned at a small table may work just as well. Remember that tables and desks are strictly for support, and should not be used to provide entertainment that distracts the child from the business at hand. Adaptors for the standard toilet seat generally do not provide adequate trunk or foot support for children with physical disabilities.

HOME MODIFICATIONS

Because activities of daily living are intimately related to home management, the physical layout of your home can be planned to ease care of your child. Ramps can be added. Counter tops, sinks, tables, and beds can be constructed or adapted to convenient heights. Doorways and hallways of adequate width are critical for children who rely on wheelchairs. Grab bars can be installed in the bathroom. Nonskid appliqués can be placed in a tub or shower for extra support and safety. Plans can be made to store vital equipment and special supplies in convenient locations for quick and easy access. Some children may require hospital beds to be managed at home, particularly those children who sleep in a particular position.

Other environmental changes can be made to maximize a child's mobility. Making these changes will be an ongoing process as your child grows and expands his or her skills. The key to modifications, as well as to any adaptive equipment, is to help children while encouraging their independence and furthering their development.

ACKNOWLEDGMENT

Contributions have been made to this chapter by Barbara Bush, R.P.T., and Peter Stack, M.S.P.T.

24

Medications May Be Necessary for Your Child

Many children with developmental disabilities take medications as part of their care. For example, children with seizure disorders take medicines to control the seizures, and youngsters with severe attention problems may take medicine to improve concentration. Many different medications are available for these and other problems. Each has advantages and disadvantages, and each has unique effects on the body, including certain adverse side effects.

This chapter discusses some of the medications commonly prescribed for children with developmental disabilities. Medicines are identified by either their trade, or common, name, with the generic name given in parentheses. How and when these medications are to be taken, how they work, and their side effects and toxic effects are briefly described. The recognition and monitoring of these side effects, and how certain medicines interact with other medications, are also discussed. First, some general information about side effects is provided.

SIDE EFFECTS

Side effects are undesirable, but not unexpected, reactions to a proper or therapeutic dose of a medicine. Some side effects occur often, whereas others are rare. Not all people will experience side effects, even when they are taking the same medication in the same amount as others who may experience serious side effects. Certain side effects, such as an upset stomach or a skin rash, are noticeable and can cause discomfort. Others may not be so obvious and may be detected only by a laboratory test or a doctor's examination. For example, some medicines may affect the child's blood count or liver function. Your doctor or pharmacist can inform you of the common side effects of particular medications. Before starting any medication, be sure to find out the signs of adverse reactions (side effects) and toxicity (overdosage). Also, if tests are needed to monitor the medication blood levels, make certain you know how often the tests must be done (see also Chapter 22).

Sometimes side effects cannot be avoided. They may have to be tolerated because it is so important that a particular medicine be administered. In general, the benefits of taking the medication should outweigh any discomfort or undesirable effects it causes. An example of a valuable medicine that causes side effects is the seizure medication Dilantin (diphenylhydantoin). It helps prevent seizures, but it may cause the gums to swell, which is called *gingival hyperplasia*.

If your child develops side effects after starting a medication, call and discuss your observations with your doctor. Your doctor needs to know about anything unusual that occurs while your child is taking a medication. Keep in mind, though, that your child's complaints may not be a side effect, but, instead, part of the illness or just a coincidence.

TOXIC EFFECTS

Toxic effects often develop when a person is taking too much medication. This is always a serious concern and must be dealt with immediately. Therefore, if a child has any unusual symptoms or is very uncomfortable, inform your physician immediately so that your child can be checked. For example, Dilantin may be absorbed at different rates by different people; at too high a level, it may cause a problem with balance (i.e., ataxia). If a toxic effect is present, the doctor will adjust the dose or change the medication. Keep in mind that two people taking the same medication and same dosage may react quite differently; one may experience toxic effects whereas the other may not.

Whenever a medication is prescribed, it is of utmost importance that the directions provided on the label be followed carefully. The directions tell how much and how often the medicine is to be taken. A good rule to follow is to consult your child's physician if you have any questions or concerns about a medication.

SEIZURE MEDICATIONS (ANTICONVULSANTS)

There are many different types of seizure disorders (see also Chapter 16). Some seizures are treated more effectively than others with specific medications. Your doctor will tell you which medication is best to use for a certain type of seizure.

Before a medication is prescribed, your child's physician or a pediatric neurologist must determine what type of seizure is occurring. Therefore, the doctor may ask for a detailed description of the seizures and then order a brainwave test.

Many children need more than one medication to control seizures effectively. For some children seizure medications are only required for 1 or 2 years, whereas others will need to take medications for their entire lives. In the beginning of treatment, it is usually difficult to predict how long a medication will be needed. Your physician will give you information about the type, severity, and expected outcomes of your child's seizure disorder.

Ordinarily, seizure medications work by quieting the brain and preventing seizure activity. In some instances, this quieting effect can help the brain to "heal" itself. In other situations, however, the injury to the brain is so severe that complete "healing" is impossible.

In order for any seizure medication to be effective, there has to be enough of it in your child's body. If too little medicine is in the body, then the quieting effect will not be strong enough to prevent seizures. If there is too much medicine, lethargy, drowsiness, sleepiness, or other symptoms may be observed. The doctor aims to prescribe just the right amount of medicine to prevent seizures, but not so much as to cause undesirable symptoms. This correct amount of medicine will provide a "therapeutic" level. When the therapeutic level has been established, the only way to maintain it is to take the medicine regularly as it is prescribed. If a child forgets to take the seizure medication, the level of the medication in the body may fall below its effective level, which in turn may lead to the recurrence of seizures. Your doctor will monitor the therapeutic level of the medication with a blood test, usually done two to four times yearly.

Levels of most seizure medications usually do not change abruptly; rather they change gradually over time. For instance, a therapeutic level usually is not reached immediately; several days of taking the proper dosage may be required. Conversely, when medicine is discontinued, it may take several days or more before the child's system is totally free of the medication. If seizures continue to occur when a therapeutic range of a seizure medication has been

reached, then the doctor may either change the medication or add one or more seizure medications in an attempt to control seizure activity.

If your child has been seizure-free for several years, the doctor may want to discontinue the medication. Children usually are weaned off a medication by reducing the dose gradually over the course of several days to weeks. An abrupt stoppage of certain seizure medications might trigger a seizure within several days of the final dose. It is important that any changes in your child's medication be made under the supervision and guidance of your physician.

The following pages describe some of the more common medications used to treat seizures.

Dilantin (Diphenylhydantoin)

Dilantin (diphenylhydantoin) is a very effective seizure medication used for the treatment of several different kinds of seizures, but particularly those that have a limb-jerking and stiffening (tonic-clonic) component. Dilantin has been used successfully for generalized seizures, in which all four limbs are involved, as well as for focal seizures, in which jerky movements are localized to one or two limbs. Dilantin also can be used to treat partial seizures, which sometimes are accompanied by unusual motor behaviors such as lip smacking or eye blinking.

Dilantin can be given in liquid, tablet, or capsule form. It usually is taken two or three times a day, but in older children it may need to be taken only once a day.

Common side effects are swollen gums, increased hair growth, and anemia. Less common side effects include dizziness, insomnia, emotional disturbances, headache, nausea, vomiting, constipation, skin rash, enlarged lymph glands, liver damage, bone softening, unsteadiness, and coarsening of facial features. Toxic effects include lethargy, sleepiness, slurred speech, poor balance, double vision, blood in the urine, and a severe rash. Call your doctor immediately if toxicity is suspected.

Your child's blood count and liver functioning should be monitored by a physician at least two to three times per year. If these tests are atypical, then Dilantin should be discontinued and another seizure medication used instead.

Dilantin often is given together with other seizure medications. This may affect its level in your child's body. Thus, close monitoring with blood tests is essential. Dilantin also should be taken with caution whenever medications to prevent blood clotting (i.e., anticoagulants) are being taken at the same time.

Phenobarbital

Phenobarbital is another effective seizure medication used for the treatment of generalized seizures. At home it can be given by mouth in liquid form, tablets, or capsules. In the hospital, it often is given intravenously or intramuscularly.

Common side effects of phenobarbital are lethargy, irritability, and/or hyperactivity. Less common side effects include dizziness, insomnia, disturbances in thinking, lowering of heart rate and breathing, nausea, vomiting, constipation, skin rash, anemia, and bone softening. Toxic effects include pronounced lethargy, sleepiness, poor balance, and a rash.

Phenobarbital often is taken together with other anticonvulsant medications similar to Dilantin. This may affect the phenobarbital level in your child's body as well as the level of the other medications. Therefore, close monitoring is required. Phenobarbital also has a tendency to decrease the effectiveness of anticoagulants, steroids, and birth control pills.

Mebaral (Mephobarbital)

Mebaral (mephobarbital) is very similar to phenobarbital, and in fact, it is converted to phenobarbital by the body. Consequently, its use, side effects, and toxicity are the same as those of phenobarbital. It is

sometimes used instead of phenobarbital because it tends to have
fewer behavioral side effects such as irritability and hyperactivity. It
is available in tablet form only.

Mysoline (Primidone)

Mysoline also resembles phenobarbital in its action and is used to
control similar types of seizures, including generalized and partial
seizures. It is dispensed in tablet and liquid form. The initial dose
is usually small and subsequently is increased over the course of
a week.

Common side effects are irritability, hyperactivity, balance problems, and vertigo (the sensation that the room is spinning). The balance problems and vertigo usually disappear with continued usage.
Less common side effects are nausea, vomiting, loss of appetite, fatigue, emotional disturbances, double vision, drowsiness, and skin
rash. The toxic effects and drug interactions are similar to those of
phenobarbital.

Tegretol (Carbamazepine)

Tegretol (carbamazepine) often is used for the treatment of partial
seizures (seizures that are accompanied by unusual behaviors). Tegretol also is given to children with generalized and focal seizures.
It comes in tablet form only and is given two to four times a day.
The dose is usually small at first and then is increased gradually in
an attempt to avoid side effects.

Common side effects are dizziness, drowsiness, unsteadiness,
nausea, and vomiting. Less common side effects include reduced
blood cell production in the bone marrow and liver toxicity. Although these side effects are rare, they are potentially very serious
and it is important to watch for them. Thus, your child's physician will want to monitor your child's blood count and liver functioning closely. These studies should be obtained two to three
times a year. Other less common side effects include emotional and
visual isturbances, ringing in the ears, pain in the limbs, retention
of urine, and cardiovascular disturbances. Toxic effects are severe
dizziness, unsteadiness, drowsiness, vomiting, restlessness, and
tremors.

Depakene (Valproic Acid)

Depakene (valproic acid) is used in controlling simple and complex
partial seizures. These are seizures that are manifested by occasional
jerking or twitching, or drop attacks, in which the child suddenly
falls to the ground. Depakene also has been found to be effective in

reducing the frequency of seizure activity in children with severe brain injury, whose brainwave studies show evidence of diffuse and widespread abnormalities. Depakene comes in liquid and capsule form, and usually it is given two to three times daily.

Common side effects of Depakene are nausea, vomiting, and indigestion. Less common side effects are liver and bone marrow toxicity, similar to effects seen with Tegretol. These are potentially serious side effects and require close monitoring of blood count and liver function by your child's physician. Other less common side effects include unsteadiness, dizziness, headache, weakness, emotional upset, skin rash, and tremors. Toxic effects are lethargy and sedation.

Due to drug interaction, Depakene can increase the sedative effect of phenobarbital and decrease the blood level of Dilantin. These effects must be monitored closely by your child's physician. If necessary, appropriate adjustments to the various medications should be made so therapeutic levels can be reached.

Klonopin (Clonazepam)

Similar to Depakene (clonazepam), this medication often is used for control of partial seizures and drop attacks. It can reduce the frequency of seizure activity in children with severe brain injury. Klonopin comes in tablet form and is given two to three times a day. The initial dose usually is small and then is increased gradually. Tolerance to the medication may develop over time; therefore, a periodic upward adjustment of the medication may be necessary.

Common side effects include drowsiness, unsteadiness, irritability, and hyperactivity. Less common side effects are confusion, depression, forgetfulness, atypical eye movements, slurred speech, increased salivation, loss of appetite, and liver problems.

Zarontin (Ethosuximide)

Zarontin (ethosuximide) is the drug of choice for the treatment of typical absence seizures. These are minor seizures characterized by brief lapses of consciousness, or "absences," that are sometimes associated with atypical eyelid movements or lip smacking (see also Chapter 16). The brainwave test shows a characteristic pattern that distinguishes absence seizures from simple or complex partial seizures. Zarontin comes in capsule and liquid form. It usually is given one to two times a day. The initial dosage of Zarontin typically is low. Then, it is increased slowly in order to avoid side effects.

Common side effects are stomach upset, loss of appetite, nausea, vomiting, cramps, and diarrhea. Less common side effects include liver and kidney disorders. Children taking this medication should have periodic blood counts, liver function studies, and urine examinations. Other less common side effects include drowsiness, lethargy, headache, irritability, unsteadiness, and sleep disturbances. In rare instances, a disease called *systemic lupus erythematosus* develops following treatment with Zarontin.

Adrenocorticotropic Hormone

Adrenocorticotropic hormone (ACTH), a drug frequently used for endocrine and rheumatic disorders, has been used successfully with a specific type of seizure disorder known as *infantile spasms, infantile myoclonic seizures,* or *hypsarrhythmia.* ACTH is not available as an oral medication and needs to be injected into muscle tissue. This can be done when the child is hospitalized, or sometimes a visiting nurse may go to the child's home to inject the medication.

Side effects of ACTH include elevated blood pressure, water retention, swelling of the face, susceptibility to infections, thinning of bones, and muscle weakness.

PSYCHOSTIMULANT MEDICATIONS

Children with attention deficit disorder with or without hyperactivity typically have difficulty focusing on activities and tend to flit from one thing to another. Poor concentration and distractibility also are observed.

Psychostimulant medications are used to reduce hyperactive behavior and attention problems by helping the child to concentrate. For a long time, doctors were baffled by the fact that stimulant medications seemed to slow down children rather than perking them up or stimulating them further. Many called this a *paradoxical effect.* Today we know that there is no paradoxical effect. These medications work in children with attention deficit disorder, with or without hyperactivity, by stimulating their brains so that they can attend better to the necessary details of an activity. When the children's distractibility is reduced, they do not jump from task to task, and their overall amount of activity is lessened.

Psychostimulant medications differ from anticonvulsant medications in that a therapeutic level is reached relatively quickly, and the medications begin to work usually within the first hour after they have been taken. However, the effects of psychostimulants do not last long, usually 4–8 hours at the most. The medicine essentially is cleared from the body overnight, and by the next morning a new dose is needed if the beneficial effects are to be achieved.

Although many studies have documented the benefits of these medications in children with attention problems and hyperactivity, these medications do not work for all children with hyperactivity. The reasons for this are unclear, but they probably relate to the fact that there are many different causes of hyperactivity. It is difficult to predict who will and who will not respond positively to psychostimulant medications. For this reason, the medications ordinarily are started on a trial basis. Initially, children are given a low dose. If no improvement is noted in the first few days, the dosage may be increased. If there still is no effect after several increases or after a similar medication has been tried, then the psychostimulant medications should be stopped and an alternative form of therapy should be sought. The therapeutic trial period should not take longer than 3 months.

If the medication does work, it can be helpful to both children and their families. However, it should not be the only form of treatment for hyperactivity. It should be thought of as one part of the total care plan. The medication alone rarely solves all behavior problems. Other helpful therapeutic interventions include family therapy, individual psychotherapy, adjustment within a child's educational setting, and a behavior modification program.

Psychostimulant medications are sometimes given only on school days, because this is when children need to pay attention the most. The medications then are withheld on weekends and holidays. However, if parents find that managing a child's behavior without medication is too difficult on weekends, it makes sense to give the medicine even on nonschool days. Generally, this helps to foster better parent–child relations.

The three medications used most often to treat hyperactivity and attention problems are Ritalin, Dexedrine, and Cylert.

Ritalin (Methylphenidate Hydrochloride)

Ritalin (methylphenidate hydrochloride) is the most frequently used psychostimulant medication. It is available in tablet form and usually is given in the morning before school and at noon. The effect of Ritalin usually wears off by the time the child arrives home from school. Sometimes a third dose is given in midafternoon so that the effect can continue beyond regular school hours.

Ritalin is also available in a sustained release form, given only once in the morning. This can be particularly beneficial for children who do not like to take their medicine at school. Many children are sensitive about their problems and do not want to draw attention by taking medication. It is important that the sustained release tablet be swallowed whole and not crushed or chewed.

Common side effects are loss of appetite, difficulty falling asleep, headaches, and stomachaches. These side effects usually are transient and pass within a few weeks. Less common side effects are nervousness, nausea, dizziness, talkativeness, moodiness, palpitations, and a possible slowing of the child's growth rate.

There are no real toxic effects, because Ritalin does not accumulate over time. Overdosage, however, can occur, as with any other medication, either by accident or on purpose. Symptoms of acute overdosage result primarily from overstimulation of the brain and include vomiting, agitation, tremors, twitching, rapid heartbeat, and palpitations.

If Ritalin is taken with anticonvulsants or antidepressant medications, the dosages of those medications may have to be decreased, because Ritalin may interfere with their elimination from the body.

Dexedrine (Dextroamphetamine Sulfate)

Dexedrine (dextroamphetamine sulfate) is available in both tablet and liquid form. The medication usually is given in the morning and at midday. A third dose may be given in the afternoon if necessary. Dexedrine also comes in a long-acting capsule (i.e., spansule), and like the sustained-release form of Ritalin, only needs to be given once in the morning. Although both Ritalin and Dexedrine have similar effects, for unknown reasons some children respond better to Ritalin, whereas others display more favorable effects than Dexedrine. Therefore, if one of the psychostimulants is ineffective, it may be worthwhile to try a different one.

The side effects and overdose symptoms of Dexedrine and Ritalin are basically the same, as are their drug interactions.

Cylert (Pemoline)

The effects of Cylert (pemoline) are similar to Dexedrine and Ritalin. Cylert usually is started at a low dose and built up gradually, so that the desired effect may not be noticed for several weeks. It is dispensed in tablet form. The duration of the effect of Cylert is longer than that of Ritalin and Dexedrine; therefore, it is given only once a day, usually in the morning. Again, for an unknown reason, a child who does not show any beneficial response to Ritalin or Dexedrine may respond well to Cylert.

Side effects and overdose symptoms of Cylert are the same as for Ritalin and Dexedrine. Blood tests that measure liver functioning should be obtained periodically on children receiving long-term therapy with Cylert.

ANTISPASTIC MEDICATIONS

Children who have physical disabilities because of cerebral palsy frequently have problems with spasticity. *Spasticity* is the tightening of muscles that occurs when the nerve cells in the part of the brain that ordinarily controls the muscles are injured. In cerebral palsy, the injured nerves stimulate the muscles continually and do not allow them to relax. Thus, the muscles of affected limbs continue to contract, and get tighter (see also Chapter 15).

Three medications are primarily used to reduce spasticity: Valium (diazepam), Lioresal (baclofen), and Dantrium (dantrolene sodium). Because each of these medications works in slightly different ways, children with a particular problem may find one of these drugs more effective than the others. To date, few comparisons have been made of the three medications to determine which works best under what circumstances.

Valium (Diazepam)

Valium (diazepam), widely known as a tranquilizer, is the medication used most often by physicians to treat symptoms of spasticity. It is available in tablet form and as an injectable liquid. Valium is started at a low dose and is built up to the point where the maximum relaxing effect is achieved with minimal tranquilizing.

Common side effects of Valium are drowsiness, fatigue, problems with balance, weakness, and dizziness. Less common side effects include confusion, constipation, depression, headache, bladder problems, speech disturbance, tremors, vision problems, and skin rashes. On rare occasions, insomnia, anxiety, hostility, and hallucinations are observed. Generally, these are seen only after long-term use of Valium. Toxic reactions include sleepiness, confusion, and unresponsiveness.

Valium may depress the function of the brain and should be taken with caution when anticonvulsants and psychotropic medications (see below) are given at the same time.

Lioresal (Baclofen)

Lioresal (baclofen) is used most often with people with paraplegia and quadriplegia who have multiple sclerosis or spinal cord trauma. Its use in children with cerebral palsy has not been well studied.

Theoretically, it may be helpful in children who have spasticity associated with spina bifida.

Lioresal comes in tablet form. It usually is given three times a day. One generally begins with a low dose and builds up to the point where there is a maximum relief of spasticity.

Common side effects are occasional drowsiness, dizziness, weakness, and fatigue. Less common side effects are confusion, headache, insomnia, low blood pressure, nausea, constipation, and bladder problems. Rarely, hallucinations and speech and vision problems are noted. Toxic effects include vomiting, weakness, lethargy, nonresponsiveness, and seizures.

Dantrium (Dantrolene Sodium)

Dantrium (dantrolene sodium) works directly on the muscle, causing it to contract less, even when receiving continued stimulation from an injured nerve. Theoretically, Dantrium appears to be the ideal treatment for spastic cerebral palsy. However, a few studies indicate that Dantrium is not any more effective than Valium in reducing spasticity.

Dantrium is available in tablet form. Like the other antispastic medications, the initial dosage is low and is increased gradually over time until an effect is seen. If the maximum dosage is reached and no positive effects are observed, the medication should be discontinued.

Common side effects are drowsiness, dizziness, weakness, fatigue, and diarrhea. Less common side effects are liver damage, stomach problems, speech disorders, urinary problems, atypical hair growth, and acne. Rarely, cardiac problems and seizures are observed.

PSYCHOTROPIC MEDICATIONS

Children with developmental disabilities may also have emotional difficulties. Some children's emotional problems are so significant that they interfere with their school performance, peer relationships, and typical body functions. Children's emotional problems often are related to difficulties in their home, school, or other environments or they may be due to intrinsic problems. In such situations, eliminating the underlying cause of the child's problems may relieve the emotional disturbance. However, this is not always possible; sometimes the psychiatric disturbance is so severe that medical intervention is required.

Medications commonly used to help individuals with emotional or psychiatric problems are called *psychotropic medications*. Two main categories of psychotropic medications are discussed here: antipsychotic and antidepressant medications.

Antipsychotic Medications

Antipsychotic medications are used in children and adolescents who show symptoms of severe psychiatric disturbance such as bizarre thinking patterns, delusions, hallucinations, confusion, aggressive behavior, agitation, and restlessness. How antipsychotic medications work to relieve some of these symptoms is not well understood. They often have a sedative effect, which tends to calm down an extremely agitated child. Recent evidence suggests that some symptoms of psychiatric problems are due to chemical disturbances in the brain. The antipsychotic medications alter the chemistry of the brain and thus improve behavior and thinking.

Like anticonvulsant medications, these medicines provide a beneficial effect when taken on a regular basis, so that adequate levels are maintained in the body. It may take a few weeks before a positive effect is seen. Specific therapeutic blood levels have not been designated for many of these medications. An adequate dosage generally is determined by the child's behavior rather than by defined blood levels.

Numerous antipsychotic medications are available. Some of the more common ones are Thorazine (chlorpromazine hydrochloride), Stelazine (trifluoperazine hydrochloride), Mellaril (thioridazine hydrochloride), Navane (thiothixene hydrochloride), and Haldol (haloperidol). All of them work in a similar way and have similar side effects.

Side effects include lethargy; sleepiness; sluggishness; weakness; dry mouth; blurred vision; and unusual muscular contractions (i.e., dystonia), which can lead to head tilting, facial grimacing, unusual tongue movements, and difficulty speaking. There may also be tremulousness, rigidity, and restlessness. Another side effect of long-term use of these medications is *tardive dyskinesia,* a condition characterized by repetitive tic-like movements of the face, tongue, lips, and sometimes the limbs. Tardive dyskinesia for which there is no known effective treatment, is more commonly seen in adults than in children.

Less common side effects are rapid heartbeat, electrocardiogram changes, a fall in blood pressure, minor liver problems, changes in blood count, breast enlargement, nasal congestion, constipation, difficulty urinating, increased perspiration, and increased salivation.

Seizures, exacerbation of psychiatric symptoms, allergic reactions, and fever are rare side effects.

These medications depress the function of the central nervous system and should be taken with caution when other medications that act similarly, such as anticonvulsant, antispastic, and antidepressant medications, are used.

Haldol (Haloperidol) Haldol (haloperidol) is a commonly used antipsychotic medication with potent sedative effects. It also is prescribed frequently for children with Tourette syndrome, a disorder in which tics of the face and extremities and bizarre vocalizations are present. The exact way Haldol works is still unclear. But like so many similar medications, Haldol may correct chemical irregularities in the brain and thus help to reduce atypical behaviors.

Haldol is available in tablet and liquid form. A trial with the medication consists of starting at the lowest possible dose once or twice a day and gradually increasing it until a significant response is noted or the side effects limit any further increase. The ideal dose is one that provides maximum therapeutic effect with minimum side effects. Because this medication is one of the antipsychotics, the side effects, toxic effects, and drug interactions are similar to those of the other antipsychotic medications described here.

Cogentin (Benztropine Mesylate) Although Cogentin (benztropine mesylate) is not an antipsychotic medication, it deserves special mention because some of the movement side effects of the antipsychotic medications such as tremors, rigidity, and dystonia can be alleviated by using Cogentin in conjunction with antipsychotic medications. Although Cogentin may diminish some of the adverse reactions, it may also cause dryness of the mouth, blurred vision, constipation, and difficulty urinating. Tardive dyskinesia may be more likely to occur when Cogentin is combined with antipsychotic medications. For these reasons, Cogentin should be used cautiously when treating children already taking antipsychotic medications. Sometimes, physicians may elect to decrease the dose of antipsychotic medication in an attempt to prevent movement side effects before adding Cogentin to the drug regimen.

Antidepressant Medications

Antidepressant medications are used in children and adolescents who manifest symptoms of severe sadness, hopelessness, and worthlessness. Sometimes poor school performance, difficult peer and family relationships, aggressive behaviors, lack of interest, withdrawal, hostility, early waking, loss of appetite, weight loss, and general slowness also are observed in depressed children.

How antidepressant medications work is not fully understood. There is some evidence that, like the antipsychotic drugs, they regulate neurochemical mechanisms and thus improve mood, sleeping, eating, and other physiological functions.

Antidepressant medications are somewhat similar to anticonvulsant and antipsychotic medications in that a certain therapeutic level must be reached before the medications become effective. It sometimes takes 2–4 weeks before any improvement is noted. These medications must be taken on a regular basis to maintain an effective drug level in the body. Blood levels of these medications can be tested from time to time and dosage adjustments made when necessary.

A number of antidepressant medications share common side effects such as constipation, dryness of the mouth, blurred vision, difficulty urinating, sleepiness, weakness, lethargy, stomach upset, and low blood pressure, which is sometimes associated with dizziness. Toxic effects may include restlessness, agitation, delirium, convulsions, and cardiac problems.

Lithium   Lithium has been used successfully in treating people with manic depression, an illness characterized by marked mood swings between depression and mood elevation. How lithium works is unclear. Again, there is some evidence that the chemical relationships of the brain are altered by this medication.

Unfortunately, lithium can be very toxic. Therefore, blood levels should be followed very closely to make sure that the medication stays within the therapeutic range. If no behavioral improvement is noted even when the medication is in the therapeutic range, it should be stopped to prevent toxic effects. Lithium is available in tablet and capsule form for oral use and generally is given three to four times daily.

Common side effects are tremors, frequent urination (particularly at night), thirst, nausea, fatigue, lethargy, and stomach upset. Less common side effects are heart and thyroid abnormalities and dizziness. Early signs of toxicity are diarrhea, vomiting, drowsiness, weakness, and loss of coordination. Later signs are giddiness, balance problems, blurred vision, ringing in the ears, and increased urine output. Serious toxic signs include seizures, confusion, stupor, heart problems, and low blood pressure. Lithium and antipsychotic medications should not be taken together.

Tofranil (Imipramine Hydrochloride)   Tofranil is one of the more commonly used antidepressant medications. It also is sometimes used to treat bedwetting (i.e., enuresis). This medication is available in tablet form. It usually is started at a relatively low dose and then increased weekly until either improvement is noted or the maximum dosage is reached. If no improvement is seen, the medication should be stopped. The use of Tofranil for enuresis is controversial because wetting often recurs when the medication is stopped and because bedwetting is such a common benign disorder.

Common side effects of Tofranil are constipation, dryness of the mouth, blurred vision, sleep disturbances, weakness, lethargy, stomach upset, low blood pressure, nervousness, and agitation. Less common side effects include heart abnormalities, anxiety, disorientation, numbness, tingling or burning sensations of the extremities, balance and coordination problems, skin rash, breast enlargement, and altered liver function. Rare side effects are seizures, blood changes, and hair loss. Toxic effects include marked drowsiness leading to unresponsiveness, balance problems, restlessness, nervousness, movement disorders, seizures, rapid or irregular heartbeat, and low blood pressure.

Decongestants should not be taken with Tofranil, and medications such as Ritalin should be taken with caution when prescribed at the same time. Tofranil increases the effect of other medications that depress brain function such as phenobarbital and Valium. Tofranil should not be given to an adolescent if alcohol or drug abuse is suspected.

Chloral Hydrate Chloral hydrate is one of the medications sometimes prescribed for sleeping problems in children. Many children with developmental disabilities have sleeping problems. Although numerous products are sold over the counter to help people get to sleep, many are not suitable for children. Chloral hydrate can help break an atypical sleeping pattern and allow a more typical pattern to take its place.

Chloral hydrate comes in capsule or liquid form. It usually is given half an hour before bedtime. This medication should not be used for more than a few weeks at a time. It can be discontinued for a week or so and then used again. It is not meant for long-term use.

Chloral hydrate also is used frequently as a sedative prior to such tests as an electroencephalogram, computed tomography scan, or special hearing tests.

Side effects of chloral hydrate include stomach upset, disorientation, incoherence, skin rash, and blood changes. Rarely, excitement, dizziness, and dependence are observed. Toxic effects are severe sleepiness leading to unresponsiveness, low blood pressure, depressed breathing, and severe stomach irritation. Chloral hydrate should be used cautiously with anticoagulants (medications that prevent blood clotting).

THYROID MEDICATIONS

A number of medications are on the market for hypothyroidism. Congenital hypothyroidism, a disease detected in infancy that can cause brain injury, results from the body's inability to produce thyroid hormone. Early treatment can prevent brain injury. Synthroid and Levothroid (levothyroxine) are two brands of thyroid hormone used most often to treat hypothyroidism. These medications perform as well as thyroid hormone produced naturally in the body. Generally, the child with hypothyroidism takes one tablet a day. Levels of thyroid hormone in the blood are monitored to ensure that the child is getting the appropriate dose.

There are no side effects to these medications, but it is possible to have overactive thyroid function, or hyperthyroidism, if the dosage is too high. Some common signs of hyperthyroidism are poor growth, diarrhea, rapid heart rate, increased body temperature, perspiration, headache, increased appetite, fatigue, overactivity, and poor sleeping.

MEDICATIONS FOR BOWEL PROBLEMS

Several groups of medications can be used to help children with physical disabilities who have bowel problems. Each group has its own mode of action.

Stool Softeners

Stool softeners may be prescribed for children who have chronic problems with constipation, fecal soiling, or impaction of the bowel. They work by either drawing water into the stool or retaining water. Water keeps the stool soft and thus helps to prevent constipation. A common stool softener is Colace (docusate sodium), which is available over-the-counter in tablet, capsule, powder, or liquid form.

Mineral Oil

Mineral oil lubricates stool, keeping it soft so that it can be moved easily through the intestines and thus be eliminated easily. Mineral oil generally is taken at bedtime. It has an unpleasant taste, but when mixed with milk, juice, yogurt, or other foods, it is less apparent. If mineral oil is to be used on a long-term basis, it is recommended that a multivitamin also be taken daily, as mineral oil has a tendency to block the absorption of fat-soluble vitamins. Mineral oil should not be taken by children with severe disabilities who might have a tendency to vomit and aspirate (taking of food or liquid into the windpipe and lungs). If aspirated, mineral oil can cause a severe form of pneumonia.

Bulk Laxatives

Bulk laxatives generally have three actions. First, they act like stool softeners, drawing water into the bowel to keep the stool soft. Second, they frequently add bulk to the stool, which stimulates elimination. Third, they usually contain an ingredient that also stimulates the intestine to move the stool through quickly. Some common laxatives include Peri-Colace, Metamucil, Senokot, and Doxidan. Side effects may include intestinal cramps or diarrhea. If used for extended periods, some laxatives may be habit-forming.

Stimulants

Dulcolax (bisacodyl) is one of the more common laxatives used for constipation. It directly stimulates the large intestine and thus enhances stool elimination. It is not as gentle as most of the just-mentioned medications, and may cause cramps in a child who is constipated.

Dulcolax is available both in tablet and suppository form. Tablets can take as long as 8 hours to work and are frequently taken at bedtime. Suppositories usually have an effect within an hour after administration. Dulcolax may be habit-forming, but may also be the only alternative for regular bowel function in some children.

Glycerin suppositories are used for younger children or when only mild bowel stimulation is required.

Enemas

Enemas are used when a child has severe constipation. A liquid solution is administered rectally, which then induces elimination. Fleet enemas are the most commonly used enemas. In addition to the regular water-like enemas, there are also mineral oil and soapsuds enemas. Elimination is usually induced within 2–5 minutes after administration. Enemas often are used when impaction is present. Cramps are the main side effect.

MEDICATIONS FOR URINARY TRACT PROBLEMS

Urinary tract infections and a condition called *spastic bladder* are common problems in children with certain developmental disabilities such as spina bifida. There are several categories of medication used to treat these problems: antibiotics, acidifying agents, and anticholinergic medications. Antibiotics combined with agents that make urine slightly acidic are used to prevent and fight infection. Anticho-linergic medications will help relax a tight or spastic bladder so that it will fill more efficiently and not cause constant dribbling of the urine. When the bladder is filled, clean intermittent catheterization can be used to empty the bladder (see Chapter 22 for discussion of catheterization).

Antibiotics

Antibiotics are used to treat and prevent infections caused by bacteria. Children who are prone to infections, or who are at risk for kidney injury due to frequent infections, are given antibiotics. Cultures of urine are taken to determine which antibiotic to use and are usually repeated later to be sure the antibiotic was effective.

Numerous antibiotics and sulfa drugs are available today. Some of the more commonly used medications for urinary tract infections include amoxicillin, ampicillin, Bactrim (trimethoprim and sulfa-methoxazole), Gantrisin (sulfisoxazole), Keflex (cephalexin), and Septra (trimethoprim and sulfamethoxazole). These medications come in tablet and liquid form and can be taken either on a short-term basis to treat an infection or on a long-term basis to prevent an infection.

The most common side effects include stomach upset with possible diarrhea, nausea, or vomiting. Bactrim, Gantrisin, and Septra may also cause serious blood problems, although this is rare. All of these medications are safe when taken over a short period to fight an infection. If Bactrim, Gantrisin, or Septra is used for long-term treatment, periodic blood counts should be obtained.

Anticholinergic Medications

Choline is a chemical found in many parts of the body. One of the actions of choline is to cause the bladder to contract. In some bladders with impaired or absent nerve function (i.e., neurogenic bladder), bladder contractions can be excessive and thus prevent the bladder from filling properly, causing continual urinary dribbling. Anticholinergic medications block the effect of choline and allow the bladder to relax and fill. The most common anticholinergic medications used for this purpose are Ditropan (oxybutynin chloride), Donnatal (phenobarbital, hyoscyamine, atropine, scopolamine), and Proxjbanthine (probantheline bromide). These medications come in tablet and liquid form.

The most common side effects are dryness of the mouth, blurred vision, decreased perspiration, increased heart rate, constipation, nausea, vomiting, drowsiness, weakness, dizziness, diffi-

culty falling asleep, and allergic reactions. Toxic effects include restlessness, excitement, psychotic behavior, low blood pressure,
decreased breathing effort, and loss of consciousness.

ACCIDENTAL INGESTION

Medications must be kept out of the reach of children, as well as
others who are at risk for ingesting them and for whom they are not
intended. If children take any medicines that have not been prescribed for them, the nearest Poison Control Center should be tele-
phoned immediately. It is also wise to have *ipecac syrup* on hand
(available from the pharmacy) should the Poison Control Center advise to induce vomiting. (Vomiting *should not* be induced with any
poisonings unless recommended by the Poison Control Center.)

CONCLUSION

Medications used appropriately can be of great help to people who
have various medical conditions. They are, in fact, life-saving in
many situations. However, despite the benefits, many medications
have potentially dangerous side effects, which must be taken into
consideration.

Whenever a medicine is prescribed, the physician's instructions
must be followed closely to achieve a therapeutic effect and to avoid
toxic effects. If suspicious symptoms are ever noticed, they should
be discussed promptly with your child's physician. It is your responsibility as a parent to monitor all medication effects, whether good
or bad. Also, as potentially beneficial as medications can be, they
will not work if they are not taken. As a parent, you must ensure
that your child is given the chance to benefit from the medicines
that are prescribed.

ACKNOWLEDGMENTS

Contributions have been made to this chapter by Daniel T. Marwil,
M.D., and Siegfried M. Pueschel, M.D., Ph.D., M.P.H.

25

Some Children May
Have to Undergo Surgery

A child with special needs requires regular medical care just like any other child. However, in addition to routine pediatric checkups, your child may need the services of one or more medical specialists. Also, on occasion your child may need to have an operation and thus require the services of a surgeon.

This chapter describes a number of surgical interventions that may be needed by children with developmental disabilities. Of course, just as there are many kinds of developmental disabilities, there are also numerous associated medical and surgical problems that can arise. The medical and surgical needs of each child are unique, and, therefore, the goals and types of treatment will vary from child to child. This chapter focuses primarily on describing surgical interventions. The characteristics and expected outcomes of some conditions necessitating surgery have been discussed in previous chapters.

Surgery has become highly specialized. Many individual surgeons are concentrating on the treatment of particular organ systems. For example, cardiac surgeons operate on the heart; orthopaedic surgeons operate on muscles, tendons, and bones; and urologists operate on kidneys, ureters, and the bladder.

GENERAL CONSIDERATIONS

Whenever surgery is planned, some general issues should be considered. For example, in nonemergency situations decisions must be made about the optimal time to perform operations. Also, factors such as the child's stage of growth and development, the possible effects of immobilization, and decreased stimulation during hospitalization must be considered. The impact of interrupting education programs and ongoing therapy must be taken into account. Families also should consider how their child reacts to unusual situations, new people, and unfamiliar, perhaps frightening, surroundings. Many children regress behaviorally during prolonged hospitalization. Recognition and anticipation of potential behavior problems may help manage, and even avoid, aberrant behaviors.

It is important to discuss with your child any anticipated surgery shortly before the operation is to take place. Explain in detail, perhaps together with the surgeon, the steps involved in admission to the hospital, preparation for surgery, and having the operation, without causing undue anxiety and fear. Be honest about possible discomfort of blood tests, the pain that may be felt after the operation, and the length of the recovery. Your child also should be told the reason for the surgery, in terms he or she can understand. Even if children do not understand all of the reasons, they usually grasp how the surgery is expected to help them. Sometimes hospitals invite children to visit and become familiar with the routines of a hospital stay, preparation for surgery, what an operating room and a recovery room look like, and what nurses do to make hospital stays more pleasant. Books that show pictures of operating rooms and describe what is going on during an operation are also available. These preparatory efforts can alleviate much of a child's anxiety and concern.

Surgery is undertaken only when it is judged that its potential benefits outweigh its risks. Before an operation, patients should be in the best health possible. Other medical problems should be treated prior to surgery. Good nutrition before surgery also is important, as nutrition plays a vital role in wound healing and resistance to infections.

ANESTHESIA

Anesthesia is a part of almost all surgical procedures. Without anesthesia, surgery would be virtually impossible, because it is through the administration of anesthetic medications that the patient's awareness of pain is altered or eliminated.

Local Anesthesia

Most people are familiar with local anesthetics such as Novocaine or Xylocaine. These medications block the pain by making the nerves numb in the area where the medication is injected. For example, if your child has a cut that needs suturing or a tooth that needs drilling, then prior to the procedure the medication is injected into the respective location.

Another form of local anesthesia is called a *nerve block*. In this case the anesthetic is injected into a specific nerve. When a nerve block is used, the entire area supplied by that nerve temporarily loses its sensation. Depending on the type and amount of local anesthesia used, the effects will wear off between 30 and 60 minutes later.

Spinal anesthesia can be thought of as a more extensive form of nerve block. When spinal anesthesia is given, a needle is used to guide a small tube between the bones of the spine into the spinal canal, which contains the spinal cord. An anesthetic then can be injected through the tube into the space around the spinal cord. This will numb all of the areas of the body supplied by nerves branching off from this level of the spinal cord and below. Also, the muscles supplied by these nerves will be paralyzed temporarily.

General Anesthesia

General anesthesia is the most frequently used type of anesthesia during major surgery. Some general anesthetics can be injected into the bloodstream, and some are gases that must be inhaled. Using these types of anesthesia, the child is unconscious during surgery and his or her muscles, including those needed for breathing, may be paralyzed. When general anesthesia is used, a tube is placed through the nose or mouth into the windpipe (i.e., trachea), permitting the anesthesia and oxygen to be given to the child during an operation.

As with any medication, general anesthesia can have side effects. In rare instances, certain anesthetics have caused liver damage. Also, a condition called *malignant hyperthermia*, in which the body's temperature rises to dangerously high levels of 105°F–107°F, has been reported in some people with specific neuromuscular diseases. However, your doctor and the anesthesiologist (medical doctor who administers anesthesia) will be aware of these potential side effects and will certainly try to avoid them.

Following general anesthesia, small segments of the lungs may collapse in some people. This condition is known as *atelectasis*. Also, the lungs' mechanisms for clearing secretions may be less efficient temporarily. This is the reason the respiratory system is considered so carefully when an operation is being planned and why coughing and deep breathing are encouraged after surgery.

NEUROSURGICAL INTERVENTIONS

Surgical Treatment of Hydrocephalus

The fluid surrounding the brain and spinal cord, the so-called *cerebrospinal fluid,* also circulates through cavities inside the brain, which are known as *ventricles.* This fluid acts as a cushion between the brain and the bones of the skull (Figures 1 and 2). Sometimes the flow of cerebrospinal fluid is blocked or is produced in excess. When this happens, the cerebrospinal fluid builds up in the ventricles of the brain, causing them to enlarge and squeeze the brain against the skull, which can cause hydrocephalus and brain injury. In a baby whose skull bones have not yet fused together, the increased pressure inside the skull can cause bulging of the soft spot, called *fontanel,* on top of the head and may lead to rapid enlargement of the head. In an older child whose skull bones have fused together, increased pressure inside the skull produces symptoms such as headache, nausea, vomiting, drowsiness, and even coma.

Hydrocephalus can be corrected surgically. To relieve the pressure inside the skull and reestablish the typical flow of cerebrospinal fluid, a neurosurgeon places a plastic tube, called a *shunt,* inside the brain. One end of the shunt is inserted into the enlarged ventricle with its excess fluid, and the other end is threaded under the skin along the neck and chest into the abdomen, where the surplus cere-

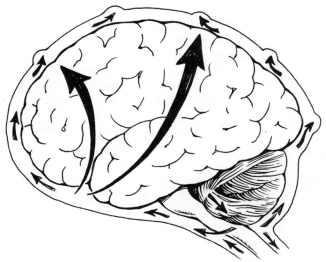

Figure 1. The arrows indicate the flow of cerebrospinal fluid around the brain.

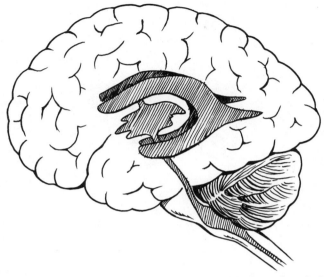

Figure 2.   The ventricles, or cavities inside the brain, in which the cerebrospinal fluid is produced.

brospinal fluid is drained. This type of shunt is called a *ventriculoperitoneal* (VP) shunt (Figure 3).

Another type of shunt, known as a *ventriculojugular shunt*, has one end inserted into the ventricle of the brain and the other one emptying into the jugular vein, a large vein in the neck. Shunts may require replacement from time to time as the child grows. Sometimes they may become infected or blocked and then need to be removed.

The shunt operation is done on an inpatient basis under general anesthesia. Children usually remain in the hospital for 5–10 days following the procedure. Before the child is discharged, parents must be taught the signs and symptoms of a malfunctioning shunt (see also Chapter 26 for discussion of Hospitalization and Aftercare).

Surgical Repair of Spina Bifida

In spina bifida (i.e., meningomyelocele), the spinal cord, its coverings called the *meninges,* and the bones of the spine or vertebrae are all damaged. A sac formed by the meninges, containing disorganized nerve tissue and cerebrospinal fluid, is exposed on the surface of the back. One of the first steps in the treatment of meningomyelocele is closing the opening in the back by a neurosurgeon. After the

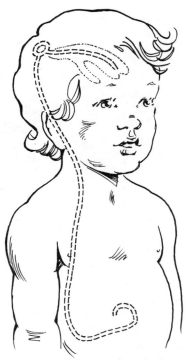

Figure 3.   The ventriculoperitoneal (VP) shunt, which is used in treatment of hydrocephalus. The shunt drains excess cerebrospinal fluid from the ventricles of the brain into the abdomen.

skin around the sac is thoroughly cleansed, the sac and its contents are removed and the skin edges are sutured together.

Surgical Treatment of Some Problems of the Brain

Brain tumors and malformations of blood vessels sometimes occur in areas of the brain where traditional surgery may be considered risky. Among the many neurosurgical procedures that can be used for brain operations there is a new one that is quite promising. The gamma knife is a precise and powerful tool using a multidisciplinary approach and requiring the combined skills of a neurosurgeon and a neuroradiologist. The gamma knife, which is not really a knife, delivers a single dose of ionizing gamma radiation with great precision to the affected brain area. This new development provides the neurosurgeon with a novel technique to treat otherwise difficult to reach brain lesions.

SURGICAL PROCEDURES FOR
THE GASTROINTESTINAL TRACT

The gastrointestinal (GI) tract is a long tube consisting primarily of the esophagus (food pipe), stomach, and small and large intestines. Food enters at one end and is broken down chemically as it passes through the intestines. Water and nutrients are absorbed into the blood stream, and residual waste is eliminated as bowel movement through the rectum.

During early embryonic development of the gastrointestinal tract, mishaps may occur resulting in birth defects. These birth defects, which can occur alone or together with specific developmental disabilities, require surgical intervention in early life. Birth defects of the gastrointestinal tract can take several forms. Three of these are discussed here: *stenosis*—a narrowing of a tube; *fistula*—an atypical connection between two parts; and *atresia*—a failure of a part of the system to develop. Hernias, which are usually due to a weakness of the abdominal wall sometimes requiring surgery, are also discussed.

Surgery for Stenosis

Pyloric stenosis is the term used to describe a narrowing at the lower end of the stomach, or pylorus. It is treated by cutting muscle fibers of the wall of the pylorus to relieve the narrowing at that point.

Narrowing of the duodenum (the part of the bowel that is close to the stomach) is called *duodenal stenosis*. In this case, surgery involves removing the stenosis and reuniting the two ends of the intestine.

In another condition, called *Hirschsprung disease*, there is a narrowing of a segment of the large bowel, caused by a lack of nerve endings. This often results in persistent constipation. Special X-ray studies, such as a barium enema, are used to identify this condition. Again, surgery is necessary; the narrow segment is cut out and the two ends of the large bowel are surgically united.

These operations are performed under general anesthesia and require a hospital stay of 1–2 weeks. Recovery takes approximately 1–4 weeks.

Surgery for Fistulas

Fistulas occur most often between the esophagus and the trachea (the latter is also known as the *windpipe*). This condition is called *tracheoesophageal fistula*. The surgeon repairs the fistula by removing the atypical connection between the esophagus and trachea. Surgery of tracheoesophageal fistulas is important in order to prevent food from entering the lungs, which may cause recurrent pneumonia.

Surgery for Atresias

A blind pouch of the esophagus, known as *esophageal atresia*, may accompany a tracheoesophageal fistula. When an atresia interrupts the continuity of the esophagus, the surgeon will attempt to connect the separated ends by sewing them together to form what is called an *anastomosis*. If a connection is impossible, a part of the intestine is used as an extension between the two ends of the esophagus.

An atresia of the duodenal segment of the bowel is another common birth defect, particularly in children with Down syndrome. Like a duodenal stenosis, a *duodenal atresia* must be repaired surgically. The operation consists of cutting out the blocked segment of bowel and rejoining the two intact ends of the intestine.

An atresia in which the anal opening at the end of the large bowel fails to form is called an *anal atresia* or *imperforate anus*. This condition may be accompanied by fistulas of other sections of the lower intestine to structures such as the urethra or vagina. In addition, kidney malformations, congenital heart disease, esophageal atresia, tracheoesophageal fistula, and bone deformities of the pelvis, spine, and the arms can be observed together with anal atresia.

Typically, the lower end of the large intestine, the rectum, passes through a funnel-shaped sling of muscles in the pelvis. If the blind end of the rectum, the imperforate anus, lies below these muscles, correction can be done in the first few days of life by creating an opening for the rectum in the usual position. If the end of the rectum lies above these muscles, then correction may require two or more operations. During the initial operation, which is usually done in the first few days of life, a *colostomy* is performed by which the colon or large bowel is attached to an opening, or stoma, on the skin of the abdomen. Through this opening stool passes to the outside and is collected in a plastic bag that is attached to the stoma. Later, when the baby is about 12–15 months of age, a second operation is performed to pull the rectum through the muscular sling and to create an opening for the rectum at the anal area. When recovery from this second procedure is complete, the opening of the colostomy is closed and the ends of the large bowel, which were separated initially at the time the colostomy was performed, are reconnected. There are variations of this surgical procedure, which depend on the individual circumstances as well as the surgeon's preference.

Surgery for Hernias

A *hernia,* or rupture, is a protrusion through a weakened area of a muscle. There are different types of hernias; for example, a *hiatal hernia* occurs when part of the stomach or bowel protrudes through the diaphragm muscle; an *inguinal hernia* results when part of the intestines pushes through muscles in the groin area; and an *umbilical hernia* is a weakness in the navel area where the umbilical cord was attached.

Hernias can become life-threatening if the protruding portion of the organ, most often a part of the intestine, gets stuck in the opening, causing an interruption of the blood supply. This condition, called *strangulation* or *incarcerated hernia,* requires immediate attention and, in many cases, emergency surgery. As a preventative measure, hernias often are repaired surgically before they become incarcerated.

Surgical repair of a hernia involves pushing the protruding part of the organ back through the opening in the muscle and closing the opening with sutures. Most umbilical hernias never cause problems and do not need surgical attention because they may close spontaneously and disappear with time.

A more serious condition, in which abdominal organs such as the liver and intestine may protrude through the front of the abdominal wall, is called an *omphalocele.* A related condition, *gastroschisis,* is a hole in the abdominal wall that occurs at a point other than the navel or umbilicus. In the case of a large omphalocele or gastroschisis, returning the organs into the abdominal cavity usually is a gradual process involving several operations. At first, if the opening is very large, a synthetic covering may be used to enclose the organs. Then, after the organs are contained within the abdominal cavity, the skin from both sides is sewn together.

SURGICAL PROCEDURES TO CORRECT FEEDING PROBLEMS

Some children have significant impairments of the muscles and nerves needed to coordinate chewing and swallowing. Problems in chewing and swallowing can lead to inadequate nutrition, choking, and aspiration of food particles into the lungs, resulting in recurrent pneumonia. For children for whom feeding by mouth is impossible, an operation called a *gastrostomy* can be performed. This procedure enables food to enter the stomach directly through a plastic tube. The surgeon creates an opening in the abdominal and stomach walls and places a gastrostomy tube through the opening into the stomach. Liquid or puréed food then can be given through the tube (see also Chapter 22).

In a condition called *gastroesophageal reflux*, the stomach contents may flow back into the food pipe or esophagus. Sometimes the material spills over into the windpipe or trachea, causing aspiration into the lungs and, subsequently, pneumonia. Gastroesophageal reflux occurs because of a weakness in the muscle that encircles the lower end of the esophagus, known as the *esophageal sphincter*. This muscle usually keeps food in the stomach from backing up into the esophagus. Severe gastroesophageal reflux may require correction by surgery. The procedure is known as *fundoplication*. In this operation, the upper part of the stomach is wrapped around the lower end of the esophagus and sewn in place.

SURGERY FOR CONGENITAL HEART DEFECTS

Not all of the congenital heart defects described in Chapter 13 require surgery because a few will correct themselves. For example, patent ductus arteriosus and small ventricular septal defects often close spontaneously. Also, the heart is able to compensate for some structural defects such as small atrial septal defects, small ventricular septal defects, and minor degrees of narrowing of pulmonic vessels and the aorta.

With severe congenital heart defects (see description in Chapter 13) such as tetralogy of Fallot, endocardial cushion defect, large atrial and ventricular septal defects, severe pulmonic and aortic stenosis, or coarctation of the aorta, the heart's ability to compensate is only partially or temporarily effective. Over time, further structural changes in the heart and pulmonary blood vessels may occur, including enlargement of the heart's chambers, thickening of the heart's walls, and increased blood pressure in the pulmonary arteries. Subsequently, as the efficiency of the circulation diminishes, the strain upon the whole body becomes obvious, and symptoms such as poor growth, shortness of breath, exercise intolerance, and frequent infections may develop. Heart surgery is necessary to prevent the downhill course.

Cardiac catheterization is a diagnostic procedure usually done before a heart defect is repaired to assess the extent of the problem. This procedure allows the cardiologist to visualize the inside structures of the heart as it pumps and to obtain oxygen concentrations and blood pressures of various parts of the heart. A detailed description of cardiac catheterization is provided in Chapter 22.

With the development of the heart–lung machine and the advent of open-heart surgery, great strides in the treatment of congenital heart disease have become possible. During open-heart surgery, blood is diverted from the heart to a machine where it is oxygenated and then returned to the child. This allows the surgeon to operate on structures inside the heart while the machine pumps the blood. Sometimes, preliminary surgery is indicated, such as *pulmonary banding*, if total correction of a severe cardiac defect is not feasible at an early age.

The type of surgery needed to correct congenital heart disease will vary according to the kind and degree of the cardiac defect present in the child. In infants with patent ductus arteriosus, surgical treatment consists of eliminating the increased flow of blood to the lungs by tying off the ductus arteriosus vessel that failed to close spontaneously after birth. Likewise, in some infants where the foramen ovale did not close spontaneously, surgical closure may be necessary.

If the problem is an opening between two chambers of the heart—for example, a ventricular septal defect—then the hole is closed by either sewing it shut directly or by patching it, depending on the size of the hole.

Valves that are either too tight, as in pulmonic stenosis and aortic stenosis, or too loose, as in mitral insufficiency, may need to be corrected by surgery. Excessive tightness of a valve can sometimes be relieved by cutting the band of fibrous tissue surrounding the valve, a procedure known as *commissurotomy*. Sometimes, he defective valve will have to be replaced with an artificial one. Similarly, a loose valve can be reconstructed surgically in an operation called *valvuloplasty*, or if necessary, the valve can be replaced. In coarctation of the aorta, the narrow portion of the blood vessel is removed and the remaining two ends sewn together.

If the problem is decreased blood flow to the lungs, as in tetralogy of Fallot, then the aim of the surgery is to deliver the oxygen-poor blood to the lungs for oxygenation. A variety of procedures have been devised to accomplish this, including connecting a branch of the aorta to a branch of the pulmonary artery or creating a connection (i.e., an anastomosis) between the aorta and the pulmonary artery. Today, total correction of tetralogy of Fallot can be accomplished. This involves enlargement of the connection between the right ventricle and the pulmonary artery and closure of the ventricular septal defect.

SURGICAL CORRECTION OF
PROBLEMS OF THE MUSCULOSKELETAL SYSTEM

Injury to the neuromuscular system including the muscles, nerves, and bones, or problems in the areas of the brain and spinal cord that control muscle function, can cause muscle dysfunction and deformities of bones and joints (for a discussion of various neuromuscular disabilities, see Chapter 18, Diseases of Muscles and Bones). Severe deformities and disabilities sometimes can be corrected or improved with surgery. Procedures that are used to treat *contractures* (shortening of muscles and tendons) caused by spasticity, hip dislocation, club foot, muscle weakness and paralysis, joint problems, and spinal deformities are described here.

Surgery for Contractures

Children with spastic cerebral palsy have overactive reflexes and tight muscles. Because of the spasticity, the child's arms and legs may be pulled into atypical positions, which often limit movements. To prevent permanent contractures, physical therapy is used in an attempt to relax and stretch muscles. Often such therapy cannot completely prevent a contracture from developing; in these cases, surgical intervention may then be necessary.

Contractures can be treated surgically by procedures to release and lengthen muscles and tendons, called *myotomy* and *tenotomy*, respectively. These procedures involve cutting either the shortened muscle or tendon to allow the affected joint to be manipulated into a central position. After the operation, a cast is applied to the affected limb to keep the joint in proper position while the cut ends of the muscle or tendon heal. When the cast is removed, physical therapy becomes important to prevent the recurrence of contractures. In some cases, myotomy or tenotomy can be done on an outpatient basis, as in heelcord lengthening. The casts usually remain on the affected limbs for 4–6 weeks. The time of recovery depends on the child's underlying neuromuscular problem and the type of surgical procedure performed. In complex situations, inpatient care is advised.

Surgical Intervention for Hip Dislocation

The unbalanced forces that spastic muscles exert on a joint also can cause dislocation of the bones at the joint. A common example is dislocation of the hip, which develops if the muscles that flex the thigh and those that pull it toward the midline are spastic. These forces tend to push the head of the bone of the upper leg, the femur,

out of its socket (Figure 4). In addition to muscle and tendon releases, it may be necessary to perform an *osteotomy* as well, to correct
the dislocation. During an osteotomy, the femur is cut transversely,
and after rotation the pieces are realigned so that the two ends of
the femur fit together. Sometimes, a wedge of bone from another
site is used to help position the cut ends of bone at the desired
angle. The bone segments are then fixed in the corrected position
with metal screws or wires.

    Congenital hip dislocation occurs in some children either as an iso-
lated defect or in association with other defects such as spina bifida.
Early treatment of a congenitally dislocated hip is aimed at repositioning the head of the femur in the joint socket, called the *acetabulum,* and keeping it there in good position (Figure 5). Frequently this
can be accomplished by casting or traction alone. In an older child,
the surgeon may have to "build" an acetabulum through osteotomies and bone grafts.

Figure 4.   A dislocated hip. The upper part of the femur, or leg bone, has slipped out of the
hip socket, shown by the arrow.

Figure 5. The arrow shows repositioning of the dislocated leg bone in its proper place in the hip socket.

Surgical Procedures for Clubfoot Deformity

Another common congenital defect of the bones is a *clubfoot*, or *equinovarus deformity*. Before surgery is performed, correction may be attempted with a serial casting procedure. If casting alone is unsuccessful, a combination of tendon releases, muscle transfers, osteotomies, and casting may be required.

Surgical Procedures for Muscle Weakness and Paralysis

Any disability that interrupts or stops the electrical impulses that travel down the nerves to a muscle can cause muscle weakness or paralysis. The degree of muscle weakness or of paralysis of a muscle or group of muscles depends on the number and kinds of nerve fibers affected. Muscles that do not receive nerve impulses do not grow well and become reduced in size, or atrophied. Sometimes, movement can be restored or strengthened by a muscle transfer operation. During this procedure an appropriate, healthy muscle that is near the weak or paralyzed muscle is separated from the bone to which it is attached. This free end then is transferred to the bony attachment of the weak or paralyzed muscle. When the transferred muscle contracts, it then produces movement at the new joint, in effect, replacing the weak or paralyzed muscle. Whether a muscle transfer is practical for a child depends on the kind of deformity present, the particular joint and limb involved, the status of the muscles available for transfer, and the type of underlying neuromuscular disorder.

Surgical Procedures for Joint Problems

When a joint is unstable—for example, the ankle in a paralyzed foot—sometimes a joint fusion, or *arthrodesis*, is performed. This operation is done both to correct the existing deformity and to prevent a potential progressive deformity. In this procedure, pieces of the bones that come together at the affected joint are removed and the joint is aligned in the desired position. This joint is then stabilized by casting. As healing progresses, the cut surfaces of the bones that are in contact with each other grow together, thus fusing the joint in the corrected position.

Surgical Correction for Spinal Deformities

The spine is composed of many small bones called *vertebrae*. The vertebrae are lined up one on top of another, creating a bony column in which the spinal cord rests. Moving from the head down, the spine is divided into four regions: cervical, which refers to the neck area; thoracic, which refers to the chest; lumbar, which refers to the lower back; and sacral, which refers to the pelvic area.

When viewed from the side, a typical spine is not straight like a broomstick, but, rather, is slightly S-shaped, with a mild curve forward of the cervical and lumbar regions (i.e., mild lordosis), and a slight curve backward of the thoracic and sacral spine (i.e., mild kyphosis).

There are three general types of spinal deformities: too much forward bend, or marked *lordosis;* too much backward curve, or marked *kyphosis;* and an atypical sideways curve, called *scoliosis* (Figure 6). The spinal abnormalities may be congenital as a result of structural abnormalities in the bones, or, more often, they may develop after birth as a complication of neuromuscular disorders such as cerebral palsy, spina bifida, or muscular dystrophy. In many children with scoliosis, the cause of scoliosis is not known; it is then called *idiopathic scoliosis.*

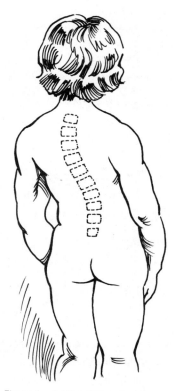

Figure 6.   Spine with scoliosis.

Children with a very mild degree of scoliosis most often do not require surgical treatment. However, these children will need regular followup to check whether the curvature is increasing with time. Sometimes electrical stimulation of the back muscles is used for mild scoliosis, although the effectiveness of this type of treatment has been questioned. Moderate degrees of scoliosis can be treated with bracing. Several different kinds of braces have been devised for this purpose. Today light-weight plastic material is used for most braces. Severe scoliosis and gradually increasing scoliosis despite bracing may require surgery. The usual procedure is a *spinal fusion*. The goal of a spinal fusion is to straighten the curve as much as possible and to prevent the vertebrae from shifting further. In order to accomplish this, metal rods called *Harrington rods* are wired along the spine to maintain proper alignment; this procedure is accompanied by bone grafts (using pieces of bone inserted along the spine that will stabilize the spine). After surgery the child must wear a plastic body jacket for 6–8 months.

SURGERY OF THE URINARY TRACT

Injury to the nerves that supply the muscles of the bladder, as in spina bifida, will impair urination. If the bladder cannot be emptied, the urine that accumulates may become infected with bacteria, and urine reflux (backing up of urine into the ureters and kidneys) may occur.

Children with spina bifida can usually prevent these complications by regularly emptying the bladder. This can be done by either pressing on the bladder—which is referred to as *Crede's maneuver*—or a tube called a *catheter* can be inserted through the urethra into the bladder at regular intervals (see also Chapter 26).

If these nonsurgical procedures are not successful in preventing reflux of urine into the ureters and injury to the kidneys, then surgery may be necessary. The goal of surgery is to provide unobstructed drainage of urine from the kidneys without the possibility of reflux. Sometimes, this is accomplished by connecting the ureters directly to a stoma (a surgically created opening on the surface of the abdomen). A plastic bag is worn over the stoma to collect the urine. If the ureters are too short or have been injured, then an ileal loop may be performed. In this operation, a piece of small intestine is used to form a connection, or conduit, between the ureters and the stoma. This operative procedure was often carried out in the past and rarely is used at the present time.

In some individuals who lack urinary sphincter control, artificial sphincters may be used, whereby a balloon-type mechanism is surgically implanted around the urethra.

SURGERY TO CORRECT HEARING DISORDERS

The structures of the ear that are primarily responsible for transmitting sound waves are the eardrum, or tympanic membrane, and the small bones in the middle ear called the *ossicles*. The inner ear, or cochlea, then transforms the sound waves into nerve impulses that are sent along the auditory nerve to the brain. In order for sound waves to be transmitted, the ear canal must be clear, the eardrum must be able to move freely, and the ossicles must work well and transmit the vibration to the inner ear. An ear canal full of wax, an immobile eardrum, ear infection, fluid in the middle ear, abnormalities of the ossicles, or any combination of these can impair hearing. For additional information on hearing problems, see Chapter 8.

The following two operative procedures can alleviate a hearing impairment:

1. In severe cases of otitis media (inflammation of the middle ear) where there is an increasing accumulation of pus, a small cut can be made in the eardrum to relieve the pressure and to drain the pus. This procedure is called a *myringotomy*.
2. In chronic serous otitis media with fluid accumulation in the middle ear, a small plastic tube, called a *ventilation* or *tympanostomy tube*, often is placed through the eardrum into the middle ear to drain the fluid from the middle ear.

SURGERY FOR THE EYE

Visual impairment may be an isolated disability or part of a complex of disabilities. Cataracts, glaucoma, and strabismus are among the more common conditions that impair vision and often are treated surgically.

Cataract Surgery

The lens is the part of the eye that focuses a visual image on the back of the eye known as the *retina*. A lens that has lost its typical transparency and has become cloudy has developed a cataract. Some dense cataracts can be identified easily, whereas others can be detected only when the eye is viewed through special instruments such as an ophthalmoscope or a slit lamp.

Cataracts as an isolated problem may be inherited or caused by trauma. Cataracts are also associated with a wide variety of disorders including congenital infections, such as congenital rubella syndrome; inborn errors of metabolism such as galactosemia, hypoparathyroidism, and diabetes mellitus; chromosome disorders such as Down syndrome; and other hereditary disorders including myotonic dystrophy.

Surgery is undertaken whenever a cataract significantly interferes with vision. Cataract surgery is done either by extraction of the affected lens or by using special, delicate instruments that pulverize the cataractous lens and then suck up and remove the debris. Following removal of the cataract, the child is fitted with either contact lenses or glasses to correct his or her vision.

Surgical Treatment of Glaucoma

Glaucoma is a condition in which there is increased pressure inside the eye. This elevated pressure can injure the retina and the optic nerve and cause permanent changes in the cornea.

The goal of surgical treatment in glaucoma is to control the pressure inside the eye. This is accomplished by draining the increased fluid in a procedure called a *goniotomy*. If this is unsuccessful, a filtering procedure known as a *trabeculectomy* is performed.

Surgical Correction of Strabismus

Strabismus is an atypical alignment of the eyes. It includes *esotropia* (cross-eyedness) in which the eyes turn inward, and *exotropia* (wall-eyedness) in which the eyes turn outward. Sometimes strabismus is due to underlying defects such as cataracts, tumors, near-sightedness (i.e., myopia), or far-sightedness (i.e., hyperopia). Also, an imbalance in the muscles that move the eyes can cause strabismus. Eye muscle surgery can correct the alignment problem. Amblyopia, or lazy eye, which often accompanies strabismus, usually is treated by patching the stronger eye. This promotes the use of the weaker eye until vision in the two eyes is equalized.

RECONSTRUCTIVE SURGERY

The goal of plastic or reconstructive surgery is to restore the typical structure and function of parts of the body that either developed atypically or have been injured by disease or trauma. Repair of a cleft lip or cleft palate is an example of a common type of reconstructive surgery.

The plastic surgeon works with soft tissues and muscles as well as with nerves and bones. Grafting of skin, muscle, and bone as well as the use of synthetic prostheses are often part of the reconstructive process. One area in which there has been major progress in recent years is in the surgical treatment of defects of the face and skull, as seen in Crouzon syndrome and Apert syndrome. The exact type of procedure performed is dictated by the extent of the structural defect present.

ACKNOWLEDGMENTS

Contributions have been made to this chapter by Katherine C. Castree, M.D., and Siegfried M. Pueschel, M.D., Ph.D., M.P.H.

26

Hospitalization and Aftercare

Being admitted to the hospital often is a frightening experience for children and their parents. With the proper information and preparation, however, a hospital stay can be made much less upsetting for you and your child.

For many children with developmental disabilities, frequent trips to the hospital are common. If your child must be admitted to a hospital, be sure you understand why it is recommended and what is to be gained from the hospitalization. If you are not familiar with certain technical terms, ask that they be explained. Also, question your child's doctor about the risks involved in any treatment or procedure planned. After all, in order to make decisions regarding your child's best care, you need adequate information about both the benefits and risks of any procedure and therapy.

Some procedures may be absolutely necessary, perhaps life-saving, leaving you little choice. Even for these procedures, you should be informed about the risks and possible side effects. Anticipated hospitalizations or surgery should be discussed with your child's pediatrician and with involved specialists.

PREPARING YOUR CHILD FOR HOSPITAL ADMISSION

If your child is old enough to understand that he or she will be admitted to the hospital, tell him or her in simple words shortly beforehand what is going to happen, why he or she is to be hospitalized, and what the outcome will be. Be honest. If you know that there will be some discomfort or something is going to be painful, tell him or her about it and offer your support and reassurance. Explain how long the pain might last, if you know, or ask the doctor to do this if he or she has a good rapport with your child.

Some hospitals have programs designed to help children get used to the hospital setting. These programs may include tours of the pediatric section of the hospital, discussion of treatment procedures, introduction to play activities, films, and other information that will prepare children for a hospital stay. You may want to check with your hospital before your child is admitted to see if such a program exists.

You also may find that books for children describing a hospital stay are helpful. Having your child talk to another child who was hospitalized or had a procedure that your child is scheduled to undergo is another way of preparing your child. Such preparation generally helps to reduce fears and apprehensions.

YOUR ROLE IN CARING FOR YOUR CHILD IN THE HOSPITAL

When your child is admitted to a hospital ward, it is a good idea to get to know the people who will be caring for him or her. Introduce yourself to the professionals who are involved in your child's care. Get to know the staff persons' names and inquire about their roles. The more interest you show in what is happening, the more likely it will be that the staff will respect the suggestions and requests you may have. If you can help with your child's care and if it does not interfere with the professional duties of the staff, do so, as it will make your child more comfortable. Many hospitals have unlimited visiting hours for parents and permit overnight stays.

Sometimes parents become frustrated and angry when the hospital staff treat their child differently than the parents do at home. Do not be afraid to discuss with the hospital staff the ways to approach your child or to explain his or her likes and dislikes. The hospital staff also want to make a child's stay as pleasant as possible. For example, if a certain position is more comfortable for your child or has been suggested to prevent pressure sores, be sure to show the staff this. You can make helpful reminders by putting a sign in colorful letters over your child's headboard, such as "Please sit me up to watch TV."

DISCHARGE PLANNING

If it has not been suggested by the hospital staff, ask to meet before discharge with the persons who have been caring for your child in

the hospital. This is particularly important if special equipment, medications, or nursing care is required at home. Such discharge planning should take place far enough in advance to allow time for special arrangements to be made.

If special equipment is needed, a social worker or nurse may be able to help you arrange for its rental or purchase. These professionals also may have valuable information about how to obtain funding for expensive equipment.

HOME CARE FOR YOUR CHILD

Learning What Is Necessary for Home Care

After a child has been discharged, parents are expected to carry out the basic care procedures at home. For example, a child might need

ongoing treatments, changes of dressings, or care of a cast. Whatever procedures are needed, they should be taught to you by the
nursing staff before your child leaves the hospital. You probably will
be asked to be with your child while a nurse demonstrates the procedure. Often, nurses ask parents to practice the procedure while
they watch.

It may be helpful to make a daily plan for your child's care at
home that is similar to the one that has been carried out in the hospital. By mapping out a daily schedule, you will be sure not to miss
giving medicine, changing a dressing, or doing any other necessary
procedures. Be sure to include some fun activities during and between care procedures. This is a good way to pass the time, and
generally will help to improve your child's spirits.

Recuperation

The recuperation period, or the time it takes the individual to resume everyday activities, depends on the nature and severity of the
disability, the type of surgery done, and the medical problem that
led to the hospitalization. The doctor can give you an idea of how
long this may be.

While the child's body adjusts to the changes brought on by an
illness or an operation and while healing takes place, frequent periods of rest will be required. This does not mean your child has to
sleep during these periods; he or she can play quietly, read, watch
television, listen to music, or do other quiet activities.

If your child must stay in bed and his or her activity is very
limited, dietary changes may be necessary to prevent constipation.
Also, after certain types of surgery, special diets may be required.
Be sure to check with the hospital and with your doctor for any
special dietary instructions.

The doctor also can give you some idea of how long your child's
activities should be restricted. Following the period of restriction, routine activities should be increased gradually until the child is able to
resume his or her usual level of functioning without fatigue. During
recuperation from surgery, particularly following orthopaedic surgery, some children will need physical therapy or special exercises.

At times, it is important for your child's progress toward recovery to be monitored by someone with training in health care. If this
is needed, a visiting nurse can be involved in home care following
hospitalization. Around-the-clock nursing care may be necessary for
some children with complex problems requiring numerous procedures. A nurse can assist you with changing dressings, equipment,
care of a cast, positioning, and other health-related concerns that

may arise. Nurses also can be a valuable link between you and other health care specialists.

Taking Care of Yourself

For severe medical problems that require constant monitoring, there are programs and facilities that can help with your child's care. Some states have pediatric nursing care centers or special programs that provide respite, babysitting, or home care for very ill children (see also Chapter 31 on Resource Development).

Many parents of ill children may feel guilty about wanting an occasional break from their responsibilities. In fact, taking a break from the strain of caring for a child with a chronic illness is not only a good idea but is often essential for stressed parents. Spending 24 hours a day, 7 days a week attending to the needs of a sick child can quickly use up all of your energy and patience. If such demands on your physical and mental resources continue unabated for a long time, it might even be harmful to your own health. Therefore, taking advantage of any available services benefits parents and children alike. You may want to check with your local health department, hospital, visiting nurse, pediatrician, health clinic, or social service department for information about respite care and other services for families.

HEALTH AIDS, ASSISTIVE TECHNOLOGY, AND TREATMENT USED DURING POSTHOSPITAL CARE

Many children leave the hospital with prescriptions for special equipment and treatment. Some types of equipment are simple to manage and require little effort on the part of the parent or caregiver. Others, however, require some training in order to operate and to keep them in proper working order. For example, you will need to become familiar with specific care procedures if your child is discharged with a plaster cast, tracheostomy, or other equipment.

Casts

If your child is discharged from the hospital with a cast, you will need to make sure that the cast is kept clean and dry. If your child is not toilet trained and the cast is near the diaper area, the edges can be protected by plastic such as Saran Wrap. The edges of the cast should be bound off or covered with adhesive tape to prevent them from causing sores to the skin. The hospital nurse or visiting nurse can show you how to do this.

Other things to watch for are stains that appear on the cast indicating possible bleeding beneath the cast. If you see this, you should call your child's doctor right away. It is a good idea to circle the area using a wax pencil or Magic Marker and to write the date and time on the edge of the circle. Then you will be able to tell if the stain is spreading, possibly indicating further bleeding.

If you note any odor, especially one that is foul smelling, from beneath the cast, report this to your child's doctor. It could indicate that an infection has developed.

If the cast is on an arm or leg, the circulation or blood flow to the area should be checked several times a day, in particular during the first few days after the cast has been applied. Ordinarily, the toes or fingers should be warm to the touch, pink in color, and should not appear swollen. The circulation can be checked by using a process called *blanching*, which means pressing the tip of a toe or finger between the thumb and the index finger. This causes the toe or finger to turn white. When you release the pressure, you should see an immediate return of pinkness to the toe or finger, which will tell you that there is adequate circulation. If the toes or fingers appear bluish-purple in color, are cold to the touch, seem to hurt, or do not blanch, then you should report this to the doctor immediately. It may mean that the cast has become too tight and is interfering with blood flow.

Shunt Care for Hydrocephalus

A shunt is a plastic tube that is used to drain excess fluid from the brain in conditions such as hydrocephalus (fluid accumulation inside the brain) or subdural effusion (fluid accumulation in localized areas surrounding the brain). During shunt implantation, one end of the tube is placed in one of the ventricles of the brain where the fluid is made or in the subdural space in case of subdural effusion. The other end is inserted into the abdominal cavity where the excess fluid can be absorbed. The rest of the tube lies just under the skin and can usually be seen and felt behind the ear, running down the side of the neck to the chest and abdomen. (For more details about shunt operation, see Chapter 25.)

If your child has a shunt, ask the neurosurgeon how to check for shunt failure and what you need to know about general shunt care. Symptoms of shunt failure include drowsiness, headache, listlessness, irritability, a high-pitched cry, vomiting, seizures, and in the case of very young babies, a bulging soft spot, or fontanel, on the top of the head. If you think that the shunt is not working and you observe these symptoms, call the physician who put the shunt in place in the hospital or take your child to the nearest hospital emergency room.

Tracheostomy

A tracheostomy is a surgical opening at the front of the throat into the windpipe (i.e., trachea) to make breathing easier. A tracheostomy is usually done when someone is having a serious breathing problem caused by a blocked airway. A tube to which a respirator can be attached is placed into the opening of the windpipe. It also provides an opening through which oxygen can be administered and mucus or secretions can be suctioned from the main passageways of the lung. Suctioning may be required on a regular basis to keep the airway open. If your child is to have a tracheostomy and particularly if your child is going home with a tracheostomy in place, you will need to be instructed in how to suction your child and how to take care of the tracheostomy.

Because tracheostomy tubes do not allow the child to talk, it becomes important to devise some way to know when the child is trying to communicate with you. Some parents become accustomed to the differences in the child's breathing pattern and can tell if the child is crying or in need of attention. Sometimes breathing or heart monitors are used at home, especially during the night to alert you if there are serious problems.

You should be aware of the signs of respiratory distress or difficulty in breathing. They include restlessness; duskiness or a bluish tint to the skin, especially around the mouth, lips, and tongue; gasping for air; rapid breathing; and limpness. Know what to do and who to call if these signs are observed: First, find out quickly whether the airway is obstructed by mucus or whether the tracheostomy tube is dislodged. If you have been well instructed, you most likely will be able to remove the obstruction by suctioning or by putting the tracheostomy tube in its proper position. If you cannot relieve the obstruction, then immediately call 911, a local rescue squad, or your child's doctor, or take your child to the closest emergency room, which ever will be the quickest way to get help for your child. Most importantly, be prepared for such emergencies.

Respirator

There are many different types of respirators. If your child requires a respirator, a respiratory therapist, nurse, or doctor can explain how it works, how to use it, and how to monitor its functioning.

A respirator may assist your child's breathing. The respirator is a machine that can push air, often mixed with oxygen, into the lungs when the lungs or other parts of the respiratory system are not functioning properly. The respirator is attached to either a tracheostomy tube or an endotracheal tube. An endotracheal tube is a plastic tube that is placed through the mouth and down the throat into the windpipe, to make a clear passageway for air to enter the lungs. Respirators also are often used during surgery.

When the respirator is no longer needed, you may hear the medical staff talking about weaning your child off the machine. Weaning means gradually decreasing your child's dependency on the respirator by giving the child alternate periods of time to breathe on his or her own. Weaning is a normal part of being taken off the respirator.

Oxygen Administration

If your child needs oxygen, it can be administered in one of several ways: by a mask, a nasal cannula, or a tracheostomy tube. Oxygen masks are usually worn over the nose and mouth. A nasal cannula is a piece of narrow plastic tubing with two short extensions that fit into the nostrils. The different methods of administering oxygen usually include the use of a fine water mist, which keeps the nasal and respiratory passages moist.

The oxygen used in hospitals ordinarily is delivered through an outlet in the wall of the child's room. If oxygen is needed at home, it is usually provided in steel flasks, tanks, or compressors, which can be serviced and maintained by a medical supply company.

Oxygen administered in the home is typically used in combination with a humidifier, oxygen concentrator, or compressor. Be sure to understand how the oxygen supply works, what the auxiliary machines are used for, and who to call if the equipment fails to work properly. Someone from the company that provided the equipment should be able to answer your questions.

Some children need certain medications mixed in a mist or aerosol solution that is inhaled into the lungs. Often these are administered through an oxygen system like the ones just described.

Suctioning

Children with respiratory problems often need to be suctioned to rid the respiratory tract of the excess mucus that is accumulating. During suctioning, one end of a small tube is placed in the respiratory tract and the other end is attached to a suction machine that uses negative pressure, like a vacuum, to suck the mucus and secretions out of the child's nose, throat, tracheostomy, trachea, and lung passages. The technique for suctioning, if your child should need it, should be taught to you by a respiratory therapist or nurse.

Cardiopulmonary Resuscitation

If your child has serious respiratory or cardiac problems, knowing cardiopulmonary resuscitation (CPR) can be very important. It may help save your child's life in a medical emergency. Courses in cardiopulmonary resuscitation are offered through most chapters of the American Heart Association and the American Red Cross.

Feeding Tubes

There are several ways to feed a child who cannot take food by mouth. Different types of tubes and other means are available.

Nasogastric Tube   If a child does not suck well or cannot eat typically, a tube may have to be passed through the nose, down the back of the throat into the esophagus (food pipe), and then into the stomach. Food, in the form of formula or other special puréed nourishment, is given through the nasogastric tube. A feeding bag or pouch is attached to the end of the nasogastric tube and then its content is drained into the stomach by gravity. When you insert the tube, it is important to make sure it is in the stomach. Tube insertion should be taught to you by the hospital staff who also will instruct you as to how often and what to feed your child.

For some children, nasogastric tube feedings are used only as a supplement. These children may continue to receive some part of their daily nourishment by mouth. Typically nasogastric tube feeding is limited to a short period of time. If feeding problems are chronic or severe, other means of feeding may be used.

Gastrostomy Tube   A gastrostomy is a surgical opening into the stomach, made through the wall of the abdomen. A gastrostomy tube is then placed into this opening. This tube has a balloon cup at its end, which is inflated after it is inserted into the stomach. This helps to hold the tube in place inside the stomach. When the gastrostomy tube is not in use, a fitted cap may be inserted into the open end of the tube or a clamp may be applied to close off the tube.

Sometimes traditional, catheter-type gastrostomy tubes are replaced with a plastic "button," which lies flat against the child's abdomen. This "button," covered by a snap-on cap, has a notched opening under the cap to which a connecting catheter is attached and locked into place. This catheter attaches to the feeding tube.

Special formulas, puréed foods, and other liquids can be given through the gastrostomy tube. The feedings may flow by gravity, or may sometimes be given by means of a special pump. The pump allows the caregiver to set the rate at which the feeding will flow.

The type of foods, and how and when they are to be administered, should be determined by the attending physician and nutritionist. You may be instructed to add different foods to your child's diet on your own, but it is always a good idea to check with your doctor before making any changes.

Central Line   A central line is a means of intravenous feeding and another way of providing nutrition. It is used when there are severe problems with the intestines and absorption of nutrients. An intravenous catheter is placed surgically into a large blood vessel such as a vein in the neck.

A special intravenous solution called *hyperalimentation* is administered for a number of hours during the day and/or night. There are procedures for cleansing the area where the tube enters the skin. Be sure to get instructions from the nurse or doctor before your child is discharged with a central line. Also, arrangements for obtaining special solutions should be made before the child goes home.

Oral Stimulation   For children fed by a nasogastric tube, gastrostomy tube, or central line, oral stimulation and good mouth care are very important. Otherwise, these children may come to dislike having things in their mouths. If possible, they should be given some food by mouth, even if it is a very small amount. This will help them to accept different tastes and textures later, as well as to keep the sucking, chewing, and swallowing mechanisms working. If your child cannot have any food by mouth, an occupational therapist or speech-language therapist can advise you about exercises and oral stimulation activities. This is particularly important if your child is expected to eat by mouth at some time in the future.

When a child is not fed by mouth, the mucous membranes (linings) of the mouth as well as the tongue and lips need special care. Good mouth care, gentle brushing of the teeth, and running your finger, covered with a soft wet cloth, over the child's gums and the insides of the cheeks can prevent problems. Lemon and glycerine swabs also can be used to clean the gums and mouth. Vaseline or similar lubricants should be applied to the lips to keep them from becoming cracked and dry.

Bladder and Bowel Aids

Children with spinal cord injuries or spina bifida or who have sustained damage to the bladder or other parts of the urinary tract may need assistance in passing urine. There are two major ways urinary elimination can be assisted: by catheterization or through an ileal loop or conduit (see also Chapter 25 on surgery). Some children will need a colostomy if specific congenital anomalies, tumors, or other gastrointestinal disorders do not allow natural elimination of stool.

Urinary Catheters   For children who have poor or no bladder control, intermittent catheterization may be necessary to prevent urinary tract infections and other complications of the kidneys. In addition, catheterization may help reduce the likelihood of children wetting their clothes. A urinary catheter is a thin plastic tube that can be inserted into the bladder to drain urine. Intermittent catheterization is carried out by a parent or other caregiver for the very young, but it is taught to older children so that they can do the procedure themselves. It involves passing the catheter through the small opening that leads to the urinary bladder. Intermittent catheterization reduces the chance of infection by preventing urine from remaining in the bladder too long or from flowing back into the ureters (tubes) that lead to the kidneys.

Ileal Loop or Conduit   With the advent of intermittent catheterization, the need for an ileal loop has decreased markedly and is rarely done today. This surgical procedure involved creating a stoma (opening) at the abdomen, through which urine was collected in a drainage bag worn over the stoma. The drainage bag attaches to an adhesive-backed wafer that sticks to the area around the stoma. The wafers are changed as necessary, and the bag is emptied periodically throughout the day (see detailed discussion in Chapter 25 on surgery).

Colostomy   A colostomy is a surgical procedure in which a stoma is created (see Chapter 25 on surgery). A small segment of bowel is surgically brought through the stoma in the abdominal wall through which stool or bowel movement are passed to the exterior of the body. A drainage bag, worn over the stoma, is used to collect the stool. This bag is emptied and cleaned at regular intervals. Good skin care around the stoma is very important because stool and secretions that are typically in the intestinal tract can be irritating to the skin. Specific care of the colostomy as well as information about nutrition can be obtained from the surgeon or nursing staff who have cared for your child in the hospital.

ACKNOWLEDGMENTS

Contributions have been made to this chapter by Carol A. Musso, B.S., R.N. and Barbara D. Remor, B.S., R.N.

V

Assessments, Education, and Resource Development

27

Assessing Developmental Disabilities
Psychological Tests and Procedures

Earlier chapters in this book have discussed the many ways developmental disabilities can be detected. This chapter describes the more complex process of assessment. The discussion focuses on evaluation of developmental and intellectual abilities and the tests and procedures used in the process. The task of assessing intellectual abilities typically belongs to the psychologist; thus, this chapter emphasizes instruments used by psychologists. The following test categories are examined:

Screening tests
Mental and intelligence tests
Developmental tests
Infant tests
Adaptive behavior scales
Achievement tests
Behavioral procedures
Personality tests and self-report inventories
Neuropsychological approaches

Tests in a number of these categories are summarized in Table 1.

Before describing the different types of instruments, a general overview of assessment is provided. It is important to be aware of what various psychological tests and procedures can and cannot tell you. Each type of test is designed to provide a particular kind of

Table 1.   Summary of commonly used tests

Test and publisher	Ages	Comments
Screening Tests		
Denver Developmental Screening Test–II Denver Development Materials, Inc. Denver, 1990	6 weeks to 6 years	Identifies possible developmental disabilities in four areas: language, gross motor, fine motor, and personal/social development.
First STEP: Screening Test for Evaluating Preschoolers The Psychological Corp. San Antonio, TX, 1993	2.9 years to 6.2 years	Brief, individually administered test to identify preschool children at risk for developmental delays in four areas: cognition, communication, motor development, and adaptive behavior.
Intelligence Tests		
Stanford-Binet Intelligence Scale (4th ed.) Riverside Publishing Co. Chicago, 1986	2 years to 18+ years	Norm-referenced intelligence test. Provides scores in four subtest areas: verbal reasoning, abstract/visual reasoning, quantitative reasoning, and short-term memory. A full-test composite score also is provided.
Wechsler Preschool and Primary Scale of Intelligence– Revised (WPPSI–R) The Psychological Corp. San Antonio, TX, 1989	3 years to 7.3 years	Norm-referenced general intelligence test. Provides a verbal IQ, performance IQ, and full-scale IQ scores. Gives a profile of strengths and weaknesses.
Wechsler Intelligence Scale for Children (3rd ed.) (WISC–III) The Psychological Corp. San Antonio, TX, 1991	6 years to 16.11 years	Norm-referenced general intelligence test. Provides scores for each subtest, a full-scale IQ score, performance IQ score, and verbal IQ score. Also provides a profile of strengths and weaknesses.
Wechsler Adult Intelligence Scale–Revised (WAIS–R) The Psychological Corp. San Antonio, TX, 1981	16 years to 74 years	Norm-referenced general intelligence test for adults. Like WISC–R, it provides a verbal IQ, performance IQ, full-scale IQ, and a profile of strengths and weaknesses.
McCarthy Scales of Children's Abilities The Psychological Corp. San Antonio, TX, 1972	2.6 years to 12.5 years	Norm-referenced test. Provides scores in five areas: verbal, perceptual performance, quantitative, memory, and

(continued)

Table 1. *(continued)*

Test and publisher	Ages	Comments
		motor. Offers a general cognitive index for total test performance.
Kaufman Assessment Battery for Children (K-ABC) American Guidance Service Circle Pines, MN, 1983	2.5 years to 12.5 years	Norm-referenced intelligence test. Designed to assess learning potential and preferred learning style. Scaled scores for mental processing subtests and composite scores are provided.
Leiter International Performance Scale Western Psychological Services Los Angeles, 1979	2 years to adult	Nonverbal intelligence test. Consists of a series of subtests requiring matching. Tasks range from simple color matching to complex patterns and analogies.
Infant Tests		
Bayley Scales of Infant Development (2nd ed.) The Psychological Corp. San Antonio, TX, 1993	1 month to 42 months	Norm-referenced test. Provides a mental developmental index, psychomotor developmental index, and infant behavior rating.
Alpern-Boll Developmental Profile Psychological Development Publications Indianapolis, IN, 1972	6 month to 12 years	Developmental scale. Uses interview format to assess abilities in five areas of functioning.
Brazelton Neonatal Behavior Assessment Scale J. B. Lippincott Co. Philadelphia, 1972	Newborn	Tests newborns' behavioral and neurological status, including responses to environmental events, organization, and behavioral state or level of arousal.
Ordinal Scales of Intellectual Development University of Illinois Press Champaign, 1975	1 month to 2 years	Developmental scale based on Piagetian theory. Contains six ordinal scales measuring level of achievement of the baby on various cognitive abilities.
Adaptive Behavior Scales		
Vineland Adaptive Behavior Scales American Guidance Service Circle Pines, MN, 1984	Birth to 18.11 years	Adaptive behavior scale. Measures communication, daily living, socialization, and motor skills. Provides standard scores and age-equivalents. Three editions are available.

(continued)

Table 1.   *(continued)*

Test and publisher	Ages	Comments
AAMR Adaptive Behavior Scales–School Edition PRO-ED Austin, TX, 1993	3 years to adult	Contains rating scale divided into two parts. The first part focuses on skills of personal independence and responsibility in daily living. Skills are grouped into nine behavioral domains. The second part focuses on social maladaptation. Has been standardized. Provides quotients and percentiles.

Achievement Tests

Peabody Individual Achievement Test–Revised (PIAT–R) American Guidance Service Circle Pines, MN, 1970	Kindergarten to grade 12	Individual achievement test. Assesses skills in mathematics, reading comprehension, spelling, and general information. Grade-equivalent and age-equivalent scores for each subtest and a composite score are available.
Wechsler Individual Achievement Test (WIAT) The Psychological Corp. San Antonio, TX, 1992	5 years to 19 years	Comprehensive battery with eight subtests: basic reading, math reasoning, spelling, reading comprehension, numerical operations, listening comprehension, and oral and written expression. Provides standard scores by age and grade, percentiles, and grade equivalents. Standardized with WISC–III allowing comparisons between achievement and ability.
Wide Range Achievement Test (3rd ed.) (WRAT–3) PRO-ED Austin, TX, 1993	5 years to adult	Individual achievement test that contains three subtests: reading, spelling, and arithmetic. Grade equivalent percentile ranks and standard scores available for each subtest.
Metropolitan Achievement Tests The Psychological Corp. San Antonio, TX, 1978	Kindergarten to grade 12	Achievement test originally published in 1930; revised most recently in 1978. Includes survey batteries for skill assessments and three instructional batteries for diagnostic purposes.

(continued)

Table 1. *(continued)*

Test and publisher	Ages	Comments
		Provides fall and spring norms for each grade level.
Iowa Tests of Basic Skills Primary Battery 1979 Multilevel Battery 1978 Riverside Publishing Co. Chicago, 1979	Kindergarten to grade 9	Achievement test battery. Assesses performance in reading, mathematics, spelling, language usage, and work study skills.

Neuropsychological Test Batteries

Test and publisher	Ages	Comments
Halstead-Reitan Neuropsychological Test Battery for Children V. H. Winston & Sons Washington, DC, 1974	9 years to 14 years	Comprehensive battery of cognitive, motor, and perceptual tests from which an index of neurological impairment is calculated. Includes 11 tests and can take 6 or more hours to administer.
Luria-Nebraska Neuropsychological Test Battery—Children's Revision Western Psychological Services Los Angeles, 1981	8 years to 12 years	Standardized test battery containing 11 subscales including gross and fine motor, tactile and visual functions, rhythm, speech, memory, reading, writing, arithmetic, and intellectual processes. Test takes approximately 2½ hours to administer.

Personality Tests and Self-Report Inventories

Test and publisher	Ages	Comments
Personality Inventory for Children—Revised Format (PIC–R) Western Psychological Services Los Angeles, 1982	3 years to 16 years	Consists of a number of brief true-false items to be completed by a parent, who answers whether each describes his or her child.
Children's Apperception Test (CAT) Western Psychological Services Los Angeles, 1980	3 years to 10 years	Consists of 10 pictures of animals shown in a variety of situations. The child is asked to describe what is happening in the pictures.
Roberts Apperception Test for Children (RATC) Western Psychological Services Los Angeles, 1982	6 years to 15 years	Norm-referenced test that measures adaptive and maladaptive functioning on 11 scales. The test pictures are realistic illustrations of children and adults in everyday activities.

(continued)

Table 1.   *(continued)*

Test and publisher	Ages	Comments
Behavior Assessment System for Children (BASC) American Guidance Service Circle Pines, MN, 1992	4 years to 18 years	A system of instruments (parent rating scales, teacher rating scales, self-report of personality) used to identify emotional and behavior disorders in children and adolescents. Provides percentiles by gender and age.
Behavioral Procedures		
Forms for Behavior Analysis with Children Research Press Champaign, IL, 1983	Children and adolescents	Contains 42 behavior assessment forms to aid professionals in making proper diagnoses and developing treatment plans. Formats include direct observation, interview, self-report, and parent report.

information, and each has limitations. Knowing a test's purpose and its limitations can help you to interpret the results more accurately.

ASSESSING DEVELOPMENTAL PROBLEMS

Assessment, or *evaluation,* refers to a careful, systematic examination of a child's skills and areas of need in order to determine current levels of functioning and future expectations. Basically, an assessment involves gathering information through observing behavior, interviewing children and families, and testing. What actually takes place during a specific assessment depends on what information the parent and evaluator want to know. In other words, the purpose of the assessment determines the types of tests and procedures, as well as the number of instruments, used. There are numerous reasons for having evaluations. One parent may want to know how a child is developing in general compared to others his or her age. Another may be concerned about a specific performance area such as speech-language or motor coordination, and the impact this may have on learning ability. Still another may want to know if the child is making progress in an intervention program. Evaluations can be tailored to answer both general and specific concerns of families and schools.

Formal testing can thus answer a variety of questions, each having a different purpose. The following list summarizes a number of assessment purposes, including diagnosis, prediction, selection, intervention, and program evaluation.

Diagnosis: To determine whether an individual has a problem and, if so, what kind

Prediction: To make a scientific guess about what is likely to happen in the future for an individual or group of individuals

Selection: To choose individuals for inclusion in a group (Selection decisions are made every day. A common example is deciding whether to hire a job applicant. In the developmental disabilities field, tests may be used to determine who may benefit from special services, or who may be ready to change from one program to another.)

Intervention: To obtain information about how a specific individual functions and to use this information to plan appropriate education or treatment programs

Program evaluation: To determine how well an education or treatment program is succeeding in achieving its goals

When testing children for possible developmental disabilities, professionals usually are concerned about diagnosis, prediction, and intervention. They want to determine whether a child has a developmental problem, and, if he or she does, the extent of the disability and the best type of care for the child.

Professionals assessing children with developmental disabilities administer tests and procedures to answer questions about children such as: Is the sequence or rate of development typical or unusually slow? Is a particular area of development affected, or is the effect observed in all areas? Can a specific disorder be recognized, and if so, are effective treatments available? Are there ways to compensate for the functional effects of a disability? Many professionals view assessment as an ongoing process in which progress toward developmental goals can be monitored through periodic assessments or recurring evaluations.

During some assessments, professionals must judge whether an individual child's performance on a test deviates from the norm, or typical performance of children of the same chronological age. This type of comparison of a specific child to average children forms the basis of many useful assessment scales. Such scales, sometimes referred to as *norm-referenced*, or *normative*, tests, are designed so results can be summarized easily and expressed as numerical scores. An intelligence test, which provides an intelligence quotient (IQ), is an example of a norm-referenced test. Many IQ tests also are standardized, which means that the procedures for administering and scoring the test are clearly specified and are performed the same way every time the test is given. When an individual's test score is significantly below the norm and parents and evaluators feel the child's performance during testing accurately represented his or her skills, then the evaluator is likely to conclude that there is a developmental problem. Minor deviations from the norm are more difficult to interpret. In some individuals, the test score will reflect a mild disability, whereas in others, it may indicate that the child was not performing up to par during the evaluation. When the findings are ambiguous, periodic retesting may be needed to get a better picture of the child's rate of development and learning.

Comparing an individual child's test score to the average is just one way to evaluate ability. Some tests compare an individual's performance to a list of skills, abilities, or achievements in specific content areas. Such instruments are referred to as *criterion-referenced* tests. Other terms to describe this type of instrument are *content-referenced* and *objective-referenced*. Many tests of academic ability and basic skills are examples of criterion-referenced tests. Professionals also observe the child's behavior during testing and inquire about adaptive (self-care) skills. Noting how a child approaches a task, interacts with the examiner, focuses on test items, and attends to events in the environment are some of the observations evaluators make during testing. Such information, along with test scores, gives a truer picture of the child's capability. For children with disabilities, the impact of the disability on opportunities to learn, the effect of adaptive equipment, and the child's attempts to compensate for the disability all must be considered during the assessment. For example, a child with severe cerebral palsy who has difficulty controlling facial muscles may not be able to speak intelligibly. Yet, the child may have developed age-appropriate skills in understanding language and in communicating in other ways. The evaluator is faced with the task of assessing the child's language abilities, whether they involve sign language, total communication (use of sign language, gestures, speech, communication boards, and so forth), use of communication boards, or other alternative systems. Regardless of the impairment, examiners of children with developmental disabilities have to assess areas of strength, areas of need, and methods of compensation. More accurate assessments allow education and intervention programs to be better tailored to the individual.

Many tests and procedures can be used effectively to assess the skills of children with disabilities. Some developmental disorders, however, are so significant or affect one area of functioning to such an extent that it becomes impossible to use certain standardized tests. In such instances, special tests or modifications to existing instruments will be necessary. In general, the greater the impairment of one or more senses—seeing, hearing, or feeling—and the greater the disruption of the child's response systems—speaking, gesturing, or moving—the harder it will be to discover the child's skills and competencies.

Evaluators of children who have developmental disabilities must consider the impact of the impairment on the child's ability to show what he or she knows. They also must consider what interpretations and generalizations can be made from results obtained from modified tests and procedures. And they must be comfortable working with children with disabilities to help them feel at ease and to encourage them to attempt tasks that may be difficult. When evaluating children from diverse cultures, evaluators must consider the child's background and experience, particularly when test norms were derived from another group's results.

TEST VALIDITY AND RELIABILITY

Psychological tests and procedures vary in length, format, and purpose. Some are administered individually; others are given to groups of people. Some are paper-and-pencil tests, others are oral, and still others involve object manipulations. Some seem like tests taken in school; others seem more like play or games.

Different tests are designed to measure various aspects of development. How well a test succeeds in measuring what it is expected to measure is called its *validity*. When selecting assessment instruments, professionals consider a test's validity. For results to be meaningful, the test first must be valid. As an example of how validity can affect findings, imagine a test of mathematical skills that only asks a child to count sets of objects. Although the test involves numbers, the child does not have to demonstrate any computational skills. Thus, the results would not be a valid measure of mathematical ability for a school-age child.

Another important consideration is test *reliability*. Reliability refers to the consistency of a test's results. A test administered twice to the same individual should yield the same or very similar results. If the findings are very different, the test should not be considered reliable. The more reliable a test, the more confidence the evaluator can have in the value of the results. Of course, individual characteristics of the child, the testing situation, and other circumstances still must be considered when interpreting the findings.

In developing tests and procedures, professionals begin with a particular theory or belief about how children grow and develop. These theories and beliefs influence what types of test items will be included, the purpose of the test, how the test is constructed, and how the results will be interpreted. It is helpful for parents and others who are the recipients of a child's test results to understand something about the test itself, how it was developed, its theoretical basis, and what it purports to measure.

TYPES OF TESTS

The majority of tests and procedures used in assessment can be classified as either *norm-referenced* or *criterion-referenced*. These terms describe how the tests were developed and whether the findings are compared to the average performances of others or to some standard criteria. Other types of tests, sometimes referred to as *process-oriented* measures, look at the specific strategies children use in solving problems or in responding to events in their environment.

Norm-Referenced Tests

As previously stated, norm-referenced tests compare an individual's test score to the average score of a group. Norm-referenced tests can be developed for any subject matter or area of functioning. Both intelligence tests and achievement tests, discussed later in the chapter, are norm-referenced tests. The norms are the average scores, or standards, against which an individual score is evaluated. They typically are found in tables in the test manual and show the expected scores for children at various ages. These comparison scores, often referred to as *age norms,* are established through painstaking research, usually with hundreds of children at each age level.

Instead of age norms, certain tests utilize grade-level norms as the standard of comparison. Thus, scores are reported as the level of functioning expected of children in a particular grade. For example, a score of 4.1 on a mathematics achievement test with grade-level norms indicates that the child's mathematic skills are equivalent to those expected of a youngster in the first month of the fourth grade.

Norms can be established for any group, such as children with a common developmental disability, medical diagnosis, or cultural background. It is important to know if the comparison group on which the test is based differs from the child being tested in important ways. If significant differences exist, the test may not be appropriate for the child, and if administered, the results could be incorrect or misleading. For example, if a child tested on a norm-referenced intelligence test is found to have a lower than expected score, at first glance you might conclude that the youngster lacks certain expected thinking abilities. But, if the child tested has a severe hearing impairment and the normative group consisted only of children with typical hearing, the appropriateness of the test and results suddenly is called into question. The child with a hearing impairment would be at a disadvantage, particularly if the test contained many oral questions and answers. The test would not be evaluating this child's thinking skills, but rather only the child's ability to answer the questions that were heard. In the same way, if the normative group included only native English-speaking children but the child being tested speaks a foreign language, then the results would be inaccurate. At times, it may be useful to know how a child who differs from the norm performs on particular test items when compared with the general population, but one must be very careful about such comparisons so that certain problems are not misdiagnosed.

Criterion-Referenced Tests

Criterion-referenced tests compare a child's performance to a specific standard or criterion. The criterion outlines what the child is expected to do and how he or she is expected to perform. Whereas the results of a norm-referenced arithmetic test might tell you how a child's performance compares to that of other children in the fifth grade, a criterion-referenced arithmetic test would show exactly what arithmetic skills the child possesses. Each kind of test is useful for different purposes.

Criterion-referenced measures concentrate on finding out what a particular child has accomplished. The test presents the child with an ordered sequence of test items. Each item is considered to represent an essential component of the area being tested. In arithmetic, items might include counting, demonstrating one-to-one correspondence, adding single-digit numbers, adding double-digit numbers, and subtracting. If a child successfully completes all questions up to adding double-digit numbers, the evaluator will know that the youngster has learned the necessary prerequisite skills but requires instruction in addition of more than one digit.

This approach can be very helpful to professionals planning education or remedial programs for specific children. Criterion-referenced tests assume, however, that the essential skills needed have been defined, analyzed, and sequenced properly for the subject being tested. More success in defining tasks in motor development, adaptive skills, and academic achievement has been achieved than has been the case for social or emotional development and thinking abilities.

Process-Oriented Measures

Certain tests are designed to assess the methods children use to solve problems or to complete tasks. Such tests often are referred to as *process-oriented* measures, as they focus on the process or strategy the child employs. An example of a strategy used by very young children working on puzzles is trial-and-error. They typically select pieces at random and try to fit them into openings on the puzzle board. Older children who have had experience with puzzles develop more efficient strategies such as looking for openings with particular shapes or finding pieces with characteristic edges, colors, or pictures.

A number of psychological tests and procedures use a process-oriented approach. Some of these are based on the work of the widely known Swiss psychologist Jean Piaget, who studied thinking strategies of young children. From his observations, he developed a theory on the development of intellectual abilities. The Ordinal Scales of Intellectual Development is an example of a process-oriented test based on Piaget's theory.

Instead of process-oriented measures, some psychologists use the term *qualitative-developmental assessment* to refer to the evaluation of a child's thinking strategies. This term indicates that it is the quality of thinking, not the quantity of knowledge, that is of interest, and it suggests that the quality of thinking changes as children develop and mature.

The following sections describe the basic categories of tests and procedures. The tests described generally are constructed as norm-referenced, criterion-referenced, or process-oriented measures. As space does not allow a description of all of the published psychological tests, only a few are highlighted here. For further reading, additional references are provided in the bibliography at the end of this book.

Screening Tests

The purpose of a screening test is to quickly distinguish individuals who are at risk for having or developing a particular problem from those who are not. The job of developmental screening tests for children is to identify those youngsters who might have a developmental disability. A screening is not the same as a detailed assessment. Screenings are designed as a fast and easy way to identify individuals who might have a problem.

Screening tests often are a first step in the assessment process. Many school systems, physicians, health centers, and visiting nurse associations routinely administer screening tests to locate children who might be in need of special services.

One of the most frequently used screening tests is the Denver Developmental Screening Test. It looks at four areas of development in children from birth to 6 years of age and can be administered in 15–20 minutes. Areas screened include the child's fine motor abilities, personal and social development, language development, and gross motor abilities. When a child fails items that 90% of children of the same chronological age successfully complete, the results are considered questionable or atypical depending on the total number of items failed. When a child passes all or most items, the results are called "normal." Children with questionable or atypical findings will need to be followed closely, with rescreening after a few weeks or perhaps a full comprehensive evaluation.

Compared to screening, a comprehensive assessment is a more detailed, more complete process that provides both descriptive and diagnostic information. An assessment should include a discussion of the factors that help, hinder, or influence a child's performance, as well as recommendations for remedial or rehabilitative programs for the child.

Mental and Intelligence Tests

Mental and intelligence tests traditionally have been among the most frequently used psychological tests. Yet, the concept and validity of intelligence testing remain controversial. Professionals disagree on definitions of intelligence, what constitutes an appropriate measure of intelligence, and how so-called intelligence tests differ from tests of school achievement. Despite the controversy, many people believe that intelligence tests have validity as assessments of the combination of abilities that enable a person to deal competently with situations according to the society's values. In short, intelligence tests attempt to measure an individual's thinking and problem-solving skills.

Mental or intelligence tests are intended to measure cognitive abilities. *Cognition* is a general term for thinking and includes sensing; perceiving; recognizing; remembering; differentiating one thing from another; developing concepts; understanding pictures, words, and numbers; judging; solving problems; and reasoning. Tests that assess cognitive skills are concerned with thinking and how a person takes in, thinks about, and uses information. Intelligence tests also frequently tap specific knowledge or facts. Items typically included in intelligence tests may ask a person to define a word, compare two pictures, sort objects into groups, make a drawing, complete a puzzle, solve a problem, answer questions, or perform other kinds of mental activities. Most intelligence tests rate a child's responses on the different test items and compare this performance rating, or score, to the average score of children of the same chronological age. The Stanford-Binet Intelligence Scale (4th ed.), Wechsler Intelligence Scale for Children (3rd ed.) (WISC–III), and the McCarthy Scales of Children's Abilities are widely known examples of this kind of test. A newer intelligence test, the Kaufman Assessment Battery for Children (K–ABC), was published in 1983. It is a useful, easy-to-administer test that gives information about a child's learning style.

Test results usually are expressed as a number, but the number alone is meaningless unless something is known about the range of possible scores and the average score for the age group. For example, if you were told a child obtained a score of 49 on a test, it would not be clear if this were a passing or failing mark or perhaps an excellent score. If you were told the maximum score possible was 50, you would know the child did very well. If 100 was the top score, then this youngster did poorly. If the youngster was 5 years old and the average score for a 5-year-old was 50, you would conclude that this child achieved what would be expected for his or her age.

Mental Age   Some intelligence test results are given as a mental age (MA) score. Mental age provides an age-equivalent for the child's test score. To illustrate, suppose that a particular test has the following norms: the average score for 5-year-olds is 50; for 6-year-olds, 55; and for 7-year-olds, 60. Then suppose a 7-year-old child was tested and obtained a score of 55; one would say that this youngster was functioning at a mental age of 6 years old on this test.

The terms *test age, functional age,* and *developmental age* mean much the same thing as *mental age.* You may see these terms used in psychological reports as well as in other developmental evaluations. They all convey the relationship between a specific child's performance and the age at which that level of ability is considered typical.

Although the concept of mental age is useful and relatively easy to understand, it has some limitations that should be kept in mind when interpreting test results.

First, a specific score means very different things when earned by children of different chronological ages. A 2-year-old who achieves a mental age of 5 years has much greater potential than a 10-year-old earning the same score.

Second, by itself mental age does not reveal anything about an individual's strengths and weaknesses. Knowing that an 8-year-old child earned a mental age of 6 years does not tell you whether the youngster does well in language tasks or has trouble in arithmetic, or perhaps has exceptional skills in object manipulations and verbal abilities. For the results to be more meaningful, you should know the mental age score expected for the child tested and something about the child's pattern of achievement on test items.

Intelligence Quotient   An intelligence quotient (IQ) is a test result expressed as a number that conveys how a child did on the test and how the performance compares to what was expected for the youngster's age.

Many tests use IQ scores. Among the most frequently used are the Stanford-Binet Intelligence Scale (4th ed.) and the Wechsler Intelligence Scales, including the Wechsler Preschool and Primary Scale of Intelligence–Revised (WPPSI–R), the Wechsler Intelligence Scale for Children (3rd ed.) (WISC–III), and the Wechsler Adult Intelligence Scale–Revised (WAIS–R). The McCarthy Scales of Children's Abilities uses a General Cognitive Index (GCI) that is basically the same as an IQ score. The Bayley Scales of Infant Development (2nd ed.) offers both a Mental Development Index (MDI) and a Psychomotor Development Index (PDI), which are similar in nature to the IQ. IQ tests have been designed statistically so that the average score, also called the *mean*, expected at each age is 100 and the standard deviation is 15 or 16 points.

The standard deviation is a standard against which specific scores can be evaluated. It describes how much better or worse an individual score is when compared to the expected score for the population. In statistics, each standard deviation above or below the average represents a percentage of the population. For example, scores falling within one standard deviation above and one standard deviation below the average, or mean, will always represent 68% of the population of interest. Scores within two standard deviations of the mean account for about 95% of the population. Figure 1 shows the standard deviations and corresponding population percentages for a test with a mean of 100 and a standard deviation of 15.

Intelligence tests and IQ scores have been shown to be related to other abilities, particularly academic achievement. Examining the patterns of correct and incorrect answers on the test can provide information about the youngster's abilities and can help clarify problem areas. IQ tests also can be used in measuring change over time.

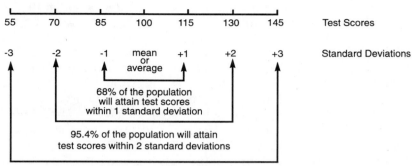

Figure 1. *Standard deviations and corresponding population percentage for a test with a mean of 100 and a standard deviation of 15.*

Intelligence tests and IQ measures also can be misunderstood and misused. Intelligence tests measure a number of skills but do not provide a complete study of abilities or characteristics. They do not tell us, for example, whether the child is creative and imaginative, musical, talented in painting or drawing, or has leadership abilities. How the child works during the test can reveal something about eagerness to achieve, interest, and concentration, but the IQ score does not tell us how motivated the child is in other situations or how hard that child will work to get something accomplished. Nor does the IQ score measure the value of a person. Whether one is kind or cruel, loving or selfish, for example, is not a matter of IQ at all. In addition, many factors may affect a child's performance on the day the test is taken and, consequently, the IQ score. Fatigue, nervousness, and illness can influence a youngster's performance.

Keep in mind, too, that some intelligence tests are known to give higher or lower IQ scores than others. Thus, there can be variations in a child's IQ simply due to the test used. IQ scores also may change over time because some tests measure different skills at different ages, children themselves change, and children may perform differently in one place than another.

It is best to regard IQ scores simply as one of many measures of a child's abilities that can be useful in planning needed educational or treatment services.

Developmental Tests

Developmental tests arrange test items into steps or periods in the order in which the child is expected to learn or acquire the skills the items represent. These tests assume that development occurs in an orderly or predictable way, that persons do not necessarily mature at the same rate, and that the level or stage of maturity can be measured by performance on certain tasks or activities.

Developmental tests usually are norm-referenced, criterion-referenced, or process-oriented, and may be used to assess cognitive, language, social-emotional, motor, or adaptive skills. One example of a developmental test is the Ordinal Scales of Intellectual Development, which measures a baby's level of achievement in six areas. The Alpern-Boll Developmental Profile is another developmental scale used to assess children from 6 months to 12 years of age.

Some developmental tests may require the child to answer questions and perform activities in a number of different skill areas. Others may use an interview or checklist format from which the examiner obtains information about the child's skills from the parent or other person who knows the child well. Test results may be reported as a developmental quotient (DQ), but findings often are described in terms of developmental age or level. A number of developmental tests are planned with educational or training activities to help the child make developmental progress when his or her developmental status has been measured.

Frequently, developmental tests are administered several times during a period of intervention, treatment, or special programming to monitor a child's progress. As children change, the kinds of learning opportunities or support services they need also can be expected to change. Assessments may need to be repeated periodically to assess changes in the child's level of functioning and to be sure that the best possible match between the child's needs and opportunities is being maintained.

Infant Tests

Assessment of infants has become increasingly important as people become more and more concerned about identifying as early as possible children who may have developmental disabilities.

Like other tests, many infant tests are norm-referenced or criterion-referenced measures. The Bayley Scales of Infant Development (2nd ed.), a norm-referenced test, is one of the most widely used infant devices. It is used with children up to 42 months of age and gives an MDI, a PDI, and an Infant Behavior Rating (IBR). The MDI is much like an IQ measure and has many of the characteristics, uses, and limitations mentioned previously.

An example of a process-oriented infant test is the Infant Psychological Development Scale, developed by Uzgiris and Hunt and based on the work of Jean Piaget. This widely known measure provides valuable information about thinking abilities considered important for all babies. The Brazelton Neonatal Assessment Scale is another type of infant test developed specifically to assess the behavioral status of newborns. It considers a newborn's responses to a variety of stimuli along with the baby's "state," or level, of arousal.

The development of tests and procedures for newborns and very young babies has occurred for a number of reasons. One is the group of discoveries by professionals showing what many sensitive parents have believed all along—that newborns and young babies are much more competent and capable of purposeful behavior than was believed previously. Another reason is the increased interest in identification and treatment of developmental problems as early as possible. Through research, professionals have learned that signs of developmental disabilities can be detected in preschool years and even in infancy. One does not have to rely solely on a baby's motor performance or the onset of language to find out what the baby knows. Other measures, such as changes in heart rate and in sucking patterns; observations of visual attention; and evaluation of an infant's abilities to attend to, recognize, understand, and remember visual and auditory stimuli, all provide valuable information about infant capabilities.

Infant tests in general use have been most successful in predicting later performance when the baby's current performance is much below what is generally expected for his or her age. Very little success has been achieved in predicting future performance with infants, particularly those younger than 1 year of age, who are developing typically. Generally, the older the child and the shorter the time between testings, the more likely that one test performance will predict the next. One reason for this seems to be that many of the items on infant tests examine motor skills, whereas tests for older children concentrate much more heavily on language and thinking skills. Although movement is important for its own sake, there is not always a direct relationship between movement and the kind of thinking that is occurring in young infants and older children.

Babies and very young children can be delightful to work with, but they are not easy to evaluate. They often need to be fed or changed, they tire easily or fall asleep, and they may become distressed when handled by an unfamiliar person. Furthermore, infant tests can be difficult to conduct. The examiner cannot ask questions or simply give the baby directions to follow. Considerable training and practice is needed to carry out the testing procedures correctly and to gain the baby's cooperation. When testing infants, knowl-

edge of typical infant development is essential, as is an awareness of developmental problems and of how they can influence the results of assessments. As with all types of assessment, if a disability is detected, it is important for the professional to be able to translate the assessment findings into programs to help the baby progress developmentally and to be able to interpret the results and recommendations clearly to the parents and other interested professionals.

Adaptive Behavior Scales

In order to gain a better understanding of how people get along in the world, we need to know about what is called their adaptive behavior. *Adaptive behavior* refers to skills in social interactions, emotional adjustment, and self-care.

In all areas of self-help skills, there is a developmental sequence of increasing independence. Most individuals learn to take care of their own needs to be fed, clothed, sheltered, and kept clean.

Social skills also are achieved in a developmental sequence. These involve tasks such as learning to respond to and interact with people, to play with games and toys, to participate in social activi-

ties, and to work at increasingly complex jobs. The ability to exchange information, ideas, and feelings with other people plays an
important part in developing social competence.

Rating scales typically are used to assess adaptive skills. The
most frequently used instruments are the Vineland Adaptive Behavior Scales and the American Association on Mental Retardation
Adaptive Behavior Scales. A psychologist goes through the rating
scale with an informant, usually a parent, who knows the individual
being evaluated very well. The parent answers questions about the
child's skills, such as "Can he feed himself neatly with a spoon and
fork?", "Can he play cooperatively at the kindergarten level?", or
"Can he wash his hands unassisted?" Some scales provide an overall
rating, which is reported in terms of age scores. Others indicate how
well an individual performs compared to a normative group in a
number of areas of functioning.

Information about adaptive behavior is crucial when a diagnosis
of mental retardation is being considered. There must be significant
impairment or delay in both adaptive behavior and cognitive ability
before a person can be diagnosed with mental retardation. The information derived from adaptive behavior scales is useful in education
programs. Teachers can see when a student needs extra instruction
to learn a skill and to achieve greater independence.

Achievement Tests

Achievement tests are used to measure what a child has learned.
Often this means the subject matter that has been learned in school
(e.g., reading, spelling, arithmetic). Like mental tests, achievement
or educational tests may be administered individually or to groups
of children. They must be both reliable and valid, and must produce
results that will give meaningful information about each child's
skills. Commonly used individual achievement tests include the Peabody Individual Achievement Test–Revised (PIAT–R) and the Wide
Range Achievement Test–Revised (WRAT–III). The Metropolitan
Achievement Tests and Iowa Tests of Basic Skills are examples of
widely used achievement batteries that often are administered in
groups. Many achievement and educational tests report scores in
terms of grade-level norms.

In order to find out which tasks a child needs to master, many
different kinds of skills may be tested. When the child's specific areas of weakness are defined, appropriate remedial programs can be
planned. The goal of remedial instruction is to improve a child's
abilities in the area of need. If the problem is one that cannot be

corrected or improved, then it is important to help the child learn alternate ways to accomplish what needs to be done.

Educational tests are usually administered by educators, including classroom teachers, resource teachers, special educators on a diagnostic team, or psychologists. Remediation, or the development of alternate methods to correct a problem, usually is done by teachers who have special training in helping children who have learning difficulties. These teachers use the information from both mental and educational tests to plan an individualized remediation program for each child.

Sometimes pretests and posttests are used to help evaluate a child's progress. Pretests are given before a specific intervention program is begun, whereas posttests are administered after the intervention to assess its effectiveness.

Behavioral Procedures

Behavioral assessment is a method of collecting and analyzing information about a child's responses to specific situations. The major goal of behavioral assessment is to measure reliably what the child does under certain circumstances or environmental conditions. The term *behavior* is used in the broadest sense and can refer to any activity of the child that is of interest. It could be anything a child says or does. *Environment* refers to those conditions that exist when the behavior occurs.

To understand the relation between behavior and the environment, behavioral psychologists first must collect the necessary information, often referred to as the *ABCs of behavior*. *A* is for antecedent, or events that happen before the behavior occurs. *B* stands for the particular behavior of interest, or what is observed. *C* is for the consequence, or what happens immediately after the child displays the behavior.

Psychologists conduct behavioral assessments to clarify a behavior problem—that is, to discover when it occurs, how often, and under what circumstances—and to devise strategies for changing or modifying the problem behavior.

Behavioral assessment typically involves direct observation. Observations are best completed in the settings where the problem behavior occurs. If direct observation is impossible for the professional, parents or others can supply the necessary information.

The measurements used in behavioral assessments usually consist of *frequency* measures, which count how often a particular behavior occurs within a given period of time in a particular setting or environment; and *duration* measures, which record how long the particular behavior lasts. These measurements may be taken continuously, counting all of the behaviors during a certain period of time; or by time sampling, counting the behaviors in a representative period of time (e.g., the first 15 minutes of each hour throughout the day, every 10 minutes during the morning, 5 minutes of each period of seat work assigned). This information is summarized, so changes in how often the behavior occurs or how long it lasts can be noted easily while a behavioral program is being conducted. Typically, these data are shown on a graph. This type of analysis provides the psychologist with the necessary information to develop a treatment strategy to bring about a change in the target behavior. Many helpful forms and surveys have been developed to ease information-gathering efforts. One source is a series of 42 behavior assessment forms developed by Joseph Cautela and his associates; these forms are contained in *Forms for Behavior Analysis with Children*.

Behavioral assessment is a very useful technique for planning ways to help an individual change. And it can be used to measure how much change has occurred. One potential drawback to behavioral assessment is that a complete, thorough analysis of behavior can be very time-consuming. However, if the assessment leads to an effective intervention for a serious behavior problem, the time is well spent.

Personality Tests and Procedures

Each individual reacts to the environment with a particular set of characteristics and behaviors that are unique. *Personality* is the term often used to refer to those patterns of behavior. People typically describe aspects of someone's personality with adjectives such as *friendly, aggressive, shy, hostile, energetic, fearful*, and *outgoing*.

Assessment of personality may be useful for a variety of reasons, such as vocational counseling or planning for treatment of emotional disorders. The following are the three basic methods of assessing personality:

1. *Observational techniques* involve systematically watching an individual in a natural setting, such as at home or in school. The information gathered may be organized in several ways—for example, by rating various characteristics and behaviors.
2. *Personality inventories* are questionnaires completed by the individual being assessed. For instance, a person might be asked to mark "True" or "False" in response to statements such as "I am often ill-at-ease in a large group of people," or "Being a success

at anything I do is very important to me." Results of inventories can be interpreted to give a description of an individual's personality. An inventory for children, such as the Personality Inventory for Children–Revised, is completed by a parent.

3. *Projective techniques* involve the presentation of stimuli such as ambiguous pictures, incomplete sentences, or inkblots. The individual is asked to respond to the stimuli—for example, to tell a story about a scene depicted in a picture, to finish the sentence, or to describe what the inkblot looks like. Projective techniques tap the individual's imagination and encourage the use of personal experiences, feelings, attitudes, and desires. The interpretation of information from projective techniques is difficult and should be done by well-trained professionals. The Children's Apperception Test and Roberts Apperception Test for Children are two projective tests in which children respond to pictures or drawings of animals, children, and adults in everyday activities.

Neuropsychological Approaches

Neuropsychological testing is an orderly way of using psychological tests and observations to study relationships between the brain and behavior (how the function of the brain affects our abilities, strengths, and weaknesses). Neuropsychological assessments may be used to detect specific problems in the brain, where the problems are located, and the impact of the problem on a person. A variety of standard neuropsychological test batteries are in use.

Areas generally assessed by neuropsychological test batteries include the sensory-perceptual systems such as vision, touch, or hearing; cognitive or thinking activities such as memory and comprehension; motor coordination; and left–right dominance patterns in use of hands, feet, and eyes. Other areas often investigated are problem solving, reasoning, concept formation, language, and emotional responses.

The tests may be interpreted in several ways: by comparing the individual's performance with others in the same group, by an analysis of the pattern of scores obtained on the various tests in the battery, or by detection of an atypical sign indicating grossly unusual functioning.

Two neuropsychological approaches frequently used are the Halstead-Reitan and Luria-Nebraska test batteries. Alternately, the examiner may construct a battery from other existing instruments. Neuropsychological testing is often quite lengthy and may be more expensive than other types of psychological testing. It is usually reserved for very special cases in which information cannot be gathered in any other way, and it is most often used along with information from physicians and other professionals.

THE PSYCHOLOGICAL REPORT

After a psychological assessment, a report of the findings should be written. The following information should be included in a psychological report and should be stated clearly and concisely:

1. The purpose of the assessment—why the child was seen
2. How the information was obtained, including the tests used and observations conducted
3. The results of the tests, interpretation of the findings, and conclusions of the assessment

In addition to the above, specific recommendations about education or treatment and about how developmental progress for that child can be encouraged should be included if the purpose of the assessment was to plan for a child who has developmental difficulties.

The psychological report should not be a simple recounting of test scores; it should also be accompanied by an interpretation. Interpretation of tests depends in large measure on the examiner's understanding of human behavior, skill in relating to the child, and knowledge of assessment techniques. The examiner must be able to describe the outcome in ways that can be understood by parents and others who will work with the child, and thus be useful to parents and professionals as they plan strategies to help the child.

Those who receive a report of psychological assessment, whether parents or other professionals, should feel free to ask for explanations if they are uncertain about why the assessment was needed, which tests or procedures were used, why these choices were made, what the results mean, or how the assessment can be used in planning interventions or education programs for the child. The more clearly the results are explained, the more likely the assessment findings will be used to benefit the child.

ACKNOWLEDGMENTS

Contributions have been made to this chapter by Ellen I. Rollins, Ed.D., Leslie E. Weidenman, Ph.D., and James A. Mulick, Ph.D.

28

Helping Children Learn

Children with developmental disabilities, particularly those with mental retardation, often learn more slowly than other youngsters. To acquire new skills and ideas, children with disabilities may need more time, practice, and opportunities than typically developing children. However, children with developmental disabilities do learn and, like all of us, they learn from their experiences. For children who are at a disadvantage because of a physical or mental disability, help from parents and professionals can foster learning.

This chapter outlines ways to help children with developmental disabilities learn. Both the types of programs available to help very young children with disabilities and the principles by which all children learn are discussed.

EARLY INTERVENTION PROGRAMS FOR INFANTS AND TODDLERS WITH DISABILITIES

Interventions for children with developmental disabilities are aimed at enhancing development and preventing or lessening problems that may result from a developmental disorder. *Early intervention* is a general term describing programs for very young children with disabilities and their families. What constitutes an early intervention program (EIP) and the age range of children served varies from state to state. In most states, early intervention applies to infants and toddlers in the birth-to-3-year-old age range. At age 3, children still requiring assistance may enter special education preschool programs or receive specialized services provided by the local school system in nursery or child care programs. PL 99-457, the Education of the

Handicapped Act Amendments of 1986, and PL 102-119, the Individuals with Disabilities Education Act Amendments of 1991, authorized early intervention programs to assist infants and toddlers with disabilities and their families. These laws extended the scope of PL 94-142, the Education for All Handicapped Children Act of 1975, which required that special education and related services be available to eligible children beginning at age 3.

How Early to Start?

Since the mid 1950s, ideas about when to begin helping children with disabilities have moved rapidly down the age scale from school age to preschool age to infancy.

In the 1960s, much interest and attention were focused on the impact of discrimination and poverty on children. From this beginning, a special concern emerged about the effects of deprivation, poor nutrition, and unusual early experiences on the development of very young children. During this time, work with preschoolers in programs such as Head Start was emphasized. Important medical advances were also made in the early diagnosis of genetic disorders and birth defects and in their care and management. Parents who wanted help for their children with developmental disorders formed parent groups and became very active in arranging the needed services. The combination of increased knowledge about and activities for children with many kinds of developmental disorders brought this population into the public awareness. As a result, programs were developed and professionals began to study the ways infants and toddlers with disabilities and their families could be helped.

Interest in early intervention has continued to grow. Today, professionals are working to discover ways to detect disabilities as early as possible and to provide the best treatment or intervention for the problems identified. This means starting to work with infants with disabilities at birth or soon thereafter, or as early as the developmental disability is detected. In addition to working directly with infants and toddlers with disabilities, programs have expanded their focus to include the entire family. Most early intervention programs now offer parent training, counseling, and support groups for families.

Recent research on the learning capacities of infants provides a sound reason for early intervention. Scientists studying very young children have found that infants are much more active learners than was previously believed. The sheer extent of the competencies of newborn and young infants that are now recognized and the amount of learning that occurs indicates that infancy is indeed an appropriate time to begin intervention. For example, scientists have learned that infants can make fine discriminations in what they hear. In 1971, researchers demonstrated that young infants can distinguish between speech and nonspeech sounds, as well as among different sounds like "pa" and "da."[1]

Such findings have caused researchers to reevaluate their ideas about typical development, the effects of various skills on each other, the consequences of impaired function, and the possibility of influencing development in beneficial ways.

Researchers also have been evaluating intervention programs to see if particular programs really are helpful. There is now little doubt that intervention can have a powerful and beneficial effect. We seem to be past the initial question: Does intervention work? Researchers now have started to ask more precise questions, such as: What are the characteristics of effective programs? How do different developmental disorders, different ages at entry, length of involvement, and level of participation affect a program's outcome? What are the consequences of particular program design, curricula, and staffing patterns?

There is much to learn about successful ways of encouraging a young child's development. No child is too young to participate in a good early intervention program. Many children are indeed helped, and numerous parents find such programs helpful for themselves as well.

Early Intervention Programs: A General Description

Early intervention programs vary widely. Differences can be found in all aspects of a program, including structure, focus, services offered, eligibility, and frequency of contact with children and families. Some programs may be primarily center-based, to which parents bring their children for individual therapy or group programming. Others may be primarily home-based, in which early intervention workers provide services for children at home and work closely with parents to design and carry out treatment programs to meet the specific needs of the child and family.

States receiving federal funds under PL 102-119 for the development and provision of comprehensive early intervention programs must meet certain basic requirements. For example, they must provide assistance to all eligible infants and toddlers with disabilities.

---

[1]Eimas, P.D., Siqueland, E.R., Jusczyk, P., & Vigorito, J. (1971). Speech perception in infants. *Science, 171,* 303–306.

Eligible children include those who are experiencing measurable delays in one or more of the following areas of development: cognitive, physical, communication, social or emotional, or adaptive skills; as well as children with a diagnosed physical or mental condition that has a high probability of resulting in a developmental disability. Children who are at risk of developing delays if no intervention is provided may also be considered eligible for services. Each participating state defines its own criteria for eligibility.

Another important aspect of the Individuals with Disabilities Education Act (IDEA) and PL 102-119 is the focus on the family as well as the child with a developmental disability. Early intervention service plans are developed collaboratively; this means that parents and family members work together with professionals to develop a program that meets the specific needs of the child and family. The resulting plan is called an individualized family service plan (IFSP), which is an agreement between program staff and the family that outlines program goals and the services that will be provided. The IFSP makes clear who will provide what services and indicates the staff member who will act as the service coordinator. The law also stresses the importance of providing the necessary services in natural settings whenever possible. The types of services that might be needed include the following: audiology, family training, physical therapy, occupational therapy, service coordination, nursing services, psychological services, social work, transportation, nutrition services, counseling, home visits, assistive technology, speech-language therapy, and special instruction.

As part of an early intervention program, a multidisciplinary team of professionals must be available to assess a child's functioning in all areas of development. Early intervention programs generally have representatives from a variety of disciplines on staff to conduct evaluations, outline the child's strengths and weaknesses, assess family needs and priorities, and work with parents and family members to develop an individualized plan of service. Typically, psychologists, social workers, educators, speech-language pathologists, occupational therapists, physical therapists, and nurses are part of early intervention teams. Many programs work closely with hospitals, clinics, or school systems and also share personnel.

Unlike traditional school programs with structured classrooms, early intervention programs, particularly home-based programs, attempt to teach families how to help their infants and toddlers within the context of everyday activities. Many effective teaching programs can be carried out during everyday activities such as diaper changes, baths, meals, and play activities. In many instances, guidance and coaching can help parents make time spent with their child even more productive and more likely to encourage development.

What to Look for in an Early Intervention Program

When choosing an intervention program, it is important for parents to familiarize themselves with the program's policies and any state regulations that govern its operation. Any state participating in the federal program outlined in the Individuals with Disabilities Education Act Amendments of 1991 (PL 102-119) must meet the requirements outlined in the law for all aspects of statewide program development, operation, monitoring, and financial management. Each state has its own set of rules and regulations to which individual early intervention programs must adhere. A review of the regulations and policies of participating early intervention programs is an excellent way for parents to learn about available services, timelines for evaluating a child's needs and developing an IFSP, and procedural safeguards that protect their rights.

If a private early intervention program is being considered, it is important to determine whether a match exists between the program services offered and the needs of the child and family. The program should be able to provide the essential services the child requires. Of course, other factors are important, too. For example, basic safety and health conditions of the program should meet regulations and parent approval. A clearly specified plan of intervention should be developed based on needs identified during assessment. Progress on program goals should be monitored regularly and reevaluations performed routinely.

In any program providing services to very young children, staff members should show interest and pleasure in working with the children. There should be sufficient staff from various disciplines to meet the basic program requirements. It also is important for parents to feel comfortable discussing their child's care with the program staff. Staff should know the levels at which the child is functioning, understand the relationship of one aspect of the child's behavior to another, and be able to participate actively in the design and implementation of a program specifically geared toward the child's skills, interests, and learning styles. This requires that program staff be keenly sensitive to the individuality in children, based on a sound understanding of human development, adequate knowledge of the kinds of problems or disorders that can occur, and a thorough knowledge of the materials, methods, and sequences of learning.

Where Are Programs Available?

Most states offer some form of early intervention program for infants and toddlers with disabilities. Many programs are administered by a state's Department of Education, Department of Health, or Department of Human Services, or by another state agency responsible for the care of persons with mental retardation and developmental disabilities.

Another source of information is the state interagency coordinating council (ICC), the body that oversees the implementation of early intervention programs under PL 102-119. ICCs are made up of parents of children with disabilities as well as professionals and administrators of agencies that deliver services to children and families.

To find out what services your state offers, try contacting the state agency for people with disabilities, the Department of Education, or local chapters of national organizations such as The Arc (formerly the Association for Retarded Citizens of the United States), United Cerebral Palsy, or Easter Seal Society. In addition, the Council for Exceptional Children keeps records about educational services that are available for young children with developmental disorders, and will provide information on request. The addresses and telephone numbers of these organizations are included in the appendix.

BASIC TEACHING STRATEGIES

Children's first and most important teachers are their parents; home, in a sense, is their first classroom. Long before children actually go to school, they learn an enormous amount with their parents' help. Basic skills such as walking, dressing, feeding themselves, talking, and playing with toys are just a sample of what children learn in their first few years. Many parents are unaware of exactly how they accomplished so much teaching in such a short time. For parents of children with disabilities, understanding how children learn and how to be an effective teacher can be very important, as effective teaching can promote development. This section of the chapter reviews basic teaching strategies.

Getting the Child's Attention

For any learning to occur, a child first has to pay attention. Paying attention involves focusing one or more of the senses on what is to be learned. Looking, listening, touching, tasting, and smelling are all examples of paying attention. Very young children attend to new and interesting things more readily than familiar, unchanging ones,

although using familiar objects in novel ways can quickly capture and hold an infant's attention.

In general, children attend more readily to things they like— things that are fun, taste good, satisfy, or provide comfort—instead of boring, unpleasant, or difficult things. Attention also is affected by one's expectations. As infants' experience broadens, they learn to anticipate changes from the cues in the environment. The cues that predict pleasurable changes generally attract attention well, but children also will attend to cues that predict unpleasant events so they can avoid them if at all possible. Parents can use cues to direct a child's attention to specific activities and learning opportunities. Examples of cues commonly used by parents and teachers are instructions and gestures.

Arranging Consequences

As soon as children are paying attention, teaching and learning can occur. The most basic principle of learning is that the consequences of our actions affect learning and behavior. This is not a difficult concept, and understanding it gives parents and teachers the most practical learning tool we know. This principle has two basic parts. The first focuses on the effects of positive consequences and is called *positive reinforcement*. It states: When a child does something that is followed immediately by a consequence the child enjoys or values, the child is more likely to perform the action again. The second concerns the effects of negative consequences or *punishment*. It states: When the immediate consequence of a child's actions is unpleasant or not valued, then the child is less likely to repeat the action. In short, positive reinforcement increases the likelihood that the behavior it follows will occur again. Punishment is the opposite—it decreases the chances that the behavior it follows will be repeated.

Different children enjoy different things, so considerable care must be taken to ensure that a particular child values a specific consequence in the anticipated way. Even parents who feel certain about their child's likes and dislikes have been surprised. An easy way for parents to test their hunches about their children's likes and dislikes is simply to observe what they do. By noticing what their children choose to play with, eat, drink, and watch on television, as well as who they elect to play with, parents can be reasonably certain about what their children find reinforcing and what they dislike. For most children, attention from parents, playing with a favorite toy, special foods, praise, and love are effective positive reinforcers. Consequences involving a loss of privileges, restricted activities, or reduced attention usually are punishing to children. Children's preferences change as they grow and develop new interests, so effective positive reinforcers and punishers also will change. Remember, you always can tell whether a consequence is a reinforcer or a punisher by observing its effect on the child's behavior. Considerations for using punishment are discussed later in the chapter.

In general, consequences have to be immediate to be effective. They also have to be provided consistently. This is particularly important when trying to teach a new skill. Children typically need lots of practice, encouragement, and positive reinforcement to learn and refine a new skill. However, once a skill has been acquired, the amount of positive reinforcement needed may decrease, as many skills become satisfying on their own. For example, once a child has mastered spoon feeding, the reward of eating is usually enough to motivate the child to feed him- or herself. Parents no longer need to provide positive consequences every time the child brings the spoon to his or her mouth. Children generally do not have to be praised to keep eating favorite foods.

Making Progress Over Time in Small Steps

Another important aspect of learning relates to the fact that learning takes time. Most tasks are made up of a sequence of steps, each of which must be learned in just the right way and in the right order.

Often, useful tasks can take a child many days or weeks to learn. Additional time is then needed for the child to refine the skills. Parents should be patient and expect their teaching efforts to be rewarded by their child's learning on a gradual but steady basis.

Because learning takes time and occurs in small steps, it may be hard to see the steady changes that are occurring. One way to be sure that progress is being made is to keep records. This may involve noting which steps in a complex skill have been mastered, the amount of time needed to complete a task, or the number of times an action has occurred.

To summarize, these basic learning principles operate all of the time and affect children and adults alike. They influence learning whether or not specific teaching is occurring. Remember, children learn from all of their experiences. Therefore, a world that contains many opportunities for exploration, play, and stimulation is an important way to ensure that learning can occur. Similarly, all of the things that parents do with children can be instructive and convey love and security, as well as the challenge of new mastery.

DISCIPLINE AND MANAGING BEHAVIOR PROBLEMS

All children initially learn the limits of acceptable behavior from the adults who care for them. Their sense of what is right and wrong develops over the years as a result of the consequences of their behavior, the direct effects of their actions, the reactions of others, and their observations of people around them.

Through discipline, parents begin teaching appropriate social behavior. Later, brothers and sisters, classmates, friends, teachers, and the extended family continue the process by providing feedback in the form of approval or disapproval for a child's actions. This is an important teaching tool. Like other consequences of behavior, the feedback functions as either positive reinforcement or punishment.

Children are keen observers of what others do. Frequently, new behaviors are learned by trying ways of acting that seem to work for others. Children tend to imitate the actions of important people in their lives, usually people in control, including parents, siblings, popular classmates, and teachers. This is one of the reasons it is so important to set good examples for children.

Children with disabilities are no different from other children in this respect. All children lack the judgment to understand the effects their behavior might have on others, and thus require the corrective feedback that parents and others can provide. Many of us treat children with disabilities or chronic illnesses as if they were exempt from discipline. This may be because people feel sorry for children with disabilities or view these youngsters as sick and helpless and, therefore, not subject to the usual rules or standards of behavior. However, unlike a temporary illness that may be associated with understandable lapses in conduct, a developmental disability in many cases represents a lifelong condition to which the child must learn to adapt. Like all of us, children with disabilities will be judged by society according to widely shared values. To the extent possible, youngsters with disabilities should learn to act and react as any child would under similar circumstances. When children with disabilities behave in ways similar to other children, they are accepted more readily into social and recreational activities that can lead to lasting relationships and enhance personal growth.

Developmental disabilities complicate the task of judging whether or not a child is behaving appropriately. In some cases, developmental delays are not associated with impairment of physical development, and affected children often physically look like others their age. People tend to expect children who look typical to behave appropriately, regardless of their ability. In other instances, marked physical disabilities are present, but without delays in intellectual development. Such children are often treated as if they had intellectual impairments. First impressions can be misleading.

Behavior problems can be extremely stressful for everyone concerned. Many parents of children with disabilities often are not sure how to view some of their children's behaviors. They often ask: Is this something I should be concerned about or is this behavior normal? Parents' concerns about how others will perceive them when their children misbehave are common and are quite natural, and in no way unique to parents of children with disabilities.

The truth is that behavior problems are common. Managing behavior problems is easier if they are considered one at a time and viewed as teaching opportunities. Most behavior problems fall into the category of common problems of childhood—for example, following family rules, using toys and household materials properly, avoiding dangerous and unhealthy substances, and performing everyday tasks. Another set of problems may be related to a child's developmental disability. These include emotional difficulties that result from the disability itself or from the way the child is treated by others.

It can be helpful to think of behavior problems as teaching problems in which there may be behavioral deficits, excesses, or a combination of the two. A behavioral deficit indicates that the child lacks a skill necessary for a particular situation, and thus, behaves inappropriately. An example of this would be a child who eats with his or her hands because he or she has never been taught to use utensils. A behavioral excess indicates that a child is doing something too often or too intensely to be tolerated. An example might be the child who cries excessively or has tantrums in order to get his or her way. A problem resulting from both deficits and excesses is described in the following example. A child becomes disruptive in the classroom when difficult work is presented for which the child lacks the prerequisite skills. Disruptions involve frequent outbursts and antics at which other children in the classroom laugh. The disruptive acts that are the result of a deficit are being reinforced by the attention of the other children.

Managing problem behavior, then, becomes a matter of setting the stage for effective teaching. The problem behavior must be well defined, so that it can be handled consistently by all involved. It is usually a good idea to count or measure a problem behavior for some time before trying to change it. This allows one to tell whether or not the consequence selected is working. If the problem behavior occurs progressively less often or lasts for shorter periods of time after the intervention is started, then the strategy for decreasing the unwanted behavior has been successful.

Selecting the specific strategy is a little more tricky. Behavioral specialists and psychologists often work with families on developing intervention strategies for problem behaviors. Behavior problems that are the result of skill deficits are best handled by teaching the required skills. Sometimes the child possesses the necessary skills, but does not exhibit them consistently. This may mean that performing the skill is not followed by satisfying consequences; that is, the behavior is not positively reinforced. Behavioral deficits of this kind can be improved upon by ensuring that the good behavior is always rewarded. Attention from parents including praise, hugs, and other expressions of appreciation and love are among the most universal positive reinforcers. Behavior that is followed by this kind of attention is usually strengthened rapidly. Parents should always consider using their attention and praise to increase desirable behavior before material reinforcers.

Unfortunately, misbehavior is often followed by parental attention. We have a tendency to ignore or take for granted good behavior and to intervene when problems develop. However, because parental attention is such a strong reinforcer, even the attention associated with anger that is lavished on a problem behavior can actually strengthen it. When no longer followed by attention, many annoying problem behaviors, such as tantrums and some mild forms of aggression, are eventually abandoned by children.

This is why many parents are encouraged to ignore problem behavior. However, this is easier said than done. Many misbehaviors or behavioral excesses cannot be ignored without the risk of harm to the child or others. Furthermore, even if parental attention had been strengthening the problem behavior accidentally, here also may have been other sources of positive reinforcement for the child's actions. For example, aggressive behavior may result in material gain or temporary resolution of a conflict. A misbehavior may actually feel good to the child when it is performed. Other sources of reinforcement for misbehavior are other people. Attention from friends and neighbors following the misbehavior can negate the effects of being ignored by parents. Finally, even if the original form of problem behavior decreases, there is no guarantee that the child will behave appropriately thereafter. There is still the question of whether the child has the ability to behave appropriately.

Instead of simply trying to eliminate the problem behavior, it is better to determine what you would like to see the child doing in its place. Then, you can go about making the occurrence of desired behavior more likely by teaching it, seeing that it is rewarded, and doing everything possible to make the misbehavior less likely to occur in the future.

Often, increasing desirable behavior serves to displace undesirable behavior, simply because the child cannot do both things at once. Another way to make misbehavior less likely is to change the environment in a way that makes it harder to do anything undesirable. When a room is child-proofed and breakable objects are placed out of reach of small children, an environmental change has been made. We are less likely to think of a child who actively explores a child-proofed environment as hyperactive or destructive. Such recautions can give us an opportunity to introduce the child to potential problems in a controlled fashion over a longer period of time.

When ignoring, displacing, or avoiding excess behavior are incomplete solutions, alternative methods are available to decrease the strength of a misbehavior directly. Self-stimulatory behavior or repetitive self-injurious acts, although relatively unusual, do occur in children with developmental disabilities and tend to be highly resistant to change. Punishment of the undesired behavior combined with reinforcement of appropriate, alternative behaviors can have fairly rapid effects on reducing misbehavior. If punishment is immediate, consistently implemented, and truly something the child dislikes, it will reduce the occurrence of the misbehavior.

There are several drawbacks to using punishment, whatever its form (e.g., loss of privileges, reprimands, extra chores). Most of us dislike using punishment so much that we delay administering it until long after the misbehavior has occurred. A comment like "Wait until your father comes home!" is one example of delayed punishment. Another drawback is that we are not always consistent with punishment. For example, we may say, "You'll be in trouble the next time you do that!" Frequently we give in to whatever it was that motivated the child's misbehavior in the first place. Another practical consideration is that what is selected as punishment may not be so undesirable from the child's point of view. These are all things that can make punishment ineffective in stopping problem behavior.

Other drawbacks include the fact that punishment does not teach anything new. It only stops or decreases behavior that it follows consistently. If no alternative is available to the child, either because of a lack of skill or a lack of opportunity, the improvement will be temporary at best. Punishment can also create fear in the child, and fear can distract the child from learning or disrupt relationships in the family. Finally, punishment given in anger can become excessive and even harmful.

These drawbacks can be overcome by never punishing without having a plan to reward an alternative, desirable behavior. In addition, many techniques have been developed to avoid the need for physical punishment. One of the most widely known of these is called *time out* from positive reinforcement. Time out has been used very successfully by numerous parents and teachers to decrease undesirable behavior. However, one must be sure that the exact nature of the time out experience truly represents the temporary withdrawal of something that the child values.

Structure has a place in every family. A large proportion of problem situations can be avoided through firm limit setting, by enthusiastic attention and appreciation for good behavior, and by providing good examples for children to follow.

Discipline is important to all children. A structured approach is sometimes needed to deal with particularly difficult problems, and many psychologists and special educators can give needed advice at such times. As with many of the teaching strategies discussed here, additional readings are available to help you adapt these approaches to your needs.

ACKNOWLEDGMENTS

Contributions have been made to this chapter by James A. Mulick, Ph.D., Leslie E. Weidenman, Ph.D., and Ellen I. Rollins, Ed.D.

29

Going to School

Like other school-age children, youngsters with developmental disabilities need appropriate education. In the past, this was not always an accepted fact, and many children with disabilities were deprived of essential educational services.

In 1975, PL 94-142, the Education for All Handicapped Children Act, became law. As a result, a free and appropriate public education (FAPE) was made available to all children with disabilities regardless of the severity of their condition. In 1986, PL 99-457 extended the provisions of PL 94-142 by providing incentives for all states to develop programs for infants and preschool children with special needs. PL 94-142 was reauthorized in 1990 and is now known as PL 101-476, the Individuals with Disabilities Education Act (IDEA). In this legislation, the word *handicap* has been replaced by the term *disability*, and *people-first* terminology has been utilized; for example, the rights of *children with disabilities*, rather than *handicapped children*, are cited. IDEA provides for special education and special related services in the least restrictive environment (LRE) to meet the unique needs of children with disabilities from ages 3 to 21. PL 102-119, the Individuals with Disabilities Education Act Amendments was passed in 1991 reauthoring PL 99-457. How children are identified as having disabilities by the school system, the educational options available, and the role of the parent as a member of a team planning for the child are discussed in this chapter.

REFERRAL PROCESS

Most children are referred to special education programs because they have difficulty keeping up with the other students in the general classroom or because they are presenting behavior problems that interfere with learning. Ordinarily, a child's name is submitted by the classroom teacher. However, referrals can also be made by parents or professionals outside of the educational system on behalf of the family. A child must be referred to be eligible for special services provided by the state with federal, state, or local monies. Most communities have Child Find programs in place that offer screening services to identify young children (beginning at 2½ years of age) who may be in need of special education services. Also, Development Evaluation Centers where children can undergo comprehensive assessments often recommend special education services for children with special needs.

ASSESSMENT

Before children can be enrolled for special education services, they must undergo a thorough evaluation. However, an evaluation cannot be initiated or acted upon by the school without written permission of the parents. From the start, therefore, you will be aware of the school's interest in identifying any academic or behavioral difficulties that your child may have. This system is designed to encourage parents to function as partners in the evaluation process. School personnel will notify you in writing about the specific tests that will be administered and the professionals who will be evaluating your child. You should also be given a copy of your rights or procedural safeguards, developed by the state's Department of Education in accordance with directives of the Individuals with Disabilities Education Act.

The purpose of your child's evaluation is to determine whether he or she needs special education services, and if so, in what areas he or she qualifies for assistance. In the process, the special methods, techniques, and materials needed in the education program are also identified. The results of the evaluation are then used as a guide in judging your child's likely future performance educationally, behaviorally, and vocationally.

In some circumstances only psychological and educational evaluations are necessary. As a general rule, evaluations are more comprehensive when it is believed that the child may need high levels of support to remain in the regular education environment. For the child who will need a more intensive level of services, the educational and psychological assessments are usually accompanied by at least a medical and a social appraisal. It is not uncommon also to include speech-language, hearing, occupational therapy, physical therapy, and psychological assessments.

A comprehensive evaluation can be accomplished in a Development Evaluation Center where professionals including pediatricians, social workers, educators, psychologists, physical and occupational therapists, audiologists, speech-language therapists, and others work together to identify the child's strengths and weaknesses.

Although requirements vary by state, there are regulations regarding the length of time it should take to complete an evaluation. These and other stipulations of state regulations are available from the director of special education in your community or from the Special Education Office in your state Department of Education.

TEAM MEETING

When an evaluation is completed, a multidisciplinary team from the school will meet and discuss the individual assessments to determine whether your child has a disability. As your child's parent, you are a member of the team. If you are not satisfied with their judgment, you have a right to disagree and request another opinion, usually at the school's expense. If it is believed that your child does not have a specific disability, he or she may not be eligible for any special education services outside of what would ordinarily be provided in the regular education program. However, if the multidisciplinary team concludes, based on the assessments, that there is a specific disability, the team and the parents are responsible for developing an individualized education program (IEP).

What constitutes a disability is usually defined in the state regulations. These regulations typically cite disabilities such as hearing impairment or deafness, speech impairment, mental retardation, visual impairment or blindness, multiply disabling conditions, orthopaedic impairments, serious emotional disturbance, learning disabilities, childhood autism, or traumatic brain injuries. Each of these categories has a specific definition. If a child has one of these disabilities, he or she is eligible for special services.

Some states consider the identification of disabilities as "labeling" the child. These states, as well as some local education agencies, have dropped these labels and have instead decided to serve children based on their educational needs. Much can be said for and against classification, labeling, and stigmatization, as was discussed in Chapter 1.

Development of an IEP for students identified as needing special services is discussed next.

THE INDIVIDUALIZED EDUCATION PROGRAM

The individualized education program (IEP) is the single most important school document about your child that you will ever possess. It is a written statement about your child's abilities and impairments, developed by you and the professionals who performed the evaluations. It contains a clear, individualized plan of instructions designed to deal with your child's disability.

Who Will Attend the IEP Meeting?

Your school must give you ample notice of the time and place of the IEP meeting. At this meeting, personnel representing the school will ask for your input. This is an important opportunity for you to provide helpful information about your child. You will be able to discuss your child's social and academic skills as well as your own expectations for him or her in school. Although many recommendations and decisions are made by various school personnel, you should know that you have an equal role in the decision-making process and play a major function in developing goals and objectives for your child.

According to IDEA, the student may attend the IEP meeting. Personnel from the school who are required to be present at this meeting include a school administrator (e.g., the special education director), the child's teacher, and members of the evaluation team. If your child will be leaving a regular education program to attend a special education setting, the receiving teacher also should be present.

In the case of a student with learning disabilities, a professional who is knowledgeable about learning disabilities may be asked to participate in this meeting. In the case of students who are 16 years of age or older, IDEA requires that an individualized transition plan (ITP) be developed as part of the individualized education program. Specifically, the act states:

> A statement of the needed transition services for students beginning no later than age 16 and annually thereafter (and, when determined appropriate for the individual, beginning at age 14 or younger), including, when appropriate, a statement of the interagency responsibilities or linkages (or both) before the student leaves the school setting.[1]

According to IDEA, transition services are defined as:

> A coordinated set of activities for a student, designed within an outcome-oriented process, which promotes movement from school to post-

---

[1]Individuals with Disabilities Education Act of 1990 (IDEA), PL 101-476. (October 30, 1990). Title 20, U.S.C. 1400 et seq: *U.S. Statutes at Large, 104,* 1103–1151.

school activities, including post-secondary education, vocational training, integrated employment (including supported employment), continuing and adult education, adult services, independent living, or community participation. The coordinated set of activities shall be based upon the individual student's needs, taking into account the student's preferences and interests, and shall include instruction, community experiences, the development of employment and other post-school adult living objectives, and when appropriate, acquisition of daily living skills and functional vocational evaluation.[2]

As an example, a vocational education teacher may attend the conference if the child is at an age when a vocational program needs to be discussed. Representatives from other agencies also might ordinarily be involved, such as a vocational rehabilitation counselor from the state's Division of Vocational Rehabilitation who might be assigned to the school. In addition, the school reserves the right to invite other professionals.

Preparing for the Meeting

To prepare for your first conference, you may wish to contact other parents regarding their experiences at IEP meetings. You may want to talk to trusted professionals and advocates for children with developmental disabilities and consider whether you would like them to accompany you. You have the right to bring anyone with you, including a friend or a representative of an advocacy and support group, to the IEP meeting. A professional who has evaluated your child or someone who has knowledge of the IEP process may be very helpful to you, as sometimes these meetings can be overwhelming and intimidating to parents.

Prior to the meeting, you should have some idea of what you want to contribute to the individualized education program and what you think would be best for your child. When considering your own recommendations, keep in mind the need to maintain the least restrictive environment (LRE), which means your child should be kept in a classroom that is as close to regular as possible, while receiving the required special services. The more special the classroom, the more restrictive or out of the mainstream the educational environment will be. All parties in an IEP meeting are supposed to work toward the goal of providing the most appropriate education for your child. All services needed by your child must be made available through your school system even if they cannot be provided locally.

If you anticipate significant disagreements with the school, you may consider the counsel of a professional outside of the school sys-

---

[2]Individuals with Disabilities Education Act of 1990 (IDEA), PL 101-476. (October 30, 1990). Title 20, U.S.C. 1400 et seq: *U.S. Statutes at Large, 104,* 1103–1151.

tem who is either an attorney familiar with educational matters or a parent advocate. With such support and proper advice, problems that might be encountered can often be resolved without the need for an impartial hearing later. If you cannot reach an agreement, however, you will need to ask for an impartial hearing, to which you are entitled under the Individuals with Disabilities Education Act.

How Will the IEP Meeting Proceed?

Usually, the director of special education will chair the IEP meeting. The school personnel who are present will be introduced to you. You may want to write down their names and positions. After such introductions, usually updates on the child's present academic skills and behavioral status are presented. Also, the child's psychomotor abilities and his or her self-help and adaptive skills are discussed. Medical, psychological, and educational assessments that have taken place previously, in addition to classroom observations, are reviewed. If your child is an adolescent, his or her vocational talents and interests will be considered through the development of the ITP. Thus, many aspects of your child's overall functioning contribute to an evaluation of his or her strengths and weaknesses.

What Is Contained in an Individualized Education Program?

Federal regulations mandate the following content for an individualized education program:

A statement of the child's present level of educational performance
A statement of the annual goals
Appropriate procedures for determining whether the short-term objectives are being achieved
A statement of specific educational and related services to be provided to the child
Identification of the providers of the various services
Dates for initiation and expected duration of services
Evaluation procedures and schedules for determining, at least annually, whether objectives are being met

Each of these statements is discussed next.

Level of Educational Performance

The first statement written in the IEP is the present level of educational performance. The term *educational* is used in a broad sense, referring not only to specific academic achievements but also to the child's behavior, special abilities, motor skills, communication capabilities, and adaptive behavior. Not all current levels of educational performance must be listed, only those relevant to your child's disability. For example, if your child's primary problem is behavioral, the specific behavioral characteristics, such as aggressive behavior toward peers, would be listed.

Annual Goals

Likewise, the annual goals and short-term objectives are only written for those educational concerns that relate to your child's special education needs. For instance, a child who has difficulties only with mathematics might receive special education or assistance from a resource teacher for this subject only.

At a minimum, the annual goals must be revised on the anniversary date of the original writing of the individualized education program. School personnel or parents may request a change in the annual goals at any time during the year and need not wait for the anniversary date.

Goals are written according to the priorities of the student's educational needs. They are based on the child's abilities and educational performance. Of course, other concerns may also affect goal selection. If, for example, a child has severe behavioral difficulties, expectations for academic growth might be conservative until the behavior is better under control. Hence, a host of variables must be considered in writing the general goals.

Short-Term Objectives

Short-term objectives are developed in conjunction with the annual goals and focus on the specific steps to be taken to reach these goals. For example, if a child does not recognize upper-case letters, the annual goal might indicate that the child will be able to name all 26 capital letters in 1 year. The short-term objectives, however, might state that the child will be able to name 7 capital letters in 10 weeks, 7 more during the following 10 weeks, and so forth until he or she reaches the final total of 26 at the end of the year. Specific criteria for such objectives might state, "The child will be able to name the upper-case letters A–G correctly 90% of the time on five occasions by a specified date." As a parent you may gauge your child's progress by using a teacher-made test that, for instance, asks your child to name each of those letters on five separate occasions, with an expectation of 90% accuracy.

For another child, the annual goal might be for the child to get dressed independently. The short-term objectives might focus on specific tasks such as putting on one's socks or shirt. For example, the objective might read, "Within a dressing routine, the child will put on a pair of tube socks with a verbal cue 80% of the time by a specified date." A subsequent goal may be to complete this task with only the visual cue of seeing the socks in a pile of the child's clothing.

School systems often will develop objectives that are written for each quarterly period, usually every 10 weeks. In this way, parents can review with the teacher the previously specified objectives to see if they have been met. If they have not been met, the teacher and parent can then discuss what might have caused this and what steps should be taken to correct the situation.

Related Services, Identification of Providers, and Scheduling

In addition to special education, other services also may be provided to your child such as occupational therapy, physical therapy, speech-language therapy, and transportation. These should be listed on the IEP, along with the names of the involved professionals. How often such services should be provided and how long the individual sessions should last must be spelled out. For example, the IEP may read, "David will receive individual speech-language therapy from the speech-language pathologist, Ms. Murray, three times a week for a 30-minute period each." Also, the date when speech-language therapy will start and the length of time that it is expected to continue should be clearly indicated.

It is important for you to know what the term *related services* entails. According to federal regulations, *related services* is defined as:

> Transportation and such developmental, corrective, and other support-ive services as are required to assist a handicapped child to benefit from special education, and includes special individualized assistance in mathematics and remedial reading, speech pathology and audiology, psychological services, physical and occupational therapy, recreation, early identification and assessment of disabilities in children, counsel-ing services, and medical services for diagnostic or evaluation purposes. The term also includes school health services, social work services in schools, and parent counseling and training.[3]

Related services usually complement the special education program in which the child is placed. For example, the school may have to provide occupational therapy services for a child with severe visual-perceptual and motor problems, or an individual with a significant orthopaedic disability may need to be trained in certain adap-

[3]Individuals with Disabilities Education Act of 1990 (IDEA), PL 101-476. (October 30, 1990). Title 20, U.S.C. 1400 et seq: *U.S. Statutes at Large, 104*, 1103–1151.

tive skills such as dressing and self-feeding. A child with spina bifida may need intermittent catheterization by the school nurse. The related services used most often are special transportation, physical therapy, occupational therapy, speech-language therapy, social work intervention, and adaptive physical education.

Inclusion in Regular Education

Because parents are included in the IEP process, every parent is in a good position to ensure that his or her child participates in an inclusive educational setting. Parents can be sure that their child's strengths are clearly described so the IEP truly reflects how these strengths can help formulate the child's inclusion in the educational setting. It is in this fashion that parents and educators can collaborate in developing a full inclusion program. A statement can be contained in the IEP about the amount of time the child will attend a regular classroom and what percentage of time each day the child will receive special services; for example, "Jane will be in a regular classroom 100% of the time but within it, special services will be provided 25% of that time."

Using the IEP as a Tool

The IEP is not a contract or legal document, and, therefore, the teachers or school cannot be held liable if a student does not progress as expected. However, school personnel must demonstrate that they made a serious attempt to help the child meet the goals and objectives specified in the IEP. Through the IEP, you may determine the progress your child makes on a yearly basis. If you observe that your child does not advance according to the specified objectives within a defined time period, or if other unforeseen circumstances (e.g., prolonged hospitalization of the child) should make the objectives unrealistic or unreasonable, you may request that the IEP be revised at any time during the school year. You may ask for another meeting and do not have to wait for the annual conference.

Although you may sign the IEP immediately at the end of the annual meeting, you also have the option to take the document home for further study and review. Read it carefully to be sure that you are comfortable with the instructional program it outlines and that it meets your child's needs. Be certain that the priorities you have identified for your child are clearly listed in the annual goals and short-term objectives. Make sure that all of the services that your child needs are detailed in this report. Finally, be positive that the principle of the least restrictive environment is followed and that your child is integrated, or included, with students without disabilities as much as possible.

If Agreement Cannot Be Reached

As mentioned, if you do not agree with the individualized education program, you have the right to request an impartial due process hearing. You should first indicate to the school authorities why you disagree with the IEP, and give them an opportunity to revise it. However, you may also reject the IEP and request a second independent evaluation of your child at the school's expense. At times, the disagreement between parent and school can be resolved on the basis of the results of the second evaluation, thus eliminating the need for a hearing. If the matter goes to a hearing, it will be conducted by an impartial hearing officer, who is from outside of the school. However, the child must remain in his or her present education program until the hearing settles the issues that are contested.

EDUCATION IN THE LEAST RESTRICTIVE ENVIRONMENT

As soon as children have been evaluated and identified as having disabilities, and an individualized education program has been developed, they must begin their specially designed education program. However, because we have come to realize that children with developmental disabilities are more like their peers without disabilities than they are different than them, the goal should be to place the child in an educational setting that is as close to regular as possible. This approach has come to be known popularly as *inclusion, mainstreaming,* or education in the *least restrictive environment.*

Actually, the words *inclusion* and *mainstreaming* are not mentioned in the Individuals with Disabilities Education Act, but *least restrictive environment* is clearly spelled out in the law. Whether the child can remain in regular education or needs a special environment depends on his or her specific needs. In developing the IEP, the multidisciplinary team and the parents decide together on the least restrictive educational alternative for a particular child.

Traditionally, the range of services has included regular education settings with resource help, self-contained special classes in regular schools, private special education day schools, residential schools, and, finally, hospitals or home-based instruction. These alternatives are discussed in the next several paragraphs but parents should know they can also advocate for full inclusion of their child in the child's neighborhood school if they feel that is the most appropriate educational setting for their child.

Probably the least restrictive environment possible for a student with special needs is to remain full-time in a regular class with special education monitoring. The special educator may function as a consultant advising the regular classroom teacher and the parents, but not providing any direct education services to the child. A child with a more serious disability, while continuing in a regular education setting, might be seen individually by a special education teacher once or twice a week for individual training in the problem area. In a slightly more restrictive educational environment, a child would be seen perhaps five times a week by a special educator who would serve as a resource teacher to the child and as a consultant to the classroom teacher and parents. For the individual with more significant needs, a regular education classroom with special services 2 hours or so per day in a resource room might be appropriate.

Although more restrictive settings exist, such as special classes within public schools, special education public and private schools, and residential schools, every effort should be made to educate the child with a disability in his or her neighborhood school with peers of the same age who do not have disabilities. This allows children to accept and understand their differences and emphasize likenesses. Social integration is an important component of a good education program. Being an integral part of everyday school life is a step toward involvement in community life. School prepares chil-dren not only academically but also for activities of daily living. Some students will need specific instruction in community living skills in order to participate in everyday life. Because not all instruc-tion needs to take place in the confines of a classroom, your child might profit more from teaching practical skills in real-life settings. Because one goal of education is to foster independence and partici-pation, children with disabilities should be involved in activities even if they are not able to perform them independently. Placement and program decisions should be based on the child's needs and the best interests of the student and his or her family.

Although the above alternatives can still be considered appro-priate for a child depending on his or her specific individual needs, there are many professionals and parents who believe that *all* chil-dren with disabilities, no matter how severe, should be educated in a regular education setting. A program of this type is described as *inclusive*. Inclusive schooling means that *all* children, regardless of disability, are educated in a regular class and that their programs are consistent with their abilities and needs in that they receive the appropriate support services to be successful in the mainstream pro-gram. This requires special and regular educators to work coopera-tively so that all students receive an appropriate education in a typi-cal environment. The child should attend the same schools as siblings, neighbors, and children of similar chronological age. The primary purpose of such an education is to provide each student with the opportunity to learn and be involved with his or her peers in the neighborhood school. Models that fit the concept of the least restrictive environment are inclusion and cooperative teaching. Co-operative teaching, or co-teaching, refers to an educational approach in which regular and former special educators work in a co-active and coordinated fashion to jointly teach academically and behavior-ally heterogeneous groups of students in inclusive settings (regular classrooms).[4]

Although the pros and cons of restrictive placement are de-bated, it is very clear that parents are the principal decision makers regarding all aspects of their child's education, as mandated by fed-eral law. Quality education programs are a shared responsibility of parents, regular educators, and special educators. The child should go to the same school as his or her neighborhood peers without disabilities. Students with disabilities should participate in regular

[4]Bauwens, J., Hourcade, J., & Friend, M. (1989). Cooperative teaching: A model for general and special education integration. *Remedial and Special Education*, *10*(2), 17–22.

school activities with similar-age peers as a natural part of their day. Special services should be provided within the regular education setting using the "integrated therapy" approach.

The student's placement and program is determined by his or her unique strengths and needs, not on the diagnostic label of the disability. The interaction of students with disabilities with their same-age peers without disabilities in academic settings is a priority.

Inclusive, or integrated, programs should not place unreasonable demands on teachers who have students with developmental disabilities. These regular education teachers will require various supports, such as inservice training, technical assistance, teacher aides, planning time, curriculum consultation, and administrative support. Instructional methods, techniques, materials, and curriculum shown to be effective with children who have disabilities should be used. Parents and educators should work as partners to monitor the goals and objectives of the individualized education program closely to ensure that they are being met and that they will ultimately result in integrated community living.

WHAT IS SPECIAL EDUCATION?

Special education refers to services provided by trained special educators who work collaboratively with regular educators. Special educators use methods, curricula, and materials that are presented, in an organized, structured, step-by-step manner. Some examples include the Visual-Auditory-Kinesthetic-Tactile (VAKT) method, which utilizes a multisensory approach to learning; and the Orton-Gillingham or other reading methods (e.g., high interest, low vocabulary readers, language experience method). Curricula that deal with the transition of secondary-level students from school to work, including daily living skills, functional acadamics, recreational opportunities, and personal-social skills, are included. Instruction is usually provided individually and in small groups, especially in the areas of reading, spelling, and mathematics, or in activities of daily living.

In addition to specially designed instruction, a great deal of help is provided in the behavioral and emotional domains. The presence of a stable and structured environment helps the student to get the most out of the program and to learn most effectively. In addition, teacher aides often participate in special education programs and may provide special tutoring. In special education, many types of adaptive equipment are available. Also, computerized systems for children with physical disabilities and other learning aids may be utilized. Equipment to enhance communication for children with a hearing impairment or deafness, electric wheelchairs for children with physical disabilities, and materials necessary for the education of children with a visual impairment or blindness are available for students with such special needs.

CONCLUSION

The Individuals with Disabilities Education Act is clear in its mission to include parents as active participants in the education of their children. Learning your child's rights, which include a free and appropriate public education, the development of an individualized education program, participation in planning an education program, instruction in the least restrictive environment, and due process procedures to settle educational disputes, is of utmost importance. The most obvious parental contribution is involvement in the planning and development of your child's education and instructional program, as the IEP cannot be written and approved without parental participation. The authors of the Individuals with Disabilities Education Act realized the pivotal role parents play as participants in the team process, a role that should help ensure an optimal education for their children.

ACKNOWLEDGMENT

Contributions have been made to this chapter by James P. McEneaney, M.Ed.

30

Legal Issues in Developmental Disabilities

In American society, knowing one's legal rights and how to protect them is becoming increasingly difficult as the legal system grows more complex. It becomes even more complicated when a parent must deal with the needs of a child who has developmental disabilities. On the one hand, the child may never be able to grasp and exercise his or her own rights adequately. On the other hand, the young person may have more ability to exercise his or her rights than the courts are prepared to recognize or grant.

This chapter does not offer you specific advice about solving legal dilemmas. Its purpose is to discuss some of the common legal issues that arise in developmental disabilities. For expert advice and opinion, there is no substitute for a competent lawyer. As a parent you should plan to consult a lawyer should legal difficulties arise that you are not prepared to handle.

BASIC RIGHTS OF PEOPLE
WITH DEVELOPMENTAL DISABILITIES

The U.S. Constitution guarantees all citizens the right to life, liberty, and the pursuit of happiness. In the past, these most basic rights often have been denied to persons with physical or mental disabilities.

The United States has undergone sweeping social changes in this century, and especially in the last 25 years. One by one, groups that have been denied their civil rights—women and racial minorities, among others—have come forward to demand social and legal equality. Among them are persons with disabilities. No longer can basic human privileges be denied to a particular group on the assumption that its members will be unable to use those privileges. Myths have been challenged and proven wrong. For example, it now is taken for granted that women are as capable as men of voting intelligently and that members of various racial and ethnic minorities can achieve economic and social independence. Similarly, persons with mental retardation can vote, hold jobs, care for their own needs, and benefit from education to a far greater extent than was once believed.

The current understanding is that citizens with developmental disabilities have the same rights as citizens without such disabilities. Parents are sometimes unaware that their sons and daughters with mental retardation deserve certain rights and privileges. Because some of these rights are easier to understand than others and because their denial has been so widespread, they warrant more detailed discussion here.

Right to Life

Above all else, people with mental retardation and other individuals with developmental disabilities have the same right to live as all other citizens. To deny this right is contrary to the most basic principles of American society. This right should not be threatened on the basis of economics, appearance, perceived or expected intellectual abilities, or the expense required to preserve life.

Right to Education

The law guarantees the right to a free and appropriate public education, and yet it was only in 1975 that this right was extended to persons with developmental disabilities. It was in 1975 that PL 94-142, the Education for All Handicapped Children Act, was passed (see Chapter 29 for more details about PL 94-142 and other legislation, including the Individuals with Disabilities Education Act [IDEA]). Prior to that time, children with mental retardation, chronic illnesses, cerebral palsy, or orthopaedic defects often remained at home and were deprived of educational services because a school was not wheelchair accessible or equipped to teach children with mental retardation. Their peers without a disability attended public schools designed for the average student. Parents of children with mental retardation paid taxes to support public education; yet, their children were denied the benefits that those taxes purchased.

Right to Freedom of Choice

Denial of choice is a particular problem for persons with mental retardation. Because of the limited intellectual abilities of persons with mental retardation, society has tended to make decisions for them or to deny them goods, services, and experiences that are available to others. It must never be assumed that individuals are incapable or undeserving because they have been categorized under the broad label of mental retardation. Like anyone else, individuals with mental retardation must be granted freedom of choice within their capacity to make decisions, and with the same limits imposed on their freedom as those on persons without mental retardation.

Right to Live in the Community

The first institutions for children with mental retardation in America began in New England in the 1800s. They sprang from the desire to educate and provide medical care to a deserving and needy minority. But the concept went awry. Institutions grew by leaps and bounds; care and training were neglected, with only custodial care being provided. Gradually, institutions became warehouses, and lifetime commitment often became the norm for persons identified as having mental retardation. Eventually, the low level of functioning of persons with mental retardation in institutions was used as evidence that most of them were incapable of acquiring the skills necessary to live in the community.

In the past, placement away from home was often recommended to parents as soon as a disability was diagnosed, particularly if the diagnosis was made at birth. Many parents of young adults with spina bifida or with Down syndrome recall that after hearing the diagnosis, institutionalization was the next thing mentioned, even though the majority of children with Down syndrome require only intermittent or limited supports and the outlook for many children with spina bifida is quite positive.

Today, placement outside of the natural home and community is done only as a last alternative, when the need is compelling, and when it clearly serves the best interests of the person with a disability. Almost every individual with mental retardation can now live and participate in the community. To meet any individual's best interests, placement in a residential facility must include habilitation, should enhance the person's life, and should be reevaluated frequently.

Right to Work

The right of persons with disabilities to work has been violated in several ways. For example, previously many have been forced to do labor in an institutional facility without reimbursement or without reimbursement to match the earnings of a person without a disability who performs the same task. In addition, many persons with developmental disabilities have been denied any opportunity to be taught work skills or to work at all. These persons, like persons without disabilities, share in the right to a fair day's pay for a fair day's labor.

Right to Contract for Goods and Property

Persons with mental retardation often are presumed to be incompetent and in need of help in making contractual arrangements. As a result, many individuals with mental retardation become wards of appointed legal guardians. Once appointed, a guardian typically becomes totally responsible for the management of the person and of his or her property. Limited guardianships that allow more freedom to the ward are gradually finding their way into the law. Overprotection of a person with a developmental disability can be as unfair as underprotection. The right to make binding legal agreements, small and large, and the right to contract should be preserved whenever possible.

Right to Equal Protection under the Law

It can be difficult for persons with mental retardation to know their rights and to take advantage of them. The services of an advocate, a responsible, impartial individual who works on someone's behalf, may be required to help a person with mental retardation know, enjoy, and benefit from his or her lawful rights, privileges, and protections. If such advocate services were not available, persons with mental retardation and other disabilities essentially would be deprived of their legal rights. For this reason, Title II of PL 94-103, the Developmental Disabilities Assistance and Bill of Rights Act of 1975, required that as of October 1, 1975, states receiving certain federal grants for persons with developmental disabilities must have a formal advocacy system for people with disabilities, and that such a system have the authority and independence needed to provide effective protection. If you are concerned about your child's rights, your local chapter of The Arc (formerly the Association for Retarded Citizens of the United States) should be able to direct you to a legal advocacy agency that can help.

Right to Nondiscrimination

In 1990, PL 101-336, the Americans with Disabilities Act (ADA), was signed into law. This legislation focuses on eliminating discrimination against individuals with disabilities and bringing them into the economic and social mainstream of American life. The four main parts of the ADA (known as Titles I–IV) are as follows:

- *Title I* stresses that individuals with disabilities should have equal opportunity to the same benefits, programs, and activities that individuals without disabilities have in settings that are as inclusive as possible. Moreover, an individual, agency, or company is not permitted to discriminate on the basis of a disability, limit the accomplishment of those with disabilities, or perpetuate discrimination against individuals because of their association with a person who has a disability.
- *Title II* incorporates many of the definitions of PL 88-352, the Civil Rights Act of 1964. It prohibits discrimination in application procedures, hiring and discharge, compensation, advancement, job training, and other privileges of employment. Title II also emphasizes that there should be reasonable accommodations for an applicant or employee whose mental or physical limitations are known.
- *Title III* applies to commerce, mass transportation, and public accommodations. It prohibits discrimination against individuals with disabilities and requires that these individuals have a right to full and equal enjoyment of services, facilities, privileges, advantages, and accommodation in any public place.
- *Title IV* provides that the Federal Communication Commission ensure that telecommunication relay services are available to the extent possible, 24 hours a day, for persons with significant hearing impairments. It ensures that individuals with hearing impairments have access to telecommunication services equal to services used by individuals without disabilities. Moreover, it prohibits discrimination to impair the development of technology to improve access to telecommunication services for individuals with disabilities.

Although not all aspects of the ADA pertain to children and adolescents, the law attempts to ensure that all individuals with disabilities can, as much as possible, enjoy life in the community and have access to facilities, employment, and public services. The main thrust of the Americans with Disabilities Act is intended to eliminate discrimination against persons with various disabilities at all levels so that they can participate fully in the mainstream of societal life.

Right to Sue

In *The Mentally Retarded Citizen and the Law*, the author writes, "The right of any citizen to gain access to the courts for the vindication of his legal rights is fundamental. It is not to be denied or curtailed without compelling justification."[1] Again, it should not be presumed that any individual does not have the ability to use the courts. Competent advocacy must be provided to aid the individual with mental retardation in making use of the legal system.

Other Civil Rights

For voting, holding public office, or serving on a jury, the requirements for persons with mental retardation should be the same as those for the general population. A truly incompetent individual will not be able to find his or her way through the procedures necessary to register to vote; will not bear the scrutiny necessary to gain public confidence and to be voted into office; and will not demonstrate sufficient understanding to be chosen for jury duty. In any society, not all voters are well informed; not all politicians are scholars; and not all jurors are entirely rational, informed, unbiased, and perfectly literate. If there is to be some minimum standard of judgment or comprehension, it should be applied to all citizens.

Right to Marry

Many states limit the right to marry for those who are labeled incompetent or intellectually limited. Enforcement of such laws varies, but is generally quite lax. There is no accurate way of predicting which marriages will be unsuccessful or end in divorce. As the record for successful marriages at all social and economic levels is far from sterling, it is hard to justify denying persons with mental retardation the right to marry.

Right to Sexual Expression

Persons with mental retardation have been the victims of myths about their sexual drive and habits, which have resulted in great hesitancy about sexual freedom for them. However, there is no evidence to suggest that persons with mental retardation and other developmental disabilities as a group differ from the norm in their sexual needs. Myths have arisen primarily because of atypical

---

[1] Kindred, M., & Kane, L. (1976). *The mentally retarded citizen and the law.* New York: Free Press.

restrictions placed on sexual expression among individuals with mental retardation, separation of the sexes, denial of privacy, exploitation, lack of teaching in "normal" and acceptable sexual behavior, and unacceptable acts by some individuals that have received widespread attention. In the past, sexual misconduct has been used as an excuse for institutionalization in some cases, and yet special education programs have offered little sex education. The need is not for greater restriction, but for more teaching and information.

Right to Bear Children

In the past, laws allowing involuntary sterilization grew from inaccurate theories about the heredity of mental retardation and the erroneous assumption that most persons with mental retardation are criminally inclined. Although there is generally a higher risk that a person with mental retardation will give birth to a child with a disability, couples with mental retardation can have children with average intelligence, just as all parents can produce offspring with mental retardation. Even in cases where typical adults are carriers of serious genetic conditions, there is no mechanism for legally restricting their right to have a child. However, genetic counseling and information concerning the risk of having a child with a developmental disability should be provided to the parents. The parent with mental retardation deserves to enjoy the same basic right in the absence of evidence of harm.

Right to Raise Children

The same argument that applies to the right of people with disabilities to bear children applies to the right to raise them. There are competent and incompetent parents at nearly all levels of intellectual ability. Proof of mental retardation is not proof of certain neglect or of harmful ignorance about childrearing. The standards for proving neglect and for assessing adequate parenting should be uniformly applied, and teaching should be provided through the educational system before the parent-to-be reaches adulthood.

To summarize, it is difficult to change assumptions that have been held for generations about persons with mental retardation and other disabilities. Double standards are no more acceptable when applied to persons with developmental disabilities than they are when applied to different races or sexes. The denial of any constitutionally guaranteed right must be based on objective and valid individual assessment. It must be demonstrated that the individual's exercise of that right will result in harm to him- or herself or others.

Discrimination against citizens with disabilities and different treatment of them have made many of these individuals *appear* to be very different. This difference has then been used to justify further discrimination. Differences between persons with mental retardation and other citizens can be diminished by minimizing differences in treatment.

ROLE OF THE ADVOCATE

Advocacy refers to any activity in which a person acts on his or her own behalf or on behalf of another to defend a cause, maintain a cause, or meet a need. In the field of developmental disabilities, there are two important types of advocacy. In *citizen advocacy*, a citizen volunteer represents the interests of another citizen who cannot do so because of some impairment. Such an advocate steps in when needs cannot be met without special assistance from a third party.

Legal advocacy is a more specific term referring to efforts to address the needs of persons with developmental disabilities by changing legislation or administrative rules, or by pursuing court action. Some legal advocacy tasks, such as representing a client in court, require a lawyer, but others do not.

Legal advocacy usually takes two forms. *Law reform advocacy* tries to achieve recognition of the basic legal rights for the population with disabilities as a whole or for a broad segment such as persons with mental retardation. In *case advocacy*, a single individual is represented in a particular dispute. Legal advocacy for persons with mental retardation is not just a privilege; it is now a right recognized by law. The logic behind the law is that only an advocate system can guarantee citizens with mental retardation basic legal rights. Without advocates, persons with mental retardation essentially would be deprived of their constitutionally guaranteed rights.

One example in which advocates can serve a critical role is in commitment cases. It now is recognized that individuals with mental retardation need legal counsel when parents or guardians institute proceedings that are intended to lead to placement in an institution. The courts view such an attempt as adversarial; they no longer assume that the parents' objective is necessarily in the best interests of the child with a disability. The individual now has a right to be represented by legal counsel in court proceedings, to dispute the grounds for commitment, to permit the court to hear the other side of the issue, and to ensure that his or her own best interests will be determined by the court.

Because of the shortage of lawyers knowledgeable in issues regarding persons with mental retardation, many states have formed agencies with full-time trained personnel. Individuals with mental retardation and their families should explore the services their home state has to offer. A good source for information about such advocacy systems is a local chapter of The Arc (see also the section about advocacy and parent empowerment in Chapter 31).

TRUSTS AND WILLS

A trust is a legal tool by which one person, the donor, can give something to a second person, the trustee, with qualifications that it must be used for the benefit of someone else, the beneficiary. It is designed to allow the donor to control the use of his or her property as he or she chooses, but is not designed to assert control over the beneficiary. Trusts are often established for persons with developmental disabilities.

There are several advantages of a trust over a gift or a will. First, the property in question does not actually belong to the beneficiary. Therefore, the trust in many cases can be arranged so that it will not cause an individual with a developmental disability to be ineligible for help from other sources. A trust can be created before the death of the parents, so that they have the opportunity to observe the plan in action during their lifetimes. This allows for changes or additional planning. It also can be reassuring to see the trust in effect. Concern about waste or misuse of funds is lessened because the terms of a trust can be detailed and enforceable. A trust is more like a contract than a gift. There can be restrictions on the use of funds, whereas it is more difficult to place legal restrictions on a gift. A trust can guard assets from mismanagement, but is less restrictive than a guardianship. It can leave the beneficiary some decision-making power. With the proper terms, the trust can be tailored to the need of the individual. The person with a developmental disability gets the maximum income from the trust while safeguarding the principal. When the trust is ended, the assets that remain can be distributed among other family members without death taxes or the expense of probate (the legal process of establishing that a will is genuine).

Willing property to a third party who does not have a disability, with provision in the will for a family member with mental retardation, is generally not recommended for a variety of reasons. It can be costly and risky, and it lacks the flexibility of a trust, which can adapt to the needs of the child as times change. Directly giving the person with mental retardation legal title to the assets by inheritance or gift is also unsatisfactory. In some cases, a person with mental retardation may be vulnerable to exploitation. Service providers can take the assets and consume the funds in compensation for their services. Moreover, the individual may become ineligible for some types of governmental assistance.

There are many variables to take into account in determining whether a trust is appropriate for your family. These include the size of the family's estate (the sum total of assets and liabilities), the severity of the disability, benefits and support systems already available to the person with a developmental disability, the cost of care for the beneficiary, the individual's potential to be self-supporting, specific abilities and limitations, educational level, and others. Although it may be difficult to find an attorney with training in estate planning for families with a member who has mental retardation, it is important to try because great care must be taken to find a reliable trustee and to set realistic terms or provisions for the trust.

Establishing a trust is complicated but valuable and highly recommended for families with adequate assets. It is of the utmost importance to identify a reliable individual as trustee or cotrustee. This should be someone who is familiar with the beneficiary's needs, and who can be relied upon to exercise care and good judgment in managing funds. The trust plan should allow the trustee flexibility to take advantage of new developments and opportunities for the beneficiary, as they arise. Provision must be made for an annual review of the trustee's accounts. The trust plan itself should be reviewed at intervals to take advantage of changes in services for persons with mental retardation or changes in trust law. When appropriate, if governmental agencies are providing for the basic life necessities of the beneficiary, the donor can and should make sure that trust funds are to be used for items not provided by other sources. Trust plans involve numerous considerations and can take many shapes. The help of an informed and competent attorney is a necessity.

COMPETENCY AND GUARDIANSHIP

Guardianship is a legal mechanism that grants an individual the legal power to make decisions for a ward, someone who is considered incapable of making these decisions on his or her own. Although guardianship is often used for deciding financial matters, it is usually granted in an all-or-nothing fashion. The ward legally is considered to lack the abilities to act on his or her own behalf; specific capacities are not considered.

The need for a guardian should be based on an individual's actual ability to make decisions in his or her own best interest. Courts historically have relied on medical testimony to determine competency, even though the issue is legal, not medical. Often in the past, no attempt was made to analyze the affected person's capabilities in regard to his or her needs. The ability of the individual with a disability to make, or to learn to make, an adequately well-informed decision on his or her own behalf was not considered or assessed. "Due process of law," the right to have any law applied fairly and reasonably and with adequate safeguards, often has been ignored. Guardianship should be used in cases where a substantial incapacity can be demonstrated, and should be limited to the particular area in which ability is lacking.

The following are the types of guardianships:

1. In a *general guardianship,* the guardian has the same relationship to the ward as a parent to a minor child. The ward is stripped

of his or her ability to make binding decisions, and the guardian assumes the role of determining the wishes and best interests of the ward, who has no personal or property rights left intact. This is the traditional form of guardianship. The ward may not be able to make legal contracts, buy or sell property, sue or be sued, engage in financial transactions, vote, marry, choose his or her place of residence, or decide for or against medical treatment without legal approval of the guardian.

2. Some states allow *guardianship of the person*, which often is sufficient to meet the ward's needs, although a general, more restrictive guardianship may have been sought. Guardianship of the person usually is not granted alone without guardianship of the property, but it may be appropriate in some cases. A guardian of the person has the power to make decisions about where and how the ward will live, as well as other judgments regarding education, training, and personal welfare.

3. A *guardian of the property* (or estate) has the power to manage property and financial affairs. The guardian may also be termed a *curator* or *conservator*.

4. A *guardian ad litem* is a special court-appointed guardian whose function is to litigate (prosecute or defend) on behalf of a person who is unable to represent him- or herself adequately. Guardians ad litem often are attorneys but are not required to be.

5. A *temporary guardian* may be appointed when a quick decision is needed (e.g., an emergency operation) to protect life or property. In such a case, the courts generally have more freedom to bypass the usual requirements of due process.

When guardianship is considered, several questions must be asked. Is it necessary? What needs to be accomplished? Can the person's interests be protected by another, less restrictive means?

Less restrictive means are becoming more available. One way is to distinguish between personal and financial affairs. Another example is the U.S. Social Security Administration's "representative payee," or "substitute payee method." This is a mechanism by which Social Security benefits are paid to someone named as a representative, on the condition that the funds will be used only for the beneficiary. Some laws permit a court to authorize a particular transaction without appointing a guardian of the property. A guardian ad litem can be appointed for the sole purpose of conducting litigation on the ward's behalf.

A *facilitative guardianship* has been proposed in which the ward maintains his or her right to decision making and the guardian assists in achieving the individual's stated goals. The person with mental retardation may need help in making minor or major purchases and contracts, in finding shelter, or in gaining access to training. The facilitative guardian functions as a guide.

Perhaps the most important alternative to guardianship is the provision of social services and involvement of the individual's service coordinator to minimize the need for any type of guardianship. Guardianship, by definition, limits the individual's choices; services, however, can expand choices. In many cases, the need for a guardian arises purely out of the lack of proper education, inability to control one's actions or behavior, lack of vocational skills, inadequate monetary management, and dietary needs. With the provision of proper services, such as homemakers and counselors, the need for control may disappear.

In all areas of life, the right of the person with a developmental disability to least restrictive alternatives is being recognized. As restrictions are lessened in other areas, it becomes obvious that guardianship laws need revision and refinement as well. The evolving, modern idea is that guardianship should be limited and invoked only as a last resort, because it involves a substantial loss of rights. How well one is able to care for oneself, not one's intellectual level, should be the primary determinant of the need for a guardian. Legal capability to care for one's own interests should be presumed in most cases, unless it can be proven that the capacity is substantially lacking. The ward should retain as much of a voice and as much self-sufficiency in his or her own affairs as possible. Guardianships should come under the scrutiny of monitoring systems. It bears repeating that guidance, training, and protective services can substantially lessen the need to place persons with disabilities under the control of guardians. The primary consideration should be the welfare of the ward, not the estate, where the good of one is incompatible with the other. As in other areas, in providing alternatives to guardianship, society is moving in the direction of developing more meaningful procedures for meeting the basic needs of persons with developmental disabilities, while ensuring their individual rights and freedoms.

ACKNOWLEDGMENTS

Contributions have been made to this chapter by Leesa H. Mann, Ph.D., and Siegfried M. Pueschel, M.D., Ph.D., M.P.H.

31

Resource Development

Services for children with special needs are found throughout the United States. Yet, the availability of services differs from region to region and state to state, and programs to meet your child's specific needs may not be immediately at your disposal. Even programs that have national chapters differ in quality on the local level, depending on the personnel involved and the community support available. This is also true in the field of education. Anyone who has moved from one town to another knows that educational standards differ from locality to locality. There is even more variability in special education. One community may take its mandate to provide special education services seriously and offer a full range of services, whereas another may interpret the law narrowly and do just enough to meet minimum standards. Also, the quality of medical care, funding sources, and the availability of parent groups and outreach programs may vary from community to community.

DETERMINING YOUR CHILD'S NEEDS

In order to obtain appropriate services for your child, it is paramount to determine his or her needs. If you are uncertain of what your child's specific needs are, you may want to request a comprehensive assessment. An evaluation clinic or a Development Evaluation Center can provide an interdisciplinary examination of your child. A complete assessment by a team of professionals, including pediatricians, neurologists, nutritionists, nurses, social workers, psychologists, educators, physical therapists, occupational therapists, speech-language therapists, and others, can identify your

383

child's strengths and weaknesses. Based on such an evaluation, the various needs of your child, including medical, educational, psychological, recreational, and other needs, can be determined.

WHERE TO BEGIN LOOKING FOR SERVICES

When you know your child's specific needs, your task is to find appropriate services to meet them. One way to begin to explore what is available is to ask the people who first brought your child's problems to your attention. Whether it is the pediatrician, school personnel, or members of an interdisciplinary team, these professionals should be able to steer you toward appropriate and available resources in your area.

If the suggestions made by these professionals are unsatisfactory, you may want to investigate on your own. Try calling your local school department and various state agencies such as the Developmental Disabilities Planning Council and state Departments of Mental Health, Mental Retardation, Health, and Human Services. You also may want to contact local chapters of national organizations such as United Cerebral Palsy Associations, Easter Seal Society, March of Dimes, and The Arc. (Addresses and telephone numbers for the national offices of these and other organizations are provided in the Resource Organizations list at the end of this book.) If your child has a specific disorder or syndrome such as spina bifida or Down syndrome, the respective parent organization often can provide you with valuable advice concerning optimal services and resources in your community. In addition, you could consult resource books that list human services in your town and state. Such guides often describe the services each agency offers, the eligibility criteria, age range, costs, and other important information.

Other parents who have children with disabilities of similar age may provide advice regarding the availability and quality of services and the personnel providing those services. You may benefit from visiting various programs in your community. After observing what each has to offer, you can make an educated decision about where you would like to enroll your child.

ADVOCACY AND PARENT EMPOWERMENT

For parents of a child with developmental disabilities, the term *advocacy* is important. Simply stated, an advocate is a person or agency who promotes, recommends, or argues in favor of a cause. With regard to children with developmental disabilities, advocacy means efforts to obtain or maintain these children's rights, privileges, and services.

Many of the services currently provided for persons with developmental disabilities originated because of the hard work of parent advocates who joined forces and requested that their children be provided the same services and education available for children without disabilities. Thus, during the past decades, numerous parent associations have developed advocacy to a fine art.

Learning to Be an Advocate: Empowering Yourself

In general, the more facts you gather, the better prepared you are to serve as an advocate. An informed person can act more effectively than one who lacks the facts. Initially, your efforts will involve identifying needs and getting in touch with knowledgeable parents and professionals. You soon will find out what needs to be done, which methods worked for others, which ones did not, and why some failed. This type of information may save you time and frustration and may assist you in making an informed decision regarding the appropriate course of action.

It also is important to familiarize yourself with the rights and laws governing the specific concerns you have identified. For example, you may want to know the extent of your medical coverage, the state regulations pertaining to special education, or how to contest your child's ineligibility for Supplemental Security Income. With each of these questions you will have to deal with a different administrative system and a different set of regulations and laws. Moreover, within each of these systems, there can be great differences between what the law provides and how the bureaucracy interprets these laws. Upon reviewing your rights and the laws, you may learn that your child is entitled to a particular service but is not getting it. If you believe that your child's rights are being violated, find out who is in charge of making the decision and what you can do to appeal. By learning how the system works, you can avoid wasting valuable time. Do not be afraid to appeal a decision because decisions made at one level may be overturned on another. If you decide to appeal, you may want to enlist the aid of an agency that specializes in advocacy (see the Resource Organizations list at the end of this book).

Advocacy Agencies

Many communities have advocacy agencies to assist persons with developmental disabilities. Advocacy in these agencies usually takes two forms: citizen advocacy and legal advocacy. Each organization may offer one or both types of advocacy.

Citizen Advocacy Citizen advocates are usually volunteers who assist individuals with developmental disabilities and their parents in obtaining services. These citizen advocates have been trained and usually are supervised by experienced people who know the steps involved in "getting through" the networks of bureaucracies. Citizen advocates also serve persons with disabilities by supporting innovative programs and encouraging change.

Legal Advocacy Legal advocacy involves helping to ensure that a person's or group's legal rights are not violated and involves more formal procedures than citizen advocacy. A legal advocacy group often employs lawyers and paralegal aides to work on individual cases or group problems. (Cases involving group problems are called *class action* suits.) Such a group can pursue litigation (use of the judicial process) if there is a violation of a person's civil rights. Legal advocacy groups are helpful in resolving problems such as determining which agency is responsible to provide the services your child requires. Correctly used, legal advocacy is a powerful resource and can lead to major changes for many children with developmental disabilities. Because parents of children with disabilities have resorted more and more to this kind of strategy, many states have been forced to improve the quality of care given to their citizens with mental retardation. This type of action also fueled the deinstitutionalization movement in the 1970s, which allowed residents of institutions to be relocated in appropriate community settings, such as group homes, supervised apartments, and independent living options. Legal advocates are often involved in legislative activity to help improve or create new services for persons with developmental disabilities.

COMMON RESOURCES

All parents are concerned about the practical issues involved in raising children, including finances, health insurance, life insurance, and many other facets of daily living. Many families of children with developmental disabilities are particularly anxious about these concerns. Many of the common issues families face as they start planning for their children with developmental disabilities are discussed in the following pages.

Specialized Health Care

Today, many options are available for health care, although the development of managed care programs has curtailed the freedom of professionals to some degree. In addition to the traditional primary care physician, who may be a general practitioner, family physician, internist, or pediatrician, there are physician assistants, nurse practitioners, physiatrists, and osteopaths, all serving as health care providers (see Chapter 4). Children with complicated health problems, including those with chronic illnesses and developmental disabilities, usually require specialized health care at one time or another. The multiple needs of children with developmental disabilities have resulted in the development of numerous medically based, multidisciplinary evaluation and treatment facilities. In such centers, professionals from a number of disciplines work together to assess the child's abilities and disabilities and develop a coordinated care plan. If your child has complex developmental problems, you may find obtaining services at such a facility easier and more efficient than seeking out each professional individually in his or her private office.

If you are unsure whether such a center exists in your area, you may want to contact your state Department of Health. The state Developmental Disabilities Planning Council also will be able to guide you. In addition, the American Association of University Affiliated Programs for Persons with Developmental Disabilities publishes *A Resource Guide to Organizations Concerned with Developmental and Related Disabilities*, which lists available programs throughout the United States. (The address of this organization is provided in the Resource Organizations list at the end of this book.)

Alternatives to Hospitalization

Not only do many children with developmental disabilities require specialized health care, but many youngsters frequently need to receive services in a hospital. Children with chronic illnesses or severe disabilities may require recurring hospitalization. However, with advances in medical technology, many of the services that once were available only in the hospital now also can be provided on an outpatient basis or even in the home. A range of services is available today that can either shorten a hospital stay or enable an individual to remain at home.

One such service is called *skilled home nursing care*. This service involves a qualified nurse visiting the home and performing any necessary or prescribed duties, such as providing intravenous hyperalimentation or catheter care, changing dressings, and giving injections. Most nurses providing home care work for profit or nonprofit agencies. Other licensed nurses provide this service on a fee-for-service basis. Medical insurance carriers often cover much of the necessary expense.

If general assistance but not nursing care is needed, a *home health aide* might be able to help. Home health aides provide personal care, such as taking temperatures and bathing, to individuals with disabilities.

Homemaker services also can be very useful, as they relieve families of housekeeping chores during busy times of the day. In addition, some of these programs provide other services such as physical and occupational therapy, nutritional counseling, and social work services.

Another resource that can be beneficial to families is *hospice care.* Hospice programs provide supportive care for patients who are terminally ill and their families. The support given by hospice workers can be invaluable during such a difficult period.

As you look for alternative services, try not to make assumptions about what an agency can or cannot provide. Often, creative thinking and perseverance by both you and agency personnel can result in provision of specialized programs that meet your family's specific needs. Be sure to inquire about costs and available funding sources. In many instances, the agencies themselves suggest means of obtaining funds to cover the costs of services. To find out more about the preceding services, contact your local visiting nurses association, hospital coordinated home care program, or home care agencies.

A note of caution must be offered with regard to medical services for children with chronic medical needs who traditionally required prolonged inpatient care. When the first edition of this book was being written, there was cause for optimism. Health care providers and third-party payors were actively exploring alternatives in developing choices for children with complex health care needs. Until that time, hospitals and allied facilities had few alternatives to long-term costly hospitalizations or skilled nursing care. New approaches to treatment led to the evolution of home care services and short-stay options.

Since the publication of the first edition of this book in 1988, skyrocketing medical costs have resulted in more stringent applications of scarce resources. As a consequence, insurance companies and third-party payors routinely fund shorter hospital stays based on the fact that home care is now deemed more appropriate. However, such resources may not be available in the community. Situations have occurred in which a child is sent home without services being available, either due to funding or personnel difficulties. For example, it may be taken for granted that a particular agency (or company) can provide a service, but the agency may be short on nurses as a result of a large caseload. In order to ensure that the family is getting necessary services, parents can contact their physician or the "discharge nurse." In addition, patient advocates or parent support groups can be important sources of information.

As is sometimes the case, a solution generates its own problems. In this instance, parents can be left without adequate coverage. Be sure you are a partner in any plan that is instituted at the time of discharge from a hospital or health care facility, and be sure there is a backup strategy should you be left without resources. For example, get a commitment from your doctor and insurance company that you can obtain an emergency admission if a home care plan begins to fail.

Residential Programs and Rehabilitation Centers

When time-limited, intensive treatment is needed for individuals with developmental disabilities or behavior disorders, a residential treatment program sometimes may be an option. Residential programs can be found in private and public institutions including hospitals, schools, and rehabilitation centers. Residential placement may be appropriate if the individual's behavioral or physical difficulties are such that he or she cannot participate in a less restrictive environment. *Generally, the option is considered only after all other community services have been tried.*

Residential programs are specialized and designed to help children with certain disabilities—for example, severe neuromuscular disabilities or emotional disorders. Types of programs and the range of services offered will depend on the facility's focus and general goals. The admission process, except for emergencies, can be long and involved and may require completing a detailed application, a multidisciplinary evaluation, interviews, and approval from the state or from a private or local funding source. Treatment philosophy, types of intervention used, staff-to-client ratio, and attitudinal concerns are important considerations to keep in mind. You will also want to evaluate the physical surroundings carefully. For more information about this kind of service, consult a directory of community services or social service agencies in your state.

Nursing Homes

At times, an individual's health problems may require ongoing nursing care, necessitating a nursing home placement. Many adult group homes are actually funded as nursing facilities because the level of care provided qualifies them as such. Nursing homes may be either privately or state operated. Like other residential programs, they differ in terms of the types of services and levels of care provided. Many areas have specialized pediatric facilities.

Before individuals are admitted to a nursing home, they must be referred by a professional, social worker, nurse, or physician, and must be certified to be in need of nursing care. The following are the different types of nursing homes:

1. *Skilled Nursing Care* services are less intensive than hospital care, but provide 24-hour inpatient nursing supervision as well as intensive rehabilitation services.
2. *Level I Intermediate Care* nursing homes provide 24-hour preventative and supportive nursing services to persons with chronic illnesses.
3. *Level II Intermediate Care* nursing homes provide minimal nursing care.
4. *Intermediate Care Facilities* for persons with mental retardation offer supervision for persons with mental retardation and nursing needs.

When looking for a nursing home for a family member with a disability, it is important to evaluate the types of services provided, how well they meet your family member's needs, the quality and attitude of the staff, and the general atmosphere of the nursing home. It is often difficult to find nursing homes or similar facilities that are geared solely to the care of children. However, such facilities are increasing in number as parents advocate for their children who have medical needs.

Nursing homes and group homes that are funded as nursing homes are highly restrictive options for care. You will probably want to avoid them at all costs. Yet, there are times when you may be left with no other alternative.

You may become ill or develop a disability and have no relatives or friends to take over your child's care. You may have some environmental problems, such as housing problems or being a single mother with a new infant. There may be no specialized foster homes or the idea of a foster home may be something you cannot tolerate. In other cases, you may be the parent of a child who requires technology assistance in an area where home nursing programs are nonexistent or in short supply.

There is a need for advocacy to provide solutions for dilemmas such as these. Until that time nursing facilities are an option in some circumstances.

LIFE INSURANCE

How to protect your loved ones financially is a major concern. In matters of life insurance, it is important to consult financial experts who are familiar with issues pertaining to people with disabilities. A child with a developmental disability can be named the beneficiary of an insurance policy. By doing so, parents assume that the child will receive care for which they have planned. Unfortunately, this may jeopardize other benefits your child may receive, such as Supplemental Security Income.

It may be difficult to obtain life insurance for a family member with a developmental disability, especially if the individual has a life-threatening illness. Because of the variability in policies, you are advised to explore the feasibility of this directly with insurance company personnel or other experts in this area.

HEALTH INSURANCE

Private Health Insurance and Health Maintenance Organizations

Several options are available for covering medical expenses. The most common resource is a private or company-sponsored policy for health insurance. You should inquire, however, about whether your child with developmental disabilities is eligible for coverage when he or she turns 21, because family policies usually cover children only until they reach adulthood. Blue Cross & Blue Shield often covers dependent children beyond the age of 18 years. Depending on the nature of the plan, adult children may be covered in full for as long as they remain a member of the member's household.

Health maintenance organizations (HMOs) in which you pay a monthly fee for medical services are also popular. The monthly fee is used to provide medical coverage for all contingencies. Your child with a developmental disability should be covered as any other family member. HMOs offer some potential limitations. Subscribers are limited to a specific list of physicians. Moreover, consulting with a specialist may not be permitted unless the managing physician agrees. In some cases, physicians share profits based on savings. Although this does not mean your child will not receive adequate care, it does create an atmosphere in which decisions to order tests, services, and medical consultations are influenced by forces other than the patient's need.

If you are locked into a health insurance plan, or even if you are considering a new plan, there are certain steps you should take.

First, learn if there are limits, or caps, on your coverage. For example, some health insurance plans say they cover 100% of mental health benefits. However, if you look closely, they may have an outpatient limit of $1,000 a year and an inpatient limit of 2 weeks. Second, get a copy of your contract. This is different from the pamphlets one usually obtains and you are entitled to it. It is technical reading but you may find details missed in the more general outlines.

Keep an accurate account of your bills and the payments the insurance company sends you. If you are denied a payment to which you believe you are entitled, appeal the decision. Sometimes an employee of the insurance company may be reluctant to make an allowance that might not be a problem for his or her supervisor. There are exceptions made in any policy. Much has been accomplished by parents who were not afraid to appeal a negative decision. If possible, arrange a face-to-face appointment as part of the appeal process and bring your child with you. Be willing to negotiate, as sometimes payors will agree to partial payments.

If you are self-employed, there are other issues and circumstances to consider. Many self-employed individuals find it difficult to afford insurance so they gamble on the premise that it will cost less to pay the medical bills as they come than to pay insurance premiums. Once you have a child with a disability, however, insurance becomes more important. There may be ways in which you can join a group plan. In group plans, the risks are distributed over a larger population. This keeps the cost down. Often you may be able to join a professional or trade association, the Chamber of Commerce, or some other group that offers a plan.

If all else fails, itemize your out-of-pocket medical and related expenses for a tax deduction. You must be able to prove you have spent a substantial portion of your income on medical expenses. Surprisingly, the IRS regulations are actually sometimes broader than medical plans in defining what a medical need is. IRS publication #520, "Medical and Dental Expenses," describes tax deduction rules related to such expenses.

Public Health Insurance

Federal and state governments have created health benefit programs for eligible individuals with certain disabilities and for those who meet other criteria, such as low income levels. At present, there are two primary programs: Medicaid and Medicare.

Medicaid is a state-run, federally reimbursed program that pays for needed medical care for eligible persons. An applicant's medical diagnosis, finances, and age are used in determining eligibility. Under current regulations, individuals with developmental disabilities and chronic medical problems are eligible for what is known as the Katie Beckett Waiver. This program enables certain persons with developmental disabilities to obtain medical coverage with no regard to their parents' income. Previously, children would be ineligible if their parents' income was in excess of a certain amount. However, there are other eligibility criteria to be met. The program is basically for children with complicated medical problems. Some states or local offices are more lenient than others in interpreting this policy. Also, some states have elected to make some individuals eligible for Medicaid under home- and community-based "waivers" in Medicaid programs. Benefits from these waivers vary from state to state despite the fact that these are federally funded programs. This is because the federal government offers states a series of mandatory requirements as well as nonmandatory options from which they can choose to design their state Medicaid plan. (It is similar to a restaurant menu from which you must order each course individually.)

Once the state plan is in effect, its provisions become a policy. State agencies develop a manual from this plan that is used by the personnel who administer the plan. The manual is an interpretation of the plan. You are entitled to copies of both the plan and the policy manual. Many times parents or advocates can reverse adverse judgments by knowing the details of both the plan and the policy or by arguing for a more liberal interpretation based on an understanding of what is proposed in the state plan.

As with most programs, in these tight economic times, governments have curtailed and continue to curtail programs so you should monitor changes in state and federal policies. You can explore these options through your Medicaid Office, Division of Mental Retardation, or, in some cases, the state Department of Health.

Medicare is a federal health insurance program for individuals who are older than 65 years or for those who are "permanently and totally disabled."

Catastrophic Health Insurance

Some states offer plans that protect their citizens against the staggering costs of catastrophic illness or injury. In this instance, the state offers financial assistance based on the parents' personal resources and the individual's resources. Your local or state departments of Health or Public Welfare will have more information on this provision.

Private Charitable
Organizations Covering Medical Expenses

Some hospitals also have programs for particular disabilities or are associated with organizations that help fund various medical conditions. The Palestine Shrine, for example, has such programs in some hospitals, but also runs its own facilities. There are private and non-profit organizations that help to pay for service for specific kinds of problems, such as the Lions Club, which is particularly concerned with vision. Other organizations may cover special equipment or specific services.

FINANCES

Raising children is expensive. Raising a child with developmental disabilities can be more expensive. Regardless of your financial situation, knowledge of various kinds of public and private financial assistance that are available on local, regional, state, and federal levels can be helpful. Obviously, new laws and programs are enacted and reenacted frequently, so it is important to keep informed about changes in them.

The best way to obtain information is to consult city, county, state, and federal agencies directly. Available services and programs change often as new laws are passed.

Various nonprofit service agencies also can be contacted. Such programs may not offer cash benefits, but may provide services such as special treatment programs, payment for equipment, or camp scholarships.

Cash Benefits

Supplemental Security Income   The federal government's Supplemental Security Income (SSI) program provides supplemental income to certain individuals with disabilities. This program was designed to assist those who may be unable to support themselves completely. The Social Security Administration is the primary agency responsible for payments. Basically, the SSI program is a jointly funded federal and state program that guarantees a minimum income to children and adults with disabilities. In addition, medical coverage is provided. Certain eligibility requirements must be met to receive benefits.

In the past, SSI program requirements were more restrictive than they are now. If you or your child have applied and have been rejected, you should consider reapplying. These changes in policy illustrate the power of advocacy.

In a case entitled *Sullivan v. Zebley*, the U.S. Supreme Court ruled that the Social Security Administration needed to alter the method it used to evaluate a child's eligibility for SSI. In essence, the court ruled that a child's disability needed to be evaluated based on his or her ability to develop and function. An individualized functional assessment is now used to determine whether a disability, or combination of impairments, seriously hinders a child from performing activities that a child without those disabilities could do.

The Supreme Court also ordered the Social Security Administration to reconsider the applications of several hundred thousand cases of children who were denied benefits after January 1, 1980. These children, known as the *Zebley* class, can have their cases reviewed even if they are adults and they may be able to receive thousands of dollars in back benefits.

In making a decision, the SSI specialist determines whether a disability can be found on a listing of impairments in the Social Security Administration's regulations. If the child's problems are the same or equal to those on the list, then the child is considered eligible. If the listing criteria fails to establish eligibility, then the disability determination specialist considers the child's ability to perform in everyday life.

Besides considering the nature of a disability, the Social Security Administration also considers a family's income level and certain resources in the case of a child under 18 who lives at home with natural or adoptive parents or is away at school but comes home enough to be considered under parental control.

This method of determining eligibility is called *deeming*. Not all income and resources are considered. Some examples of income that are not deemed are Veterans Administration pensions, foster care payments, income used to make court-ordered child support payments, and Aid to Families with Dependent Children (AFDC) payments. Homes and pension funds are examples of other resources that are not deemed.

When a child turns 18, he or she can apply independently and the parents' income or resources is not considered. A child who is considered ineligible due to deeming should reapply.

If you or your child would like to apply for SSI, contact the Social Security Administration office. Information about your child's disability and level of functioning will be needed to evaluate eligibility. The examiner will request reports from agencies, school departments, and physicians who have evaluated or treated your child. Make sure the various professionals include information about the test procedures and the signs and symptoms used in arriving at a diagnosis. All information should be clear and objective. When the documentation is received, it will be assigned to a specialist at the Disability Determination Service Branch of the Social Security Administration.

Aid to Families with Dependent Children, General Public Assistance, and Other Forms of Public Aid   Other state and local programs that provide financial or medical assistance to eligible individuals and families include the federally funded, state-run Aid to Families with Dependent Children, General Public Assistance (GPA), or Medical Assistance. To learn more about what is available and the eligibility requirements, contact your local, county, or state Public Welfare Departments or other social service agencies. Some states offer cash or medical supplementation to parents who adopt children with disabilities.

Although finding sources of assistance can be difficult, you should at least try. Do not assume that a program does not exist or that your child or family is ineligible. It never hurts to investigate the resources in your area. For example, there may be a little-known city fund for paying transportation costs for persons with disabilities or a special fund for holiday baskets. Knowing what resources exist increases your choices when a particular need arises.

Other Services

Certain private, nonprofit organizations offer financial aid to people with disabilities. Some agencies serve the population in general, whereas others focus on specific disabilities or a particular need. Religious groups, community action programs, the American Red Cross, the Salvation Army, and others provide social and health care services. Many communities have mental health clinics, family service agencies, and counseling if you need mental health services. Also, organizations such as the Muscular Dystrophy Association, the Cystic Fibrosis Foundation, United Cerebral Palsy Associations, and the March of Dimes offer specialized services that may assist you. These and other organizations are included in the list of Resource Organizations at the end of this book.

RECREATION

Day-to-day recreation activities are another concern of families who have children with developmental disabilities. To begin exploring recreational opportunities, start with your local recreational department or community center. Church groups, YMCA, YWCA, Boy Scouts of America, and Girl Scouts of America also can provide assistance. The Arc and Special Olympics, Inc., often sponsor athletic activities and fitness programs for persons with mental retardation and other developmental disabilities. Camping experiences—either day or residential camping—provide recreation for children and their families.

Whenever possible, begin with recreational programs that are available to the general public. Do not assume that because your child has a particular disability, he or she will not be accepted. If you find that your child cannot be safely accommodated by a regular program, you may want to look into programs specifically designed to serve persons with developmental disabilities.

SUMMARY

In summary, there are a large number of social services and resources available. Often, we do not realize that the services we need do exist until we begin looking for a particular program or we begin to notice an unmet need. Identifying the need and then searching in the community takes time and energy. Creativity and endurance are essential. Some states have information and referral services or community councils that will make your task easier. Becoming informed is the only way to assess whether a service exists in your community. If it does not exist, perhaps you need to take the initiative to foster its development. Many of the most successful programs for children with special needs are the result of motivated parents and interested professionals who joined forces and advocated for specific services.

ACKNOWLEDGMENTS

Contributions have been made to this chapter by Sarah J. Gossler, M.S.W., and James C. Bernier, M.S.W.

Resource Organizations

ACCENT on Information
P.O. Box 700
Bloomington, IL 61702
(309) 378-2961
(309) 378-4420 (FAX)

Adopt a Special Kid (AASK)
2201 Broadway, Suite 702
Oakland, CA 94612
(510) 451-1748
(510) 451-2023 (FAX)

Alexander Graham Bell Association for the Deaf
3417 Volta Place, NW
Washington, DC 20007-2778
(202) 337-5220 (Voice/TTY)

Alliance of Genetic Support Groups
35 Wisconsin Cr. #440
Chevy Chase, MD 20815-7015
800-336-GENE
(301) 652-5553
(301) 654-0171 (FAX)

American Academy of Pediatrics
141 Northwest Point Blvd.
P.O. Box 927
Elk Grove Village, IL 60009-0927
(708) 228-5005

American Alliance for Health, Physical Education, Recreation and Dance
1900 Association Drive
Reston, VA 22091
(703) 476-3400
(703) 476-9527 (FAX)

American Association for the Advancement of Science
Project on Science, Technology, and Disability
1333 H St., NW
Washington, DC 20005
(202) 326-6672 (Voice/TDD)
(202) 371-9849 (FAX)

American Association on Mental Retardation (AAMR)
444 N. Capitol St., NW, Suite 846
Washington, DC 20001
(202) 387-1968
(202) 387-2193 (FAX)

American Association of University Affiliated Programs for Persons with Developmental Disabilities
8430 Fenton St., Suite 410
Silver Spring, MD 20910
(301) 588-8252
(301) 588-2842 (FAX)

American Athletic Association for the Deaf
3701 Harrison Blvd., 2nd Floor
Ogden, UT 84403-2040
(801) 393-7916 (Voice/TTY)
(801) 393-2263 (FAX)

American Bar Association Center on Children and the Law
1800 M St., NW
Suite 200 South
Washington, DC 20036
(202) 331-2250
(202) 331-2225 (FAX)

American Civil Liberties Union (ACLU) Children's Rights Project
132 W. 43rd St.
New York, NY 10036
(212) 944-9800
(212) 302-7035
(212) 921-7916 (FAX)

American Council of the Blind
1155 15th St., NW, Suite 720
Washington, DC 20005
800-424-8666
(202) 467-5081
(202) 467-5085 (FAX)

American Deafness and Rehabilitation Association
P.O. Box 251554
Little Rock, AK 72225
(501) 868-8850 (Voice/TTY)
(501) 868-8812 (FAX)

American Foundation for the Blind
15 W. 16th St.
New York, NY 10011
800-AFB-LINE
(212) 620-2147 (in NY only)
(212) 620-2158 (FAX)

American Heart Association
7272 Greenville Ave.
Dallas, TX 75231-4596
(214) 373-6300
(214) 706-1341 (FAX)

American Occupational Therapy Association, Inc.
1383 Piccard Drive
Rockville, MD 20850
(301) 948-9626
(301) 948-5512 (FAX)

American Physical Therapy Association (APTA)
1111 N. Fairfax St.
Alexandria, VA 22314
800-999-2782, ext. 3210 (information services)

American Printing House for the Blind (APH)
P.O. Box 6085
Louisville, KY 40206-0085
(502) 895-2405 (Phone & FAX)

American Self-Help Clearinghouse
St. Clares-Riverside Medical Center
25 Pocono Rd.
Denville, NJ 07834-2995
(201) 625-7101
(201) 625-9053 (TDD)
(201) 625-8848 (FAX)

American Society for Deaf Children (ASDC)
2848 Arden Way
Sacramento, CA 95825-1373
800-942-ASDC
(916) 482-0120 (TDD)
(916) 482-0121 (FAX)

American Speech-Language-Hearing Association (ASHA)
1801 Rockville Pike
Rockville, MD 20852
(301) 897-5700 (Voice/TDD)
(301) 571-0457 (FAX)

Associated Services for the Blind
919 Walnut St.
Philadelphia, PA 19107
(215) 627-3501
(215) 922-0692 (FAX)

Association of Birth Defect Children
827 Irma St.
Orlando, FL 32803
800-313-ABDC
(407) 629-1466 (Phone & FAX)
(407) 245-7035

Association for the Care of Children's Health (ACCH)
1910 Woodmont Ave., Suite 300
Bethesda, MD 20814
(301) 654-6549
(301) 986-4553 (FAX)

Association for Children with Down Syndrome
2616 Martin Ave.
Bellmore, NY 11710
(516) 221-4700
(516) 221-4311 (FAX)

Association for Education and Rehabilitation of the Blind and Visually Impaired
206 N. Washington St.
Alexandria, VA 22314
(703) 548-1884
(703) 683-2926 (FAX)

Association on Higher Education and Disability (AHEAD)
P.O. Box 21192
Columbus, OH 43221
(614) 488-4972 (Voice/TTY)
(614) 488-1174 (FAX)

Association of Neurometabolic Disorders
5223 Brookfield Lane
Sylvania, OH 43560-1809
(419) 885-1497

Autism Network International
P.O. Box 448
Syracuse, NY 13210-0448

Autism Research Institute
4182 Adams Ave.
San Diego, CA 92116

Autism Society of America
8601 Georgia Ave., Suite 503
Silver Spring, MD 20910
(301) 565-0433
(301) 565-0834 (FAX)

Avenues
P.O. Box 5192
Sonora, CA 95370
(209) 928-3688

Barrier-Free Design Centre
Access Place Canada
College Park
4044 Yonge St.
Toronto, Ontario, M5B 2H4
  CANADA
(416) 977-5010
(416) 977-5225 (TDD)
(416) 977-5264 (FAX)

Boy Scouts of America
1325 Walnut Hill La.
Irving, TX 75062
(214) 580-2000

Canadian Association for Community Living
4700 Keele St.
Kinsmen Bldg.
North York, Ontario, M3J 1P3
  CANADA
(416) 661-9611
(416) 661-2023 (TDD)
(416) 661-5701 (FAX)

Canadian Down Syndrome Society
12837 76th Ave., Suite 206
Surrey, British Columbia, V3W 2V3
  CANADA
(604) 599-6009
(604) 599-6165 (FAX)

Canadian Hearing Society
271 Spinea Rd.
Toronto, Ontario, M5R 2V3
  CANADA
(416) 964-9595
(416) 964-0023 (TDD)
(416) 323-4750 (FAX)

Canadian National Institute for the Blind
1929 Bayview Ave.
Toronto, Ontario, CANADA M4G 3E8
(416) 480-2500
(416) 480-7699 (FAX)

Canadian Rehabilitation Council for the Disabled
45 Sheppard Ave. E., Suite 801
Willowdale, Ontario, CANADA M2N 5W9
(416) 250-7490
(416) 250-7490 (TDD)
(416) 229-1371 (FAX)

Candlelighters Childhood Cancer Foundation
7910 Woodmont Ave., Suite 460
Bethesda, MD 20814
800-366-2223 (TTY)
(301) 657-8401
(301) 718-2686 (FAX)

Captioned Films/Videos
5000 Park St. N.
St. Petersburg, FL 33709
800-237-6213 (Voice/TTY)
(813) 541-7571

Center on Human Policy
Syracuse University
200 Huntington Hall
Syracuse, NY 13244-2340
(315) 443-3851
(315) 443-4338 (FAX)

Centers for Disease Control National AIDS/HIV Hotline
800-342-AIDS (2437)
800-344-SIDA (7432) (Spanish access)
800-AIDS-TTY (1-800-243-7889) (Deaf Access)

Centers for Disease Control National AIDS Information Clearinghouse
P.O. Box 6003
Rockville, MD 20849-6003
800-458-5231
800-243-7012 (TTY/TDD)
(301) 738-6616 (FAX)

Children and Adults with Attention Deficit Disorders (CH.A.D.D.)
49 NW 70th Ave., Suite 109
Plantation, FL 33317
(305) 587-3700
(305) 587-4599 (FAX)

Children's Brain Diseases Foundation
350 Parnassus Ave., Suite 900
San Francisco, CA 94117
(415) 565-6259
(415) 863-3452 (FAX)

Children's Defense Fund
25 E St., NW
Washington, DC 20001
(202) 628-8787
(202) 662-3520 (FAX)

Christian Council on Persons with Disabilities
7120 West Dove Ct.
Milwaukee, WI 53223
(414) 357-6672 (Phone and FAX)

Clearinghouse on Disability Information
Office of Special Education and Rehabilitative Services (OSERS)
U.S. Dept. of Education
Room 3132, Switzer Bldg.
Washington, DC 20202-2524
(202) 708-5366

Cleft Palate Foundation
1218 Grandview Ave.
Pittsburgh, PA 15211
(412) 481-1376
1-800-24-CLEFT
(412) 481-0847 (FAX)

Coalition on Sexuality and Disability, Inc.
122 East 23rd St.
New York, NY 10010
(212) 242-3900 (answering service; staff will return calls)

Compassionate Friends
P.O. Box 3696
Oak Brook, IL 60522-3696
(708) 990-0010
(708) 990-0246 (FAX)

**Cornelia de Lange Syndrome
Foundation, Inc.**
60 Dyer Ave.
Collinsville, CT 06022
(203) 693-0159

**Council for Exceptional Children
(CEC)**
1920 Association Drive
Reston, VA 22091-1589
(703) 620-3660
(703) 264-9494 (FAX)

Council on Family Health
225 Park Ave., South, 17th Floor
New York, NY 10003
(212) 598-3617
(212) 598-3665 (FAX)

Cystic Fibrosis Foundation
6931 Arlington Rd.
Bethesda, MD 20814
800-FIGHT CF (344-4823)
(301) 951-4422
(301) 951-6378

Deafness Research Foundation
9 E. 38th St.
New York, NY 10016
(212) 684-6556
(212) 684-6559 (TTY)
(212) 779-2125 (FAX)

Deafpride
1350 Potomac Ave., SE
Washington, DC 20003
(202) 675-6700 (Voice/TTY)
(202) 547-0547 (FAX)

**DIRECT LINK for the disABLED,
Inc.**
P.O. Box 1036
Solvang, CA 93464
(805) 688-1603 (Voice/TDD)
(805) 686-5285 (FAX)

**Disabilities Rights Education and
Defense Fund (DREDF)**
2212 Sixth St.
Berkeley, CA 94710
(510) 644-2555 (Voice/TDD)
(510) 841-8645 (FAX)

Dyslexia Research Institute, Inc.
4745 Centerville Rd.
Tallahassee, FL 32308
(904) 893-2216
(904) 893-2440 (FAX)

**Early Recognition Intervention
Network (ERIN)**
P.O. Box 637
Carlisle, MA 01741
(508) 287-0920 (Phone and FAX)
(617) 329-5529 (Answering machine)

Epilepsy Foundation of America
4351 Garden City Drive
Landover, MD 20785-2267
800-EFA-1000
800-332-2070 (TDD)
(301) 459-3700
(301) 577-4941 (FAX)

ERIC Clearinghouse on Disabilities and Gifted Education
1920 Association Drive
Reston, VA 22091-1589
800-328-0272
(703) 264-9474
(703) 620-3660 (TDD)
(703) 264-9494 (FAX)

Exceptional Parent
209 Harvard St., Suite 303
Brookline, MA 02146
(617) 730-5800
(617) 730-8742 (FAX)
(617) 730-9856 (TDD)

**Families of Children Under Stress
(FOCUS)**
3813 Briargreen Ct.
Doraville, GA 30340
(404) 934-7529

FEDCAP Rehabilitation Services, Inc.
211 W. 14th St.
New York, NY 10011
(212) 727-4200
(212) 727-4384 (TDD)
(212) 727-4374 (FAX)

Federation for Children with Special Needs
95 Berkely St., Suite 104
Boston, MA 02116
800-331-0688 (in MA only—Voice/TTY)
(617) 482-2915 (Voice/TTY)
(617) 695-2939 (FAX)

Federation of Families for Children's Mental Health
1021 Prince St.
Alexandria, VA 22314-2971
(703) 684-7710
(703) 836-1040 (FAX)

Fighters for Encephaly Defects Support (FEDS)
3032 Brereton St.
Pittsburgh, PA 15219
(412) 687-6437

5p- Society
(Cri du chat syndrome)
11609 Oakmount
Overland Park, KS 66210
(913) 469-8900

Gesell Institute of Human Development
310 Prospect St.
New Haven, CT 06511
(203) 777-3481
(203) 776-5001 (FAX)

Girl Scouts of the U.S.A.
830 Third Ave.
New York, NY 10022
(212) 940-7500

Guillain-Barré Syndrome Foundation, International
P.O. Box 262
Wynnewood, PA 19096
(610) 667-0131
(610) 667-7036 (FAX)

Hearing Aid Helpline
20361 Middlebelt Rd.
Livonia, MI 48152
800-521-5247 (U.S. and Canada)
(810) 478-4520 (FAX)

Hereditary Disease Foundation
1427 7th St., Suite 2
Santa Monica, CA 90401
(310) 458-4183
(310) 458-3937 (FAX)

Howard University Center for Sickle Cell Disease
2121 Georgia Ave., NW
Washington, DC 20059
(202) 806-7930
(202) 806-4517 (FAX)

Hydrocephalus Association
870 Market St., Suite 955
San Francisco, CA 94102
(415) 776-4713

Hydrocephalus Support Group
P.O. Box 4236
Chesterfield, MO 63006
(314) 532-8228

Independent Living Aids, Inc.
27 E. Mall
Plainview, NY 11803
(516) 752-8080
(516) 752-3135 (FAX)

In Door Sports Club, Inc.
1145 Highland St.
Napoleon, OH 43545
(419) 592-5756

IN*SOURCE, Indiana Resource Center for Families with Special Needs
833 Northside Blvd
Bldg. #1-Rear
South Bend, IN 46617
800-332-4433 (in IN only; Voice and TDD)
(219) 234-7101
(219) 234-7279 (FAX)

Institute for Child Behavior Research
4182 Adams Ave.
San Diego, CA 92116

International Organization for the Education of the Hearing-Impaired
3417 Volta Place, NW
Washington, DC 20007
(202) 337-5220 (Voice/TDD)
(202) 337-8314 (FAX)

International Rett Syndrome Association
9121 Piscataway Rd., Suite 2B
Clinton, MD 20735
(301) 856-3334
(301) 856-3336 (FAX)

International Shriners Headquarters
2900 Rocky Point Drive
Tampa, FL 33607
800-282-9161 (in FL only)
800-237-5055 (in U.S.)
(813) 281-8113 (FAX Hospital Administration)
(813) 281-0300

Job Accommodation Network (JAN)
West Virginia University
918 Chestnut Ridge Rd., Suite 1
P.O. Box 6080
Morgantown, WV 26506-6080
800-526-7234
800-ADA-WORK
800-526-2262 (CANADA)
(304) 293-5407 (FAX)

Joseph P. Kennedy, Jr., Foundation
1350 New York Ave., NW, Suite 500
Washington, DC 20005-4709
(202) 393-1250
(202) 737-1937 (FAX)

Judge David L. Bazelon Mental Health Law Center
1101 15th St., NW, Suite 1212
Washington, DC 20005
(202) 467-5730
(202) 467-4232 (TTY)
(202) 223-0409 (FAX)

Keshet-Jewish Parents of Children with Special Needs
3525 W. Peterson, Suite T-17
Chicago, IL 60659
(312) 588-0551
(312) 588-5825 (FAX)

Learning Disabilities Association of America
4156 Library Rd.
Pittsburgh, PA 14234
(412) 341-1515
(412) 341-8077
(412) 344-0224 (FAX)

Learning Disabilities Association of Canada
323 Chapel St., Suite 200
Ottawa, Ontario, K1N 7Z2
CANADA
(613) 238-5721
(613) 235-5391 (FAX)

Lethbridge Society for Rare Disorders
#2-740-4 Ave. South
Lethbridge, Alberta, 0N4 T1J
CANADA
(403) 329-0665

March of Dimes Birth Defect Foundation
1275 Mamaroneck Ave.
White Plains, NY 10605
(914) 428-7100
(914) 428-8203 (FAX)

Mobility International
P.O. Box 10767
Eugene, OR 97440
(503) 343-1284 (Voice/TDD)
(503) 343-6812

Mothers United for Moral Support, Inc. (MUMS)
150 Cluster St.
Green Bay, WI 54301
(414) 336-5333

Muscular Dystrophy Association
3561 E. Sunrise Dr.
Tuscon, AZ 85718-3208
(602) 529-2000
(602) 529-5300 (FAX)

National Association of Developmental Disabilities Councils
1234 Massachusetts Ave., NW, Suite 103
Washington, DC 20005
(202) 347-1234
(202) 347-4023 (FAX)

National Association for Parents of the Visually Impaired
P.O. Box 317
Watertown, MA 02272-0317
800-562-6265

National Association for Perinatal Addiction Research and Education (NAPARE)
200 N. Michigan
Chicago, IL 60601
(312) 541-1272
(312) 541-1271 (FAX)

National Association of Private Schools for Exceptional Children
1522 K St, NW, Suite 1032
Washington, DC 20005
(202) 408-3338
(202) 408-3340 (FAX)

National Association of Protection and Advocacy Systems
900 Second St., NE, Suite 221
Washington, DC 20002
(202) 408-9514
(202) 408-9520 (FAX)
(202) 408-9521 (TDD)

National Association of State Directors of Developmental Disabilities Service
113 Oronoco St.
Alexandria, VA 22314
(703) 683-4202

National Association for Visually Handicapped
22 W. 21st St., 6th Floor
New York, NY 10010
(212) 889-3141
(212) 727-2932 (FAX)

National Association of Work Force Development Professionals
1620 I St., NW
Washington, DC 20006
(202) 887-6120
(202) 887-8216 (FAX)

National Attention Deficit Disorder Association (NADDA)
19262 Jamboree Rd.
Irvine, CA 92715
(membership in NADDA)
P.O. Box 488
West Newbury, MA 01985
800-487-2282

National Autism Hotline/Autism Services Center
605 Ninth St.
Prichard Bldg.
P.O. Box 507
Huntington, WV 25710-0507
(304) 525-8014
(304) 525-8026 (FAX)

National Birth Defects Center
40 Second Ave.
Waltham, MA 02154
(617) 466-9555
(617) 487-2361 (FAX)

National Braille Association, Inc.
3 Towline Circle
Rochester, NY 14623-2513
(716) 473-0900
(716) 427-0263 (FAX)

National Captioning Institute (NCI), Inc.
1900 Gallows Rd.
Vienna, VA 22182
800-533-9673
800-321-8337 (TDD)
(703) 917-7600

National Catholic Office for Persons with Disabilities
P.O. Box 29113
Washington, DC 20017
(202) 529-2933 (Voice/TDD)
(202) 529-4678 (FAX)

National Center for Education in Maternal and Child Health
38th and R Sts., NW
Washington, DC 20057
(202) 625-8400

National Center for Law and the Deaf
Gallaudet University
800 Florida Ave., NE
Washington, DC 20002-3695
(202) 651-5373 (Voice/TDD)

National Center for Learning Disabilities (NCLD)
381 Park Ave., S, Suite 1420
New York, NY 10016
(212) 545-7510
(212) 687-7211
(212) 545-9665 (FAX)

National Center for Stuttering, Inc.
200 E. 33rd St.
New York, NY 10016
800-221-2483
(212) 532-1460

National Center for Youth with Disabilities
University of Minnesota
Box 721
420 Delaware St., SE
Minneapolis, MN 55455-0392
(612) 626-2825
(612) 626-2134 (FAX)
(612) 624-3939 (TDD)

National Clearinghouse on Postsecondary Education for Individuals with Disabilities
HEATH (Higher Education and Adult Training for People with Handicaps) Resource Center
One Dupont Circle, Suite 800
Washington, DC 20036-1193
800-333-6293
800-54H-EATH
(202) 939-9320
(202) 833-4760 (FAX)

National Committee for Citizens in Education
900 Second St. NE, Suite 8
Washington, DC 20002
(202) 544-9495

National Council on Independent Living
2111 Wilson Blvd., Suite 405
Arlington, VA 22201
(703) 525-3406
(518) 274-1979
(703) 525-3409 (FAX)

National Down Syndrome Congress (NDSC)
1605 Chantilly Drive, Suite 250
Atlanta, GA 30324
800-232-6372
(404) 633-1555
(404) 633-2817 (FAX)

National Down Syndrome Society
666 Broadway, Suite 810
New York, NY 10012
800-221-4602
(212) 460-9330
(212) 979-2873 (FAX)

National Easter Seal Society
230 West Monroe St., Suite 1800
Chicago, IL 60606
800-221-6827
(312) 726-6200
(312) 726-4258 (TDD)

National Federation of the Blind
1800 Johnson St.
Baltimore, MD 21230
(410) 659-9314
(410) 685-5653 (FAX)
(410) 752-5011 (Computer Bulletin
    Board)

**National Foundation of Dentistry
    for the Handicapped**
1800 Glen Arm Place, Suite 500
Denver, CO 80202
(303) 298-9650
(303) 298-9649 (FAX)

**National Foundation for Jewish
    Genetic Diseases**
250 Park Ave., Suite 1000
New York, NY 10177
(212) 371-1030

National Fragile X Foundation
1441 York St., Suite 2156
Denver, CO 80206
800-688-8765
(303) 333-6155
(303) 333-4369 (FAX)

National Gaucher Foundation
1424 K St., NW, 4th Floor
Washington, DC 20005
(202) 393-2777

National Handicapped Sports
National Headquarters
451 Hungerford Dr., Suite 100
Rockville, MD 20850
(301) 393-7505
(301) 217-0963 (TDD)
(301) 217-0968 (FAX)

**National Head Injury Foundation
    (NHIF)**
1776 Massachusetts Ave., NW,
    Suite 100
Washington, DC 20036-1904
800-444-6443 (Helpline)
(202) 296-6443
(202) 296-8850 (FAX)

**National Hydrocephalus Foun-
    dation**
400 N. Michigan Ave., Suite 1102
Chicago, IL 60611-4102
(815) 467-6548

**National Information Center for
    Children and Youth with Dis-
    abilities (NICHCY)**
P.O. Box 1492
Washington, DC 20013
800-695-0285 (Voice/TDD)
(202) 884-8200
(202) 884-8441 (FAX)

**National Information Center on
    Deafness**
Gallaudet University
800 Florida Ave. NE
Washington, DC 20002-3695
(202) 651-5051
(202) 651-5052 (TDD)
(202) 651-5054 (FAX)

**National Information Center for
    Educational Media (NICEM)**
P.O. Box 40130
Albuquerque, NM 87196
800-468-3453
(505) 265-3591
(505) 256-1080 (FAX)

**National Information System and
    Clearinghouse Center for Devel-
    opmental Disabilities**
University of South Carolina
Benson Bldg.
Columbia, SC 29208
800-922-9234
800-922-1107 (in SC only)
800-777-6058 (FAX)

**National Institute of Neurological
    Disorders and Stroke**
9000 Rockville Pike, Bldg. 31
Room 8A-16
Bethesda, MD 20892
(301) 496-5751
(301) 402-2186 (FAX)

National Library Service for the Blind and Physically Handicapped
Library of Congress
1291 Taylor St., NW
Washington, DC 20542
(202) 707-5100
(202) 707-0744
(202) 707-0712 (FAX)

National Mental Health Association
1021 Prince St.
Alexandria, VA 22314-2971
800-969-6642
(703) 684-7722
(703) 684-5968 (FAX)

National Network to Prevent Birth Defects
Box 15309 SE Station
Washington, DC 20003
(202) 543-5450
(202) 543-4791 (FAX)

National Neurofibromatosis Foundation
141 Fifth Ave., Suite 7-S
New York, NY 10010-7105
800-323-7938
(212) 460-8980 (Voice/TDD)
(212) 529-6094 (FAX)

National Organization on Disability
910 16th St., Suite 600
Washington, DC 20006
800-248-ABLE
(202) 293-5960
(301) 229-1187 (in MD only)
(301) 293-7999 (FAX)
(301) 293-5968 (TDD)

National Organization for Rare Disorders (NORD)
100 Route 37
P.O. Box 8923
New Fairfield, CT 06812-8923
800-999-NORD
(203) 746-6518
(203) 746-6481 (FAX)
(203) 746-6972 (TDD)

National Parent Network on Disabilities (NPND)
1600 Prince St., Suite 115
Alexandria, VA 22314
(703) 684-NPND
(703) 684-6763 (Voice/TDD)
(703) 836-1232 (FAX)

National Rehabilitation Clearinghouse
816 W. 6th St.
Oklahoma State University
Stillwater, OK 74078
(405) 624-7650
(405) 624-0695 (FAX)

National Rehabilitation Information Center
8455 Colesville Rd.
Silver Spring, MD 20910
800-346-2742 (Nat. Rehab.)
800-227-0216 (Voice/TDD)
(301) 588-9285 (Able Data)
(301) 587-1967 (FAX)

National Scoliosis Foundation, Inc.
72 Mt. Auburn St.
Watertown, MA 02172
(617) 926-0397
(617) 926-0398 (FAX)

National Self-Help Clearinghouse
Grad. School/University Center
CUNY
25 West 43rd St., Room 620
New York, NY 10036
(212) 642-2944
(212) 642-1956 (FAX)

National Society to Prevent Blindness
500 E. Remington Rd.
Schaumburg, IL 60173
800-221-3004
(708) 843-2020
(708) 843-8458 (FAX)

National Spinal Cord Injury Association
545 Concord Ave., Suite 29
Cambridge, MA 02138
800-962-9629 (Hotline)
(617) 935-2722

National Spinal Cord Injury Hotline
Montebello Hospital
2201 Argonne Drive
Baltimore, MD 21218
800-526-3456
(410) 366-2325

National Tay-Sachs and Allied Disease Association
2001 Beacon St., Suite 204
Brookline, MA 02146
(617) 277-4463
(617) 277-0134 (FAX)

National Tuberous Sclerosis Association
8000 Corporate Drive, Suite 120
Landover, MD 20785
800-225-NTSA
(301) 459-9888
(301) 459-0394 (FAX)

National Wheelchair Athletic Association
3595 E. Fountain Blvd., Suite L1
Colorado Springs, CO 80910
(719) 574-1150

Orton Dyslexia Society
8600 LaSalle Rd.
Chester Bldg., Suite 382
Baltimore, MD 21286-2044
800-ABCD-123 (800-222-3123)
(410) 321-5069 (FAX)
(410) 296-0232

PACER Center, Inc. (Parent Advocacy Coalition for Educational Rights)
4826 Chicago Ave., South
Minneapolis, MN 55417-1055
800-53PACER (in MN only)
(612) 827-2966 (Voice/TDD)
(612) 827-3065 (FAX)

PAM Assistance Centre
601 Maple St.
Lansing, MI 48906-5038
800-274-7426
(517) 371-5897
(517) 371-5898 (FAX)

Parents of Chronically Ill Children
1527 Maryland St.
Springfield, IL 62702
(217) 522-6810 (Voice and TDD)

Parent Educational Advocacy Training Center
10340 Democracy Lane
Fairfax, VA 22030
(703) 691-7826 (Voice/TTY)
(703) 691-8148 (FAX)

Prader-Willi Foundation, Inc.
223 Main St.
Port Washington, NY 11050
800-253-7993
(516) 944-3173 (FAX)

Prader-Willi Syndrome International Information Forum
40 Holly Lane
Roslyn Heights, NY 11577
800-358-0682
(516) 484-7154 (FAX)

President's Committee on Employment of People with Disabilities
1331 F St., NW
Washington, DC 20004-1107
(202) 376-6200
(202) 376-6205 (TDD)
(202) 376-6219 (FAX)

President's Committee on Mental Retardation (PCMR)
330 Independence Ave.
Cohen Bldg., Room 5325
Washington, DC 20201
(202) 619-0634
(202) 205-9519

Project STAR
1800 Columbus Ave.
Roxbury, MA 02119
(617) 442-7442
(617) 442-1705 (FAX)

Research and Training Center for Accessible Housing
North Carolina State University
School of Design
Box 8613
Raleigh, NC 27695-8613
(919) 515-3082
(919) 515-3082 (TDD)
(919) 515-3023 (FAX)

Scoliosis Research Society
6300 N. River Rd., Suite 727
Rosemont, IL 60018-4226
(708) 698-1627
(708) 823-0536 (FAX)

Self Help for Hard of Hearing People (SHHH)
7910 Woodmont Ave., Suite 1200
Bethesda, MD 20814
(301) 657-2248
(301) 657-2249 (TDD)
(301) 913-9413 (FAX)

Siblings Information Network
The A.J. Pappanikou Center on Special Rehabilitation
62 Washington St.
Middletown, CT 06457-2844
(203) 344-7500
(203) 344-7595 (FAX)
(203) 344-7590 (TDD)

Siblings for Significant Change
United Charities Bldg.
105 E. 22nd St., Room 710
New York, NY 10010
(212) 420-0776
(212) 677-0696 (FAX)

Sickle Cell Disease Association of America, Inc.
3345 Wilshire Blvd., Suite 1106
Los Angeles, CA 90010
800-421-8453
(213) 736-5455
(213) 736-5211 (FAX)

Signing Exact English (SEE) Center for the Advancement of Deaf Children
P.O. Box 1181
Los Alamitos, CA 90720
(310) 430-1467 (Voice/TTY)
(310) 795-6614 (FAX)

Social Security Administration (SSA)
1350 New York Ave., NW, Suite 500
Washington, DC 20005-4709
(202) 523-0412

Special Olympics International
1350 New York Ave., NW, Suite 500
Washington, DC 20005-4709
(202) 628-3630
(202) 737-1937 (FAX)

Special Recreation, Inc.
362 Koser Ave.
Iowa City, IA 52246-3038
(319) 337-7578
(319) 353-6808

Spina Bifida Association of America
4590 MacArthur Blvd., NW, #250
Washington, DC 20007-4226
800-621-3141
(202) 944-3285
(202) 944-3295 (FAX)

Spina Bifida Association of Canada
220-388 Donald St.
Winnepeg, Manitoba, R3B 2J4
CANADA
(204) 957-1794

Team of Advocates for Special Kids (TASK)
100 W. Cerritos Ave.
Anaheim, CA 92805
(714) 533-TASK
(714) 533-2533 (FAX)

**Technical Assistance for Special
Populations Program (TASPP)**
National Center for Research in
Vocational Education
University of Illinois Site
345 Education Bldg.
1310 S. Sixth St.
Champaign, IL 61820
(217) 333-0807
(217) 244-5632 (FAX)

**The Arc (formerly Association for
Retarded Citizens of the United
States)**
500 E. Border St., Suite 300
Arlington, TX 76010
800-433-5255
(817) 261-6003
(817) 277-0553 (TDD)
(817) 277-3491 (FAX)

**The Association for Persons with
Severe Handicaps (TASH)**
1121 Greenwood Ave., N.
Seattle, WA 98115
(206) 361-8870
(206) 361-9208 (FAX)

**THRESHOLD-Intractable Seizure
Disorder Support Group**
26 Stavola Rd.
Middletown, NJ 07748-3728
(908) 957-0714

Tourette Syndrome Association
42-40 Bell Blvd.
Bayside, NY 11361
(212) 224-2999
(718) 279-9596 (FAX)

**Trace Research and Development
Center**
1500 Highland Ave., S-151
Madison, WI 53705-2280
(608) 262-6966
(608) 263-5408 (TDD)
(608) 262-8848 (FAX)

Treacher Collins Foundation
P.O. Box 683
Norwich, VT 05055
800-823-2055
(802) 649-3050

**United Cerebral Palsy Associa-
tions, Inc.**
1522 K St., NW, #1112
Washington, DC 20005-1202
800-872-5827
(202) 842-1266 (Voice/TTY)
(202) 842-3519 (FAX)

**U.S. Architectural Transportation
Barriers Compliance Board**
1331 F St., NW, Suite 1000
Washington, DC 20004-1111
800-USA-ABLE
(202) 272-5447 (FAX)
(202) 272-5449 (TDD)

Wheelchair Sports, U.S.A.
3595 E. Fountain Blvd., Suite L1
Colorado Springs, CO 80910
(719) 574-1150
(719) 574-9840 (FAX)

World Rehabilitation Fund
386 Park Ave. S, Suite 500
New York, NY 10016-4901
(212) 725-7875
(212) 725-8402 (FAX)

References and Suggested Readings

In order to become more effective medical and educational advocates for their children, many parents try to improve their understanding of disabilities and their rights as the parents of children who have disabilities. It is difficult to recommend any one book or article on any given subject in this book. Articles in medical journals are not always easily available, use complex terminology, or provoke undue anxiety. Local bookstores do not always stock books that deal with developmental issues, and parents may not want to order a book without being sure it addresses their particular concerns.

Although availability of resources varies according to geographical location, there are several approaches that should be considered when seeking further information. Your physician may have written information about diagnoses that he or she frequently encounters. Many physicians also have access to on-line computer searches that review the most recent information in medical journals; such access can be particularly helpful with rare disorders. National and local organizations often have pamphlets relating to the population of children and families they serve (see Chapter 31 and Resource Organizations).

State and local education departments should have written material to help parents know their rights with regard to their child's education. Early interventionists, teachers, and special education program directors can be very helpful in directing parents to materials that can be individualized to promote a child's developmental

413

progress. Community colleges often offer courses in child development for those who want a broader understanding of developmental issues. Colleges and universities that include courses in education as part of their curricula usually have a range of suitable references.

Public libraries continue to be an excellent starting point, as well. A good reference librarian will know how to obtain information from many sources. Most libraries have computerized systems to find information in their own library, and many also have interlibrary loan arrangements. Thus, the references that follow are only suggestions.

PART I: CHILDREN WITH SPECIAL NEEDS, THEIR PARENTS, AND THE PROFESSIONALS WHO CARE FOR THEM

Chapter 1: Who Are the Special Children?

Batshaw, M.L. (1991). *Your child has a disability. A complete sourcebook of daily and medical care.* Boston: Little, Brown.

Batshaw, M.L., & Perret, Y.M. (1992). *Children with disabilities: A medical primer* (3rd ed.). Baltimore: Paul H. Brookes Publishing Co.

Darling, R.B., & Darling, J. (1982). *Children who are different: Meeting the challenges of birth defects in society.* New York: C.V. Mosby.

Ross, B. (1977). *Our special child: A guide to successful parenting of handicapped children.* New York: Walker & Co.

Chapter 2: Discovering Your Child Has a Problem

Batshaw, M.L., & Perret, Y.M. (1992). *Children with disabilities: A medical primer* (3rd ed.). Baltimore: Paul H. Brookes Publishing Co.

Pueschel, S.M., & Pueschel, E.V. (1988). The child with Down syndrome: The impact on the family. In V. Dmitriev & P.L. Oelwein (Eds.), *Advances in Down syndrome* (pp. 215–227). Seattle, WA: Special Child Publications.

Thompson, R.J., & O'Quinn, A.N. (1990). *Developmental disabilities—Etiologies, manifestations, diagnosis, and treatments.* New York: Oxford University Press.

Veen, S., Ens-Dokkum, M.H., & Schreuder, A.M. (1991). Impairments, disabilities and handicaps of very preterm and very-low-birth-weight infants of five years of age. *Lancet, 330,* 33–36.

Chapter 3: Developmental Disabilities Are a Family Affair

Bernier, C.J. (1990). Parental adjustment toward a disabled child: A family system perspective. *Families in Society: The Journal of Contemporary Human Services, 71,* 589–596.

Featherstone, H. (1980). *A difference in the family: Life with the disabled child.* New York: Basic Books.

Goldfarb, L.A., Brotherson, M.J., Summers, J.A., & Turnbull, A.P. (1986). *Meeting the challenge of disability or chronic illness—A family guide.* Baltimore: Paul H. Brookes Publishing Co.

Miller, N.B. (1994). *Nobody's perfect: Living and growing with children who have special needs.* Baltimore: Paul H. Brookes Publishing Co.

Pearlman, L., & Scott, K.A. (1981). *Raising the handicapped child.* Englewood Cliffs, NJ: Prentice Hall.

Powell, T.H., & Gallagher, P.A. (1993). *Brothers & sisters—A special part of exceptional families* (2nd ed.). Baltimore: Paul H. Brookes Publishing Co.

A reader's guide: For parents of children with physical or emotional disabilities. (Publication Number [HSA], 77-5290). Washington, DC: U.S. Government Printing Office.

Singer, G.H.S., & Powers, L.E. (1993). *Families, disability, and empowerment: Active coping skills and strategies for family interventions.* Baltimore: Paul H. Brookes Publishing Co.

Turnbull, A.P., & Turnbull, H.R., III. (1990). *Families, professionals, & exceptionality—A special partnership.* Columbus, OH: Charles E. Merrill.

Chapter 4: Parents and Professionals: A Working Partnership

Mulick, J.A., & Pueschel, S.M. (1983). *Parent–professional partnerships in developmental disability services.* Cambridge, MA: Ware Press.

Mulliken, R.K., & Buckley, J.J. (1983). *Assessment of multihandicapped and developmentally disabled children.* Cambridge, MA: Aspen Systems.

Turnbull, A.P., & Turnbull, H.R., III. (1986). *Families, professionals, and exceptionality—A special partnership.* Columbus OH: Charles E. Merrill.

PART II: COMMON PROBLEMS AND DISABILITIES IN CHILDREN WITH SPECIAL NEEDS

Chapter 5: Mental Retardation

American Association on Mental Retardation. (1992). *Mental retardation: Definition, classification, and systems of supports* (9th ed.) Washington, DC: Author.

Kaufman, S.Z. (1988). *Retarded isn't stupid, Mom!* Baltimore: Paul H. Brookes Publishing Co.

O'Shaughnessy, E. (1992). *Somebody called me a retard today . . . and my heart felt sad.* New York: Walker & Co.

Pueschel, S.M. (1990). *A parent's guide to Down syndrome: Toward a brighter future.* Baltimore: Paul H. Brookes Publishing Co.

Seltzer, G.B. (1983). Systems of classification. In J.L. Matson & J.A. Mulick (Eds.), *Handbook of mental retardation* (pp. 143–156). Elmsford, NY: Pergamon.

Szymanski, L.S., & Tanquay, P.E. (1980). *Emotional disorders of mentally retarded persons: Assessment, treatment, and consultation.* Baltimore: University Park Press.

Chapter 6: Attention-Deficit/Hyperactivity Disorder

Barkley, R.A. (1990). *Attention-deficit hyperactivity disorder—A handbook for diagnosis and treatment.* New York: Guilford Press.

Coleman, W.S. (1988). *Attention deficit disorders, hyperactivity & associated disorders: A handbook for parents and professionals* (5th ed.). Madison, WI: Calliope Books.

Conners, C.K., & Wells, A.C. (1986). *Hyperactive children*. Beverly Hills: Sage Publications.

Galvin, M. (1988). *Otto learns about his medicine: A story about medication for hyperactive children*. New York: Brunner/Mazel.

Quinn, P., & Stern, J.M. (1993). *Putting on the brakes. Young people's guide to understanding attention deficit hyperactivity disorder*. New York: Brunner/Mazel.

Quinn, P., & Stern, J. M. (1993). *The "putting on the brakes" activity book for young people with ADHD*. New York: Brunner/Mazel.

Wodrich, D.L. (1994). *Attention deficit hyperactivity disorder: What every parent wants to know*. Baltimore: Paul H. Brookes Publishing Co.

Chapter 7: Learning Disabilities

Catts, H.W. (1991). Early identification of dyslexia: Evidence from a follow-up study of speech-language impairment in children. *Annals of Dyslexia, 41*, 163–177.

Gallico, R., & Lewis, M.E.B. (1992). Learning disabilities. In M.L. Batshaw & Y.M. Perret, *Children with disabilities: A medical primer* (3rd ed., pp. 365–385). Baltimore: Paul H. Brookes Publishing Co.

Gillett, J.W., & Temple, C. (1990). *Understanding reading problems—Assessment and instruction* (3rd ed.). Boston: Little, Brown.

Hammill, D.D. (1990). On defining learning disabilities: An emerging consensus. *Journal of Learning Disabilities, 23*(2), 74–84.

Stevens, S.H. (1984). *Classroom success for the learning disabled*. Winston-Salem, NC: John F. Blair Publisher.

Chapter 8: Sensory Disorders

American Speech-Language-Hearing Association. (1990). Guidelines for screening for hearing impairments and middle ear disorders. *Asha, 32* (Suppl 2), 17–24.

Dekker, R., & Koole, F.D. (1992). Visually impaired children's visual characteristics and intelligence. *Developmental Medicine & Child Neurology, 34*, 123–133.

Glaser, J.S. (Ed.). (1990). *Neuro-ophthamology* (2nd ed.). Philadelphia: J.B. Lippincott.

Northern, J.L., & Downs, M.P. (1991). *Hearing in children* (4th ed.). Baltimore: Williams & Wilkins.

Wong, V.C. (1991). Cortical blindness in children: A study of etiology and prognosis. *Pediatric Neurology, 7*, 178–185.

Chapter 9: Communication Disorders

Kaiser, A.P., & Gray, D.B. (1993). *Communication and language intervention series: Vol. 2. Enhancing children's communication: Research foundations for intervention*. Baltimore: Paul H. Brookes Publishing Co.

Kumin, L. (1994). *Communication skills in children with Down syndrome—A guide for parents*. Baltimore: Woodbine House.

Shewan, C.M., & Malm, K.E. (1990). The prevalence of speech and language impairments. *Asha, 32*, 108.

Warren, S.F., & Reichle, J. (1992). *Communication and language intervention series: Vol. 1. Causes and effects in communication and language intervention*. Baltimore: Paul H. Brookes Publishing Co.

Chapter 10: Autism: A Pervasive Developmental Disorder

Amenta, C.A., III. (1992). *Russell is extra special: A book about autism for children.* New York: Brunner/Mazel.

Callanan, C.R. (1990). *Since Owen. A parent-to-parent guide for care of the disabled child.* Baltimore: The Johns Hopkins University Press.

Hart, C.A. (1993). *A parent's guide to autism. Answers to the most common questions.* New York: Pocket Books.

Koegel, R.L., Rincover, A., & Egel, A.L. (1982). *Educating and understanding autistic children.* San Diego: College Hill.

Park, C.C. (1982). *The siege. The first eight years of an autistic child.* Boston: Little, Brown.

Powers, M.D. (Ed.). (1989). *Children with autism: A parent's guide.* Rockville, MD: Woodbine House.

Schopler, E., & Mesibov, G. (1984). *The effects of autism on the family.* New York: Plenum.

Smith, M.D. (1990). *Autism and life in the community: Successful interventions for behavioral challenges.* Baltimore: Paul H. Brookes Publishing Co.

PART III: INHERITED AND ACQUIRED DEVELOPMENTAL DISABILITIES

Chapter 11: Chromosome and Genetic Disorders

Borgaonkar, D.S. (1989). *Chromosomal variation in man: A catalog of chromosomal variance and anomalies* (5th ed.). New York: Alan R. Liss.

Buyse, M.L. (1990). *Birth defects encyclopedia.* Dover, MA: Center for Birth Defects Information Services.

Emery, A.E.H., & Rimoin, D.L. (1900). *Principles and practice of medical genetics* (2nd ed.). New York: Churchill Livingstone.

Gardner, R.J.M., & Sotherland, G.R. (1989). *Chromosome abnormalities and genetic counseling.* New York: Oxford University Press.

Hall, J.G. (1990). Genomic imprinting: Review and relevance to human diseases. *American Journal of Human Genetics, 46,* 857–873.

Jones, K.L. (1988). *Smith's recognizable patterns of human malformation: Genetic, embryologic, and clinical aspects* (4th ed.). Philadelphia: W.B. Saunders.

Lott, I.T., & McCoy, E.E. (1992). *Down syndrome: Advances in medical care.* New York: Wiley-Liss.

Pueschel, S.M. (1990). *A parent's guide to Down syndrome: Toward a brighter future.* Baltimore: Paul H. Brookes Publishing Co.

Pueschel, S.M., & Pueschel, J.K. (Eds.). (1992). *Biomedical concerns in persons with Down syndrome.* Baltimore: Paul H. Brookes Publishing Co.

Thompson, M.W., McInnes, R.R., & Willard, H.F. (1991). *Genetics in medicine* (5th ed.). Philadelphia: W.B. Saunders.

Chapter 12: Environmental Events

Lehr, E. (1990). *Psychological management of traumatic brain injuries in children and adolescents.* Rockville, MD: Aspen Publishers.

Scola, P. (1991). Infections. In J.L. Matson & J.A. Mulick (Eds.), *Handbook of mental retardation* (2nd ed.) (pp. 151–157). Elmsford, NY: Pergamon.

Chapter 13: Birth Defects

Burton, B.K., Schulz, C.J., & Burd, L.I. (1992). Limb anomalies associated with chorionic villus sampling. *Obstetrics and Gynecology, 79*, 726–730.

Feingold, M., & Pashayan, H. (1983). *Genetics and birth defects in clinical practice*. Boston: Little, Brown.

Fraser, F.C. (1989). Mapping the cleft lip genes: The first fix? *American Journal of Human Genetics, 45*, 345–347.

Jones, K.L. (1988). *Smith's recognizable patterns of human malformation: Genetic, embryologic, and clinical aspects* (4th ed.). Philadelphia: W.B. Saunders.

MRC Vitamin Study Research Group. (1991). Prevention of neurotube defects: Results of the medical research council vitamin study. *Lancet, 338*, 131–137.

Rekate, H.L. (1991). Neurosurgical management of the newborn with spina bifida. In H.L. Rekate (Ed.), *Comprehensive management of spina bifida* (pp. 1–28). Boca Raton, FL: CRC Press.

Chapter 14: Problems in the Newborn Period

Fenichel, G.M. (1990). *Neonatal neurology* (3rd ed.). New York: Churchill Livingstone.

Stevenson, D.K., & Sunshine, P. (1989). *Fetal and neonatal brain injury: Mechanisms, management, and the risks of practice*. Toronto, Ontario, Canada: B.C. Decker.

Taeusch, H.W., & Yogman, M.W. (Eds.). (1987). *Followup management of the high-risk infant*. Toronto, Ontario, Canada: Little, Brown.

Chapter 15: Cerebral Palsy

Kurtz, L.A. (1992). Cerebral palsy. In M.L. Batshaw, & Y.M. Perret, *Children with disabilities: A medical primer* (3rd ed., pp. 441–469). Baltimore: Paul H. Brookes Publishing Co.

Rang, M. (1990). Cerebral palsy. In R.T. Morrisey (Ed.), *Lovell & Winter's pediatric orthopedics* (3rd ed., pp. 465–506). Philadelphia: J.B. Lippincott.

Chapter 16: Seizure Disorders

Menkes, J.H. (1990). *Textbook of child neurology* (4th ed., pp. 602–674). Philadelphia: Lea & Febiger.

Wyllie, E. (Ed.). (1993). *The treatment of epilepsy: Principles and practice*. Philadelphia: Lea & Febiger.

Chapter 17: Neurological Disorders with Associated Skin Findings

Jones, K.L. (1988). *Smith's recognizable patterns of human malformation: Genetic, embryologic, and clinical aspects* (4th ed.). Philadelphia: W.B. Saunders.

Riccardi, M.D., & Eichner, J.E. (1986). *Neurofibromatosis: Phenotype, natural history, and pathogenesis*. Baltimore: The Johns Hopkins University Press.

Swaiman, K.F. (1989). *Pediatric neurology: Principles and practice*. St. Louis: C.V. Mosby.

Chapter 18: Diseases of Muscles and Bones

Buyse, M.L. (1990). *Birth defects encyclopedia.* Dover, MA: Center for Birth Defects Information.

Morrissy, R.T. (Ed.). (1990). *Lovell & Winter's pediatric orthopedics* (3rd ed.). Philadelphia: J.B. Lippincott.

Pueschel, S.M., & Solga, P.M. (1992). Musculoskeletal disorders. In S.M. Pueschel & J.K. Pueschel (Eds.), *Biomedical concerns in persons with Down syndrome* (pp. 147–157). Baltimore: Paul H. Brookes Publishing Co.

Siegel, I.M. (1986). *Muscle and its diseases: An outline primer of basic science and clinical methods.* Chicago: Yearbook Medical Publishers.

Tachdjian, M.O. (1990). *Pediatric orthopedics* (2nd ed.). Philadelphia: W.B. Saunders.

Chapter 19: Metabolic Disorders

Cotton, R.G.H. (1990). Heterogeneity of phenylketonuria at the clinical, protein, and DNA levels. *Journal of Inherited Metabolic Diseases, 13,* 739–750.

Doherty, L.B., Rohr, F.J., & Levy, H.L. (1991). Detection of phenylketonuria in the very early newborn specimen. *Pediatrics, 87,* 240–244.

Levy, H.L. (1986). Phenylketonuria—1986. *Pediatrics in Review, 7,* 269–275.

Scriver, C.R., Beaudet, A.L., Sly, W.S., & Valle, D.R. (1989). *The metabolic basis of inherited disease* (6th ed.). New York: McGraw-Hill.

Seashore, M.R. (1990). Neonatal screening for inborn errors of metabolism: Update. *Seminars in Perinatology, 14,* 431–438.

Chapter 20: Endocrine Disorders

Hung, W. (1991). *Clinical pediatric endocrinology.* St. Louis: C.V. Mosby.

PART IV: SPECIAL CARE FOR YOUR CHILD: PROCEDURES, ASSISTIVE DEVICES, AND MEDICAL AND SURGICAL TREATMENTS

Chapter 21: Strategies for Helping Your Child

Baker, B.L., & Brightman, A.J. (1989). *Steps to independence. A skills training guide for parents and teachers of children with special needs* (2nd ed.). Baltimore: Paul H. Brookes Publishing Co.

Clark, L. (1985). *SOS help for parents: A practical guide for handling common everyday behavior problems.* Bowling Green, KY: Parents Press.

Fraser, B.A., & Hensinger, R.N. (1983). *Managing physical handicaps: A practical guide for parents, care providers, and educators.* Baltimore: Paul H. Brookes Publishing Co.

Handleman, J.S., & Harris, S.L. (1986). *Educating the developmentally disabled: Meeting the needs of children and families.* San Diego: College Hill.

Horner, R.H., Meyer, L.H., & Fredericks, H.D.B. (Eds.). (1986). *Education of learners with severe handicaps: Exemplary service strategies.* Baltimore: Paul H. Brookes Publishing Co.

McMorrow, M.J., Foxx, R.M., Faw, G.D., & Bittle, R.G. (1986). *Looking for the words—Teaching functional language strategies.* Champaign, IL: Research Press.

Musselwhite, C.R. (1986). *Adaptive play for special needs children: Strategies to enhance communication and learning.* San Diego: College Hill.

Chapter 22: Tests and Procedures

Antonarakis, S.E. (1989). Diagnosis of genetic disorders at the DNA level. *New England Journal of Medicine, 320,* 153–163.

Burton, B.K., Schulz, C.J., & Burd, L.I. (1992). Limb anomalies associated with chorionic villus sampling. *Obstetrics and Gynecology, 79,* 726–730.

Filkins, K., & Russo, J.F. (1990). *Human prenatal diagnosis.* New York: Marcel Dekker.

Harrison, M.R., Golbus, M.S., & Filly, R.A. (1990). *The unborn patient: Prenatal diagnosis and treatment.* Philadelphia: W.B. Saunders.

Miller, W.A. (1988). Prenatal genetic diagnosis. In S.M. Pueschel & J.A. Mulick (Eds.), *Prevention of developmental disabilities* (pp. 114–129). Cambridge, MA: Academic Guild Publishers.

Northern, J.L., & Downs, M.P. (1991). *Hearing in children* (4th ed.). Baltimore: Williams & Wilkins.

Chapter 23: Adaptive Equipment

Bergen, A.F., & Colangelo, C. (1985). *Positioning the client with CNS deficits: The wheelchair and other adaptive equipment* (2nd ed.). Valhalla, NY: Valhalla Rehabilitation Publications.

Finnie, N. (1975). *Handling the young cerebral palsy child at home* (2nd ed.). New York: E.P. Dutton.

Fraser, B.A., Hensinger, R.N., & Phelps, J.A. (1990). *Physical management of multiple handicaps: A professional guide* (2nd ed.). Baltimore: Paul H. Brookes Publishing Co.

Jones, S., & Clark, S. (1982). *Adaptive positioning equipment: Directory of available services.* (Available from Georgia Retardation Center, 4770 North Peachtree Road, Dumwoody, Georgia 30338)

Letts, R.M. (1991). *Principles of seating the disabled.* Ann Arbor, MI: CRC Press.

Paciorek, M.J., & Jones, A.J. (1994). *Sports and recreation for the disabled.* Carmel, IN: Cooper Publishing Group.

Rowley-Kelly, F.L., & Reigel, D.H. (Eds.). (1993). *Teaching the student with spina bifida.* Baltimore: Paul H. Brookes Publishing Co.

Williamson, G.G. (1987). *Children with spina bifida: Early intervention and preschool programming.* Baltimore: Paul H. Brookes Publishing Co.

Chapter 24: Medications May Be Necessary for Your Child

Craig, C.R., & Stitzel, R.E. (Eds.). (1990). *Modern pharmacology* (3rd ed.) Boston: Little, Brown.

Chapter 25: Some Children May Have to Undergo Surgery

Jones, P.G., & Woodward, A.A. (1986). *Clinical pediatric surgery* (3rd ed.). Melbourne, Australia: Blackwell Scientific Publications.

Maher, B.W. (1992). *Pediatric anesthesia.* Philadelphia: J.B. Lippincott.

Tachdjian, M.O. (1990). *Pediatric orthopedics* (2nd ed.). Philadelphia: W.B. Saunders.

Chapter 26: Hospitalization and Aftercare

Knafl, K.A., Cavallari, K.A., & Dixon, D.M. (1988). *Pediatric hospitalization: Family and nurse perspectives.* Glenview, IL: Scott, Foresman.

PART V: ASSESSMENTS, EDUCATION, AND RESOURCE DEVELOPMENT

Chapter 27: Assessing Developmental Disabilities: Psychological Tests and Procedures

Fewell, R.R. (1983). Assessing handicapped infants. In S.G. Garwood & R.R. Fewell (Eds.), *Educating handicapped infants* (pp. 143–169). Rockville, MD: Aspen Publishers, Inc.

McLoughlin, J.A., & Lewis, R.B. (1986). *Assessing special students* (2nd ed.). Columbus, OH: Charles E. Merrill.

Mullikin, R.K., & Buckley, J.J. (1983). *Assessment of multihandicapped and developmentally disabled children.* Cambridge, MA: Aspen Systems.

Simeonsson, R.J., (1986). *Psychological and developmental assessment of special children.* Newton, MA: Allyn & Bacon.

Ulrey, G., & Rogers, S.J. (1982). *Psychological assessment of handicapped infants and young children.* New York: Thieme-Stratton.

Wodrich, D.L., & Kush, S.A. (1990). *Children's psychological testing: A guide for nonpsychologists* (2nd ed.). Baltimore: Paul H. Brookes Publishing Co.

Wodrich, D.L., & Joy, J.E. (Eds.). (1986). *Multidisciplinary assessment of children with learning disabilities and mental retardation.* Baltimore: Paul H. Brookes Publishing Co.

Chapter 28: Helping Children Learn

Baker, B.L., Brightman, A.J., Heifetz, L.J., & Murphy, D.L.M. (1976). *Behavior problems.* Champaign, IL: Research Press.

Becker, W.C. (1971). *Parents are teachers: A child management program.* Champaign, IL: Research Press.

Cautela, J.R., & Groden, J. (1978). *Relaxation—A comprehensive manual for adults, children, and children with special needs.* Champaign, IL: Research Press.

Cutler, B.C. (1993). *You, your child, and "special" education: A guide to making the system work.* Baltimore: Paul H. Brookes Publishing Co.

Evans, I.M., & Meyer, L.H. (1985). *An educative approach to behavior problems: A practical decision model for interventions with severely handicapped learners.* Baltimore: Paul H. Brookes Publishing Co.

Foxx, R.M., & Meyer, L.H. (1973). *Toilet training persons with developmental disabilities.* Champaign, IL: Research Press.

Handleman, J.S., & Harris, S.L. (1986). *Educating the developmentally disabled: Meeting the needs of children and families.* San Diego: College Hill.

Meyer, L.H., & Evans, I.M. (1989). *Nonaversive intervention for behavior problems: A manual for home and community.* Baltimore: Paul H. Brookes Publishing Co.

Chapter 29: Going to School

Blackman, H., & Peterson, D. (1989). *Totally integrated neighborhood schools.* La Grange, IL: La Grange Department of Special Education.

Cutler, B.C. (1993). *You, your child, and "special" education: A guide to making the system work.* Baltimore: Paul H. Brookes Publishing Co.

Falvey, M.A. (1989). *Community-based curriculum: Instructional strategies for students with severe handicaps* (2nd ed.). Baltimore: Paul H. Brookes Publishing Co.

Ford, A., & Davern, L. (1989). Moving forward with school integration: Strategies for involving students with severe handicaps in the life of the school. In R. Gaylord-Ross (Ed.), *Integration strategies for students with handicaps* (pp. 11–31). Baltimore: Paul H. Brookes Publishing Co.

Orelove, F.P., & Sobsey, D. (1987). *Educating children with multiple disabilities: A transdisciplinary approach.* Baltimore: Paul H. Brookes Publishing Co.

Stainback, W., & Stainback, S. (Eds.) (1990). *Support networks for inclusive schooling: Interdependent integrated education.* Baltimore: Paul H. Brookes Publishing Co.

Wilcox, B., & Bellamy, G.T. (1982). *Design of high school programs for severely handicapped students.* Baltimore: Paul H. Brookes Publishing Co.

Winton, P.J., Turnbull, A.P., & Blacher, J. (1984). *Selecting a preschool: A guide to parents of handicapped children.* Baltimore: University Park Press.

Chapter 30: Legal Issues in Developmental Disabilities

Apolloni, T., & Cooke, T.P. (Eds.). (1984). *A new look at guardianship: Protective services that support personalized living.* Baltimore: Paul H. Brookes Publishing Co.

Cooke, R.E. (1991). Ethics and developmental disabilities. In A.J. Capute & P.J. Accardo (Eds.), *Developmental disabilities in infancy and childhood* (pp. 251–259). Baltimore: Paul H. Brookes Publishing Co.

Effland, R.W. (1976). Trusts and estate planning. In M. Kindred, J. Cohen, D. Penrod, & T. Shaffer (Eds.), *The mentally retarded citizen and the law* (pp. 115–132). New York: Macmillan.

Kindred, M. (1976). Guardianship and limitations upon capacity. In M. Kindred, J. Cohen, D. Penrod, & T. Shaffer (Eds.), *The mentally retarded citizen and the law* (pp. 62–87). New York: Macmillan.

Tucker, B.P., & Goldstein, B.A. (1993). *Legal rights of persons with disabilities.* Horsham, PA: LRP Publications.

Vitello, S.J., & Soskin, R.M. (1985). *Mental retardation: Its social and legal context.* Englewood Cliffs, NJ: Prentice Hall.

Zuckerman, D., & Chrmatz, M. (1992). *Mental disability law—A primer: A comprehensive introduction to the field.* Washington, DC: Commission on Mental and Physical Disability Law.

Chapter 31: Resource Development

Larson, G., & Kahn, J. (1990). *Special needs/special solutions: How to get quality care for a child with special health needs.* St. Paul, MN: Life Line Press.

Manes, J., & Carty, L. (1991). *SSI: New opportunities for children with disabilities.* Washington, DC: Mental Health Law Project.

Peterson, R., & Tenenbaum, D. (1992). *Fighting back health insurance denials.* Madison, WI: Center for Public Representation.

Rosenfeld, L.R. (1994). *Your child and health care: A "dollars & sense" guide for families with special needs.* Baltimore: Paul H. Brookes Publishing Co.

Index

423